The Governance of China

IV

XI JINPING

The Governance
of China

IV

FOREIGN LANGUAGES PRESS

First Edition 2022

ISBN 978-7-119-13094-1
© Foreign Languages Press Co. Ltd, Beijing, China, 2022
Published by Foreign Languages Press Co. Ltd
24 Baiwanzhuang Road, Beijing 100037, China
http://www.flp.com.cn
Email: flp@CIPG.org.cn
Distributed by China International Book Trading Corporation
35 Chegongzhuang Xilu, Beijing 100044, China
P.O. Box 399, Beijing, China
Printed in the People's Republic of China

Publisher's Note

Since the 18th National Congress of the Communist Party of China (CPC) in 2012, China's Communists, with Xi Jinping as their chief representative, have continued to adapt the basic tenets of Marxism to China's realities and to its traditional culture. As a result, Xi Jinping Thought on Socialism with Chinese Characteristics for a New Era has been developed. It represents Marxism applied to contemporary China and the 21st century. It also represents the essence of Chinese culture combined with the ethos of the Chinese nation in the new era. It marks a new step forward in adapting Marxism to the Chinese context.

At the Sixth Plenary Session of the 19th CPC Central Committee in 2021, it was emphasized that the Two Affirmations – of Xi Jinping's core position on the Party Central Committee and in the Party as a whole, and of the guiding role of Xi Jinping Thought on Socialism with Chinese Characteristics for a New Era – reflect the common aspirations of the whole Party, the military and all the Chinese people, and that they are of great significance to the future of the Party and the country in the new era, and to the rejuvenation of the Chinese nation.

The world is experiencing a pandemic and a scale of change unseen in a century, and is entering a stage of turbulence and reform. In response to an unprecedented level of risks and challenges, the CPC Central Committee with Xi Jinping at its core has given overall consideration to the domestic and international situation. It has succeeded in striking a balance between development and security, and between carrying out effective epidemic prevention and control and maintaining economic and social development. It has united the whole Party and the whole country and led them in meeting challenges head-on and with great strength and self-reliance. China has won the battle against extreme poverty, achieved the First Centenary Goal of building a moderately prosperous society in all respects on schedule, and celebrated the centenary of the CPC. It has sounded the bugle call to march towards the Second Centenary Goal – building China into a modern socialist country. It will deliver new and greater achievements with flying colors on the journey to national rejuvenation.

Xi Jinping has led the Party and the people in the effort to respond to changes and open up new prospects by freeing the mind, seeking truth from facts, maintaining the right political orientation, breaking new ground, and making a penetrating analysis and acute assessment of major theoretical and practical issues concerning the development of the Party and the country in the new era. Employing originality in vision and a full range of ideas and strategies, he has provided answers to questions concerning the present and future of China and its people, and the wider world.

The first three volumes of *Xi Jinping: The Governance of China* have played an important role in explaining the Party's innovative theories, in inspiring people to work harder, and in presenting China to the rest of the world. They have thereby opened a window for the international community to better understand China.

The Publicity Department of the CPC Central Committee and the State Council Information Office, with the support of the Research Institute of Party History and Literature of the CPC Central Committee, and China International Publishing Group, have compiled a fourth volume of *Xi Jinping: The Governance of China*. This volume is designed to help officials and the public better understand and apply Xi Jinping Thought on Socialism with Chinese Characteristics for a New Era, to impress upon them the decisive nature of the Two Affirmations, to strengthen their commitment to the Four Consciousnesses, the Four-sphere Confidence, and the Two Upholds, and to guide them to forge ahead in unity and with greater resolve on a new journey in the new era. It is also intended that this volume will keep the international community abreast of the latest developments in President Xi's thoughts, give them a better understanding of how the Chinese people have succeeded under CPC leadership and how they will continue to succeed in the future, and explain the development path that China has chosen and its approach to and theory of governance.

This volume contains a compilation of 109 of Xi Jinping's spoken and written works from February 3, 2020 to May 10, 2022, along with 45 photographs taken since January 2020. It is divided into 21 sections by topic, with the articles in each section arranged in chronological order. For ease of reading, notes are provided at the end of relevant articles.

CONTENTS

Socialism with Chinese Characteristics in the New Era

Overall CPC Leadership

The People First

Whole-Process People's Democracy

Socialist Rule of Law

Advanced Socialist Culture

Development and Security

One Country, Two Systems and National Reunification

A Global Community of Shared Future

Global Governance and Multilateralism

High-Quality Belt and Road Cooperation

Party Self-Reform for Social Transformation

Socialism with Chinese Characteristics in the New Era

Speech at the Ceremony Marking the Centenary of the Communist Party of China

July 1, 2021

Comrades and friends,

Today, the first of July, is a great and solemn day in the history of both the Communist Party of China and the Chinese nation. We gather here to join all Party members and all the Chinese people in celebrating the centenary of the Party, looking back on the glorious journey it has traveled over 100 years of struggle, and looking ahead to the bright prospects for the rejuvenation of the Chinese nation.

To begin, let me extend warm congratulations to all Party members on behalf of the CPC Central Committee.

On this special occasion, it is my honor to declare on behalf of the Party and the people that through the continued efforts of the whole Party and the entire nation, we have realized the First Centenary Goal of building a moderately prosperous society in all respects. This means that we have brought about a historic resolution to the problem of absolute poverty in China, and we are now marching in confident strides towards the Second Centenary Goal of building China into a great modern socialist country in all respects. This is a great and glorious achievement for the Chinese nation, for the Chinese people, and for the Communist Party of China.

Comrades and friends,

The Chinese nation is a great nation. With more than 5,000 years of history, China has made an indelible contribution to human civilization. After the Opium War of 1840, however, China was gradually reduced to a semi-colonial, semi-feudal society and went through a period of suffering worse than it had ever previously known. The country endured intense humiliation, the people were subjected to great pain, and the Chinese civilization was plunged into darkness. Since that time, national rejuvenation has been the greatest dream of the Chinese people and the Chinese nation.

To save the nation from peril, the Chinese people put up a courageous fight. As noble-minded patriots sought to pull the nation together, a series of uprisings occurred – the Taiping Rebellion[1] (1851-1864), the Reform Movement of 1898, the Boxer Uprising[2] (1899-1900) and the Revolution of 1911 – and a variety of plans were devised to ensure national survival, but all of these ended in failure. China was in urgent need of new ideas to lead the movement to save the nation and a new organization to rally revolutionary forces.

With the salvoes of Russia's October Revolution in 1917, Marxism-Leninism was brought to China. Then in 1921, as the Chinese people and the Chinese nation were undergoing a great awakening and Marxism-Leninism was becoming an essential component of the Chinese workers' movement, the Communist Party of China was born. The founding of a communist party in China was an epoch-making event, which profoundly changed the course of Chinese history in modern times, transformed the future of the Chinese people and nation, and altered the global landscape.

Since the very day of its founding, the Party has made seeking happiness for the Chinese people and rejuvenation for the Chinese nation its aspiration and mission. All the struggle, sacrifice and creation through which the Party has united and led the Chinese people over the past hundred years has been tied together by one ultimate goal – bringing about the rejuvenation of the Chinese nation.

– To realize national rejuvenation, the Party united the Chinese people and led them in fighting bloody battles. With unyielding determination, we achieved great success in the New Democratic Revolution (1919-1949).

Through the Northern Expedition (1926-1928), the Agrarian Revolutionary War (1927-1937), the War of Resistance Against Japanese Aggression (1931-1945), and the War of Liberation (1946-1950), we fought armed counter-revolution with armed revolution, toppling the three mountains of imperialism, feudalism and bureaucrat-capitalism, and establishing the People's Republic of China (PRC), which made the people masters of the country. We thus secured our nation's independence and liberated our people.

The victory of the New Democratic Revolution put an end to China's status as a semi-colonial, semi-feudal society. It brought to an end the total disunity that existed in old China, all the unequal treaties imposed on our country by foreign powers, and all the privileges that imperialist powers enjoyed in China. It created the fundamental social conditions for realizing national rejuvenation.

Through tenacious struggle, the Party and the Chinese people showed the world that the Chinese people had stood up, and that the day when the Chinese nation could be abused and oppressed by others was gone forever.

– To realize national rejuvenation, the Party united the Chinese people and led them in endeavoring to build a stronger China with a spirit of self-reliance, achieving great success in socialist revolution and construction.

By carrying out socialist revolution, we eliminated the exploitative and repressive feudal system that had persisted in China for thousands of years, and established socialism as our basic system. In the process of socialist construction, we overcame subversion, sabotage, and armed provocation by imperialist and hegemonic powers, and brought about the most extensive and profound social changes in the history of the Chinese nation. This great transformation of China from a poor, populous and backward country in the East into a socialist country laid down the fundamental political conditions and the institutional foundations necessary for realizing national rejuvenation.

Through tenacious struggle, the Party and the Chinese people showed the world that the Chinese people were capable of dismantling the old world and building a new one, that only socialism could save China, and that only socialism could enable China to develop.

– To realize national rejuvenation, the Party united the Chinese people and led them in freeing the mind and forging ahead, achieving great success in reform, opening up, and socialist modernization.

We established the Party's basic guidelines for the primary stage of socialism, resolutely advanced reform and opening up, neutralized risks and overcame challenges from every direction, and founded, upheld, safeguarded and developed socialism with Chinese characteristics. This led to a major turnaround with far-reaching significance in the history of the Party since the founding of the People's Republic of China. This enabled China to transform itself from a highly centralized planned economy to a socialist market economy brimming with vitality, and from a country that was largely isolated to one that is open to the outside world in every respect. It also enabled China to achieve the historic leap from a country with relatively backward productive forces to the world's second largest economy, and to make the historic transformation of raising the living standards of its people from bare subsistence to an overall level of moderate prosperity, and then ultimately to moderate prosperity in all respects. These achievements fueled the push towards national rejuvenation by providing institutional guarantees imbued with new energy, as well as the material conditions for rapid development.

Through tenacious struggle, the Party and the Chinese people showed the world that by pursuing reform and opening up, an essential step in making China what it is today, China had made great strides and caught up with the times.

– To realize national rejuvenation, the Party has united the Chinese people and led them in pursuing a great struggle, a great project, a great cause, and a great dream through a spirit of self-confidence, self-reliance and innovation, achieving great success for socialism with Chinese characteristics in the new era.

Following the Party's 18th National Congress, socialism with Chinese characteristics entered a new era. In this new era we have upheld and strengthened the Party's overall leadership, ensured a holistic approach to the Five-sphere Integrated Plan[3] and coordinated implementation of the Four-pronged Comprehensive Strategy[4], upheld and improved the system of socialism with Chinese characteristics, modernized China's system and capacity for governance, continued to exercise rule-based governance over the Party, and developed a sound system of intra-Party regulations. We have overcome a long list of major risks and challenges, fulfilled the First Centenary Goal, and defined strategic steps for achieving the Second Centenary Goal. All the historic achievements and changes in the Party and the country have provided the cause of national rejuvenation with more robust institutions, stronger material foundations, and a source of inspiration for seizing the initiative.

Through tenacious struggle, the Party and the Chinese people have shown the world that the Chinese nation has achieved the tremendous transformation from standing up and growing prosperous to becoming strong, and that China's national rejuvenation has become an unstoppable process.

Over the past hundred years, the Party has united the Chinese people and led them in writing the most magnificent chapter in the millennia-long history of the Chinese nation, embodying the dauntless spirit that Mao Zedong expressed when he wrote, "Our minds grow stronger for the martyrs' sacrifice, daring to make the sun and the moon shine in the new sky."[5] The great path we have pioneered, the great cause we have undertaken, and the great achievements we have made over the past century will go down in the annals of the Chinese nation and of human civilization.

Comrades and friends,

A hundred years ago, the pioneers of communism in China established the Communist Party of China and developed the great founding spirit of the Party, which is comprised of the following principles: upholding truth and ideals, staying true to our original aspiration and founding mission, fighting bravely without fear of death, and remaining loyal to the Party and faithful to the people. This spirit is the Party's source of strength.

Over the past hundred years, the Party has carried forward this great founding spirit. Through its protracted struggles, it has developed a long line of inspiring principles for China's Communists and tempered a distinct political character. As time moves steadily forward, the spirit of the Party has been passed on from generation to generation. We will continue to promote our glorious traditions and sustain our revolutionary legacy, so that the great founding spirit of the Party will be passed down from generation to generation and carried forward.

Comrades and friends,

We owe all that we have achieved over the past hundred years to the concerted efforts of the Chinese Communists, the Chinese people, and the Chinese nation. China's Communists, with comrades Mao Zedong, Deng Xiaoping, Jiang Zemin and Hu Jintao as their chief representatives, have made tremendous and historic contributions to the rejuvenation of the Chinese nation. To them, we express our deepest respect.

Let us take this moment to cherish the memory of comrades Mao Zedong, Zhou Enlai, Liu Shaoqi, Zhu De, Deng Xiaoping, Chen Yun, and other veteran revolutionaries who contributed so much to China's revolution, construction and reform, and to the founding, consolidation and development of the Communist Party of China; let us cherish the memory of the revolutionary martyrs who bravely laid down their lives to establish, defend and develop the People's Republic; let us cherish the memory of those who dedicated their lives to reform, opening up, and socialist modernization; let us cherish the memory of all the men and women who fought tenaciously for national independence and the liberation of the people in modern times. Their great contributions to our country and our nation will be immortalized in the annals of history, and their noble spirit will live on forever in the hearts of the Chinese people.

The people are the true heroes, for it is they who write history. On behalf of the CPC Central Committee, I would like to offer my highest respects to workers, farmers and intellectuals across the country; to other political parties, prominent individuals without party affiliation, people's organizations, and patriotic figures from all sectors of society; to all members of the People's Liberation Army, the People's

Armed Police Force, the public security police, and the fire and rescue services; to all socialist working people; and to all members of the united front. I would like to extend my sincere greetings to compatriots in the Hong Kong and Macao special administrative regions and in Taiwan as well as overseas Chinese. And I would like to express my heartfelt gratitude to all those from around the world who have shown friendship to the Chinese people and understanding and support for China's endeavors in revolution, construction and reform.

Comrades and friends,

Our Party's founding mission is easy to define. Ensuring that we stay true to that mission is much more difficult. By learning from history, we can understand why powers rise and fall. Through the mirror of history, we can find where we currently stand and gain foresight into the future. Looking back on the Party's 100-year history, we can see why we were successful in the past and how we can continue to succeed in the future. This will ensure that we act with greater resolve and purpose in staying true to our founding mission and pursuing a better future on the new journey that lies before us.

As we put conscious effort into learning from history to create a bright future, we must never lose sight of the following:

– We must uphold the firm leadership of the Party. China's success hinges on the Party. More than 180 years of the history of modern China, a century of Party history, and more than seven decades of the People's Republic of China – all provide ample evidence that without the Communist Party of China, there would be no new China and no national rejuvenation. The Party was chosen by history and the people. The leadership of the Party is the defining feature of socialism with Chinese characteristics and constitutes the greatest strength of this system. It is the foundation and lifeblood of the Party and the country, and the crux upon which the interests and wellbeing of all Chinese people depend.

On the journey ahead, we must continue to uphold and strengthen the Party's overall leadership. We must be deeply conscious of the need to maintain political commitment, think in terms of the general picture, follow the core leadership of the CPC Central Committee, and act in accordance with its requirements. We must remain confident in the path, theory, system and culture of socialism with Chinese characteristics. We must uphold the core position of the general secretary on the Party Central Committee and in the Party as a whole, and uphold the authority of the Central Committee and its centralized, unified leadership. Always conscious of the country's most fundamental interests, we must strengthen the Party's capacity to conduct sound, democratic and law-based governance, and ensure that it plays to the full its core role in providing overall leadership and coordinating the efforts of all sides.

– We must unite the Chinese people and lead them in working ceaselessly for a better life. The country is the people and the people are the country. As we have fought to establish and consolidate our leadership over the country, we have in fact been fighting to earn and keep the people's support. In the people, the Party has its roots, its lifeblood, and its source of strength. The Party has always represented the fundamental interests of all Chinese people; it stands with them in the best and the hardest of times and shares a common destiny with them. The Party has no special interests of its own – it has never represented any individual interest group, power group, or privileged stratum. Any attempt to divide the Party from the Chinese people or to set the people against the Party is bound to fail. More than 95 million Party members and more than 1.4 billion Chinese people will never allow such a thing to come to pass.

On the journey ahead, we must rely closely on the people to create history. Upholding the Party's fundamental purpose of wholeheartedly serving the people, we will stand firmly with the people, implement the Party's mass line, respect the people's creativity, and practice a people-centered philosophy of development. We will develop whole-process people's democracy, safeguard social fairness and justice, and resolve the imbalances and insufficiencies in development and the most pressing difficulties and problems of greatest concern to the people. In doing so, we will make more notable and substantive progress towards achieving well-rounded human development and common prosperity for all.

– We must continue to adapt Marxism to the Chinese context. Marxism is the fundamental ideology upon which our Party and country are founded; it is the very soul of our Party and the banner under which it strives. The Communist Party of China upholds the basic tenets of Marxism and the principle of seeking truth from facts. Taking into consideration China's realities and the general trends in the world, and through a process of painstaking experiments, we have succeeded in adapting Marxism to the Chinese context and the needs of our times in guiding the Chinese people as we advance our great social transformation. At the fundamental level, the capability of our Party and the strengths of socialism with Chinese characteristics are attributable to the fact that Marxism works.

On the journey ahead, we must continue to uphold Marxism-Leninism, Mao Zedong Thought, Deng Xiaoping Theory, the Theory of Three Represents, and the Scientific Outlook on Development, and fully implement the Thought on Socialism with Chinese Characteristics for a New Era. We must continue to adapt the basic tenets of Marxism to China's specific realities and its traditional culture. We will use Marxism to observe, understand and steer the trends of our times, and continue to develop the Marxism of contemporary China and in the 21st century.

– We must uphold and develop socialism with Chinese characteristics. We must follow our own path – this is the bedrock that underpins all the theories and practices of our Party. More than that, it is the conclusion our Party has drawn from its struggles over the past century. Socialism with Chinese characteristics is a fundamental achievement of the Party and the people, forged through innumerable hardships and great sacrifices, and it is the right path for us to achieve national rejuvenation. As we have upheld and developed socialism with Chinese characteristics and driven coordinated progress in material, political, cultural, ethical, social and eco-environmental terms, we have pioneered a new and uniquely Chinese path to modernization, and created a new model for human progress.

On the journey ahead, we must adhere to the Party's underlying theories, basic guidelines, and fundamental principles, and implement the Five-sphere Integrated Plan and the Four-pronged Comprehensive Strategy. We must expand all-round reform and opening up, ground our work in this new development stage, apply the new development philosophy in full, to the letter and in all fields, and foster a new development dynamic. We must promote high-quality development and achieve greater self-reliance in science and technology. We must ensure that our people run the country, continue to govern based on the rule of law, and uphold the core socialist values. We must ensure and increase public wellbeing in the course of development, promote harmony between humanity and nature, and take well-coordinated steps towards making our people prosperous, our nation strong, and our country beautiful.

The Chinese nation has fostered a splendid civilization over 5,000 years or more. The Party has also acquired a wealth of experience through its endeavors over the past 100 years and during more than 70 years of governance. At the same time, we are also eager to learn from the fruitful experience of other cultures, and we welcome helpful suggestions and constructive criticisms. We will not, however, accept condescending sermons from those who feel they have the right to lecture us. The Party and the Chinese people will keep moving confidently forward in broad strides along the path that we have chosen for ourselves, and we will make sure that China's destiny, development and progress remains firmly in our own hands.

– We must accelerate the modernization of national defense and the armed forces. A strong country must have a strong military; only then can it guarantee the security of the nation. While it was engaged in violent struggle, the Party came to recognize the irrefutable truth that it must command the gun and build a people's military of its own. The achievements of the people's military on behalf of the Party and the people have been remarkable. It is a strong pillar that safeguards our socialist country and preserves national dignity, and a powerful force for protecting peace in our region and beyond.

On the journey ahead, we must fully implement both the Party's philosophy on strengthening the military and our military strategy for the new era, maintain the Party's absolute leadership over the people's armed forces, and follow a Chinese path to military development. We will take comprehensive measures to reinforce the political loyalty of the armed forces, to strengthen them through reform and technology and the training of competent personnel, and to run them in accordance with the law. We will elevate our people's armed forces to world-class standards so that we are equipped with greater capacity and more reliable means for safeguarding our national sovereignty, security, and development interests.

– We must continue working to build a global community of shared future. Peace, concord and harmony are goals that China has pursued and carried forward for more than 5,000 years. The Chinese nation does not carry aggressive or hegemonic traits in its genes. The Party cares about the future of humanity, and wishes to move forward in parallel with all progressive forces around the world. China has always worked to safeguard world peace, contribute to global development, and preserve international order.

On the journey ahead, we will remain committed to promoting peace, development, cooperation, and mutual benefit, to an independent foreign policy of peace, and to the path of peaceful development. We will work to build a new model of international relations and a global community of shared future, promote the high-quality development of the Belt and Road Initiative through joint efforts, and use China's new achievements to provide the world with new opportunities. The Party will continue to work with all peace-loving countries and peoples to promote the shared human values of peace, development, fairness, justice, democracy and freedom. We will continue to champion cooperation over confrontation, to open up rather than closing our doors, and to focus on mutual benefits rather than zero-sum games. We will oppose hegemony and power politics, and strive to keep the wheels of history rolling towards bright horizons.

We Chinese are a people who uphold justice and are not intimidated by threats of force. As a nation, we have a strong sense of pride and confidence. We have never abused, oppressed or subjugated the people of any other country, and we never will. By the same token, we will never allow any foreign force to abuse, oppress or subjugate us. Anyone who would attempt to do so will find themselves on a collision course with a great wall of steel forged by over 1.4 billion Chinese people.

– We must carry out the great historic struggle with many new features. Having the courage to fight and the fortitude to win is what has made our Party invincible. Realizing our great dream will require hard work and perseverance. Today, we are closer than ever before to the goal of national rejuvenation, and more confident and more capable of making it a reality. But we must be prepared to work harder than ever to get there.

On the journey ahead, we must maintain stronger vigilance and always be prepared for potential danger, even in times of calm. We must adopt a holistic approach to national security that balances development and security imperatives, and implement the national rejuvenation strategy within a wider context of the unprecedented changes taking place in the world. We need to acquire a full understanding of the demands that changes and challenges in Chinese society impose upon us, and the new issues and problems stemming from a complex international environment. We must be both brave and adept in carrying out our struggle, forging new paths, and building new bridges wherever necessary to take us forward.

– We must strengthen the great unity of the Chinese people. In the course of our struggles over the past century, the Party has always considered the role of the united front to be essential. We have constantly consolidated and developed the broadest possible united front, combining all the forces that can be united, mobilizing all positive factors that can be mobilized, and pooling as much strength as possible for collective endeavors. The patriotic united front is an important means for the Party to bring together all the sons and daughters of the Chinese nation, both at home and abroad, for the goal of national rejuvenation.

On the journey ahead, we must ensure great unity and solidarity and balance commonality and diversity. We should strengthen theoretical and political guidance, build broad consensus, bring together the brightest minds, expand common ground, and seek convergence of interests, so that all Chinese people, both at home and overseas, can focus their ingenuity and energy on the same goal and come together as a mighty force for national rejuvenation.

– We must continue to advance the great new project of strengthening the Party. A hallmark that distinguishes the Communist Party of China from other political parties is the courage to undertake self-reform. An important reason why the Party remains so vital and vibrant despite having undergone so many trials and tribulations is that it practices effective self-supervision and full and rigorous self-governance. It has thus been able to respond appropriately to the risks and tests of different historical periods, to ensure that it always remains at the forefront of the times even as profound changes confront us at home and sweep the global landscape, and to stand firm as the core of the nation.

On the journey ahead, we must keep firmly in mind the old adage that it takes a good blacksmith to forge good tools. We must demonstrate greater awareness of the fact that full and rigorous self-governance is a never-ending journey. We must continue to advance the great new project of strengthening the Party with its political development as an overarching principle. We must tighten the Party's organizational system, work hard to train high-caliber officials who have both moral integrity and professional competence, remain committed to improving Party conduct, upholding integrity, and combating corruption, and root out any elements that would harm the Party's progressive and wholesome nature and any viruses that would erode its health. We must ensure that the Party preserves its essence, color and character, and see that it always serves as the strong leadership core in upholding and developing socialism with Chinese characteristics in the new era.

Comrades and friends,

We will stay true to the letter and spirit of the One Country, Two Systems policy, under which the people of Hong Kong govern Hong Kong, and the people of Macao govern Macao, both with a high degree of autonomy. We will ensure that the central government exercises overall jurisdiction over Hong Kong and Macao, and implement legal systems and enforcement mechanisms for the two special administrative regions to safeguard national security. While protecting China's sovereignty, security, and development interests, we will ensure social stability in Hong Kong and Macao, and maintain lasting prosperity and stability in the two special administrative regions.

Resolving the Taiwan question and realizing China's complete reunification is a historic mission and an unshakable commitment of the Communist Party of China. It is also a shared aspiration of all the sons and daughters of the Chinese nation. We will uphold the one-China principle and the 1992 Consensus[6], and advance towards peaceful national reunification. All of us, compatriots on both sides of the Taiwan Straits, must come together and move forward in unison. We must take resolute action to utterly defeat any move towards "Taiwan independence", and work together to create a bright future for national rejuvenation. No one should underestimate the resolve, the will, and the ability of the Chinese people to defend their national sovereignty and territorial integrity.

Comrades and friends,

The future belongs to the young, and our hopes also rest with them. A century ago, a group of young progressives held aloft the torch of Marxism and searched assiduously in those dark years for ways to rejuvenate the Chinese nation. Since then, under the banner of the Communist Party of China, generation after generation of young Chinese have devoted their youth to the cause of the Party and the people, and remained in the vanguard of the drive to rejuvenate the nation.

In the new era, our young people should make it their mission to contribute to national rejuvenation and aspire to greater pride, confidence and assurance in their identity as Chinese, so that they can live up to the promise of their youth and the expectations of our times, our Party, and our people.

Comrades and friends,

A century ago, at the time of its founding, the Communist Party of China had just over 50 members. Today, with more than 95 million members in a country of more than 1.4 billion people, it is the largest governing party in the world and enjoys tremendous international influence.

A century ago, China was in decline and withering away in the eyes of the world. Today, the image it presents to the world is one of a thriving nation that is advancing with unstoppable momentum towards rejuvenation.

Over the past century, the Communist Party of China has secured extraordinary achievements on behalf of the people. Today, it is rallying the Chinese people and leading them on a new journey towards realizing the Second Centenary Goal.

To all Party members,

The Central Committee calls on every one of you to stay true to our Party's original aspiration and founding mission and stand firm in your ideals and convictions. Acting on the aims of the Party, you should always maintain close ties with the people, empathize and work with them, stand with them through good times and testing times, and continue working tirelessly to realize their aspirations for a better life and to bring still greater glory to the Party and the people.

Comrades and friends,

Today, a hundred years on from its founding, the Communist Party of China is still in its prime, and remains as determined as ever to achieve lasting greatness for the Chinese nation. Looking back on the path we have traveled and forward to the journey that lies ahead, it is certain that with the firm leadership of the Party and the great unity of all the Chinese people, we will achieve the goal of building a great modern socialist country in all respects and fulfill the Chinese Dream of national rejuvenation.

Long live our great, glorious and correct Party!
Long live our great, glorious and heroic people!

Notes

[1] Also known as Taiping Heavenly Kingdom Movement. – *Tr.*

[2] Also known as Yihetuan Movement. – *Tr.*

[3] This is China's overall plan for building socialism with Chinese characteristics, that is, to promote coordinated progress in the economic, political, cultural, social and eco-environmental fields.

[4] This is China's strategic plan for building socialism with Chinese characteristics, that is, to make comprehensive moves to achieve moderate prosperity in all respects, to further reform, to advance the rule of law, and to strengthen Party self-governance. Now that China has achieved moderate prosperity in all respects, the strategy has been changed to adopting comprehensive measures to build a modern socialist country in all respects, to further reform, to advance the rule of law, and to strengthen Party self-governance.

[5] Mao Zedong: "Shaoshan Revisited", *Mao Zedong Poems*, Chin. ed., Central Party Literature Publishing House, Beijing, 1996, p. 110.

[6] This refers to an oral agreement reached at a November 1992 meeting between the Association for Relations Across the Taiwan Straits representing the mainland and the Straits Exchange Foundation based in Taiwan. The meeting discussed how to express the one-China principle in negotiations on general affairs, and agreed that "both sides of the Straits belong to China and both sides will work together for the realization of reunification of the country".

Explanation of the Resolution of the CPC Central Committee on the Major Achievements and Historical Experience of the Party over the Past Century[*]

November 8, 2021

On behalf of the Political Bureau of the 19th Central Committee of the Communist Party of China, I will now brief you on the Resolution of the CPC Central Committee on the Major Achievements and Historical Experience of the Party over the Past Century, and related issues.

I. Considerations on the Agenda of the Sixth Plenary Session of the 19th CPC Central Committee

Our Party has always attached great importance to reviewing its historical experience. As early as in the Yan'an period (1935-1948), Mao Zedong pointed out, "We will not be able to achieve greater success unless we have a clear understanding of our history and of the roads we have traveled."[1]

In 1945, on the cusp of securing final victory in the War of Resistance Against Japanese Aggression, the Sixth CPC Central Committee convened its Seventh Plenary Session and adopted the Resolution on Certain Questions in the History of Our Party. The Resolution reviewed the history of the Party and the experience it had gained and lessons it had learned since its founding in 1921, in particular those in the period between the Fourth Plenary Session of the Sixth Central

---

[*] Speech at the Sixth Plenary Session of the 19th CPC Central Committee.

Committee in January 1931 and the Zunyi Meeting in January 1935. It drew conclusions on major historical issues, leading to a broad consensus among all Party members, particularly high-ranking officials, on fundamental questions pertaining to the Chinese revolution. It served to strengthen the solidarity of the Party, paved the way for the convocation of the Seventh CPC National Congress in 1945, and enabled a significant advance in the Chinese revolution.

When our country entered a new period marked by the launch of reform and opening up in 1978, Deng Xiaoping noted, "The experience of successes is valuable, and so is the experience of mistakes and defeats. Formulating principles and policies in this way enables us to unify the thinking of the whole Party so as to achieve a new unity; unity formed on such a basis is most reliable."[2]

In 1981, at its Sixth Plenary Session, the 11th Central Committee adopted the Resolution on Certain Questions in the History of Our Party Since the Founding of the People's Republic of China. The Resolution reviewed our Party's history in the period before the founding of the People's Republic in 1949 and summarized the experience it had gained in the course of socialist revolution and construction (1949-1978).

The Resolution evaluated certain major events and important figures. In particular, it gave a proper appraisal of Mao Zedong and Mao Zedong Thought. It drew a clear distinction between right and wrong and corrected the erroneous "Leftist" and Rightist viewpoints existing at the time. Through the Resolution, the Party came to a clear consensus and was more united than ever in support of a forward-looking approach. All this provided a strong impetus for reform, opening up, and socialist modernization.

Seventy-six years have passed since the adoption of the Party's first resolution on historical issues, and 40 years since the second. The past four decades have witnessed tremendous progress in the country and tremendous advances in the Party's theory and practice.

We have now arrived at a new historic milestone. As we look back and set our sights on the future, we have a need for an objective review of our Party's major achievements and historical experience over the past century, especially those in the 40-plus years of reform and opening up, and the subjective conditions are right.

The Party's central leadership considers it important in both a practical and historical sense to have a comprehensive review of the major achievements and historical experience of the Party over the past century, as we celebrate its centenary and the fulfillment of the First Centenary Goal of building a moderately prosperous society in all respects by 2021, and move on towards the Second Centenary Goal of building China into a great modern socialist country by 2049. This review will help build a broader consensus and stronger unity in will and action among all members, rally all the Chinese people, and lead them to new successes in building socialism with Chinese characteristics in the new era.

The central leadership understands that there are many issues that merit our careful study, as our Party has gone through an extraordinary journey over the past century, covering a long period of time and a wide range of fields. As a general requirement, we need to review our history and understand the underlying dynamics of its development so as to prepare for the future with greater confidence.

To this end, we need to relive the glories of the Party and appreciate how it has succeeded in rallying the Chinese people and leading them to so many magnificent achievements. We need to take stock of the invaluable experience the Party has gained in carrying out revolution, construction and reform, and summarize the theories and practices that have proved successful in advancing the cause of the Party and the country since the 18th CPC National Congress in 2012.

To put it more clearly, we need to revisit the Party's century-long history of leading the people in carrying out revolution, construction and reform. We need to review the Party's great historical course of achieving one victory after another, and the successes it has achieved in the interests of the country and the nation.

We need to revisit the Party's century-long history in which it has advanced Marxism in the Chinese context by adapting the basic tenets of Marxism to China's realities and traditional culture, and we need to gain a deeper understanding of the Party's innovative theories for the new era.

We need to revisit the Party's century-long history in which the Party has maintained unity and upheld the authority of the Central Committee and its centralized, unified leadership. We need to appreciate the significance of reinforcing the Party's political foundations, which is a distinctive feature and political strength of a Marxist party such as ours.

We need to revisit the Party's century-long journey in pursuit of happiness for the Chinese people and rejuvenation of the Chinese nation. We must always bear in mind that the Party and the people are inextricably connected and rise and fall together. Only with this understanding can we Party members better devote ourselves to the wellbeing of the people and rely on them in our endeavors.

We need to revisit the Party's century-long journey in which it has grown stronger through self-improvement and self-reform. We must never falter in exercising full and rigorous self-governance of the Party, and we must see this as an ongoing endeavor, in order to make sure that the Party always remains a strong leadership core in the endeavor to uphold and develop Chinese socialism in the new era.

We need to reflect on the past in order to understand historical patterns and trends, to be able to take timely actions in advancing the cause of the Party and the country in the new era, and to build greater courage and strength in order to keep to our set goals and stride ahead with pride and confidence.

The central leadership considers it essential to follow the methodology of dialectical and historical materialism in the review of the Party's major achievements and its experience over the past century. We need to look at the Party's history in the context of the times and all relevant events, and from an objective and developmental perspective.

We need to look at the Party's history rationally and from a broad perspective so as to accurately identify the underlying trends and defining features of the CPC's evolution.

We need to put in perspective the mistakes our Party made and setbacks it encountered on its way forward. We should draw experience from our successes and learn lessons from our mistakes so as to achieve new victories.

We need to be resolute in setting things straight, taking a clear-cut stance against historical nihilism, strengthening ideological guidance and theoretical analysis, and clearing up confusion and misunderstandings over some major questions in the Party's history.

The central leadership has made it clear that the following are the top priorities in drafting the resolution to be adopted at this session:

First, the resolution must focus on the Party's major achievements and experience over the past century.

Our Party has already produced two resolutions on historical issues, settling controversies on major issues in Party history in the period from its founding to the early stage of reform and opening up. Their basic points and conclusions remain valid.

Since reform and opening up was introduced in 1978, the Party and the country have by and large made smooth progress in the right direction, achieving results that have earned worldwide acclaim, despite encountering certain problems. In view of this, the draft resolution to be adopted at this session should focus on a review of the Party's major achievements and experience over the past century. This will help pool our wisdom, strengthen our unity, and boost our confidence and morale.

Second, the resolution must highlight the new era in advancing Chinese socialism.

This resolution should place emphasis on the new era, mainly reviewing the historic achievements and shifts in the cause of the Party and the country, and the latest experience that the Party has gained during this period. This is because the two previous resolutions on historical issues were devoted to Party history during three earlier phases: the period of the New Democratic Revolution, the period of socialist revolution and construction, and the period between the

Third Plenary Session of the 11th CPC Central Committee in 1978 and its Sixth Plenary Session in 1981.

Concerning the achievements and experience gained during the new period of reform, opening up, and socialist modernization, the Central Committee has already conducted thorough reviews on the occasions of the 20th and 30th anniversaries of the Third Plenary Session of the 11th CPC Central Committee. I also gave a systematic analysis of this period in my speech at a gathering to celebrate the 40th anniversary of reform and opening up.

Therefore, the resolution before us needs to focus on the new era when we advance socialism with Chinese characteristics, along with a brief summary of Party history prior to the 18th CPC National Congress based on existing reviews and conclusions. This will further fortify the confidence of all Party members, and help them to focus on our current endeavors, forge ahead on the new journey with greater strength of purpose, and contribute even more in the new era.

Third, the resolution's appraisal of major events, significant meetings, and important figures must be consistent with the Party Central Committee's existing conclusions.

The previous two resolutions and a substantial body of important Party literature document the major events, meetings, and figures in Party history prior to its 18th National Congress, and contain well-considered conclusions on historical issues. These points and conclusions are to be upheld in the new resolution.

Since 2012, I have spoken about Party history and the Party's conclusions on historical issues on a number of important occasions, including events marking the 95th anniversary of the founding of the Party, the 90th anniversary of the founding of the People's Liberation Army, the 70th anniversary of the founding of the People's Republic of China, and in particular the Party's centenary. These statements represent an updated understanding on the part of the Central Committee of the Party's century-long history. This updated understanding needs to be reflected in the new resolution.

II. The Drafting Process

In March this year, the Political Bureau decided that the Sixth Plenary Session of the 19th CPC Central Committee would focus on a comprehensive review of the Party's major achievements and historical experience in its century-long history.

To this end, a working group was established to draft the document under the auspices of the Standing Committee of the Political Bureau. I am head of this group, and my colleagues Wang Huning and Zhao Leji serve as its deputy heads. The group's membership is composed of other Party and state leaders, as well as leading officials from relevant central departments and localities.

On April 1, the Central Committee issued the Circular on Soliciting Opinions on the Agenda of the Sixth Plenary Session of the 19th CPC Central Committee of Focusing on a Full and Systematic Review of the Major Achievements and Historical Experience of the Party, in order to seek comments and suggestions from Party members and non-Party figures as appropriate.

From their feedback, we can see unanimous agreement among all localities, departments and sectors consulted, that the decision of the 19th CPC Central Committee to focus its Sixth Plenary Session on a comprehensive review of the Party's major achievements and historical experience over the past century is a well-considered one and is of historic and strategic significance.

They believe the decision reflects the Party's firm resolve to stay true to its original aspiration and founding mission and remain as vibrant as ever. It demonstrates the Party's keen understanding of the general trends of history, its strong sense of mission and purpose, and its commitment to advancing the cause of the Party and the country. It also embodies the Party's broad and farsighted vision, its willingness to learn from history, and its commitment to remaining firmly grounded in reality while setting its sights on the future.

They expressed their unanimous endorsement of the Central Committee's decision to focus the session on a review of the Party's major achievements and historical experience over the past century. They have also come up with many constructive comments and suggestions on what issues should be covered in the resolution.

They all agree that in its century-long history the Party has united the Chinese people and led them in a continued endeavor to carry out revolution, construction and reform. They agree that the Party and the people have achieved successes that will go down in the annals of the Chinese nation, world socialism, and human society. They agree that the Party and the people have fundamentally changed the course of the Chinese nation's history in modern times and written a great chapter in the history of world socialism, adding new dimensions to Marxism. They agree that the Party and the people have made great progress towards national rejuvenation, made a significant contribution to human progress, and gained a wealth of invaluable experience on this great journey. All of these merit a systematic review.

The localities, departments and sectors involved in the consultation suggest that in reviewing the Party's major achievements and historical experience over the past century, we should focus on the historic achievements and shifts in the new era, and the latest experience gained during this period.

Under the planning of the Central Committee, the drafting group first carefully studied the Party's major historical documents. Following a thorough review of all major issues in the Party's history and giving full consideration to the comments and suggestions collected from those consulted, the group subsequently began to draft the resolution.

In accordance with a decision made at a meeting of the Political Bureau, the text of the draft resolution was distributed on September 6 to selected Party members, including retired senior Party officials, for consultation. We also sought opinions from the central committees of other political parties and the All-China Federation of Industry and Commerce and prominent individuals without party affiliation.

The feedback we have received provides full endorsement of the text of the draft resolution and its general framework and main content. They all agree that the most salient feature of the document is its focus on facts and its respect for history.

They also agree that the document highlights the Party's commitment to its original aspiration and founding mission in all its endeavors over the past century. It is a fact-based document and its descriptions and appraisals of major events, meetings and figures are consistent with those in the Party's existing historical documents. It also demonstrates the Central Committee's updated understanding of Party history in the period after the Party's 18th National Congress.

Under the subheading, "Historical Significance of the Party's Endeavors over the Past Century", the document provides a comprehensive, in-depth and systematic summary of the Party's historic contribution to China and humanity.

Under the subheading, "Historical Experience of the Party's Endeavors over the Past Century", the document summarizes the Party's experience in the past and also highlights its significance for guiding ongoing and future endeavors.

All localities, departments and sectors consulted agree that this draft resolution represents a political declaration of China's Communists to stay true to their original aspiration and founding mission, and their commitment to upholding and developing socialism with Chinese characteristics in the new era. It is a guideline for the Party to create a brighter future and achieve national rejuvenation by learning from history.

They also agree that the draft resolution is imbued with the same spirit as the two previous resolutions on historical issues, while also reflecting the spirit of the times. It will inspire the whole Party to strive harder on the journey ahead.

Over the course of soliciting opinions, we received many valuable comments and suggestions from the localities, departments and sectors consulted. The drafting group analyzed these opinions and suggestions individually and incorporated as many of them as possible. Following multiple discussions and careful consideration, a total of 547 revisions were made to the preliminary draft. The revised draft therefore fully reflects the input of those consulted. During the drafting process, the Standing Committee of the Political Bureau met three times and the Political Bureau twice for the purpose of discussing and finalizing the draft. The current draft for your consideration is a product of these meetings.

III. The General Framework and Main Content of the Document

In addition to a preamble and a conclusion, the document has seven sections.

1. A Great Victory in the New Democratic Revolution

This section outlines the major tasks of the Party during the New Democratic Revolution period, namely opposing imperialism, feudalism and bureaucrat-capitalism, and working for the nation's independence and the people's liberation, so as to create the fundamental social conditions necessary for realizing national rejuvenation.

It analyzes the historical background to the founding of the Party, and highlights the revolutionary struggle waged by the people under the Party's leadership and its great achievements in the early days of the Party and during the periods of the Great Revolution (1924-1927), the Agrarian Revolutionary War (1927-1937), the War of Resistance Against Japanese Aggression (1931-1945), and the War of Liberation (1946-1950). It also highlights the Party's major achievements in establishing Mao Zedong Thought, and initiating and advancing the great project of strengthening the Party.

It emphasizes that founding the People's Republic of China, achieving national independence, and securing the people's liberation represented China's great transformation from a millennia-old feudal autocracy to a people's democracy. Through these achievements, gained by tenacious struggle, the Communist Party of China and the Chinese people showed the world that China had stood up and the time in which the Chinese nation could be abused and oppressed by others was gone and would never return. This marked the beginning of a new epoch in China's development.

2. Socialist Revolution and Construction

This section specifies the Party's major tasks during this period, which were to realize the transformation from new democracy to socialism, carry out socialist revolution, promote socialist construction, and lay down the fundamental political conditions and the institutional foundations necessary for national rejuvenation.

It reviews the Party's great achievements during the period following the founding of the People's Republic of China, in which the Party led the people in surmounting many challenging obstacles to consolidate the newly-established state power, completing the process of socialist transformation, establishing the socialist system, launching large-scale socialist construction on all fronts, and breaking new ground in foreign affairs.

It recaps the efforts of the Party to build up its capacity as the governing party, and summarizes the preliminary experience gained in this regard. It gives a rational appraisal of Mao Zedong Thought based on a summary of the creative theories put forward by the Party during this period.

The section also highlights the achievements of the Chinese people under the Party's leadership, which brought about a great transformation from a poor, backward and populous Eastern country to a strong socialist nation. Through these achievements, gained by tenacious struggle, the Communist Party of China and the Chinese people showed the world that the Chinese people were not only capable of dismantling the old world but also of building a new one, and that only socialism could save China and develop China.

3. Reform, Opening Up, and Socialist Modernization

This section recounts the major tasks of the Party during this period, which were to continue exploring the right path for building socialism in China, unleash and develop productive forces, lift the people out of poverty and help them become prosperous in the shortest time possible, and fuel the push towards national rejuvenation by providing new, dynamic institutional guarantees as well as the material conditions for rapid development.

It highlights the great significance of the Third Plenary Session of the 11th CPC Central Committee, and documents the historic contribution of China's Communists with Deng Xiaoping, Jiang Zemin and Hu Jintao as their chief representatives. It reviews the spectacular progress and resounding successes of the Party during this period as it led the people in restoring order in all sectors, developing the theory of socialism with Chinese characteristics, advancing reform, opening up and socialist modernization, effectively responding to the many challenges to China's overall reform, development and stability, promoting national reunification, safeguarding world peace, pursuing common development, and launching and advancing the great new project of strengthening the Party.

This section commends the great achievements of the Party and the people during this period, which made possible the Chinese nation's tremendous advance from standing up to becoming prosperous. Through these achievements, gained by tenacious struggle, the Communist Party of China and the Chinese people showed the world that reform and opening up was a crucial move in making China what it is today, that socialism with Chinese characteristics is the right path towards development and prosperity, and that China has caught up with the times in great strides.

4. A New Era of Socialism with Chinese Characteristics

This section outlines the major tasks of the Party during this period: completing the First Centenary Goal of building a moderately prosperous society in all respects, launching a new journey to realize the Second Centenary Goal of turning China into a great modern socialist country, and continuing to advance towards the great goal of national rejuvenation.

It elaborates on the new era in advancing socialism with Chinese characteristics, which represents a new phase in China's development. It reviews the Party's achievements in theoretical innovation since its 18th National Congress, and thoroughly analyzes the conditions, risks and challenges faced by the Party in the new era.

With a focus on the original ideas, transformative practices, new breakthroughs, and landmark accomplishments over the past nine years, the section reviews the great achievements and historic shifts in the new era in 13 areas:

- upholding the Party's overall leadership;
- exercising full and rigorous self-governance of the Party;
- pursuing economic development;
- expanding reform and opening up;
- reinforcing the political foundations;
- advancing law-based governance;
- driving cultural progress;
- promoting social progress;
- spurring eco-environmental progress;
- strengthening national defense and the armed forces;
- safeguarding national security;
- upholding the One Country, Two Systems policy and promoting national reunification;
- bolstering the diplomatic front.

The section emphasizes that the great achievements of the people under the leadership of the Party during this period provide better institutional conditions, stronger material foundations, and a source of inspiration for realizing national rejuvenation. Through these achievements, gained by tenacious struggle, the Communist Party of China and the Chinese people have shown the world that the Chinese nation has achieved the tremendous transformation from standing up and becoming better off to growing in strength.

5. The Historical Significance of the Party's Endeavors over the Past Century

Based on a thorough review of the Party's major achievements over the past century, this section highlights the significance of the Party's endeavors from a broad perspective:

- fundamentally transforming the future of the Chinese people;
- opening up the right path for achieving rejuvenation of the Chinese nation;
- demonstrating the vitality of Marxism;

- exerting a profound influence on the course of world history;
- making the CPC a forerunner of the times.

It spells out the CPC's historic contribution to the Chinese people, the Chinese nation, Marxism, human progress, and the development of Marxist political parties.

This five-point summary is rooted in China's experience, but represents a vision for the future of humanity. It reflects the close bond between the CPC and the Chinese people and nation, the connections between the CPC and Marxism, world socialism, and human society, and the underlying logic behind the Party's history, theory and practice in the past 100 years.

6. The Historical Experience of the Party's Endeavors over the Past Century

The historical experience of the Party is of fundamental and far-reaching significance. This section summarizes this experience from 10 perspectives:

- upholding the Party's leadership;
- putting the people first;
- advancing theoretical innovation;
- staying independent;
- following the Chinese path;
- maintaining a global vision;
- breaking new ground;
- standing up for ourselves;
- promoting the united front;
- remaining committed to self-reform.

These 10 points form a systemic, interconnected and indivisible whole. They are critical to the continued success of the Party and the people. They are the source of the Party's strength, and are the very reason why the Party has always been able to take timely actions. They are essential for the Party to preserve its progressive and wholesome nature and always stand at the forefront of the times.

This section reiterates that the 10 points represent valuable practical experience the Party has gained on its century-long journey and they are intellectual treasures created through the joint efforts of the Party and the people. We must all cherish them, uphold them over the long term, and continue to enrich and develop them in practice in the new era.

7. The Communist Party of China in the New Era

This section focuses on the Second Centenary Goal of building China into a great modern socialist country in all respects. It calls on all Party members to make unremitting and resolute efforts to advance the rejuvenation of the Chinese nation and never to let up until we reach our goals, bearing in mind that the last leg of the journey marks the halfway point only.

It emphasizes the importance of adhering to the Party's underlying theories, basic guidelines, and fundamental principles, and of grounding our work in this new development stage, applying the new development philosophy, fostering a new development dynamic, and pursuing high-quality development. It calls for coordinated nationwide efforts to make our people prosperous, our nation strong, and our country beautiful.

It reiterates the need to forever maintain the Party's close ties with the people and the need to better realize, safeguard and advance the fundamental interests of all the people. It reminds us that one may thrive in adversity and decline in times of ease. It requires us to see things from a long-term, strategic perspective, and always remain mindful of potential dangers, and inspires us to continue the great new project of strengthening the Party in the new era. It emphasizes that we must nurture the people who will carry on the cause of the Party from generation to generation.

It calls on the whole Party, the military, and all our people to bear in mind the glories and hardships of yesterday, rise to the mission of today, and live up to the great dream of tomorrow. It also calls on us to learn from history, work hard, forge ahead for a better future, and make tireless efforts to realize the Second Centenary Goal and the Chinese Dream of national rejuvenation.

Comrades,

The key task of the present session is to review and adopt the resolution. I hope that in doing so, you will act in accordance with the requirements of the central leadership, and adopt a holistic perspective on the past, the present, and the future of our Party.

I also hope you will carry out in-depth discussions on the draft resolution, draw on our collective wisdom, and come up with constructive ideas and suggestions.

Let us work together to make this session a great success and do our best to improve the draft.

Notes

[1] Mao Zedong: "How to Study the History of the CPC", *Collected Works of Mao Zedong*, Vol. II, Chin. ed., People's Publishing House, Beijing, 1993, p. 399.

[2] Deng Xiaoping: "Reform and Opening to the Outside World Can Truly Invigorate China", *Selected Works of Deng Xiaoping*, Vol. III, Eng. ed., Foreign Languages Press, Beijing, 1994, p. 232.

Adapt Marxism to China's Realities and Keep It Up-to-Date*

January 11, 2022

The Party Central Committee has organized this study session focusing on the resolution adopted at the Sixth Plenary Session of the 19th CPC Central Committee. The session is designed to help you study the resolution and understand its guiding principles. This will serve as an opportunity to further review, study and disseminate Party history, to better draw on the experience of our Party over the past hundred years, and to carry forward the great spirit of our forerunners in creating the CPC. With more confidence in our history, with greater unity and solidarity, and with a renewed fighting spirit, the whole Party and all the Chinese people will press ahead firmly and fearlessly towards our Second Centenary Goal.

To stay at the forefront of the times, a nation must always be guided by the right theories and thoughts. How does the CPC succeed? Why does Chinese socialism work? Because Marxism works. Because Marxism is adapted by the CPC to the Chinese context, kept up-to-date, and employed to guide our cause.

In the resolution, we have a comprehensive review of how the Party has adapted Marxism to China's realities and kept it fresh over a period of 100 years, which is the main thrust of the resolution and which we must study earnestly and understand fully.

Marxism points the way for advancing human society. It is a powerful theoretical weapon for us to understand the world and its

---

* Main points of the speech at the opening ceremony of a study session on implementing the decisions of the Sixth Plenary Session of the 19th CPC Central Committee, attended by principal officials at the provincial and ministerial level.

underlying trends, seek the truth, and change the world. Marxism is not a set of rigid dogmas, but a guide to action that must evolve as the situation changes. Whether Marxism can serve its guiding role depends on whether its basic tenets are adapted to the conditions in China and the features of the times. In a fast-changing world and a fast-growing country, we cannot be fettered to old conventions and rigid thinking, and we must be bold enough to update our theory. If we cannot answer questions concerning the present and future of China and its people and the wider world, we will lose momentum in advancing the cause of the Party and the country, Marxism will wither, and people will lose faith in it.

What contemporary China is experiencing is an innovative social transformation unique in history. In this context, the magnitude of our tasks to advance reform and development and to maintain stability, the multitude of problems, risks, and challenges we face, and the difficulties involved in the governance of the country are all unprecedented. As the world experiences change on a scale unseen in a century, a plethora of questions need to be answered in theory and in practice. We need to gain a keen appreciation of the underlying trends of the times, and stand boldly at the forefront of human development. We should listen to the people, respond to their needs, continue to free our minds, seek truth from facts, and maintain the right political direction and break new ground. We should develop Marxism while upholding its basic tenets, combine them with the best of our traditional culture, and apply them in China's context, so that Marxism can continue to work in solving problems in China in the new era.

The Party's history over the past century tells us that for the cause of the Party and the people to progress, we must have a thorough understanding of the principal challenge facing our society and properly identify our central task. Only when this is done can the cause of the Party and the people progress smoothly. Otherwise our cause will suffer setbacks.

The resolution presents a full analysis of the Party's strengths in focusing on China's principal challenge and central task when advancing work on all fronts. An important theme of the resolution is the review of how the Party has studied and understood the principal challenge and central task over the past century. We should pay particular attention to this when we study the resolution to ensure that we understand it fully. When dealing with complex situations and difficult problems, or tasked with a demanding workload, no one will do well by trying to attend to major and minor issues at one and the same time. We should have a good knowledge of the overall situation, and know full well what challenges we face. Then we will focus on the principal challenge and the central task, and address the main aspects of the principal challenge first, hence laying the groundwork for the solution of other problems. By making breakthroughs in key areas we will drive overall economic development and social progress to a new level, and come closer to the goal of developing China into a great modern socialist country in all respects.

Strategic issues are fundamental to a political party and a country. Accurate judgment and sensible planning help us gain the strategic initiative crucial to the success of the cause of the Party and the people. At every critical moment over the past hundred years the Party has responded to crucial issues of historical significance from a strategic perspective, making sound assessments and defining political strategies accordingly. This has ensured our success in dealing with numerous risks and challenges along the way.

The resolution summarizes how the Party has always attached great importance to strategies and tactics, and how it has conceived sound strategies and tactics in the century since its founding. It is an important part of the resolution that we must study earnestly; we must ensure we understand it fully.

Strategic thinking is all about judgment and decision-making. It requires us to take into consideration the overall situation, long-term interests and underlying trends. Ours is a major political party governing a large country and working for a great cause. We must be able to think strategically and plan accordingly. A sound strategy is to be executed through proper tactics, which are dictated by the former and serve the former. They are in a dialectical relationship, in which the strategy stays consistent while the tactics can be flexible. In planning their work and devising policy measures, local authorities and government departments should make sure that their work plans, arrangements and policy decisions conform with the Party's theories, guidelines, principles and policies, and they must correct any deviation as soon as it appears. Strategic decisions made by the Party Central Committee must be enforced fully, faithfully and unconditionally.

Over the past hundred years, our Party has led the people to victory after victory, and its vigor and vitality have never been diluted by hardships or obstacles. It has won the people's support because it faces its own shortcomings squarely, has the courage to correct itself, and always maintains its progressive and wholesome nature. In increasing its creativity, cohesiveness and capabilities, the CPC has preserved its character as a Marxist political party. The resolution gives a full review of the Party's experience in self-governance and self-reform, to which the Party has paid great attention and in which it has made steady progress over the past hundred years. This is an important thread going through the resolution that we must study earnestly to ensure we understand it fully.

To maintain our nature as a Marxist political party under new circumstances, we must be self-driven, know clearly for whom we exercise governance and power and for whose interests we work, and take a firm stance on these fundamental issues. All Party members must have political integrity, observe the code of conduct in public office, and apply high moral standards in their private lives. They should be clean and honest in office and in private life, work selflessly and diligently for the public, live frugally to cultivate morality, and maintain political integrity.

The key to self-reform is to have the will to admit our own shortcomings and the courage to redress them. Now, our fight against corruption has secured an overwhelming victory on strong foundations, but we cannot allow ourselves any respite. We must remain committed to self-reform, and persevere in the never-ending journey of full and rigorous governance of the Party. We must continue to improve Party conduct, build clean government, and fight corruption to the end in the spirit of "leaving our mark in the steel we grasp and our print on the stone we tread". Not for one minute will we let our guard drop in this prolonged, uphill battle. There will be zero tolerance for anyone who violates Party discipline and the law.

In the resolution, there is a full review of the education campaign on CPC history, which calls on the whole Party to uphold a materialist approach to history and adopt a correct outlook on our Party's history. We should learn from our history to know why we succeeded in the past, and see how we can continue to succeed in the future. This will help strengthen our resolve in fulfilling our founding mission, and in upholding and developing Chinese socialism in the new era.

The education campaign on CPC history is an important political initiative launched at the Sixth Plenary Session of the 19th CPC Central Committee, and should be implemented in full. The Party's third resolution on its history reflects new perspectives on our understanding. We should pay special attention to them while studying the resolution, in order to have a better understanding of the Party's achievements and experience over the past hundred years. The education campaign has been a success. We must take stock of the successful experience gained from the campaign and turn it into a regular and institutionalized practice so that the results can be consolidated and extended.

The whole Party should focus on studying and implementing the guiding principles of the Sixth Plenary Session of the 19th CPC Central Committee, and drive the education campaign on CPC history to new heights, so as to have a better understanding of our cause, firmer commitment to our ideals, higher standards of integrity, and greater determination to turn what has been gained from studying history into concrete actions. All Party members should study Party history, reflect on our guiding principles, do solid work, and break new ground. They should arm themselves with the Party's new theories and enforce the Central Committee's decisions and plans.

We should study the resolution in earnest, so as to understand the Party's glorious history, its perseverance in fulfilling its founding mission, the significance and experience of its hundred-year struggle, and the importance of building a better future by drawing on history. Through study sessions of the theory study groups in Party committees and Party leadership groups, officials should take the lead in studying history on a regular basis. We should also leverage training institutions for officials to promote the study of Party history. Party history should be made a compulsory course for Party schools (academies of governance) and executive leadership academies for every semester. Party history should also be made available as part of school courses on moral and political education for young students to learn in classrooms, so that students can learn sound values and ethics. We should take advantage of our revolutionary heritage, strengthen education on our traditions and on patriotism to cultivate moral integrity in young people, and inspire society to love the Party and the country. Through the mechanisms established in the campaign "I do solid work for the people", Party organizations and members should continue to help solve problems that concern the people most, and carry our Party's mass line into the new era.

The Way Forward in the New Era[*]

March 5, 2022

As we look back on the journey the Party and the people have traveled since the 18th CPC National Congress in 2012, we are all the more convinced of the following:

First, upholding overall Party leadership is the only way to advance socialism with Chinese characteristics. As long as we uphold overall leadership by the Party and the authority of the Party Central Committee and its centralized, unified leadership, we will be able to ensure stronger political cohesion and greater confidence in the Party and across the nation. We will be able to gather strength to keep to the correct political direction, work together to overcome difficulties, and remain the most reliable core of the nation when problems arise.

Second, socialism with Chinese characteristics is the only path to national rejuvenation. As long as we remain committed to this path, we will be able to meet our people's aspirations for a better life and achieve common prosperity for all.

Third, solidarity is the only route for the Chinese people to achieve historic successes. We will surely overcome all challenges on our way forward and create new successes that will attract international acclaim, as long as we the Chinese people unite as one under the leadership of the Party, and have the courage and capacity to confront difficulties.

Fourth, implementing the new development philosophy is the only way for China to grow stronger in the new era. As long as we fully, accurately and faithfully apply the new development philosophy,

---

* Main points of the speech at the deliberation session of the Inner Mongolia delegation to the Fifth Session of the 13th National People's Congress.

create a new development dynamic, promote high-quality development, and strengthen our self-reliance in science and technology, we will grow more competitive, achieve sustainable development, and keep hold of the initiative in an environment of fierce and increasing international competition.

Fifth, full and rigorous self-governance is the only way for the Party to maintain its vitality and realize the Second Centenary Goal. China's success hinges on our Party, so we must ensure that the Party practices strict self-governance in every respect. As long as we continue to carry forward the great founding spirit of the Party, have the courage to reform ourselves, remove all harmful elements that might damage the Party's progressive and wholesome nature, and treat all viruses that erode its health, we will be able to ensure that the Party does not change or betray its nature.

Overall CPC Leadership

Keep Matters of National Significance to the Fore[*]

April 20, 2020-March 1, 2022

I

We must be politically aware, and build a clear understanding of matters of national significance by paying close attention to the Central Committee's main concerns and priorities, by fully understanding what matters most to the Party and the country, and by seeing clearly what we must uphold. We must not pay lip service to the Four Consciousnesses[1], the Four-sphere Confidence[2], and the Two Upholds[3]. We must act on them.

(from the speech during a visit to Shaanxi Province,
April 20-23, 2020)

II

Leading officials must have a clear understanding of matters of national significance in analyzing problems and making decisions. Build a strategic vision and think about the overall situation, rather than being short-sighted and focusing only on local interests. Learn to integrate local and departmental work into the overall undertakings of the Party and the state, contributing to both local and overall development.

(from the speech at the opening ceremony of a training program for
younger officials at the Central Party School [National Academy of
Governance] on October 10, during its 2020 fall semester)

---

[*] Excerpts from speeches made between April 20, 2020 and March 1, 2022.

III

With a clear focus on matters of national significance, Party members and officials at all levels, particularly leading officials, must strengthen their political stance and commitment to the Party, and reinforce Party consciousness. When we have problems to solve or decisions to make at work, we must first and foremost consider them from the political perspective – checking against the Party Constitution, regulations on internal Party activities, and Party disciplinary regulations to see what we should do or are allowed to do before taking action. This is the only way that we can withstand tests, resist temptation, and become rational political actors. This is exactly as an old saying goes: "A person without virtue has no high aspirations; a person without talent has no keen insights."[4]

(from the speech at the Fifth Plenary Session of the 19th CPC Central Commission for Discipline Inspection, January 22, 2021)

IV

Only with a sound political perspective can we build a thorough understanding of the Central Committee's major policies, decisions and plans, and work with foresight and initiative. It is imperative for officials at all levels, especially those in senior positions, to constantly improve their political acumen, understanding and capacity to deliver. Officials must be very clear about the priorities of the country and strictly follow the Central Committee's guiding principles when conceiving major strategies, formulating major policies, planning major tasks, and implementing major programs. We should regularly examine ourselves against our goals and standards, and promptly rectify any deviation.

(from the speech at the 27th group study session of the Political Bureau of the 19th CPC Central Committee, January 28, 2021)

V

This year is important as we have just embarked on the march towards the Second Centenary Goal of building a modern socialist country in all respects, and we will soon convene the 20th CPC National Congress. We must follow to the letter the guiding principles of the 19th CPC National Congress and of all the plenary sessions of the 19th CPC Central Committee, strengthen our commitment to the Four Consciousnesses, the Four-sphere Confidence and the Two Upholds, have a better understanding of matters of national significance, and closely follow the Party's central leadership in thinking, action and political commitment.

(from the instruction to the work reports of some officials, February 2022)

VI

We should be fully conscious of all matters of national significance, and analyze problems and take actions from an overall strategic perspective. In doing all our work, we must first and foremost implement the decisions and plans of the Central Committee. We must never damage overall interests for the sake of local interests, or harm fundamental and long-term interests for the sake of short-term interests.

(from the speech at the opening ceremony of a training program for younger officials at the Central Party School [National Academy of Governance] on March 1, during its 2022 spring semester)

Notes

[1] This refers to maintaining political commitment, thinking in terms of the general picture, following the core leadership of the CPC Central Committee, and acting in accordance with its requirements.

[2] This refers to confidence in the path, theory, system and culture of socialism with Chinese characteristics.

[3] This refers to upholding General Secretary Xi Jinping's core position on the CPC Central Committee and in the Party as a whole, and upholding the authority of the Central Committee and its centralized, unified leadership.

[4] Wang Chong: *Discourses Weighed in the Balance* (*Lun Heng*). Wang Chong (27-c. 97) was a philosopher, thinker and literary critic in the Eastern Han Dynasty.

Strengthen Our Political Acumen, Understanding and Capacity to Deliver[*]

December 24-25, 2020

We are going to celebrate the centenary of our Party next year. From the epoch-making founding of the CPC all the way to the establishment of the PRC that opened a brand new chapter, from the reform and opening up that brought nationwide change all the way to the post-18th CPC National Congress era that witnessed historic achievements and transformations in the undertakings of our Party and our state, the fundamental reason for a century of successes is that the Party has remained true to its original aspiration and founding mission to seek happiness for the Chinese people and rejuvenation for the Chinese nation. To sustain this original aspiration and founding mission and guarantee enduring success in the undertakings of the Party and the people, we must reinforce political awareness, look at problems from a political perspective, grasp the overall political situation, and improve our political acumen, understanding and capacity to deliver.

Taking a clear political stance is a distinctive feature of a Marxist party and also a political strength that our Party has valued from the outset. In exercising leadership in governance, the key is to keep to the correct political orientation, preserve the political character of the Party, and forge ahead on the path of building socialism with Chinese characteristics. We members of the Political Bureau of the CPC Central Committee must be adept at observing and dealing with problems from a political perspective, in the same way as we do in shooting –

---

[*] Main points of the speech at a meeting of criticism and self-criticism among members of the Political Bureau of the 19th CPC Central Committee.

knowing the range, aligning the sights, and aiming at the bullseye – to make political awareness an inner part of our thinking rather than a requirement imposed from the outside.

A clear political stance requires sound political acumen. One point has been constantly proved in the historical process of revolution, construction and reform under the leadership of the Party: Political proactivity is the most favorable form of proactivity, while political passivity is the most dangerous form of passivity. To improve political acumen, we must prioritize national political security, secure the people's interests, uphold and develop Chinese socialism, and increase our capacity for evaluating changing situations, identifying the true nature of issues, telling right from wrong, mitigating risks, and rising to challenges.

As members of the Political Bureau of the CPC Central Committee, we must be capable of reflecting on issues of fundamental significance to the overall and long-term undertakings of the Party and the state, strengthen our efforts in drawing up strategic, systemic and proactive plans, and stay sober-minded and insightful when dealing with major issues or making critical decisions. We must have the ability to distinguish political problems from everyday work, have a keen eye for sensitive matters and tendencies that might trigger political issues, learn to understand the political logic behind complex contradictions and relationships, and maintain our political stance and direction.

A clear political stance requires good political understanding. Leading officials, particularly high-ranking ones, who shoulder political responsibilities must have a thorough understanding of the guidelines of the Central Committee, and follow them closely in analyzing situations and improving their work. In other words, they must always align themselves with the requirements of the Central Committee. As the key organizers and leaders of the implementation of these guidelines, we members of the Political Bureau of the CPC Central Committee must work harder to increase our political understanding and to fully understand matters of national significance and our role in relation to such matters.

A clear political stance requires the capacity to deliver. Leading officials, particularly high-ranking ones, must uphold the guidelines of the Central Committee, respond promptly to its calls, fully implement its decisions, put a stop to anything it prohibits, and resolutely uphold its authority and centralized, unified leadership without hesitation or deviation. We must make preparations for worst-case scenarios, focus on solving problems in our work, be sharp and quick in foreseeing and identifying potential threats, and take preventive measures. We must increase our sense of responsibility and act accordingly, and face up to and resolve problems when they arise.

A clear political stance requires strict discipline. We members of the Political Bureau of the CPC Central Committee must exercise consistent self-cultivation and self-discipline, maintain self-respect, conduct self-examination, stay alert and motivated, maintain the strictest discipline even when unsupervised, guard against temptation, identify erroneous ideas from the outset, and be cautious in making friends. To preserve our integrity, we must cherish our moral principles as we do our lives. We must set an example in restraining family members and opposing the exploitation of privilege.

Strengthen Overall CPC Leadership in Socialist Modernization*

January 11, 2021

CPC leadership is the defining feature of Chinese socialism, in which the combinations of theoretical and practical innovation and of confidence in the system and culture feature most prominently. Together they evolve into strengths in politics, theory, system and culture that boost development. The implementation of decisions of the Fifth Plenary Session of the 19th CPC Central Committee should operate in parallel with those of the Fourth Plenary Session. In modernizing China's governance system and capacity, we must unify the political strengths of overall Party leadership, the institutional strengths of Chinese socialism, and the theoretical strengths of our new development philosophy. While exercising the Party's leadership in socialist modernization, we must make its division of functions more rational, reinforce its systems and mechanisms, and render its operations and management more efficient.

The implementation of the decisions of the Fifth Plenary Session of the 19th CPC Central Committee determines the overall development of the undertakings of the Party and the state in the coming five to 15 years and even longer. The Recommendations for Formulating the 14th Five-Year Plan for Economic and Social Development and Long-Range Objectives Through the Year 2035 adopted at the meeting is rich in content: It lays out guiding principles, strategic thoughts, overall plans, and specific requirements. It includes both strategies for

---

* Part of the speech at a study session on implementing the decisions of the Fifth Plenary Session of the 19th CPC Central Committee, attended by principal officials at the provincial and ministerial level.

implementation since the 18th CPC National Congress in 2012, and major new judgments and strategic measures. Without hard effort you will not gain a good grasp of this report, and without a good grasp you will miss the point and fail to enforce it effectively. Leading officials at all levels, particularly those in senior positions, must study the original text paragraph by paragraph, and have a good understanding of the key points and innovative proposals while bearing the overall picture in mind. You should carry forward the good tradition of combining theory with practice, consider both the current situation and long-term development, and increase enthusiasm, initiative and creativity in work.

I have emphasized on many occasions that high-ranking officials must make themselves into Marxist statesmen and stateswomen, and leading officials at all levels must take a clear political stance. Not long ago, I reiterated this at a meeting of criticism and self-criticism among members of the Political Bureau. Economic work has never been abstract or isolated; it is a network of specifics. Officials at all levels, and particularly those in senior positions, must consider the overarching goal of national rejuvenation in the context of change on a scale unseen in a century, improve their political acumen, understanding and capacity to deliver, and bear in mind matters of national significance. You must improve your political ability, strategic vision, and professionalism in understanding the new development stage, acting on the new development philosophy, and creating the new development dynamic. You should readily take on responsibilities, and fully implement decisions and plans of the Central Committee.

In leading this huge Eastern country with over one billion people towards socialist modernization, our Party must seek truth from facts, pursue progress while ensuring stability, advance our work in a coordinated manner, and intensify efforts in forward thinking, overall planning, strategic deployment, and comprehensive progress. Thus we can achieve rapid, efficient and safe development while maintaining quality, structure and scale. No region or ethnic group will be left behind when the whole country is working hard towards the goal of realizing all-round socialist modernization. At the same time, we must understand that regional disparities and imbalanced development make concurrent modernization impossible. So we should encourage the most capable regions to take the lead and support other regions to this end.

The Spring Festival is approaching. Local Party and government officials must pay more attention to Covid-19 prevention, and ensure security, stability, people's wellbeing, and supply of goods. You should identify problems early, attend to details, make real efforts to neutralize risks, and create a peaceful and harmonious social environment. You must make Covid-19 prevention and control regular and consistent, fully and carefully implementing the necessary measures to bring sporadic cases under quick and effective control. You must undertake a full review of any social tension, increase your analytical capability, and avoid or mitigate all potential risk factors through a proactive approach. Supply of energy and other goods, and transport safety must be ensured during the Spring Festival. A sound prevention and control system must be put in place to combat all crimes endangering people's lives and property and ensure social stability. Problems that might trigger incidents of social disturbance such as defaulting on payments to construction enterprises and delaying rural migrant workers' wages must be settled quickly.

Comrades, a statement made by Deng Xiaoping in 1992 often rings in my ears: "If we can make China a moderately developed country within a hundred years from the founding of the People's Republic, that will be an extraordinary achievement. The period from now to the middle of the next century will be crucial. We must immerse ourselves in hard work: We have difficult tasks to accomplish and bear a heavy responsibility."[1]

Now, the tasks and responsibilities fall on us. We must step forward to take on these responsibilities, unite the people, lead them to work diligently, and deliver results that live up to the expectations of the Party, the people and history.

Notes

[1] Deng Xiaoping: "Excerpts from Talks Given in Wuchang, Shenzhen, Zhuhai and Shanghai", *Selected Works of Deng Xiaoping*, Vol. III, Eng. ed., Foreign Languages Press, Beijing, 1994, p. 370.

Reinforce Our Party's Political Foundations for Unity and Solidarity[*]

November 11, 2021

Unity and solidarity are our Party's lifelines and the keys to our historic achievements over the past century. We have always kept our political foundations strong by guiding Party members to increase their political awareness and hold to the correct political direction and stance. All Party members have closely followed the Party's political guideline and are unified in thinking as a capable organization with an iron will and coordinated action.

Our Party has grown mature and strong over a long course. In the early days of the revolution it lacked a functional central leadership to unite the Party as one, resulting in repeated frustrations, and at some points even jeopardizing the cause. The Zunyi Meeting in 1935 laid the groundwork for establishing the leading position within the Central Committee of the correct Marxist line chiefly represented by Mao Zedong. The first generation of the Party's collective central leadership with Mao at the core started to take shape, ensuring success in the Party's later endeavors. History and our experience have proved that the unity and solidarity of the Party determines the future of the Party and the people and secures the fundamental interests of the country. It is our foundation and must be ensured at all times and under all circumstances.

To govern the world's biggest political party and most populous country, we must uphold the Party's centralized, unified leadership and the Central Committee's authority, and ensure that the Party exer-

---

* Part of the speech at the second full assembly of the Sixth Plenary Session of the 19th CPC Central Committee.

cises overall leadership and coordinates work in all areas. Since the 18th CPC National Congress in 2012, we have addressed problems of weakened, ineffective and marginalized measures in upholding Party leadership that had existed for some time, and called on the whole Party to take responsibility in upholding the Party's centralized, unified leadership. With constant improvements in the Party's leadership system, the whole Party has become more unified in thinking, with greater political solidarity and more concerted action. The resolution adopted at this plenary session reiterates the importance of strengthening the centralized, unified leadership of the Central Committee, requiring the whole Party to act consistently with the Central Committee and remain strong as iron on its march forward.

Unity and solidarity require absolute loyalty from all Party members. Loyalty to the Party is the political character essential to China's Communists. It should be sincere, unconditional and absolute, allowing no room for maneuver. All Party members, especially leading officials, must remain fully aligned with the Central Committee in political stance, orientation, principles and path. They must be loyal to the Party and the people, to the Party's ideals and convictions, to its original aspiration and founding mission, to its organization, and to its theories, guidelines and policies. They must strictly observe the Party's political discipline and rules, and uphold the Central Committee's centralized, unified leadership in thinking, action and political principles.

Loyalty to the Party is not an empty slogan and cannot be perfunctory. It calls for action in executing the Central Committee's decisions and plans, in performing one's duties diligently and effectively, and in following discipline and rules in daily life. Party members must respond promptly to the Central Committee's calls, fully implement its decisions, and put a stop to anything it prohibits. This should be unconditional and no deviation is allowed. All Party members should stay on the right track, and join their forces to forge a strong synergy.

The People First

Always Put the People First[*]

May 22, 2020

The CPC has its foundations in the people and maintains a close bond with the people. The people-centered philosophy of development embodies our Party's ideals and convictions, its nature and purpose, and its aspiration and founding mission. It is also the result of an in-depth reflection on the Party's development and practical experience. The fundamental goal for the Party since its founding, in uniting the people and leading them in revolution, construction and reform, is to give them a better life. The Party has never wavered in pursuing this goal no matter what challenges and pressure it faces, no matter the sacrifice and the cost. The people-centered philosophy of development is not an empty slogan, but a principle that underpins all our decisions and plans, and every aspect of our work.

First, always put the people first.

As an ancient Chinese said, "A sovereign who shares the interests of the people will have their support; a sovereign who denies the interests of the people will provoke their opposition."[1] The Constitution of the CPC states clearly that the Party has no special interests of its own and it shall, at all times, give top priority to the interests of the people. This salient feature distinguishes our Party, a Marxist party, from many others.

Confronted by the rapid spread of Covid-19, from the very beginning we have stated clearly that people's lives and health should be our top priority. We have mobilized the best doctors, the most advanced equipment, and the most urgently needed resources across

---

[*] Main part of the speech at the deliberation session of the Inner Mongolia delegation to the Third Session of the 13th National People's Congress.

the country, and committed ourselves fully to the treatment of the sick. All the costs of the treatment are borne by the state. We act on our belief that the people come first, and life matters most. We are willing to protect people's lives and health at any cost.

At present, China faces growing pressure in preventing inbound cases and guarding against domestic resurgence. It is necessary to tighten epidemic prevention and control and improve the regularized epidemic response mechanism to prevent domestic resurgence.

Second, rely on the people.

The people are our greatest strength in governance. Under the unified leadership of the CPC Central Committee, the whole country has been mobilized and has joined the battle against Covid-19, and governments at all levels and the whole of society are involved, establishing an impermeable network and forming an indestructible force for joint prevention and control. Considering the national interest and the general situation, the people have consciously subordinated their own needs to the overall interests of epidemic control, becoming the fundamental force in the battle.

As an ancient Chinese said, "If you can employ the strength of the people, you will be invincible under Heaven; if you can employ the wisdom of the people, no sage will be cleverer than you."[2] China's socialist democracy is the most broad-based, genuine and effective democracy that safeguards the fundamental interests of the people. We must uphold people's democracy and better integrate the people's wisdom and strength into the undertakings of the Party and the people.

The Inner Mongolia Autonomous Region was the first ethnic autonomous region in China. I hope you will uphold and improve the system of regional ethnic autonomy, strengthen exchanges and interactions among different ethnic groups, accelerate the pace of economic and social development, and continue to take the lead in promoting ethnic unity and progress.

We must rely closely on the people in coordinating epidemic control with economic and social development. The epidemic has had a substantial impact on China's economic and social development, but the economic fundamentals for stable and long-term progress have not changed. A coin has two sides. The epidemic is a crisis, but to some extent it has generated new opportunities. It is necessary to take proactive action and launch effective measures to press ahead with major projects, support market players, accelerate industrial restructuring, and improve grassroots governance. Targeted efforts should be made in mapping out major plans, reforms and policies that will serve as drivers of high-quality development and high-efficiency governance. This way, we will keep the initiative and achieve progress in our response to the crisis.

Third, constantly work for the benefit of the people.

The purpose of economic and social development is, in the final analysis, to fulfill the people's desire for a better life. We must ensure that the people live and work in peace and contentment, and we must work hard to address practical issues of public concern, including employment, education, social security, medical care, housing, pension, food safety, and public order. We must make concrete efforts year after year to deliver tangible results and real benefits to the people.

Inner Mongolia announced in March that all of its impoverished counties had emerged from poverty. Further efforts should be made to consolidate and expand progress in poverty alleviation through economic development and employment, to provide effective follow-up support for relocation of the poor from inhospitable areas, and to integrate poverty alleviation into rural revitalization. The epidemic has increased the pressure on employment this year. We must succeed in generating employment for key groups including graduating college students, rural migrant workers, and demobilized military personnel.

The epidemic has exposed weaknesses and shortcomings in our public health system. Immediate action must be taken to improve the public health system and the system for preventing, controlling and treating serious epidemics, to reinforce community-level epidemic response capacity in both urban and rural areas, and to carry out extensive public health campaigns, so as to better protect people's lives and health.

We must consider serving the people and working for their well-being to be our primary political goal. The Party measures job performance of its members by how much good they have done for the people. Party members and officials, particularly senior ones, must be aware that the power in their hands and the positions they hold are entrusted by the Party and the people, and can only be used for advancing the Party's undertakings for the benefit of the people. Leading officials at all levels must take the right attitude towards power, job performance and career, and take concrete actions to benefit the local people during their term in office, rather than indulging their vanity, pursuing unearned prestige, or achieving worthless outcomes.

For example, eco-environmental protection is of vital importance to the people. The eco-environmental conditions in Inner Mongolia have a critical impact not only on the life and development of all ethnic groups in the region, but also on the eco-environmental security of the north, northeast and northwest of the country, and on the nation as a whole. Over the years, you have carried out key environmental projects, fought a tough battle against pollution, and taken important steps to build a beautiful Inner Mongolia. Local officials and people have persevered for more than 60 years in controlling the Mu Us Desert, 70 percent of which has been brought under control. The local environment as a whole is improving. What a great achievement!

We should remain confident in our eco-environmental strategy, and prioritize eco-environmental protection and green development. We should take comprehensive measures to improve the eco-environment in key locations such as the Yellow River Basin, Hulun Lake, Wuliangsu Lake, Daihai Lake, Wuhai Lake and the surrounding areas. Efforts to improve the quality of air, water and soil should continue in this region, so as to further fortify the green barrier in north China.

Fourth, take root in the people.

To achieve long-term governance, our Party must maintain close ties with the people, think and act in their interests, and share weal and woe with them. Since the 18th CPC National Congress held in 2012, we have exercised full and strict governance over the Party. Firm action has been taken to combat corruption and the Four Malfea-sances of favoring form over substance, bureaucratism, hedonism and extravagance. We have launched education campaigns among all Party members to increase awareness of honoring the Party's mass line and its original aspiration and founding mission. Our goal is to educate and guide Party members and officials to share the future with the people, and stay truly connected to them. To achieve this goal, we should make every effort to combat corruption and oppose any tendency towards favoring form over substance and bureaucratism. And we should prevent any disengagement from the people, which may lead to a loss of public support.

Notes

[1] *Guan Zi*. This is a collection of writings attributed to Guan Zhong. Guan Zhong (?-645 BC), also known as Guan Zi, was a statesman of the State of Qi in the early Spring and Autumn Period.

[2] Chen Shou: *Records of the Three Kingdoms* (*San Guo Zhi*). Chen Shou (233-297) was an official and historian of the Western Jin Dynasty.

The People's Support Is Our Top Political Priority*

September 17, 2020

The sudden outbreak of Covid-19 represented a challenge to our efforts to fulfill the 13th Five-year Plan (2016-2020) and achieve the annual targets and tasks set at the start of this year. Making people's lives and health our top priority, we waged an all-out people's war on the virus. After making initial progress in containing its spread, we coordinated epidemic prevention and control with the reopening of the economy, to restore economic and social order as soon as possible. On September 8 we held a grand gathering in Beijing to award national medals and honorary titles of the PRC, the highest state honors, to outstanding individuals and groups in the fight against the epidemic. I delivered a speech at the meeting.

Since the flood season began this year, severe floods have occurred in the Yangtze and Huaihe river basins. At times, water in major rivers and lakes exceeded the warning level, and some places were severely affected. The central leadership made timely arrangements for flood control and disaster relief. Under the guidance and coordination of the central departments concerned, the affected provinces, including Hunan, have done their best in flood control and disaster relief and sped up post-disaster recovery and reconstruction.

Looking at the whole world, we are in the front ranks in both epidemic response and economic recovery. Achieving this success has been no easy matter.

What impresses me most is that, in the face of urgent and difficult tasks and dangerous and severe challenges, our people have always

* Main part of the speech at a meeting with grassroots representatives.

acted with one heart, united their efforts, and fought tenaciously. They have made a great contribution. These victories of our Party and our country are all victories won by our people, who are the true heroes.

The people's expectation for a better life is what drives us forward. Sound guidelines, policies and development plans must accord with the will, aspirations and expectations of the people. They should come from the people and serve their interests. Over the decades, our Party has always required relevant departments to conduct in-depth research and studies at the grassroots level and to understand and gather information firsthand before issuing important guidelines and policies and making major decisions and arrangements. Seeking truth from facts is an important element of our Party's guiding principles. When our Party was headquartered in Yan'an in the 1930s and 1940s, Mao Zedong emphasized, "Communists should set an example in being practical"[1], and "for only by being practical can they fulfill their appointed tasks"[2]. He pointed out that to conduct research and studies, "first, direct your eyes downward, do not hold your head high and gaze at the sky"[3]; "second, hold fact-finding meetings"[4]. The formulation of the Five-year Plan involves all aspects of economic and social development, and is closely related to the work and life of the people. It is necessary to strengthen top-level design and at the same time collect ideas from the people, encouraging all sectors of society to submit opinions and suggestions in various ways.

Among the representatives of grassroots officials and the public present here, some are from rural areas, urban communities and enterprises; some are from the fields of education, science and technology, health care, the judiciary, and law enforcement; some are delegates to Party congresses, deputies to people's congresses and members of the Chinese People's Political Consultative Conference (CPPCC) at various levels, model workers, and poverty alleviation officials; some are from the New Social Group[5]; some are migrant workers, couriers, and online store owners. You all work on the front line of reform and development in various sectors. You are directly involved in economic and social activities, and have most frequent contact with the public.

Thus you have a more realistic perception and experience of how effectively the Party's guidelines and policies are implemented. Your opinions and suggestions can better reflect the grassroots reality and express the people's wishes.

You have just made some very good speeches, going straight to the point and offering a wealth of valuable opinions and suggestions. They are all fresh and practical. They help us to understand more about the situation at the grassroots. Departments concerned must study them thoroughly and make full use of them.

Not long ago, we launched an online activity to solicit opinions on the 14th Five-year Plan (2021-2025). Officials and the public have paid careful attention and participated extensively. Many of the opinions and suggestions were directly addressed to me, as I welcome letters from the public. These opinions and suggestions reflected problems of general concern, which have also been referenced in your contributions. They should be duly addressed in the Central Committee's recommendations for formulating the 14th Five-year Plan.

Now I would like to share with you some of my thoughts.

First, make best use of the favorable environment and build momentum for development.

The 14th Five-year Plan period is the first five-year period in our country's new journey towards a modern socialist country after achieving moderate prosperity. At present and for a period to come, our country is still in an important period of strategic opportunity for development, but both the opportunities and the challenges we face will be subject to further changes. The world today is undergoing change on a scale unseen in a century, whose evolution has been exacerbated by the Covid-19 pandemic. The international landscape is more complex, economic globalization is facing opposition, and unilateralism and protectionism prevail in some countries. We have to seek development in a world with more uncertainties and instabilities. China has entered a stage of high-quality development and has good prospects for economic growth. At the same time, it still faces a prominent problem of imbalanced and insufficient growth, and many shortcomings and weaknesses still hamper high-quality development. Whatever the difficulties, challenges, obstacles and changes, we shall never cover them up, avoid them, turn a blind eye to them, panic, or become confused. I have said on many occasions that the rejuvenation of the Chinese nation will be no easy task. It will not be achieved by simply banging drums and gongs. Glory comes from adversity. No country or nation can achieve modernization easily.

Despite the deep and complex changes that have taken place in the internal and international environment, the fundamentals of long-term stability and progress in our economy remain unchanged. Our economy is still solid and resilient with great potential and significant scope for readjustment, and it is supported by many policy tools. These basic features have not changed, nor have the strengths and conditions behind our development. China has the world's largest and most comprehensive manufacturing system, with strong production capacity and the ability to provide complete supporting facilities and services. It has a super-large domestic market, and huge potential demand for investment. We must effectively analyze the general situation, and understand the general trends of development. We should follow the fundamental principle of pursuing progress while ensuring stability, uphold the new development philosophy, and coordinate development and security. We will move faster to create a double development dynamic with the domestic economy as the mainstay and the domestic economy and international engagement providing mutual reinforcement.

Second, uphold the people-centered philosophy of development.

The people's support is our top political priority. Our Party serves the people wholeheartedly, honors its commitment to serving the public good, exercises power in the interests of the people, and considers it our goal to meet the people's aspirations for a better life. These principles have been both stated and followed over almost 100 years.

During the Long March in the 1930s, when the Red Army passed through Shazhou Village, in Wenming Township of Rucheng County, three female soldiers cut their only quilt in half and gave one half to a poor villager. This story has since been remembered and retold. In the fight against Covid-19, we have, from the very beginning, stated explicitly that people's lives and health should be regarded as the top priority. To limit the spread of the virus to the greatest extent possible, we have mobilized the best medical workers, the most advanced equipment, and the most urgently needed resources from across the country, all of which have been devoted to treating patients, with all the costs covered by the government.

When mapping out the 14th Five-year Plan, we must follow the principle that development is for the people and its fruits should be shared by the people. Efforts should be made to improve people's daily lives and make up for shortcomings while ensuring high-quality development. We must focus more on issues of public concern that affect people's lives, take more targeted measures, and ensure effective implementation to solve each and every one of them, so that the people will have a growing, guaranteed, and sustained sense of gain, fulfillment and security.

Third, strengthen Party organizations and governments at the grassroots level.

If the foundation is not solid, the building trembles. Only with strong Party organizations and governments at the grassroots level can the foundations of Chinese socialism be solid.

During the 14th Five-year Plan period, greater efforts should be made in our foundational work to improve grassroots governance. We should strengthen and improve the Party's overall leadership over grassroots work and improve grassroots organizations in rural areas, so as to provide strong political and organizational guarantees for comprehensive rural revitalization. We should strengthen and reform grassroots social governance, and carry on and improve the Fengqiao model[6] in the new era – building stronger urban and rural communities, strengthening grid-based management and services, and improving the mechanism to prevent, mediate and resolve social conflicts and disputes by multiple means at the grassroots level. All of this will contribute to social stability.

Fourth, be role models as grassroots representatives.

The achievement of moderate prosperity is not the end, but the starting point of a new life and a new round of hard work. The people have wisdom and infinite creativity. We need to organize, mobilize and unite them and fully arouse their enthusiasm and initiative. Party members and officials should play an exemplary role; deputies to people's congresses should form closer ties with the people; CPPCC members should maintain contact with and serve the people in their respective sectors; and rural workers who have become prosperous should work harder to lead others forward, so that all are united in striving for a new and better life.

Finally, I want to emphasize that the achievements of our socialist country have not fallen like manna from Heaven, nor have they been granted by others. They have been achieved by our people through hard work, wisdom and courage under the leadership of the Party. For a country with a population of 1.4 billion, individual contributions gather into an earth-shaking force. If everyone can do one thing or one job well, the cause of the Party and the state will advance one step further. All of you are from the grassroots or the front line, and you represent various sectors and industries. You should have firm ideals and convictions, and study hard to improve yourselves. You should work hard in a pragmatic manner, taking one step at a time and handling every piece of work, big or small, with the utmost care and attention. I believe you will experience greater fulfillment in life through hard work, and together we will create a happy life and bright future for all.

Notes

¹ Mao Zedong: "The Role of the Chinese Communist Party in the National War", *Selected Works of Mao Zedong*, Vol. II, Eng. ed., Foreign Languages Press, Beijing, 1965, p. 198.

² *Ibid.*

³ Mao Zedong: "Preface and Postscript to *Rural Surveys*", *Selected Works of Mao*

Zedong, Vol. III, Eng. ed., Foreign Languages Press, Beijing, 1965, p. 11.

[4] *Ibid.*, p. 12.

[5] This refers to groups of people that have emerged with the development of the socialist market economy, mainly management and technical personnel in private and foreign-funded enterprises, those working in intermediary agencies and social organizations, freelancers, and new media professionals. – Tr.

[6] In the early 1960s, the officials and citizenry of Fengqiao Town in Zhejiang Province created the Fengqiao practice, which emphasized solving problems in situ rather than passing them up to higher authorities. The practice has developed quickly over the intervening decades, especially after the 18th CPC National Congress and is now a model for promoting community-level governance and social harmony. Relying on the people, the Party committee and government devote their efforts to preventing disputes and solving problems, so as to maintain social stability and promote development.

Earn and Keep the People's Support in Consolidating Party Leadership[*]

June 25 and September 14, 2021

I

Our Party has won the people's wholehearted support because it has always stayed true to its original aspiration and founding mission, and faithfully observed its fundamental purpose of wholeheartedly serving the people. This is also why our Party was able to grow in strength from a small and fragile organization, rise time and again after setbacks, and fight its way through dangers. The people are the root of our vitality, the foundation of our governance, and the source of our strength.

I have reiterated on many occasions that the country is its people, and the people are the country. As we have fought to establish and consolidate our Party's leadership over the country, we have in fact been fighting to earn and keep the people's support. My purpose is to warn all Party members that having served in office as long as we have, no danger is greater than forgetting our founding mission or distancing ourselves from the people. As long as we stay together with and work for the people, they will steadfastly follow the Party's leadership and the Party will be able to flourish. All members should further the understanding of our original aspiration in the context of the Party's history, follow the people-centered development philosophy,

---

[*] Excerpts from two speeches made on June 25 and September 14, 2021.

and never waver in our drive towards national rejuvenation.

*(from the speech at the 31st group study session of
the Political Bureau of the 19th CPC Central Committee,
June 25, 2021)*

II

Reviewing this rich revolutionary history, we see how the older generation of revolutionaries "gave top priority to the interests of the Party", "stood with the overwhelming majority of the working people", and "sat on the side of the people". Their devotion to serving the people is of great educational value. The reason why our Party was able to lead the people to victory in the revolution is that the Party won their support, and many hundreds of millions of people chose to side firmly with us. We must carry forward our revolutionary traditions and fine conduct, and always put the people's interests first. We should stay true to the Party's original aspiration and founding mission, follow the mass line, and respect the people's principal position. We should always stand with the people and think and act in their interests.

*(from the speech during a visit to the site of the former office of
the CPC Suide Prefectural Committee in Yulin, Shaanxi Province,
September 14, 2021)*

The People's Concerns Are My Concerns, and the People's Expectations Are My Goals*

December 31, 2021

In a large and populous country, we have our own list of priorities. The myriad of things we attend to all boil down to matters concerning every household. During my visits to different places, I have seen and heard a lot of things which I find very inspiring and rewarding. Every time I visit people in their homes, I ask if they still have any difficulties, and I remember everything they share with me.

The people's concerns are my concerns, and the people's expectations are my goals. Having spent long years in the countryside when I was young, I know precisely what poverty feels like. Thanks to the sustained efforts of the Chinese people from generation to generation, those who once lived in poverty no longer have to worry about food or clothing, or access to education, housing and medical insurance. Realization of a moderately prosperous society in all respects and elimination of extreme poverty is what the Party has delivered to our people, and it is also our contribution to the world. To ensure that everyone leads a better life, we must never rest on what we have achieved, and there is still a long way to go.

* Part of the 2022 New Year message.

Our Party's Mission Is to Serve the People[*]

January 26, 2022

Our Party's mission is to serve the people and to improve their lives.

Your village is in the Lüliang Mountains, near the Yellow River, and across the river is Shaanxi Province. In the late 1960s, I was sent to work as a farmer in Shaanxi's Yanchuan County, which is not far from here. Its hilly terrain and ravines are similar to the landscape here. The Loess Plateau is our home, and the home of our ancestors. It has nurtured our Chinese civilization.

In the past, people of my age led a hard life. Even those living in cities wore patched clothes. I used to spin and weave during my farming years. In the past, I was always dismayed and concerned to see how hard life was for some people. But now, our rural areas have changed significantly. Food, clothing, and consumer goods have all improved, and the lack of basic necessities that troubled the Chinese for several thousand years has been addressed once and for all.

During this trip to Shanxi, I have been to two villages. I am delighted to see that you now lead a life of contentment. Yet we still have a long way to go. We have accomplished our First Centenary Goal, and are now on a journey towards the Second Centenary Goal. That is to build China into a modern socialist country in all respects. This goal, however, cannot be realized without modernizing agriculture and rural areas. We should pool our efforts to consolidate gains in poverty elimination with endeavors to revitalize the countryside.

---

* Part of the speech during a visit to Linfen, Shanxi Province.

In this way, we will help our rural people to live a modern life with a bright future.

The sole aims of the CPC in governance are to meet the needs of the people, and give its all in serving them and striving for their wellbeing. This has never changed throughout its hundred years of history. Numerous revolutionary martyrs and forefathers sacrificed their lives for the cause or committed themselves to the reform and development of the country. We owe all our achievements to them.

We will stay true to the Party's original aspiration and founding mission and do solid work, generation after generation, so that by the centenary of the PRC in 2049, our nation will stand taller and stronger in the East and make a greater contribution to humanity.

Confront Challenges Head-On

Keep Up the Fight to
Achieve National Rejuvenation*

September 3, 2020

The Communist Party of China and the Chinese people have grown and gained strength in the course of our struggle. Our fighting spirit has been apparent in the whole process of the country's revolution, construction and reform. Our country is now at the critical stage of national rejuvenation, and of reform and opening up. We can expect to encounter all sorts of challenges on the way forward. We must maintain our commitment, step up to the fight, and confront these challenges, whatever difficulties may lie ahead.

We must counter any risks and threats that endanger Party leadership, the socialist system, the sovereignty, security and development interests of our country, our core national interests and principles, the fundamental interests of our people, the realization of the Two Centenary Goals[1], and the rejuvenation of the Chinese nation. We must allow ourselves no respite until victory is won.

We will prove that the rejuvenation of the Chinese nation is a process that cannot be halted. We, the Chinese people, will never allow any force or any person to impose their will on China, change our course forward, or obstruct our efforts to create a better life.

---

* Part of the speech at a meeting to commemorate the 75th anniversary of the victory of the Chinese People's War of Resistance Against Japanese Aggression and the Global War Against Fascism.

Notes

[1] At its 18th National Congress in November 2012, the CPC put forward the Two Centenary Goals for building socialism with Chinese characteristics – to build a moderately prosperous society in all respects by the centenary of the CPC in 2021 and to build China into a modern socialist country by the centenary of the PRC in 2049. At its 19th National Congress in October 2017, the CPC drew up a two-step strategy for the Second Centenary Goal. In the first stage from 2020 to 2035, we will build on the foundations of the moderately prosperous society with a further 15 years of hard work to see that basic socialist modernization is realized. In the second stage from 2035 to the middle of the 21st century, having achieved basic modernization, we will work hard for a further 15 years and develop China into a great modern socialist country that is prosperous, strong, democratic, culturally advanced, harmonious, and beautiful. At the ceremony marking the centenary of the CPC on July 1, 2021, General Secretary Xi Jinping declared that China had succeeded in eradicating extreme poverty and achieving the First Centenary Goal of building a moderately prosperous society in all respects, and would move forward towards the Second Centenary Goal of building a modern socialist country.

Carry Forward the Spirit of the War to Resist US Aggression and Aid Korea in the Great Historic Struggle*

October 23, 2020

China's resounding victory in the War to Resist US Aggression and Aid Korea (1950-1953) was a declaration that the Chinese people had stood upright and tall in the East. It was a significant milestone in China's progress towards national rejuvenation, with great and far-reaching impact on China and the wider world.

Through this war, the Chinese people foiled the aggressors' plan to destroy China in its infancy with the troops it had sent to the PRC border. As Mao Zedong said, "Throw one hard punch now to avoid taking a hundred punches in the future." The newly-founded People's Republic stood firm and the imperialists were deterred from any further invasion attempts. The war safeguarded our territorial integrity, secured peace for our homeland, and fully demonstrated the Chinese people's iron will in confronting a hegemonic power.

Through this war, we the Chinese people ended our century-long history of humiliation following the Opium War of 1840. We would no longer allow ourselves to be trampled on or dependent upon others. We bid farewell to the image of "the sick man of East Asia". We did ourselves proud and felt truly heartened. The victory fully displayed the Chinese people's unyielding spirit and indomitable will as we united as one.

Through this war, we the Chinese people shook the world with

---

* Part of the speech at a meeting to commemorate the 70th anniversary of the Chinese People's Volunteers' entry into the War to Resist US Aggression and Aid Korea.

our victory over the aggressors. The victory helped to establish the PRC's position in Asia and in the international arena and highlight its status as a major country. It changed the world's perception of China and demonstrated the Chinese people's determination to safeguard world peace.

Through this war, our people's army gained important military experience and emerged stronger and braver. The victory also enabled the army's transition from single service combat forces to integrated combat forces and greatly accelerated the modernization of China's national defense and military. It made very clear to the world the combat effectiveness of our armed forces and their heart and will to fight and win.

Through this war, the strategic landscape of post-World War II Asia and even the world was profoundly changed. The victory gave a tremendous boost to the struggle of oppressed nations and people around the world for national independence and liberation, and to human progress and world peace. It left the world in no doubt that no country or military, no matter how powerful it might be, can prevail if it stands against the trend of world development, abuses the weak, pursues a regressive agenda, or indulges in aggression and expansion. The victory proved once again that right will triumph over might, and that peace and development represent the irresistible tide of history.

In the great and momentous War to Resist US Aggression and Aid Korea, the valiant Chinese People's Volunteers forged a great spirit of patriotism, heroism, optimism, loyalty, and internationalism.

Patriotism inspired them to uphold the interests of the country and the people above all else and put their lives on the line to defend the dignity of the country and the nation.

Revolutionary heroism motivated them to fight tenaciously and fearlessly.

Revolutionary optimism encouraged them to keep up their morale despite hardships and difficulties.

Loyalty to the revolutionary cause reinforced their devotion to missions entrusted by the nation and the people.

The spirit of internationalism stimulated them to fight for peace and justice for humanity.

The great spirit of the War to Resist US Aggression and Aid Korea extends through time and space and continues to flourish. We must carry it forward from generation to generation.

– Regardless of how times may change, we must forge the national character to defy oppression and fight hegemony. Seventy years ago, a war started by the imperialist aggressors reached China's door. The Chinese people knew well that it was imperative to send the aggressors a message they would understand: War must be fought to deter aggression, force must be met with force, and a victory is the best way to win peace and respect.

We the Chinese people do not provoke others, nor do we shy away from trouble. We do not give in to fear or yield in the face of difficulties and dangers. The Chinese nation will never cower before threats, or be subdued by oppressors.

– Regardless of how times may change, we must pool the indomitable national strength that unites us all. In this war, driven by patriotism, the Chinese people fought shoulder to shoulder against the enemy, demonstrating our strength to the world. The war made it clear that "the Chinese people are now organized, they are not to be trifled with. Once provoked to anger, they will respond with a will."[1]

– Regardless of how times may change, we must forge a national spirit of devotion and the courage to risk our own lives for the interests of the country. On the cruel Korean battlefield, the Chinese People's Volunteers shed blood and even laid down lives while confronting a strong and fierce rival. Poor in steel but with an iron will, they wrote an earth-shaking epic defeating an enemy rich in steel but weak in will.

They charged forward braving the storm of gunfire and shells, stood their ground under artillery barrage, hurled themselves against the machine-gun slits of dugouts, and used their bodies as ladders. After exhausting their supplies and ammunition, they advanced to their death against the enemy lines carrying explosive charges or

Bangalore torpedoes. They persevered in spite of hunger or cold, withstood the test of fire and flame to conceal the position of their units, and remained undaunted under the assaults of the US air force.

Yang Gensi, Huang Jiguang and Qiu Shaoyun are just a few of more than 300,000 heroes from 6,000 heroic units. They made a vow: Right behind our back is the motherland; we cannot afford to take one step back. This immense courage and the spirit of devotion struck fear into the enemy.

– Regardless of how times may change, we must forge ahead and continue innovating on the basis of what has worked in the past. Those who are innovative and creative can always make breakthroughs and achieve victory.

Facing an unfamiliar enemy on a new battlefield, the Chinese People's Volunteers made the most of flexible strategies and tactics – "You fight your way and I will fight mine. You have atomic bombs to launch and I have grenades to fire."[2] No matter what pressure we come under, no matter what challenges and risks may lie ahead, we the Chinese people will always fight our way out and prevail, displaying our tremendous courage, wisdom and will.

Over the six decades since victory in the war, unprecedented changes have taken place in China under the robust CPC leadership. Chinese socialism has entered a new era and the Chinese nation has achieved a tremendous transformation from standing up to becoming better off and growing in strength.

Today, we are approaching a historic milestone in realizing the Two Centenary Goals, when the victory of the first, building a moderately prosperous society in all respects, is in sight, and the prospects of the second, building a modern socialist country in all respects, are promising. The road ahead, however, will not be smooth. We must not forget the grueling route to victory in this war. We must maintain our mettle and courage, and display wisdom in our endeavor. We must press ahead with tenacity in spite of all difficulties and advance the great historic cause of socialism with Chinese characteristics for a new era.

To commemorate the great victory and advance the great historic cause, we must do the following:

— We must uphold the Party's leadership and make it even stronger. Victory in this war proved once again that no other political force in China could match the CPC in pooling the strength of millions to fight for national rejuvenation and for the happiness of the people, and to win one victory after another, no matter what sacrifice it might entail. So long as we bear in mind our Party's original aspiration and founding mission, press ahead with the great new project of strengthening the Party in the spirit of self-reform, and strengthen the Party's ability to provide political leadership and theoretical guidance, and to organize and inspire the people, we will make it the strong and reliable spine of our nation.

— We must remain committed to a people-centered philosophy. We must do everything in the interests of the people and rely on them in everything we do. History is created by the people. The strength of our Party and our military comes from the people. We must uphold the Party's fundamental goals of serving the people wholeheartedly, working for their benefit, and fulfilling our responsibilities to them.

We must always seek to meet the people's desire for a better life, and forever maintain our close ties with them. So long as we stand firmly on the side of the people and uphold their principal position, we will spark their mighty and indomitable force and produce new and splendid chapters in the history of China's national rejuvenation.

— We must promote economic and social development and continue to build up our overall national strength. Backwardness left us vulnerable to attack; only development can make us strong.

Over the past seven decades since the founding of the PRC, we have achieved progress that took the developed countries several centuries. Our economic growth has staggered the world. We are now entering a new development stage that brings us new opportunities and challenges. We will achieve higher-quality development that is more efficient, equitable, sustainable and secure, and create new miracles, so long as we ensure a holistic approach to the Five-sphere

Integrated Plan and coordinated implementation of the Four-pronged Comprehensive Strategy, embrace the new development philosophy, and create a new development dynamic.

– We must quicken the pace in modernizing our national defense and armed forces, and build the people's army into a world-class force. Without a strong military, a country cannot be strong. To uphold and develop socialism with Chinese characteristics, we must coordinate our efforts in both development and security, and in building a prosperous country and a strong military.

We must implement the Party's philosophy on strengthening the military and our military strategy for the new era, and uphold absolute Party leadership over the people's armed forces. We must strengthen the political loyalty of the armed forces and build their capacity through reform, science and technology, and training of competent personnel, and run the military in accordance with the law. We must improve the strategic ability of the armed forces to safeguard national sovereignty, security, and development interests, and help them better fulfill their missions in the new era. So long as we step up efforts to develop national defense and the armed forces in keeping pace with the times and march towards the Party's goal of building a strong military, we will ensure greater strategic support for national rejuvenation.

– We must safeguard world peace and justice and work to build a global community of shared future. The Chinese nation always values amity and friendship with neighbors. As a responsible major country, China upholds the common values of humanity, including peace, development, equity, justice, democracy and freedom. We follow the principle of achieving shared growth through consultation and collaboration in global governance, and commit ourselves to peaceful, open, collaborative and common development. As long as we keep to the path of peaceful development and endeavor to build a global community of shared future with the peoples of other countries, there will be a bright future for peace and development.

Our world belongs to the peoples of all countries. Difficulties and challenges confronting the world can only be addressed and overcome when all countries pull together. Peace, development and win-win cooperation are the right way forward. In today's world, no unilateralism, protectionism or extreme self-interest will ever succeed. No blackmailing, blockading or applying maximum pressure on others will ever work. Attempts to throw one's weight around and self-centered, hegemonic and abusive actions against others are doomed to fail. They will lead nowhere.

China upholds a national defense policy that is defensive in nature, and the Chinese military has always been a staunch force for maintaining world peace. China will never seek hegemony or engage in expansion, and it will resolutely oppose hegemonism and power politics. China will never tolerate any threat to its sovereignty, security and development interests, or allow any force to violate or divide its sacred territory. The Chinese people will respond to any such attacks with head-on blows.

A review of this great war fought 70 years ago gives us limitless determination and greater confidence in continuing our great historic struggle with many new features. Let us unite more closely around the CPC Central Committee, carry forward the great spirit of this war, and march forward brimming with confidence on the new journey towards a modern socialist China and the Chinese Dream of national rejuvenation.

Notes

[1] Mao Zedong: "Our Great Victory in the War to Resist US Aggression and Aid Korea and Its Significance", *Collected Works of Mao Zedong on the Military*, Vol. VI, Chin. ed., Military Science Publishing House, Central Party Literature Publishing House, Beijing, 1993, p. 355.

[2] Mao Zedong: "War Situation in Korea and Our Principles", *Collected Works of Mao Zedong*, Vol. VI, Chin. ed., People's Publishing House, Beijing, 1999, pp. 93-94.

Fight for a Bright New Future[*]

March 1, 2021

Being ready for the fray is a distinctive quality of our Party. It is through struggle that our Party has developed to its present state, and that is what will create a bright future. The risks and challenges confronting us now are no less than those we faced in the past, as we enter a new stage of building an all-round modern socialist country and create a new development dynamic under the guidance of the new development philosophy.

You younger officials should broaden your experience of struggle, hone your skills in work and improve yourselves during this process, and finally become brave and capable fighters. Strengthen your resolve with a resilient and indomitable spirit, and stand firm in the face of difficulties and setbacks. Be adept in the struggle, with an ability to identify the general trend from the tiniest of clues, an ability to perceive the essence through the appearance, an ability to accurately identify the need for, successfully respond to, and actively bring about change, and an ability to spot opportunities before others to gain the initiative.

You must improve your strategic planning, grasp overall trends, address principal challenges and the key aspects of challenges in order of importance and urgency, and make judicious arrangements to gain firm control in any struggle.

You should have plans in place for worst-case scenarios, and

---

* Main points of the speech at the opening ceremony of a training program for younger officials at the Central Party School (National Academy of Governance) during its 2021 spring semester.

conduct regular, comprehensive analyses to identify possible risks. Learn from experience and past mistakes, understand how different phenomena interact, and draw inferences about general cases from particular instances, so as to build up your fighting skills.

Be Prepared for the Great Struggle[*]

November 11, 2021

We must have a keen sense of responsibility, and build the will and ability to continue the great struggle. An ancient Chinese philosopher observed, "The weak-minded cannot be wise; the dishonest cannot succeed."[1]

Founded amid domestic turmoil and foreign aggression, our Party has been tempered through numerous tribulations, and grown strong by surmounting difficulties. It does not fear powerful enemies or any risk or challenge; it has the courage to fight and the mettle to win. To fulfill its historic duty to the cause of the Party and the people, it has never flinched before formidable enemies or backed down in the face of severe challenges on its path. It fears no sacrifice or setback.

In the years of the revolutionary war, the Party took on the mission of national independence and people's liberation, and fought fearlessly in an arduous battle against domestic and foreign enemies. Opposing imperialism and feudalism, it brought the Great Revolution (1924-1927) to a climax. Getting back to its feet after suffering bloody massacres, it launched the armed struggle and the Agrarian Revolution (1927-1937). For the greater good of the nation, the CPC formed a united front with the Kuomintang to resist Japanese aggression. In the subsequent civil war started by Kuomintang reactionaries, it defeated 8 million Kuomintang troops. In its 28 years of struggle, the Party made tremendous self-sacrifices on behalf of the people.

After 1949, when the People's Republic of China was founded,

---

* Part of the speech at the second full assembly of the Sixth Plenary Session of the 19th CPC Central Committee.

our Party faced severe tests and challenges from inside and outside its organizations, at home and abroad, both natural and manmade. With a strong sense of mission and great courage, our Party made the correct choices at critical junctures, unflinchingly stood up to all tests, and led the people in a determined struggle to victory. Under its leadership, the Chinese nation has stood up, become better off, and grown in strength.

In the 1950s, under provocation and the threat of force from the imperialist US, the richest and most powerful country in the world, the Party's central leadership faced a critical choice – whether to send troops to aid Korea. Mao Zedong said it was one of the toughest decisions he had ever made. Determined to "throw one hard punch now to avoid taking a hundred punches in the future", the central leadership made the historic decision to aid Korea against US aggression and defend the new-born PRC, even though it would hamper domestic reconstruction. By making this necessary move, China stopped the foreign aggressors at its doorstep and secured its national borders.

In the late 1980s and early 1990s, during a period of dramatic change in Eastern Europe, the Communist Party of the Soviet Union collapsed and the Soviet Union disintegrated, dealing a severe blow to world socialism. Political disturbance also occurred in our country in the late spring and early summer of 1989. In response, our Party relied on the people and took resolute measures to win a life-and-death battle, showing strong resolve and historic commitment. We withstood the sanctions of the West, and kept to the correct path of reform and development and socialism with Chinese characteristics. Deng Xiaoping said, "So long as socialism does not collapse in China, it will always hold its ground in the world."[2] I also said, "If CPC leadership and Chinese socialism had collapsed in that domino reaction or for any other reason, socialism would again have stumbled in the dark for a prolonged period, which would certainly have blocked the Chinese nation's journey towards rejuvenation."

History is a continuous progression divided into different stages. Each stage creates a particular mission, and each generation has a certain responsibility. Since the Party's 18th National Congress in 2012, we have been fully aware that upholding and developing Chinese socialism in the new era will be an arduous task but a great social transformation. Hostile forces will not sit back and let us achieve national rejuvenation smoothly. This is why I have repeatedly emphasized that we must carry out the great historic struggle with many new features. We must be prepared to make even greater efforts, and keep guard against and defuse major risks at all times.

Over the past few years, we have adopted proactive and preemptive strategies to deal with risks and challenges, taking resolute measures to tackle those that threaten the Party's governing status and the stability of state power, or undermine the country's core interests and the people's fundamental interests. In defusing the major threats that could have delayed or interrupted China's rejuvenation process, we have shown great determination and courage, solved many longstanding, complex problems, and accomplished many long-sought and elusive goals. We have undergone these experiences together, which are fully summarized in the resolution adopted at this plenary session.

Our Party has fought to create history, and will continue to fight to win the future. On the new journey, we will only face more daunting tests and unimaginable turbulence in a prolonged struggle to complete the Second Centenary Goal. Confronted by major risks, and powerful opponents, it is unrealistic to think confrontation can be avoided, nor will it help to fear it or evade it.

"Those skilled in warfare make sure they are invincible and miss no chance of overwhelming their enemies."[3] Meeting challenges head-on is the only way to survive, to develop, and to win dignity. Retreat, compromise or concession will only lead to defeat and humiliation.

We must understand the features of this great historic struggle and be clear on our targets. We must be courageous, stick to the right pathway, maintain the initiative, understand how to fight, and build up the spirit and capacity to do it. We are determined to overcome all difficulties by effectively addressing challenges, defusing risks, removing obstacles, and solving problems on the way forward, and we are resolved to win this great new struggle in the new era.

Notes

[1] *Mo Zi.* This is a collection of writings by Mo Di and other scholars of the Mohist school of thought. Mo Di (c. 468-376 BC), also known as Mo Zi, was a philosopher, thinker and statesman of the Warring States Period, and the founder of the Mohist school.

[2] Deng Xiaoping: "We Must Adhere to Socialism and Prevent Peaceful Evolution Towards Capitalism", *Selected Works of Deng Xiaoping*, Vol. III, Eng. ed., Foreign Languages Press, Beijing, 1994, p. 334.

[3] *The Art of War (Sun Zi).* This is a book on military strategy and tactics attributed to Sun Wu. Sun Wu (dates unknown), also known as Sun Zi, was a military strategist in the late Spring and Autumn Period (770-476 BC).

Epidemic Response and Socio-Economic Development

Priorities in Epidemic Prevention and Control*

February 3, 2020

Our novel coronavirus prevention and control is directly related to people's lives and health, economic development, social stability, and opening up. To contain the virus and win this battle we must race against time, fight with confidence, strength and unity, and adopt a science-based approach and a targeted response. The current priorities in our work are as follows:

First, strengthen unified leadership. We need to ensure a coordinated national response. Party committees and governments at all levels must follow the unified command, coordination and arrangements of the Party's central leadership to ensure proper execution of orders. Provincial authorities and central departments are generally doing well in carrying out the decisions and plans of the central leadership. But there are still some weaknesses and problems, and we need to direct our attention to them, make improvements, and close loopholes. Virus prevention and control is not only a medical and health issue. It is a battle across various fields, and all sectors should engage in the battle and strive for victory. The situation is constantly changing, leading to new developments and challenges in every aspect of our work. We need to keep close track of the situation, make timely analyses, respond promptly, and act with resolve.

When taking measures to contain novel coronavirus, provincial authorities and central departments should take into account not only their own needs, but also the impact on virus response in key regions and at the national level. We should not hesitate to criticize those who

---

* Part of the speech at a meeting of the Standing Committee of the Political Bureau of the 19th CPC Central Committee on novel coronavirus response.

fail to effectively implement the decisions and plans of the central leadership, and we should urge them to rectify their conduct immediately. In the case of those who are insubordinate and do not obey the unified command and arrangements, those who shirk their responsibilities, only make a perfunctory effort, or pass the buck, we should hold those individuals directly in charge accountable, and in serious cases, look into the responsibilities of the principal Party and government leaders. Those found guilty of malfeasance or dereliction of duty must be punished in accordance with Party discipline and the law.

Second, strengthen virus prevention and control in key regions. Only when we succeed in bringing this virus under control in key regions can we turn the tide across the country. We must focus on coordinating prevention and treatment forces across regions, pool medical resources and protective equipment on the front line, and prioritize the needs of medical workers and patients.

Hubei Province, and especially Wuhan City, remains the top priority in our national effort to contain the novel coronavirus – most infected people in other parts of our country have had contact with people from Hubei. As long as we keep the virus in Hubei under control, we will be able to ensure overall stability in the country as a whole. Within Hubei, we must continue to strengthen prevention and control in all respects. The principle of early detection, reporting, quarantine and treatment should be strictly applied. In addition, novel coronavirus surveillance should be heightened, infected people must be hospitalized and treated in designated medical facilities, and all close contacts are required to remain under medical observation at home. At the same time, we must enforce stricter measures to prevent the virus from spreading beyond Hubei. We closed all outbound channels, including planes, trains, highways and waterways, which played an important role in the national fight against novel coronavirus. But we cannot ignore the potential hazard from the outflow of people before the restrictions were implemented.

Recently, novel coronavirus has been spreading rapidly in the neighboring provinces of Hubei and in provinces with large population flows, as shown in the fast-growing number of new cases. To contain the virus, local Party committees and governments must fulfill their responsibilities. Grid-based community management should be strengthened, a thorough screening is to be carried out to ensure no one is left unchecked, and stricter, more targeted, and more effective measures should be adopted. To prevent the coronavirus from spreading through the movement of population, we need to identify risks and weaknesses in the management of people returning from seriously infected regions, emphasize the responsibilities of the authorities in places of departure and arrival, and carry out strict health monitoring for passengers and disinfection and ventilation of transport stations. Beijing holds a position of unique importance, but it now faces increasing pressure as a large number of people are now returning. To put a brake on the spread of the coronavirus, we must improve our response measures, reinforce management of key groups, cut mobile sources of infection, and reduce population flows and close personal contact.

Third, increase the admission and cure rates and reduce the infection and fatality rates, which is currently our crucial task. Hospitals solely for admitting and treating coronavirus patients should be completed and brought into service as soon as possible. We must continue to dispatch medical personnel from all over the country to Wuhan and the rest of Hubei as needed, while ensuring their own physical and mental health. We must arrange the disposition of these professionals based on overall plans, gathering together the most competent and the most experienced to coordinate the treatment of severe cases and reduce mortality. Where conditions permit, areas of high incidence of the disease can adopt the Xiaotangshan Hospital model[1] to strengthen treatment. In the treatment of severe cases, prompt efforts should be made to replicate the most effective practices of other hospitals.

Fourth, redouble our efforts in scientific research. Novel coronavirus cannot be beaten without science. It is essential that we scientifically determine the origin of the virus, identify the infection sources and transmission routes as quickly as possible, keep close track of virus mutations, and develop the appropriate response strategies and measures. As I said back in 2016, we should encourage competition to make breakthroughs in core technologies in key fields. Anyone who can make such breakthroughs should be given the opportunity regardless of their background.

With regard to the R&D of vaccines and medicines, it is recommended to incentivize universities, research institutes and companies, and to combine R&D with clinical practice and virus prevention and control to accelerate this science-based process. Subject to ensuring national security, data concerning the virus and cases should be shared in our scientific and technological circles, with the exception of those that are confidential for legal reasons. We should bring together specialists in clinical medicine, epidemiology and virology to study the transmissibility, infectiousness, and some other vital features of the novel coronavirus and to achieve effective results as soon as possible. Experts and researchers are encouraged to sharpen their sense of responsibility and professional duty, so that they generate more professional opinions and suggestions based on scientific research.

Notes

[1] This is a countermeasure to curb the spread of infectious respiratory illnesses. Temporary hospitals meeting infection-control standards are built to admit infected patients, and medical workers and resources are gathered there to provide them with the best treatment. In April 2003, Beijing built the Xiaotangshan Hospital to treat SARS cases to control the spread of the disease. As a response to the Covid-19 epidemic, the Huoshenshan and Leishenshan hospitals in Wuhan and the central government-aided emergency hospital in Hong Kong were built following this model.

Reinforce CPC Central Leadership over the Epidemic Response[*]

February 23, 2020

When the coronavirus struck, the CPC Central Committee responded to the emergency immediately, exercising overall leadership over all fronts in the epidemic response and making timely decisions.

On January 7, I presided over a meeting of the Standing Committee of the Political Bureau of the CPC Central Committee and issued instructions on our epidemic response. On January 20, I issued further instructions requiring Party committees and governments at all levels and the competent authorities to put people's lives and health above all else and take resolute and effective action to stem the spread of the virus.

On January 25, the first day of the Chinese New Year, I presided over another meeting of the Standing Committee of the Political Bureau on epidemic control and made further plans to mobilize more resources to contain the virus. We decided to set up the Central Leading Group for Coronavirus Response, and send a central steering group to Hubei Province to oversee the local epidemic response. We also instructed the State Council to make well-coordinated efforts through its joint prevention and control mechanism.

After that, I chaired three more meetings of the Standing Committee of the Political Bureau and one meeting of the Political Bureau, all to discuss ways to conduct epidemic control and reopen the economy.

---

* Part of the speech at a meeting on coordinating the epidemic response with economic and social development.

On February 10, I inspected epidemic prevention and control work in Beijing. I talked online to frontline health workers in Wuhan City and the rest of Hubei, and heard the reports of the central steering group and the Hubei epidemic response command center. I also chaired meetings of the Central Commission for Law-based Governance, the Central Cyberspace Affairs Commission, the Central Commission for Further Reform, and the Central Commission for Foreign Affairs, setting requirements for response measures on different fronts.

The Party Central Committee issued the Notice on Strengthening Party Leadership and Providing Strong Political Support for the Epidemic Response. I have closely followed progress in virus control and given verbal and written instructions daily. With timely planning and action by the Central Leading Group for Coronavirus Response, specific directions and coordination from the central steering group, strong coordination by the State Council joint prevention and control mechanism, and strenuous efforts by Party committees and governments at all levels, a powerful synergy has been formed in the race to fight the virus.

True heroes will emerge in times of adversity. In this arduous battle, members and officials of Party organizations at all levels have rushed to the front and fought fearlessly as the vanguard.

Our health workers have proved their dedication to their profession, shouldering this daunting mission and working around the clock to save lives. Officers and soldiers of the People's Liberation Army have swiftly responded to the call of duty and fought some of the toughest battles, demonstrating their loyalty to the Party and the people.

Our people have stood together in solidarity. The people of Wuhan and other parts of Hubei, in particular, put the greater interests of the country in the first place and have shown unmatched perseverance and tenacity in their support for epidemic control.

Police officers, epidemic control workers, and community workers have worked around the clock. Media workers have rushed to the front line to cover the battle heedless of the risks they face. A vast number of volunteers have made a major contribution through their devotion and service.

All Party and government ministries, departments and commissions have fulfilled their duties. They include those in charge of public health, development and reform, industry and information technology, commerce, foreign affairs, international communications, transport, agriculture and rural affairs, emergency management, finance, culture and tourism, science and technology, education, market regulation, social security and basic medical insurance, natural resources, the eco-environment, state-owned assets, and forestry and grasslands, those responsible for discipline inspection, supervision over the exercise of state power, Party organization, public communications and united front work, and those responsible for judicial, prosecuting and public security affairs.

People's congresses at all levels, CPPCC national and local committees, and people's organizations have actively taken on their responsibilities and lent strong support to epidemic control. All sectors of society and our compatriots in Hong Kong, Macao, Taiwan, and overseas have donated money and supplies, extending a helping hand when it was most needed.

Strengthen Covid-19 Control and Promote Economic and Social Development*

February 23, 2020

The economy and society, being dynamic in nature, cannot stop functioning for long. While ensuring effective Covid-19 control, we should resume the operation of enterprises and public institutions and restore the normal order of people's work and life in places that are less affected by coronavirus. This is necessary in order to ensure adequate supplies for disease control, people's livelihoods, and social stability. This is essential for us to meet the goals for this year's economic and social development, finish the building of a moderately prosperous society in all respects, and meet the goals of the 13th Five-year Plan for Economic and Social Development. It is also important to our opening up initiative and to global economic stability.

Covid-19 will inevitably exert a negative impact on the economy and society. In such a challenging time, we must be more confident about our development in the long run and view it from a comprehensive and dialectical perspective. Generally speaking, our economy has maintained a positive trend despite the occurrence of Covid-19, which will not last long and will be brought under control. To achieve this year's goals of socio-economic development, we must unleash our great potential and momentum by turning pressure into motivation and crisis into opportunity, by restoring the normal order to business and people's lives, by taking solid measures to stabilize employment, finance, foreign trade, inbound investment, domestic investment, and market expectations, and by strengthening policy adjustment.

* Part of the speech at a meeting on strengthening Covid-19 control and economic and social development.

First, adopting a region-specific, tiered and targeted approach to reopen the economy.

The outbreak of Covid-19 made it hard for us to pool resources in a short time to control it. Now, when the situation has stabilized, we also face two challenges – strengthening Covid-19 control, and reopening the economy. A one-size-fits-all approach for different places will impede the restoration of economic and social order. However, relaxing controls indiscriminately will only put all our gains at risk. Based on these considerations, at the meeting of the Standing Committee of the Political Bureau on February 12, I proposed a region-specific, tiered and differentiated approach for coronavirus control in less affected areas. Now 1,396 counties and districts, 46 percent of the total number in the country, have no confirmed cases, and some counties and districts only have a few cases and basically no new cases. The authorities of these low-risk localities should quickly shift their focus to preventing inbound transmission and restoring their economic and social order. The authorities in medium-level risk areas should reopen the economy as progress in Covid-19 control allows, and those in high-risk areas should continue to focus on Covid-19 control. As the situation continues to improve, the authorities of provinces that meet the criteria should lower their response levels and make the appropriate adjustments.

Second, adjusting macroeconomic regulation.

Macro policies, which are an effective way of making counter-cyclic adjustments, should be exercised with the right pace and intensity to offset the adverse impacts of Covid-19, protect the economy from an excessive slowdown, and prevent short-term impacts from turning into directional change. We should give the proactive fiscal policy another boost, and see that subsidized interest rates, large-scale fee reductions, and tax deferrals deliver benefit to enterprises as soon as possible. We should continue to make phased and targeted tax and fee reductions, lend more support to some sectors in resuming operation, and help micro, small and medium-sized businesses survive these difficult times. The surplus funds of some central government departments should be pooled and used on Covid-19 control and key expenditures. Larger transfer payments should be made to localities whose government revenues are affected more by Covid-19, to ensure pay for local government employees, keep the government functioning, and meet people's basic living needs. The issuance of special local government bonds should be expanded in scale, and the structure of local government budgetary investment should be improved. A prudent monetary policy should be pursued with greater flexibility as called for, support for the resumption of the operation of the real economy should be strengthened, current financial support policies should be fully used, and new policy measures should be enacted at the right time. To help businesses that are returning to work to repay debts, ensure capital turnover and expand financing, we should provide financial support, such as special credit lines for key Covid-19 control areas, more severely affected industries, private businesses, and micro and small businesses. We should adjust the schedule for repayment of capital and interest by enterprises, facilitate loan extension and renewal, and reduce or appropriately exempt loan interest to micro and small businesses, so that they will not run out of operating funds.

Third, taking forceful and comprehensive measures to stabilize employment.

We should give priority to employment, adjust policy measures as conditions change, ease corporate burdens, keep jobs stable, and expand employment. We should implement policies that support the special reduction and exemption of social insurance contributions, return unemployment insurance premiums to enterprises that have protected jobs despite difficulties, and provide subsidies to people who have just joined the workforce or started businesses. More targeted measures should be taken based on the conditions of localities and industries, to support those enterprises experiencing severe labor shortages, those struggling to protect jobs, and key groups of people having difficulty finding employment. Migrant workers in low-risk localities should be encouraged to return to work, and door-to-door pick-up services should be provided to transport them from their homes to their destinations. We should support flexible employment in various forms, and help individual businesses reopen as soon as possible. We should promote online unemployment registration and online application for unemployment insurance benefits, and make sure all eligible individuals get their benefits in full. We should help graduating college students find jobs by providing services related to graduation, recruitment, job application, and acceptance.

Fourth, eradicating extreme poverty as planned.

Poverty eradication is scheduled for this year. We already face a tough challenge. Now we must work harder to offset the impact of Covid-19 and spare no effort in our fight against poverty. Direct channels should be established between source locations of migrant workforce and their employment destinations, and we should help migrant workers from poor areas resume work in an orderly fashion. We should help leading enterprises and workshops involved in poverty alleviation to resume operations, so as to create jobs locally. We should help farmers in poor areas find buyers for their agricultural and livestock products. We should move faster to establish a mechanism for preventing people from falling back into poverty, and take timely steps to help those who have fallen back into poverty due to Covid-19 or other reasons, to ensure their basic living needs are met.

Fifth, promoting the resumption of business operations.

We should take a region-specific, tiered and targeted approach to Covid-19 control, which means removing transport bottlenecks to enable unimpeded movement of people and logistics and ease controls on freight. We should see that workers can return to their jobs, raw materials can reach factories, and finished products are delivered. The industrial chain is an interlocked system requiring the functioning of all links. If one link fails to function, both upstream and downstream businesses will be affected. Production and distribution links of the industrial chain across regions should be closely connected, so that they can resume operations at the same time. We should expand effective domestic demand, work faster on ongoing and new projects, ensure the supply of labor, land and capital, make good use of central government budgets for investment, special bond funds, and policy finance, and invest in sectors where it is mostly appropriate. Covid-19 poses both a challenge and an opportunity for industrial development. While some traditional industries are bracing for a negative impact, smart manufacturing, unmanned delivery, online consumption, health care, and other emerging industries have great potential for growth. We should take advantage of this opportunity to upgrade traditional industries and develop emerging industries.

Sixth, losing no time in carrying out spring farming.

Spring farming has started from south to north. We must solve pressing problems affecting production, circulation and provision of agricultural materials in time for sowing and plowing. Agricultural production must also begin in Hubei and other badly-affected provinces, adjusted to local conditions. Excessive restrictions on farmers working in open fields should be lifted to ensure timely planting. We must continue to strengthen control over African swine fever, HPAI and other major animal epidemics, and develop animal husbandry and aquaculture.

Seventh, meeting basic living needs.

Covid-19 has directly affected people's incomes; this plus growing prices may make life harder for some people. Provincial governors must ensure the supply of rice and other staple foods, and city mayors the supply of meat and vegetables. We must watch closely the impact of Covid-19 on supply and demand, ensure the supply of daily necessities, and keep prices from rising too fast. Vital services should continue during Covid-19 control, and services that people need most in daily life should be resumed in an orderly fashion. Relief for groups in need should be strengthened, and local authorities may give higher special price subsidies if they have the ability to do so. Special attention should be given to families of Covid-19 patients and families who have lost members to meet their basic living needs. Government officials should pay more visits to elderly people with no family, children from poor families, and people with serious diseases and disabilities who are in isolation at home. Acts in violation of social ethics must be prevented. Treatment and medicines should be provided for patients suffering from acute and severe conditions, patients with chronic diseases, and all other patients seeking medical care.

Eighth, ensuring normal foreign trade and foreign investment operations.

We should ensure the smooth operation of industrial and supply chains in foreign trade, and maintain our share of the international market. We should make good use of export tax rebates, export credit insurance, and other trade policy tools that comply with due criteria, and expand export credits and relax the conditions for insurance underwriting and claims as appropriate. We should streamline customs clearance procedures, cut port, inspection and quarantine charges, and provide more convenient foreign exchange services. Local governments are encouraged to retain existing foreign investment and attract more investment, and launch key projects. We should further open up finance and other services, continue to improve the business environment, and attract and retain foreign investment, so as to boost international confidence in long-term investment and business operations in China.

Turn the Fighting Spirit Against Covid-19 into a Powerful Force for National Rejuvenation[*]

September 8, 2020

The great strategic success we have achieved in the fight against Covid-19 is a testament to the strengths of the leadership of the CPC, China's socialist system, the Chinese people and the Chinese nation, our profound cultural heritage, and our sense of mission as a responsible major country. This success has significantly boosted the confidence, pride, unity, and cohesion of the entire Party and all the Chinese people. It will inspire us to keep forging ahead over all obstacles on our journey in the new era.

In the fierce battle against Covid-19, the Chinese people and the Chinese nation have shown extraordinary mettle and fought courageously for victory. While fighting the virus, we have put life above all else, rallied the entire country, braved danger, respected science, and stood together through adversity.

– Putting life above all else embodies the Chinese people's deep-rooted tradition of compassion and the people-centered philosophy of China's Communists.

As an ancient Chinese philosopher said, "Compassion means loving and helping others."[1] Human compassion will prevail over the merciless virus. Life is the most precious of all things, for we only live once; once lost, life can never be restored. When lives are at stake, we must protect them at all costs, a promise we are capable of delivering because the fundamental mission of our Party is to serve the people wholeheartedly, and because ours is a socialist country run by the people.

* Part of the speech at a national gathering to honor outstanding individuals and groups in the fight against the Covid-19 epidemic.

We took the decisive step of closing outbound traffic from Wuhan City and the rest of Hubei Province, and put in place control measures unprecedented in their stringency. This was a decision that required enormous political courage and a strong sense of responsibility, but we were prepared to do whatever it took to protect the lives of the people. From newborn babies just 30 hours old to elderly people over the age of 100, and from international students to other foreign expatriates in the country, every life was fully protected, valued and respected. All this best illustrates the people-centered governance philosophy of our Party, the Chinese ethos and ethics that human life is invaluable, and the Chinese people's reverence for life.

– Rallying the entire country embodies the great strength of unity that enables us to stand together through thick and thin.

Despite the huge physical and mental stress caused by the mortal threat of the virus and long stretches of time under quarantine, our people refused to back down in the face of challenges and dangers. In their own ways, they bravely contributed to epidemic control, either rushing to the front line or holding firm at their posts.

Our people across the country united as one with a single purpose in mind. We knew what was at stake: the wellbeing of every one of us, the common interests of our communities, and the safety of our nation. Doctors and nurses in white coats, military personnel in green uniforms, police officers in blue gear, and volunteers in red vests all played their part. Party members rushed to the front line, and their pledge to keep fighting until the virus was defeated has shown their loyalty to the Party and the people. The 1.4 billion Chinese have stood together shoulder to shoulder, side by side, and proved an important truth: In unity there is strength.

– Braving danger embodies the indomitable will of the Chinese people to overcome whatever difficulties we encounter.

At the moment of crisis when Covid-19 struck, everyone responded heroically. People fighting the virus on various fronts rose to the challenge, put themselves in harm's way, and risked their own lives. They performed their duty with compassion and protected others with their own lives. Among them was a hospital president who, himself infected, gave up the chance to save his own life so he could give hope to other patients. There was a husband who could not give his wife the wedding he had promised. There was a mother who lost her life at her post saving others, and never returned home to her young child.

The Chinese have confronted the rampant virus head-on, like explorers pushing into the mountains undaunted by the presence of stalking tigers, and together we have written a moving epic. The reason that the Chinese nation has been able to thrive despite countless disasters is never because of a savior, but thanks to hundreds of millions of ordinary people stepping forward to brave the dark for others.

– Respecting science embodies the Chinese character of pragmatism and innovation.

Faced with an unknown infectious disease, we maintained a rational mindset and attitude, and followed the laws of science in all respects and throughout the process of decision-making, treatment, research, and social governance. In the absence of proven effective medicines, we used both Western medicine and traditional Chinese medicine, and upgraded national diagnostic and treatment protocols eight times. We identified traditional Chinese and Western medicines and treatment methods that have proved effective in clinical practice, including the Three TCM Drugs and Three Herbal Formulas[2], and they have been adopted or used as references by several countries.

We raced to build temporary treatment centers, conducted vaccine research through multiple technical approaches, carried out nucleic acid testing on a massive scale, traced infections with big data, introduced health code verification, implemented differentiated, tiered response measures tailored to different localities, and promoted the orderly resumption of work. All the results have justified our respect for rational thinking, and equipped us with powerful scientific and technological tools to help us defeat the epidemic.

– Standing together through adversity embodies the Chinese

people's love for peace, and commitment to looking out for others.

A noble cause is never a lonely pursuit, and compassion knows no borders. Upholding the belief that all countries are members of one and the same family, we take responsibility for the lives and health of the Chinese people; we also make due contribution to global public health security. We have launched the most wide-ranging and intense emergency humanitarian assistance campaign since the founding of the PRC in 1949, and have contributed to the global fight against Covid-19 on an ongoing basis. China has proved to be a responsible major country that honors its word, values friendship, upholds justice, and champions integrity – a country committed to pursuing a more harmonious world and building a global community of shared future.

Just as inner strength is indispensable for individuals, it is also essential for nations. Indeed, only with inner strength can a nation stand tall and firm while weathering the tide of challenging times. The ability to overcome difficulties demands not only material resources but also an indomitable will. The great spirit that we have forged in the battle against Covid-19 is deeply rooted in the character of the Chinese nation and our cultural genes. It carries and builds on patriotism, collectivism, and socialism, and illustrates and enriches the ethos of both our nation and our times. We should promote this great spirit in our society and turn it into a powerful force for building a modern socialist country and realizing the rejuvenation of the Chinese nation.

"To know the flavor of a thing, one must taste it; to know what lies ahead on a path, one must walk it."[3] In this heroic battle against the coronavirus, we have accumulated important experience, and gained deep insights.

– The fight against Covid-19 has once again demonstrated that the strong leadership of the Communist Party of China is the pillar that the people can rely on when crisis strikes.

Our Party comes from the people and has its roots among them. Everything it does is for the people, and it relies on the people in everything it does. The Party has thus earned the wholehearted and unwavering support of the public, which provides a broad and solid foundation for its leadership and governance of the country.

When the virus struck, the central leadership immediately called on all Party members to rush to the front line, and keep the Party flag flying high in the battle against the virus. This fully demonstrates the sense of mission and strength of character of China's Communists. Throughout the battle, Party members across the country have kept the original aspiration and founding mission of our Party firmly in mind and lived up to their exemplary role. Over 25,000 outstanding individuals swore their oaths and joined the Party on the front line.

It is precisely because of the leadership of the Party and the support given to the Party by the people across the country, that China has achieved rapid economic growth and lasting social stability, a remarkable achievement by any standard. With this leadership and support we have responded swiftly to emergencies such as floods, earthquakes, and the SARS epidemic, and emerged from the battle against Covid-19. History and our experience have shown that as long as we uphold and strengthen the Party's overall leadership, and reinforce its ability to provide political leadership and theoretical guidance, to organize and inspire the people, and to maintain close bonds between the Party and the people, we will create a powerful synergy that enables us to deal with all complexities, risks and challenges.

– The fight against Covid-19 has once again demonstrated that the unyielding will of the Chinese people is the source of strength that enables us to overcome all obstacles and difficulties as we move forward.

Hard times have put us to the test and made us stronger. It is by facing all odds with tenacity and perseverance that we have been able to resist foreign aggression, fight to keep our country together when it was being torn apart, build the country up from a base of utter destitution, and keep pace with a changing world. This is why the Chinese nation now stands tall and proud among the nations of the world.

For centuries, the Chinese people have been known for resilience, cohesiveness, tenacity and creativity, and we are all proud to be called Chinese. History and our experience have shown that as long as we rely on the people, do everything with their interests in mind, and encourage their indomitable will and determination, we will be able to forge stronger unity and bring new glory to our nation.

– The fight against Covid-19 has once again demonstrated that the strengths of China's socialist system make it possible for us to defuse risks, resolve challenges, and strengthen the governance of our country.

An important criterion for judging the success and strengths of a country's system is whether it is able to mobilize the whole nation to respond to major risks and challenges. With China's socialist system, we have a great capacity to mobilize, coordinate, and take action, as well as a unique ability to pool resources to complete major, difficult, and urgent undertakings. The fight against Covid-19 is a vivid illustration of the strengths of China's state and governance systems. History and our experience have shown that as long as we uphold and improve China's socialist system, modernize China's governance system and capacity, and fully leverage the ability of our system to respond to risks and challenges, we will be able to withstand the trials we face, turn challenges into opportunities, and emerge stronger time and time again.

– The fight against Covid-19 has once again demonstrated that the robust strength our country has built up since the founding of the People's Republic has given us the confidence to navigate stormy seas with composure.

Over the years, China has built up solid material foundations, a complete system of industries, strong scientific and technological capabilities, and abundant medical resources, all of which have underpinned our effective epidemic response. After the virus struck, we took swift action to mobilize people and supplies, intensify research, and gather and transport essential materials. At the height of the epidemic much of China's economic and social development was put on hold, but people's lives were not seriously affected and society generally carried on as normal. This is, in essence, attributable to the composite national strength that China has built up since the founding of the People's Republic – and particularly since the launch of reform and opening up in 1978 – and to China's ability to fully leverage this strength in times of crisis.

History and our experience have shown that we will be able to ensure that the great ship of Chinese socialism can cleave the waves and sail steadily into the future, as long as we continue to unleash and develop productive forces, build our economic strength, scientific and technological capabilities, and composite national strength, give people a stronger sense of gain, fulfillment and security, and steadily boost the material foundations for upholding and developing Chinese socialism and realizing the rejuvenation of the Chinese nation.

– The fight against Covid-19 has once again demonstrated that the core socialist values[4] and traditional Chinese culture are a powerful force for inspiring our people, rallying their support, and pooling their strength.

Cultural confidence is the most essential, profound, and enduring source of strength for a country. A culture featuring the pursuit of excellence and virtue serves as a crucial bond bringing the people and the nation to stand together as one. Throughout history, we Chinese have always cherished deep feelings for our nation, the same way as we do for our family. We hold dear the values of putting one's interests aside for the common good, fulfilling one's duties to secure the future of the nation, standing together through times of adversity, looking out for one another, and respecting the elderly and caring for the young. We also believe that with freedom comes self-restraint, and with rights come responsibilities.

In the fight against Covid-19, the 1.4 billion Chinese have forged a powerful line of defense by acting with a keen sense of responsibility, self-discipline, dedication, compassion, unity and solidarity. History and our experience have shown that as long as we foster and live by the core socialist values and keep the best of traditional Chinese culture alive, we will be able to create a wellspring of inspiration and motivation for all the people across the country to forge ahead together.

– The fight against Covid-19 has once again demonstrated that the endeavor to build a global community of shared future has wide appeal, and it is the right approach in tackling humanity's common challenges and shaping a more prosperous and beautiful world.

In a way, Covid-19 is a wakeup call for the world, reminding us that our destinies are intertwined and that no country can afford to go it alone in the face of such a major crisis. What we should do is to work together as a team. Those who act out of self-interest, assign blame to others, twist facts, or call black white will end up harming not only their own country and people, but many other peoples around the world. History and our experience have shown that as long as all countries are committed to building a global community of shared future, upholding multilateralism, and boosting unity and cooperation, the people of the world will be able to meet whatever challenges we face and make this planet a beautiful home for all of us.

Changes on a scale unseen in a century are gripping the world at an accelerating pace, and the tasks of advancing reform, promoting development, and maintaining stability are arduous. As we move on from the First Centenary Goal towards the Second Centenary Goal, we must fully implement our Party's underlying theories, basic guidelines, and fundamental principles, and act on the general principle of pursuing progress while ensuring stability. We must follow the new development philosophy and focus on creating the new development dynamic. We must pay sufficient attention to both domestic and international imperatives, pursue development while safeguarding security, and modernize our system and capacity for governance. This will enable us to continuously advance the cause of the Party and the state.

In the coming period, we must focus on the following tasks:

– We will steadfastly implement regularized control measures and work to prevail over Covid-19.

The virus is still spreading around the world. In our country, the risk of sporadic cases and local surges still exists. Fully defeating this virus thus requires a consistent effort. We must remain vigilant, work tirelessly, and take comprehensive and effective steps to prevent both

inbound cases and domestic resurgence. We must adopt normal-
ized and targeted control measures, and be ready to address isolated
emergencies. We must not, under any circumstances, let the hard-won
progress we have made against the epidemic go to waste.

We need to step up our efforts to develop medicines and vaccines,
carry out extensive public health campaigns, upgrade public health
facilities, and raise the cultural and ethical quality of the whole nation.
We must ensure public health and epidemic control in all communities
so that they will form a strong line of defense against the virus across
the country.

– We will take solid steps to stabilize the Six Fronts[5] and guarantee the Six Priorities[6] so as to meet our goals of eradicating extreme
poverty and building a moderately prosperous society.

We need to boost confidence and redouble our efforts to make
up for lost time and repair the damage caused by the coronavirus. We
will put in place medium- and long-term mechanisms for coordinating
epidemic response with economic and social development.

We will continue to prioritize supply-side structural reform, extend
reform and opening up, and expand domestic demand as a strategic
pivot. We should protect and boost the vigor of market entities, fully
implement macro policies to deliver their intended effects, and reinforce the stability and competitiveness of industrial and supply chains.

We will mobilize resources and intensify efforts to resolve prominent problems and strengthen weak links in poverty elimination. We
will always bear in mind the interests of our people, help them resolve
difficulties they encounter in employment, income, education, social
security, medical insurance, and housing, and take solid steps to ensure
and improve their wellbeing.

– We will move more quickly to strengthen weak links in our
governance and provide sound institutional safeguards for the health
and safety of the people.

Covid-19 is an intense challenge to our system and capacity for
governance. We should act swiftly to address problems, plug loopholes, and reinforce weak points in our institutions and mechanisms,

so as to raise our ability to tackle major public health emergencies.

We will build a robust public health system, improve our disease prevention and control system, and establish a major epidemic prevention, control and treatment system that works in times of both peace and emergency. We will strengthen legal safeguards and scientific and technological support for public health, upgrade our capacity for stockpiling emergency supplies to ensure their provision, and consolidate community-level efforts to underpin interdepartmental and society-wide prevention and control.

We will improve the systems for urban governance and for urban and rural grassroots governance, embrace a vision of comprehensive urban health management, and make overall social governance more efficient. We should stay alert to biorisks and upgrade our country's capacity for biorisk management.

– We will uphold the vision of a global community of shared future and work with the international community to tackle global challenges that are growing in severity.

China will continue to promote international cooperation against the coronavirus, support the WHO's leading role in the global response, and share with other countries its experience in Covid-19 prevention, control and treatment. As the largest supplier of medical supplies, we will continue to provide assistance to vulnerable countries and regions, and contribute to building a global community of health for all.

We will expand mutually beneficial cooperation with other countries, continue to promote economic globalization, uphold the multilateral trading system, and maintain the secure and smooth functioning of global industrial and supply chains, thus making our contribution to the speedy recovery of the global economy.

We are ready to work with other countries to establish more inclusive global governance, build more effective multilateral mechanisms, and pursue more active regional cooperation. We will work together to address regional disputes and global issues such as terrorism, climate change, cybersecurity threats, and biorisks, in a common pursuit of a brighter future for humanity.

– We must always have plans in place for worst-case scenarios, stay vigilant against potential dangers, and effectively forestall and defuse any risks we may encounter on the road ahead.

Just as a rainbow appears after rain, opportunities are born out of challenges; this embodies an eternal law of dialectics. Never in the hundred years of Party history, the seven decades of the People's Republic, or the four decades of reform and opening up, have we experienced completely untroubled waters. Success and progress are reserved for those who face challenges head-on rather than looking for an easy way out.

We must gain a full understanding of major domestic and international trends, strengthen strategic, systematic, and forward-thinking research and planning, and be prepared, in both thought and deed, to face long periods of change in the external environment. We must foster new opportunities amid crises and open up new horizons on a shifting landscape.

We must maintain our fighting spirit, gathering the courage and capability to surmount all difficulties. We should adapt our tactics to evolving circumstances, rally all available forces, and mobilize all favorable factors as we strive towards new victories in the great historic struggle with many new features.

"Just as Heaven maintains vigor through movement, a gentleman makes unremitting efforts to perfect himself."[7] A nation is great because it never gives up, never retreats, and never stops moving forward. No matter what setbacks it faces, it will keep fighting for a better future.

The Chinese people have experienced both hardship and glory in our 5,000 years of civilization, and we will continue to forge ahead on our great journey in the new era. No force or individual can stop the Chinese people from seeking a better life.

Let us unite closer, carry forward the heroic spirit against Covid-19, and forge ahead with resolve. Let us strive to reach our goals of building a moderately prosperous society in all respects and winning the battle against poverty, and achieve new and historic successes in building a modern socialist country.

Notes

[1] *Zhuang Zi.* This is a collection of writings by Zhuang Zhou and other scholars. Zhuang Zhou (c. 369-286 BC), also known as Zhuang Zi, was a Taoist philosopher in the Warring States Period.

[2] The Three TCM Drugs are Jinhua Qinggan Granules, Lianhua Qingwen Capsules/Granules, and Xuebijing Injection; the Three Herbal Formulas are Lung Cleansing and Detoxifying Preparation, Dampness Resolving and Detoxifying Preparation, and Lung Diffusing and Detoxifying Preparation.

[3] Liu Ji: *Anadiploses* (*Ni Lian Zhu*). Liu Ji (1311-1375), also known as Liu Bowen, was a statesman and writer of the Ming Dynasty.

[4] The core socialist values: Prosperity, democracy, civility and harmony are values that underpin our nation; freedom, equality, justice, and the rule of law are values that buttress our society; patriotism, dedication, good faith, and amity are values that underlie individual conduct.

[5] The Six Fronts are employment, finance, foreign trade, inbound investment, domestic investment, and market expectations.

[6] The Six Priorities are jobs, daily living needs, food and energy security, industrial and supply chains, the operation of market players, and the smooth functioning of grassroots government.

[7] *Book of Changes* (*Zhou Yi*), also known as *I Ching* (*Yi Jing*). This book is one of the Confucian classics.

Respond to Covid-19 with a Dedicated Effort*

March 17, 2022

Since May 2020 when we started to conduct Covid-19 prevention and control on a regular basis, we have spared no effort to prevent both inbound cases and domestic resurgence. We have improved our targeted response capabilities and taken region-specific, tiered and differentiated prevention and control measures. We have also acted swiftly to stamp out local outbreaks whenever they occurred. Our efforts have protected people's lives and health to the greatest possible extent. China has continued to lead the world in both economic development and epidemic prevention and control, and this fully demonstrates our country's strong epidemic response capabilities and the strengths of CPC leadership and China's socialist system.

Perseverance will be rewarded. All provincial authorities, central departments, and sectors should be fully aware of the complexity and difficulty of epidemic prevention and control, and the volatility of the epidemic at home and abroad. We should mobilize, be of one mind, stay confident, and respond to Covid-19 with dedicated efforts. We should always put the people and their lives first, take a science-based and targeted approach to implement the dynamic zero-Covid policy, and act promptly to curb the spread of the virus.

We should continue our science-based and targeted Covid-19 response, and improve response measures. We should expedite the research and development of vaccines, medicines, and rapid test reagents, and make our response more targeted. We should always be confident in our response strategy, pursue progress while ensuring

---

* Main points of the speech at a meeting of the Standing Committee of the Political Bureau of the 19th CPC Central Committee.

stable performance, and promote economic and social development while containing the disease. We should also adopt more effective measures, ensure the most effective response possible at reasonable cost, and minimize the impact of Covid-19 on society and the economy.

Towards a Modern Socialist Country

Major Points on the Recommendations of the CPC Central Committee for Formulating the 14th Five-Year Plan for Economic and Social Development and Long-Range Objectives Through the Year 2035[*]

October 26, 2020

The Recommendations in this draft report present some important points. I would like to offer brief explanations on several of them.

First, on promoting high-quality development.

According to the Recommendations, China should focus on promoting high-quality development during the 14th Five-year Plan period (2021-2025). This is based on a sound assessment of the stage, environment, and conditions for our country's development: that China is still in the primary stage of socialism and will remain so for a long time to come; that China is still the largest developing country in the world; that development remains the CPC's top priority in governance. It should be emphasized that during the new era and at the new stage we must follow the new development philosophy and ensure high-quality growth. Today the principal challenge facing Chinese society is the gap between the people's growing expectation for a better life and imbalanced and insufficient development. All challenges and problems impeding our development derive from the

* Part of the Explanation of the Recommendations of the Central Committee of the Communist Party of China for Formulating the 14th Five-Year Plan for Economic and Social Development and Long-Range Objectives Through the Year 2035 made at the Fifth Plenary Session of the 19th CPC Central Committee.

quality of growth. Therefore, we must place more emphasis on the quality of growth, so as to improve the quality and effectiveness of development.

The world is undergoing change on a scale unseen in a century, and the external environment for our development is becoming increasingly complex. To avoid or address all kinds of risks and hazards, and proactively act against the challenges arising from the changes in external circumstances, the key is to manage our own affairs well. We need to raise the quality of growth, improve international competitiveness, build our composite national strength and our capability to withstand risks, and safeguard national security, so as to ensure economic stability and sustainability and social harmony and order. We should achieve high-quality development in the economy, society, culture, the eco-environment, and all other fields.

When we focus on promoting high-quality development, we must follow the new development philosophy. We will take supply-side structural reform as the main theme, put quality and effectiveness first, transform the development model, and improve the quality, efficiency and drivers of economic growth, so that the fruits of development will become real benefits enjoyed by all the people, and their desire for a better life will be consistently met.

Second, on creating a double development dynamic with the domestic economy as the mainstay and the domestic economy and international engagement providing mutual reinforcement.

This is a strategic decision designed to raise our economic level in keeping with the times, and to give ourselves a new edge in international economic cooperation and competition. Since the launch of reform and opening up in 1978, and especially after China's accession to the World Trade Organization in 2001, we have become more deeply involved in the global economy, rising as "the world's factory" with both ends of the production process – the supply of resources and the sale of products – on the international market. This has contributed enormously to our rapid growth and the improvement in people's lives. In a changing global political and economic landscape in recent years, globalization is meeting with growing opposition; some countries are moving rapidly towards unilateralism and protectionism, and traditional international engagement is weakening. In such circumstances, we must build on firm domestic foundations for development and exploit the domestic market as an engine for economic growth. With a population of 1.4 billion and a per capita GDP exceeding US$10,000, China has become the largest consumer market in the world, with more potential to boost consumption than any other country. We have encountered various external risks and threats since reform and opening up. However, we have always managed to withstand risks by doing well on the home front with a focus on domestic development.

To create the new development dynamic, we must focus on driving domestic demand. Our production, distribution, circulation and consumption should depend more on the domestic market, and form a virtuous cycle in the national economy. To this end, we will continue supply-side structural reform, adapt the supply system more closely to domestic demand, eliminate bottlenecks in economic flows, and upgrade the industrial and supply chains. In doing so, we will make the domestic market the major source of aggregate demand, and boost a higher-level dynamic equilibrium in which demand drives supply and supply creates demand. The new development dynamic is not a closed loop but a blend of domestic and international economic flows. A large-scale domestic economy that functions smoothly will certainly attract resources from all over the world. This will both satisfy domestic demand and develop our industrial and technological capabilities, opening up a new horizon for China's participation in international economic cooperation and competition.

Third, on economic growth targets during the 14th Five-year Plan period and through the year of 2035.

During the process of soliciting opinions, some regions and departments suggested setting a clear growth rate target for the 14th Five-year Plan period, and the goal of doubling GDP or per capita income through 2035. Based on careful research and calculation of our capabilities and conditions for economic development, the drafting group believes that it is feasible for our country to maintain long-term steady growth, and China will very likely become a high-income economy according to the current threshold by the end of the 14th Five-year Plan period and double its GDP or per capita income by 2035. However, we should be aware that the world economy may stagnate due to the potential instability and uncertainty of the external environment in the coming years, the potential threats to our domestic economic growth, and the impact of the Covid-19 pandemic. We have therefore decided to place more emphasis on optimizing the economic structure in the medium and long-term plan, and guide all sectors to prioritize the quality and effectiveness of development in their work.

The Central Committee makes recommendations to determine the general direction and overall strategies. The draft report defines qualitative objectives which in turn point to specific quantifiable requirements for the 14th Five-year Plan and the 2035 vision. The relevant quantitative goals can be set on the basis of careful calculation when formulating the Outline for the 14th Five-Year Plan for Economic and Social Development and Long-Range Objectives Through the Year 2035.

Fourth, on promoting common prosperity for all.

As an essential requirement of socialism and a shared aspiration of the people, common prosperity is our ultimate goal in social and economic development. Since the founding of the PRC in 1949, and especially following the launch of reform and opening up, our Party and our people have worked without respite on the path to common prosperity, and the country's standard of living has steadily improved. After the 18th CPC National Congress in 2012 we made poverty elimination our top priority, and eventually succeeded in bringing all rural residents living below the current poverty line out of poverty, which represents a major step towards common prosperity. Today, imbalanced and insufficient development is still a prominent problem, and the development and income gaps between urban and rural areas and between different regions remain wide. Common prosperity is a long-term goal. However, following the realization of a moderately prosperous society in all respects, as we start on a new journey towards a modernized socialist country by every measure, we must give greater priority to this task, and devote more active, sustained, practical and effective efforts. In this regard, the draft report states that "more obvious and substantive progress will have been made towards common prosperity for all" by 2035 in the long-range plan, and lays emphasis on "firmly promoting common prosperity" in the section on improving the quality of people's lives, along with some other important requirements and measures. Our Party has used these expressions for the first time in a plenary session document to direct the orientation and define the goals. They are based on the realities and conform to the laws governing development, striking a balance between what is necessary and what is feasible, so that we may implement them better and more proactively as we advance nonstop on the path towards common prosperity.

Fifth, on synergizing development and security.

We have become more aware that security is a prerequisite for development and development guarantees security. Our country is exposed to the risk of various problems and dangers now and in the future, and risks – both foreseeable and unforeseeable – are on the increase. We must ensure both development and security, be better aware of the opportunities and risks we face, and always have plans in place to respond to worst-case scenarios. We should think harder and more deeply, close loopholes, strengthen areas of weakness, and make preemptive moves to deal with various risks and challenges, so as to ensure smooth progress in our socialist modernization drive.

Based on the above analysis, the draft report devotes a special section to the work of ensuring both development and security and of modernizing national defense and the armed forces. It emphasizes the need for a holistic approach to national security, for strengthening the national security system and capabilities, and for consolidating the national security shield.

Sixth, on persevering with systems thinking.

The draft states that systems thinking is a principle that must be followed for economic and social development during the 14th Five-year Plan period.

Since the 18th CPC National Congress, the Central Committee has been planning and pushing forward all undertakings of the Party and the state in a systematic and coordinated manner. In line with the new realities we face, it has formed a series of new plans and policies, and led all Party members and the Chinese people onward to new successes. In this process, systems thinking provides a fundamental method of thinking and working.

Once we achieve moderate prosperity in all respects, we will begin a new journey towards the goal of building a modern socialist country. We will face in-depth and complex changes in our development environment. The problem of imbalanced and insufficient development will remain, and the conflicts in economic and social development are tangled and complex. We must commit ourselves to systems thinking when drafting plans and addressing these challenges, make efforts to achieve progress in various fields, and advance socialist modernization in a comprehensive and coordinated manner.

Seventh, on the realization of a moderately prosperous society in all respects, and the time to announce it. After entering the 21st century, our Party set a goal to be achieved by its centenary: to build a higher-level moderately prosperous society in an all-round way to the benefit of over one billion people. This was a solemn promise to the Chinese people.

Since the Central Committee defined the strategy for building a moderately prosperous society at the initial stage of reform and opening up, we have worked hard over several decades to meet the people's desire for a better life. During the 13th Five-year Plan period (2016-2020), which was the decisive stage for realizing this goal, new successes have been achieved. We have focused on top priorities, addressed shortcomings, and overcome weaknesses. We have also taken solid steps to forestall and defuse major risks, carried out targeted poverty elimination, and prevented and controlled pollution.

The outbreak of Covid-19 had a detrimental impact on our economic and social development. However, under the firm leadership of the Central Committee and through the joint efforts of all the people, we have achieved a strategic success in the prevention and control of the epidemic. China leads the world in reviving the economy and restoring social order. Major economic indicators have rebounded, and livelihoods have been guaranteed. It is estimated that our GDP will exceed RMB100 trillion this year, and our standard of living will improve significantly. All the rural population living below the current poverty line will be raised from poverty. All the objectives for development set in the 13th Five-year Plan will be fulfilled on time, and the goal of building a moderately prosperous society in all respects will be achieved as scheduled.

As the building of a moderately prosperous society is still in progress, the draft report expresses that "a decisive victory has been achieved in building a moderately prosperous society in all respects". Sometime in the early months of next year, the Central Committee will make a systematic assessment and review of our work towards the goal before officially announcing that it has been successfully completed.

March Towards the Second Centenary Goal*

October 29, 2020

Through generations of hard work, we are now very close to the First Centenary Goal of building a moderately prosperous society in all respects, and to eradicating absolute poverty. We will embark on our journey towards the Second Centenary Goal next year.

At this critical moment, we should know that we have built up considerable development momentum, and that we have all the foundations, conditions and abilities to secure another great victory. But at the same time we need to be alert to the unprecedented complexity of an environment in which various problems overlap, and risks and challenges are escalating. We should adopt a historical and holistic approach, have a sound view on future development, and see through the mass of complexities influencing international and domestic affairs. Remaining calm in the face of danger, we should seek to turn crises into opportunities, open up new dimensions in our work, and achieve our strategic goal of national rejuvenation, while dealing with global change on a scale unseen in a century.

From an international perspective, these changes are still gathering momentum and the environment is becoming increasingly complex. On the one hand, peace and development remain the underlying trends of our times, a new revolution in science, technology and industry continues to develop, the international balance of power is undergoing profound readjustment, and the idea that humanity belongs to one community of shared future has taken deep root in people's hearts.

---

* Part of the speech at the second full assembly of the Fifth Plenary Session of the 19th CPC Central Committee.

On the other hand, instability and uncertainties are spreading globally, the Covid-19 pandemic will have far-reaching consequences, opposition to globalization is on the rise, populism and xenophobia are gaining ground, unilateralism, protectionism and hegemony are posing a threat to world peace and development, and profound and complex changes are reshaping the international economic, political, cultural, security, and scientific and technological landscape. We should correctly understand the key factors that will determine the course of these unprecedented changes, and look to seize the strategic initiative.

Domestically, we enjoy many strengths and favorable conditions for further development, while facing a number of difficulties and challenges. It is essential to take a comprehensive, dialectical and long-term perspective, and open up new areas for development.

First, we should have an in-depth understanding of how the principal challenge facing Chinese society is evolving, and devise a more systematic solution to imbalanced and insufficient development. Currently the major problems affecting China's development are as follows:

- Our capacity for innovation cannot satisfy the need for high-quality development.
- As the foundation of the country, agriculture is not strong enough.
- The urban-rural divide, regional disparity and income inequality are all considerable.
- There is much work to do in eco-environmental protection.
- There are shortcomings in social governance and social security.

All these problems stem from our country's imbalanced and insufficient development. This imbalance is manifested between regions, fields and sectors, and imposes restraints on overall development. Insufficient development makes China's all-round socialist modernization a time-consuming and difficult endeavor.

In order to address these issues, we must adhere to the world view and methodology of dialectical and historical materialism. They represent the principal challenge facing our society, and it will be impossible for us to resolve them at a stroke. Only an active and sustained effort will bear fruit. We must aim to solve problems and reach our goals, and adopt a holistic approach. We should spare no effort to consolidate our foundations, leverage our strengths, and address our weaknesses, so as to promote the comprehensive, balanced and sustainable economic and social development of our country.

Second, we should truly understand the people's expectation for a better life, and target our solutions at imbalanced and insufficient development. Shortages and insufficient supply, which plagued our economy in the past, have been fully addressed. The people's expectations have evolved in general from satisfying basic needs to improving the quality of life, and their demands at different levels and in various areas are becoming more diverse. Some non-pressing problems in the past have become more severe today as the people's expectations have risen. We should be more aware of these problems, and our ability to solve them has to increase accordingly. We should ensure and improve the people's wellbeing through development, address the most pressing and immediate issues that concern them the most, better meet their desire for a better life, promote well-rounded personal development and comprehensive social progress, and achieve more substantial progress in promoting prosperity for all.

Third, we should be well aware of the fundamentals of our long-term economic growth, and be more confident in addressing imbalanced and insufficient development. At present, the economy is facing unprecedented difficulties under the combined impact of periodical and structural factors, short-term and long-term problems, and the Covid-19 epidemic and external pressure. However, the epidemic will not last forever, and the virus can be contained; external pressure compels us to strengthen our capacity for independent innovation, and the economic fundamentals sustaining our country's sound development remain unchanged. Firm Party leadership and the strength of our socialist system in concentrating resources on major projects guarantee our country's steady and sustainable economic growth and social stability. For a long time, the solid material foundations we have laid, a wealth of talent, a complete industrial system, strengths in science and technology, and the world's largest market with the greatest potential have underpinned our economic growth and our defenses against external risks.

With a comprehensive analysis of the domestic and international situation, we are still in an important period of strategic opportunity which will continue, but the challenges and opportunities keep changing. When we first spoke of a period of strategic opportunity, we referred to the first two decades of this century. Now, after 20 years, how shall we address new challenges and opportunities? This is a major issue we need to consider. In the past it was easier to seize the opportunities as we sailed with the current; it has become harder now as we are moving forward against the wind. It was not difficult to identify risks and challenges in a relatively stable environment; now we are facing a volatile and complex global situation. Geopolitical challenges, like high waves, submerged reefs, and numerous undercurrents, require us to better adapt to changes. In the past, our lower-level development could be seen as more complementary to other countries; now at a much higher level, we have become more competitive with others.

Therefore, our judgment is that there currently exist both crises and opportunities. Opportunities are nurtured in crises, and crises can turn into opportunities. The opportunities are more strategic and promising; the challenges are more complex and bear on our overall situation. The challenges are unprecedented, but they can turn into extraordinary opportunities if we respond with ingenuity. The Covid-19 epidemic is such an example. We still remember the urgency and the intense pressure when it broke out earlier this year. More than six months have passed; far from being beaten down by the virus, with our exemplary anti-epidemic effort we will be the only major economy to restore growth this year. Our country's comprehensive strength and international influence have risen significantly despite the epidemic. We should reflect on the reasons for this and learn from the whole experience.

In short, the 14th Five-year Plan period (2021-2025) will be a critical time for China. To achieve further and greater development we should seize opportunities while guarding against potential risks. We should accurately understand the current changes we face, seize the initiative in building an effective response, and ultimately be the ones to seek change. We should be bold and set our sails for a headwind, and be ready to turn crises into opportunities. On the journey towards a modern socialist country in all respects, a great beginning beckons.

Follow the Chinese Path to Modernization[*]

October 29, 2020

China's socialist modernization has many particular characteristics. There is no such a thing as a single authorized model of modernization, nor a universally applicable standard of modernization. Deng Xiaoping once said, "The modernization we are striving for is modernization of a Chinese type. The socialism we are building is a socialism with Chinese characteristics."[1] While sharing some common characteristics with other countries, our modernization has some unique features adapted to the realities of China.

First, our modernization is for a huge population. Success in modernizing a country of 1.4 billion people – a population that exceeds in size the combined total of all the developed countries – will completely change the international landscape and have a far-reaching impact on humanity.

Second, our modernization aims at common prosperity for everyone, which is an essential requirement of Chinese socialism. Committed to the people-centered philosophy of development in our drive for modernization, we have proactively addressed regional divides, disparities between urban and rural areas, and the gap in income distribution. We have promoted social fairness and justice, worked towards common prosperity for all our people, and stood firmly against polarization between rich and poor.

Third, our modernization balances material and cultural-ethical progress. It upholds the core socialist values, strengthens education on ideals and convictions, spreads splendid traditional culture, boosts

* Part of the speech at the second full assembly of the Fifth Plenary Session of the 19th CPC Central Committee.

people's moral strength, and fosters material abundance and the well-rounded development of all.

Fourth, our modernization features a harmonious coexistence between humanity and nature. When we modernize our country, we strive to synergize material and eco-environmental progress, and follow a path of sound development that ensures growth, better lives, and a good environment; otherwise the pressure on resources and the environment will simply become unbearable.

Fifth, our modernization follows a path of peaceful development. Some of the old capitalist countries pursued modernization through violent exploitation of colonies and at the cost of other countries' development. In contrast, our modernization emphasizes mutual benefit with other countries, strives for a global community of shared future, and works to deliver peace and development to humanity.

Past experience shows that the Chinese path to modernization fits China's realities. It respects the laws governing the development of socialism and human society. We should press ahead with our modernization to drive forward our national rejuvenation and contribute more to humanity.

Notes

[1] Deng Xiaoping: "We Are on the Right Track and Our Policies Will Not Change", *Selected Works of Deng Xiaoping*, Vol. III, Eng. ed., Foreign Languages Press, Beijing, 1994, p. 39.

Speech at the National Conference to Review the Fight Against Poverty and Commend Outstanding Individuals and Groups

February 25, 2021

Comrades and friends,

Today, at this conference, we solemnly declare that through the efforts of the whole Party and the entire nation, China has secured a complete victory in its fight against absolute poverty in this important year, with the centenary of the Communist Party of China fast approaching.

All of the 99 million rural residents, who were lying below the current poverty line, have emerged from poverty, as have the 832 counties and 128,000 villages. All regional poverty has been eliminated, and the arduous task of eradicating absolute poverty has been completed, representing yet another astounding achievement. This is a great and glorious success for the Chinese people, for the CPC, and for the Chinese nation.

Here, on behalf of the CPC Central Committee, I would like to extend my warm congratulations to the exemplary individuals and groups who have been honored. My greatest respect goes to all those who have contributed to the fight against poverty, including:

- Party, government, and military bodies at all levels;
- enterprises and public institutions;
- village-level organizations, Party members, officials, and people in rural areas;
- first secretaries and members of resident work teams in villages and volunteers;

- various political parties, federations of industry and commerce, and prominent individuals without party affiliation;
- people's groups;
- other people from all sectors of society.

Finally, I would like to express heartfelt gratitude to our compatriots in the Hong Kong Special Administrative Region, the Macao Special Administrative Region, and Taiwan, as well as those overseas who have actively supported and participated in the fight against poverty, and to foreign governments, international organizations, and friends from all over the world who have shown concern and offered support for China's poverty reduction efforts.

Comrades and friends,

Poverty is a problem that has long plagued humanity. Throughout history, combating poverty has remained an important matter of governance for countries around the world. The history of China is a chronicle of the Chinese people's struggle against poverty. A deep longing to see the people free of poverty and well fed and clothed was expressed by great historical figures such as Qu Yuan who lamented, "Long did I sigh to hold back tears; saddened I am by the grief of my people."[1] Du Fu wrote forlornly, "If only I could build a house with thousands upon thousands of rooms, I would bring all the poor people on the earth under its roof and bring smiles to their faces."[2] Dr Sun Yat-sen yearned to see "every family living in plenty, with not a single person left behind"[3].

From the middle of the 19th century, China suffered political upheaval and incessant conflict due to the decadence of feudal rule and the aggression of Western powers. As the Chinese people struggled to earn their livelihood, the nightmare of poverty became an even greater torment. Escaping poverty thus became their constant goal and an important part of realizing the Chinese Dream of national rejuvenation.

From the outset, the CPC has pursued its mission of seeking happiness for the people and rejuvenation for the Chinese nation. It has shown steadfast commitment, uniting the people and leading them in a long and arduous struggle for a better life.

During the New Democratic Revolution (1919-1949), the CPC united the peasants and led them in overthrowing local tyrants and dividing up the land, put into effect the policy of "land to the tiller", and helped liberate those living in destitution. Winning broad support from the vast majority of the people, it went on to secure victory in the Chinese revolution and ultimately founded the People's Republic of China. This created the political base for eradicating poverty in China.

After the founding of the PRC in 1949, the CPC united the people and led them in completing the socialist revolution, establishing and developing socialism as the country's fundamental system, and engaging in national construction. It mobilized the people and encouraged them to be self-reliant and work hard to bring order to the country and make it strong. This laid solid foundations for shaking off poverty and improving the lives of the people.

After the launch of reform and opening up in 1978, the CPC united the people and led them in carrying out well-conceived and well-organized initiatives for development-driven poverty alleviation on a massive scale, and devoted itself to releasing and developing productive forces and to ensuring and improving public wellbeing, achieving remarkable and unprecedented results in the process.

Since the 18th CPC National Congress in 2012, the Central Committee has made it clear that in building a moderately prosperous society in all respects, the most arduous tasks are to be found in rural areas, particularly impoverished rural areas, and that this goal cannot be considered complete unless these areas have reached moderate prosperity. The Central Committee has also emphasized that poverty is not compatible with socialism, and that if impoverished areas were to remain poor and unchanged for a long time with no noticeable improvement to people's lives, then there would be no grounds for asserting the superiority of China's socialist system. This, too, would be contrary to socialism, and therefore we must lose no time in the fight against poverty.

At the end of 2012, not long after the Party's 18th National Congress, the Central Committee stated, "The measurement for moderate prosperity lies in the rural areas." It pledged that not a single poverty-stricken area or individual would be left behind, and this launched the battle against poverty in the new era.

In 2013, the Central Committee introduced the concept of targeted poverty alleviation and created new working mechanisms for poverty alleviation.

At the Central Conference on Poverty Alleviation and Development in 2015, overall requirements were raised for fulfilling the objectives of the fight against poverty. Standards were set in six areas to ensure the precision of the work: identifying the poor accurately, arranging targeted programs, utilizing capital efficiently, taking household-based measures, dispatching first Party secretaries based on village conditions, and achieving the set goals. The Central Committee launched five key measures through which people would be lifted out of poverty: new economic activities, relocation from uninhabitable areas, recompense for eco-protection, education, and social assistance for basic needs. This sounded the call for a general offensive to win the battle against poverty.

At the 19th CPC National Congress in 2017, comprehensive plans were drawn up to achieve targeted poverty alleviation, as poverty, pollution, and major risks had been identified as the targets of three critical battles. To achieve the goal of building a moderately prosperous society in all respects, the CPC focused its efforts on breaking through the last strongholds of absolute poverty and securing a decisive victory in this battle.

In 2020, the Central Committee called on the whole Party and the entire nation to work even harder and with greater determination, to effectively meet the challenges posed by Covid-19 and severe flooding, and to march with full confidence towards the final victory in the battle against poverty.

Over the past eight years, the Central Committee has made the battle against poverty a top priority in national governance and a fundamental component of moderate prosperity, and mobilized all the people to work to this end. With determination, endurance, and the courage to take on tough challenges, the Party and the people have liberated one stronghold after another from the grips of poverty, achieving a great and historic success.

– The entire rural poor population has emerged from poverty, a key contribution towards the goal of building a moderately prosperous society in all respects.

Every year since 2012, an average of more than 10 million people, equivalent to the population of a medium-sized country, have escaped from poverty. Poor people have seen their incomes grow by a significant margin, while their basic food and clothing needs have been guaranteed and their access to compulsory education, basic medical services, and safe housing and drinking water has been ensured. More than 20 million poor people with health issues have received proper treatment, and families that were once haunted by the specter of serious illness have been freed from that burden. Nearly 20 million impoverished people have received subsistence allowances or assistance and support for the extremely poor; more than 24 million people with disabilities who faced financial difficulties, and people with severe disabilities, have received living or nursing subsidies. More than 1.1 million impoverished people have become forest wardens, earning their livelihood by protecting the environment.

Whether on the snowy plateau, in the gobi desert, or under the shade of cliffs and mountains, the poverty eradication campaign has reached every corner of the country, helping countless people transform their future, realize their dream, and find a better life.

– Areas that have been the target of poverty elimination efforts have taken great strides to catch up in terms of economic and social development, and experienced dramatic and historic change.

In impoverished areas, the pace of development has accelerated, economic strength has grown, and infrastructure has developed in leaps and bounds. At the same time, great progress has been made with social programs, and long-standing problems that have made it hard in the past for people to move around, attend school, seek medical attention, access safe drinking water and electricity, and communicate with the outside world have finally been resolved. School dropouts from registered poor families during the compulsory education stage have come back to school.

Where conditions permit, all towns, townships, and villages have been connected to paved roads and provided with bus and postal services. An additional 1.1 million kilometers of rural roads have been built or upgraded, and 35,000 kilometers of new rail lines have been built. Reliability of power grids in impoverished rural areas has reached 99 percent, while 100 percent of poor villages on major grids are now connected to three-phase power. The provision of both fiber optics and 4G connections to poor villages has surpassed 98 percent.

Unsafe housing occupied by 7.9 million households, representing almost 26 million poor people, has been renovated; 35,000 residential communities and 2.66 million housing units have been built for more than 9.6 million people who have emerged from poor, isolated and backward places.

Many villagers have bid farewell to rope crossings as bridges are built over the rift valleys, to bitter and saline water as they now have clean water to drink, and to houses built of beaten earth and straw that were exposed to the elements, as they have moved into bright and spacious new homes built of brick and tile.

Millions of children from poor families now have more equitable educational opportunities, and no longer have to endure the daily trek to class now that they can board at school.

All the 28 ethnic groups with smaller populations have been lifted out of poverty. Some of these ethnic groups, who transitioned directly from primitive to socialist society after the founding of the PRC, skipping forward a thousand years of social evolution, have now made a second historic leap from poverty and backwardness to all-round moderate prosperity. All of the last strongholds of poverty in deeply impoverished areas have been breached, and in the areas that have exited poverty, beauty and change can be seen everywhere one goes.

– People who have shaken off poverty are thriving, with the confidence and courage to rely on themselves.

The fight against poverty has yielded gratifying results both in the material sense and the psychological sense. Those who have been lifted out of poverty have been instilled with the drive to keep pushing forward, while the core socialist values and healthy conduct have spread and taken root in society. The desire to do hard, solid work and build a happier life with one's own hands has become the norm in poverty-stricken areas.

Party Secretary Mao Xianglin of Xiazhuang Village in Wushan County, Chongqing, led the locals in a seven-year effort to carve a path along precipitous cliffs to the outside world. He said, "It was gratifying to widen and lengthen the mountain path inch by inch and foot by foot. Even if our generation has to endure poverty and hardship for another decade, we are resolved to ensure that the next generation lives a better life."

Zhang Shundong, a disabled yet determined villager from Pingzi Village in Dongchuan District, Kunming, Yunnan Province, said, "Though we are impaired physically, we are not impaired in spirit. We still have brains to think and hands to work."

The mental fortitude of poor people has been honed and reinforced in the fight against poverty. Now with firmer confidence, keener minds, and greater ambition, their external and internal transformation is complete.

– The relationships between the Party and the public and between officials and ordinary people have improved significantly, consolidating the foundations of CPC governance in rural areas.

Heeding the call of the Central Committee, Party members and organizations at all levels have spared no effort to accomplish their missions, and taken action to make good on their promises. In the fight against poverty, which has been no less of a battle despite the lack of gunsmoke, they have sown with painstaking effort and harvested rich results. Poverty alleviation officials have worked for others at the expense of their own families, and formed bonds of friendship and cooperation with the impoverished people they have served. They have worked tirelessly and put in extra hours all year round, endured the strain and fatigue of their posts, and stepped up at crucial moments to face challenges head-on, visiting countless families across the country through their effort and devotion. They have made their way up the highest mountains, trekked the most perilous roads, visited the most remote villages, and stayed with the poorest families. Wherever the need was greatest, that is where they have been found, hard at work.

Here I would like to quote two village officials:

"As long as I am still standing, I will always work for the people of this village. I will see them live a better life."

"As a CPC member, I must lead the people in weeding out the roots of poverty."

Grassroots Party organizations have played their key role. In their efforts to strengthen the CPC and promote poverty eradication, they have honed their best qualities, become stronger and more cohesive, and added to their capacity for governance. People in poverty-stricken areas have listened to the Party, sensed its support, and followed its lead. Here are a few relevant quotes:

"With Party members taking the lead and us following that lead, there is hope that poverty will be eliminated."

"We love to hang the national flag, because there is no better symbol of good fortune."

"Just as he who drinks the water cannot forget who has dug the well, we cannot forget the Party for helping us escape poverty."

All this is evidence that the relationships between the Party and the public and between officials and ordinary people have been greatly strengthened.

– China has set an example and made a significant contribution to global poverty reduction.

Casting off poverty has always been a prominent issue in global development and governance. Since the launch of reform and opening up, China has lifted 770 million rural poor out of poverty according to current standards, and contributed to more than 70 percent of global poverty reduction during this period according to the World Bank's international poverty line.

It should be highlighted that even with severe global poverty and increasing polarization between rich and poor in certain countries, China has achieved the poverty reduction target set in the UN 2030 Agenda for Sustainable Development 10 years ahead of schedule, winning wide acclaim from the international community.

We have actively conducted international cooperation on poverty reduction, fulfilled our international obligations, provided other developing countries with all possible assistance, and acted as a champion for global poverty reduction.

No other country throughout history has been able to lift hundreds of millions out of poverty in such a short period of time. This achievement is China's, but it also belongs to the world, and has contributed Chinese strength to the development of a global community of shared future.

Over the past eight years, I have presided over seven central conferences on poverty alleviation, carried out more than 50 inspection tours on poverty alleviation work, and visited 14 contiguous impoverished areas. In the process, I have endeavored to see poverty in its rawest form, and to find out how poverty alleviation measures are being carried out, providing tangible assistance to the people who really need it and delivering genuine outcomes. I have spoken with poor people face to face and in great detail about their lives, and experienced first-hand the tremendous changes brought about by the fight against poverty. In places across the country, I have seen people who have escaped poverty smiling from the heart. These smiles are the greatest affirmation of the fight against poverty, the best possible reward for the dedicated work of Party members and officials, and the ultimate tribute to the revolutionaries and martyrs that came before us.

Comrades and friends,

Trying times make heroes out of ordinary men and women.

Millions of officials have devoted themselves to the battle against poverty, and done hard and solid work. They have empathized with impoverished people, lived in their villages, and worked alongside them. They have given their prime to the cause of poverty elimination, and performed many exemplary deeds.

Among them are:

- Li Baoguo, who dedicated himself to poverty alleviation in the Taihang Mountains for 35 years, like the "foolish old man" in the ancient fable who conquered the mountains through his persistence;
- Zhang Guimei, who ignited hope among girls living deep in the mountains through her commitment to education;
- Huang Dafa, who made good on his promise that he would complete his village canal, even if it cost him his life;
- Huang Wenxiu, who returned from the city to work in her hometown, lighting a new path for young people in the new era;
- Huang Shiyan, who fought poverty with his life and fell in the line of duty;
- all the other exemplary individuals and groups being honored here today.

Allow me to quote some of them:

"On the road that has led millions upon millions of people out of poverty, I was really just a tiny cobblestone. Though we went through bitter hardship to get where we are today, its acrid aftertaste has been dispelled by the sweetness of success."

"Farmers will only trust you and listen to you if you show them that you are not out for personal gain."

"You are only truly capable if you can take what you have learned and put it into practice on this land."

In the fight against poverty, more than 1,800 Party members laid down their lives for the ideals that we as Communists have always cherished. Their sacrifice will go down in history and will never be forgotten by the Party, the people, or our country. Party committees and governments at all levels should show care and compassion to the families of those who have given their lives, and do all they can to make their noble spirit and their exploits widely known. They should serve as examples to inspire officials and the public to make brave new advances towards the Second Centenary Goal.

Comrades and friends,

We have won international acclaim for our achievements in the fight against poverty. These achievements would not have been possible without the strong leadership of the CPC, the Chinese people's spirit of self-reliance and hard work, the solid material foundations laid down since the founding of the PRC and particularly since the launch of reform and opening up, the perseverance and dedication of one official after another, and the concerted efforts of all the Party members and all the Chinese people.

Based on our national conditions and our understanding of the structures underlying poverty alleviation, we have adopted a series of distinctive policies and measures, established a whole set of effective policies, working mechanisms and systems, pioneered a unique Chinese path to poverty reduction, and formed a Chinese theory on fighting poverty.

– We have upheld the leadership of the CPC to provide solid political and organizational guarantees for the fight against poverty.

We have upheld the centralized, unified leadership of the Central Committee over the fight against poverty, and planned and promoted related initiatives as part of the Five-sphere Integrated Plan and the Four-pronged Comprehensive Strategy. We have strengthened the working mechanism under which the central leadership makes overall plans, provincial authorities assume overall responsibility, and city and county authorities take charge of implementation. We have worked to ensure that secretaries of Party committees at the provincial, city, county, township, and village levels tackled poverty alleviation as a major priority, and that all Party members were mobilized in the fight.

We have put in place a system whereby top leaders of the Party and government bodies take full responsibility for the fight against poverty, with the leaders of 22 provincial-level administrative units in the central and western regions signing pledges to the central authorities that they would achieve their objectives. Furthermore, we arranged that Party and government chiefs of impoverished counties would not be moved to new posts while poverty eradication efforts were ongoing in their areas.

We have worked to build up village organizations led by the Party organization at the same level, and to strengthen village-level Party organizations so that they can be more effective in leading the people out of poverty. We have sent our best teams to the main battlefields of the fight against poverty, assigning 255,000 work teams and more than 3 million first secretaries and officials to villages nationwide, where they worked on the front lines alongside nearly 2 million town and township officials and millions of village officials. The bright red flag of the CPC has always flown high on the main battlefields of the fight against poverty.

The CPC has proved that it has unparalleled capacity to lead, organize and implement, and that it is the most reliable force for uniting the people and guiding them to overcome difficulties and forge ahead. As long as we are steadfast in our commitment to upholding the leadership of the Party, we will be able to overcome any difficulties or obstacles on the road ahead and fulfill the people's aspirations for a better life.

– We have adhered to the people-centered development philosophy, and followed the path of common prosperity without deviation.

To quote an ancient Chinese historian, "The key to running a country is to first enrich the people."[4] We have always stood on the side of the people, and consistently emphasized that eradicating poverty, improving the people's lives, and achieving common prosperity are essential requirements of socialism. They are important manifestations of the CPC's commitment to its fundamental purpose of serving the people wholeheartedly, and major responsibilities of the Party and the government.

We have made public satisfaction an important measure for the effectiveness of poverty eradication initiatives, and focused our efforts on addressing the basic needs of the poor. We have given full play to the guiding role of government investment, cutting back on a number of other major projects to ensure funding for poverty eradication. Over the past eight years, central, provincial, city and county governments have earmarked a total of almost RMB1.6 trillion for poverty alleviation, of which RMB660.1 billion came from the central government.

The critical battle against poverty was launched in 2012. The following are some of the funds that have been directed to poverty alleviation:

- more than RMB440 billion from land transfer between and within provinces to ensure cropland acreage and proper land use for construction;
- more than RMB710 billion in microloans and RMB668.8 billion in re-lending to help the poor;
- RMB9.2 trillion in loans for targeted poverty alleviation;
- more than RMB100.5 billion of government fiscal support and non-governmental financial help provided by nine eastern provinces and municipalities to the areas with which they were collaborating on poverty alleviation;
- over RMB1 trillion invested in poverty-stricken areas by designated enterprises from the eastern region.

We have integrated government funds for rural development, strengthened scrutiny over funds for poverty alleviation, and ensured that the money is used where it is needed most. These investments have provided strong capital guarantees for winning the fight against poverty.

Our experience demonstrates clearly that for the undertakings of the Party and country to be accomplished, all initiatives must serve one immutable goal – realizing, defending and developing the fundamental interests of the people, while a conscious effort must be made to ensure that reform and development offer greater benefits to all the people in a fair way. As long as we follow the people-centered development philosophy and keep working year by year to tackle one issue after another, we will be able to make clear and substantial progress in achieving common prosperity for all our people.

– We have leveraged the strengths of China's socialist system in pooling resources behind major undertakings and are united in will and action to fight poverty.

We have mobilized the whole Party, the entire nation, and all sectors of society to join the war against poverty. This has allowed us to bring together the strength of the Party, the government, the military, the public, and the academic community across the country, and channel it towards the fight.

We have reinforced collaboration between the eastern and western regions on poverty alleviation, encouraged provinces, cities and counties to pair up with their counterparts and provide assistance, and promoted the flow of talent, capital and technology to impoverished areas.

We have organized and launched poverty alleviation assistance to designated areas, involving all central Party and government departments, the other political parties, people's organizations, state-owned enterprises, and the armed forces. We have ensured that all key counties under the national development-driven poverty alleviation initiative can turn to somebody for help.

Different industries and sectors have brought their specializations to bear to fight poverty through the development of local businesses, science and technology, education, cultural programs and health services, and by boosting the consumption of products and services from poor areas. Private enterprises, social organizations, and individual citizens have enthusiastically participated in poverty alleviation initiatives, and the "10,000 enterprises helping 10,000 villages" campaign has built up great momentum.

We have established a comprehensive setup for poverty alleviation in which government-sponsored projects, sector-specific programs, and societal assistance supplement each other, as well as a social poverty alleviation system featuring coordination between regions, departments and organizations in which all of society participates.

The tens of millions of positive actions that have helped the poor demonstrate the tremendous compassion of our society, and have merged to form an unstoppable force.

CPC leadership and our socialist system have proved to be the fundamental guarantees for withstanding risks and challenges and overcoming difficulties through concerted efforts. As long as we uphold the leadership of the CPC and follow the path of Chinese socialism, we will be able to confront other serious challenges like poverty eradication, and advance from victory to victory.

– We have followed a targeted strategy in poverty alleviation, and eliminated the root causes of poverty through development.

We have emphasized that a targeted approach is the crux of the fight against poverty. We have committed to precise work in poverty alleviation in terms of the management of target groups, allocation of resources, and provision of assistance, and set up a national registration system to ensure that resources have reached the people and the places that truly needed them. To identify the targets of poverty alleviation, determine who to help and how to help, and make clear how to apply an exit mechanism for those who have emerged from poverty, we have adopted a set of targeted policies tailored to individual villages, households, and people, to their specific conditions, and to the circumstances that made them poor in the first place, so that we can address the root causes of poverty with precision.

We have demanded meticulous efforts to ensure that poverty alleviation work hits the target, addresses the problem at its roots, and gets to the families who need it, so that the average progress does not mask cases of individual hardship. Through our commitment to development-driven poverty alleviation, under which development is the fundamental approach to eliminating poverty, we have improved conditions and boosted capacity for development, bringing about a shift in poverty alleviation from simply injecting help into poverty-stricken areas to enabling these areas to help themselves. This has made development the most effective means of eliminating poverty, and the most reliable path towards a better life.

We have maintained a keen focus on education as an essential vehicle for helping people out of poverty and towards prosperity, emphasizing that no child should be deprived of education or opportunities and lose out before the race has even begun because they are poor. We have worked hard to give every child the chance to excel in life, and done our best to break the chain of intergenerational poverty.

Targeted poverty alleviation has proved to be the "magic weapon" for winning the battle against poverty, while the development-driven approach has emerged as the distinctive feature of China's path to poverty reduction. As long as we stick to targeted and rational methods, impose precise requirements on our work, and continue to address imbalanced and insufficient development through development itself, we will be able to provide a sound path forward and lasting momentum for economic and social development and for improving people's lives.

– We are committed to mobilizing the enthusiasm, initiative and creativity of impoverished people so that they have the drive to lift themselves out of poverty.

The ancient Chinese philosopher Han Fei Zi said, "The key to achieving your aspirations lies not in overcoming others but in overcoming your own weaknesses."[5] Similarly, to shake off poverty, the poor must shake off the mindset of poverty. We have focused on making the people's desire for a better life a strong source of motivation in the fight against poverty. We have helped poor people build the confidence and capacity to help themselves, and seen that their pockets are full and their minds are keen, while encouraging them to lift themselves out of poverty and change their lives by relying on their own hard work and tenacity. We have helped them understand that it is better to put in hard work now than spend more hard years waiting, that they will achieve prosperity as long as they believe in themselves, and that even the weakest in the flock can catch up through perseverance. Our encouragement has warmed their hearts and stirred them into action.

To quote two individuals who have risen from poverty:

"Now that the state policies are in place, as long as we get to work rather than sit by and wait, we can surely create better lives for ourselves."

"Life has changed me, and I have changed my life."

The people have shown themselves to be the real heroes, and boosting their own drive to be self-reliant and work hard has been vital in arming them to create better lives for themselves. As long as we continue to work for the people, rely on them, respect their principal position and creativity, and tap into their wisdom and strength, we will achieve even greater success.

– We have promoted the virtues of solidarity and mutual help, creating an atmosphere in which all of society helps those in need.

We have encouraged all of society to practice the core socialist values and to keep alive the traditional Chinese virtues of looking out for one another, coming together in times of difficulty, and helping those in need. We have guided all sectors of society in showing care for the poor and concern for the cause of poverty reduction, and in committing themselves to the campaign. We have refined mechanisms for mobilizing society, set up platforms for society-wide participation, and created new forms of social assistance, so that everybody has the desire, the ability, and the tools to help.

The core socialist values and China's fine traditional culture have proved to be a powerful force for rallying people's support and pooling their strength. As long as we remain firm in our moral values, as long as we continue to inspire positive energy that will drive all of society towards goodness and excellence, we will be able to equip the Chinese nation with an inexhaustible source of inner strength with which we can cleave the waves and sail forward.

– We have persevered with a realistic and pragmatic approach when confronting tough challenges, in order to ensure that our poverty alleviation initiatives reach those who truly need help.

We have incorporated the requirement to enforce full and rigorous Party self-governance throughout the process and in every aspect of the fight against poverty. With steely determination, we have carried the fight to the end. We have highlighted the need to follow a pragmatic approach, strictly enforce established rules, and avoid becoming bogged down in red tape or being deflected by impractical measures or superficial, eye-catching initiatives. We have resolutely opposed approaches that do not address problems properly, indiscriminate distribution of resources without regard for priorities, unrealistic projects pursued solely for show, and pointless formalities and bureaucratism; instead we have focused all of our work on addressing the problems of the poor. We have put in place the most rigorous assessments and evaluations possible, worked to address corruption and misconduct in the field of poverty alleviation, and established a comprehensive monitoring system, so that the results of our poverty eradication efforts stand the test of time and win the approval of the people.

By devoting the majority of our energy to following through with our plans and committing ourselves to doing solid and hard work, we have ensured victory in the fight against poverty. As long as we keep making concrete efforts for the good of our country and our people, we will be able to realize the grand blueprint for building a fully modern socialist country one step at a time.

The important knowledge and experience we have gained have shaped China's theory on poverty alleviation. They are the latest achievement in adapting Marxist theory on poverty to the Chinese context, and a valuable resource that must therefore be preserved and developed over the long term.

Comrades and friends,

A great cause breeds a great spirit, and is in turn guided by it. Our struggle against poverty has forged such a spirit, through which we have all come together, put our all into the fight, made precise and pragmatic efforts, launched pioneering initiatives, overcome difficulties, and worked hard to live up to the people's expectations. This is a vivid representation of the nature and purpose of the CPC, the determination of the Chinese people, and the essence of the Chinese nation, a concentrated reflection of patriotism, collectivism, and socialism, a full manifestation of China's spirit, values, and strength, and a confirmation of our great national spirit and our readiness to respond to the call of the times. The whole Party, the entire nation, and all of society should carry forward the spirit of the battle against poverty, continue to unite and fight heroically, overcome any difficulties and risks that lie on the road ahead, and achieve new and greater victories in upholding and developing socialism with Chinese characteristics.

Comrades and friends,

Our complete victory in the fight against absolute poverty signifies that a substantial step forward has been made in the CPC's efforts to unite the people and lead them in the pursuit of a better life and common prosperity. At the same time, however, shaking off poverty is not the finish line, but rather the starting point of a new quest and a new endeavor. We still have a long way to go to solve the problem of imbalanced and insufficient development, narrow the gap between urban and rural areas and between regions, and achieve well-rounded development and common prosperity for all our people. We cannot therefore be complacent or rest on our laurels; we must build on our current momentum, make further efforts, and keep fighting.

As an old Chinese saying goes, "The most difficult part of victory is not the winning, but the sustaining."[6] We must take concrete steps to consolidate and expand upon the outcomes of the fight against poverty as part of our effort to promote rural revitalization, so that the foundations of poverty eradication are more solid and the effects are more sustainable. We will carefully monitor populations that are at risk of lapsing or relapsing into poverty, and work to ensure early detection, early intervention, and early assistance. We will see that businesses and industries in areas that have escaped poverty are fostered through long-term support to boost sustainable, locally-driven development.

We will improve follow-up support for people who have been relocated from inhospitable areas, facilitate their employment through multiple channels, strengthen social management, and promote their integration into new communities. To buttress counties that have emerged from poverty, we will institute a transition period during which the main poverty alleviation support policies will generally remain in place. We will continue and improve systems for stationing first secretaries and work teams in villages, promoting cooperation between the eastern and western regions, facilitating assistance through pairing programs, and providing social assistance, and make corresponding adjustments as our circumstances and tasks evolve.

The Central Committee has decided that timely arrangements should be made for follow-up assessments on the consolidation of poverty eradication outcomes, and that Party committees and governments at all levels should be held accountable for consolidating these achievements, so as to ensure that people do not return to poverty in large numbers.

Rural revitalization is a major strategy for bringing about our national rejuvenation. New circumstances and requirements arise as we seek to ground ourselves in this new development stage, apply the new development philosophy, and foster a new development dynamic. Under the new circumstances and requirements, to address problems related to agriculture, rural areas, and rural people will be our Party's top priority. The development of agriculture and rural areas will come first. We will follow a Chinese socialist path to rural revitalization, and continue to narrow the development gaps between urban and rural areas and between regions, so that low-income people and less developed areas can share in the fruits of development and catch up in the process of modernization rather than falling behind.

Comprehensively implementing the rural revitalization strategy will be no less of a challenge than the fight against poverty in terms of depth, breadth and difficulty. We must therefore improve our policies, working mechanisms, and systems. We will adopt more forceful measures and pool more formidable strength to accelerate agricultural and rural modernization, promote quality and efficiency in agriculture, make rural areas attractive places to live and work in, and see that rural residents become more prosperous.

On our new journey towards a modern socialist country, we must raise the common prosperity of all our people to a more prominent position, doing consistent, results-oriented work as we make more active and effective efforts towards this goal. We must promote the well-rounded development of individuals together with all-round social progress, and ensure that our people always have a strong sense of gain, fulfillment and security.

Comrades and friends,

Looking back, we have achieved a great and historic success in solving the problem of absolute poverty that plagued the Chinese nation for thousands of years, and we have created a miracle in the history of poverty reduction. Looking ahead, we are now striving towards the goal of building an all-round modern socialist country. The journey will be long, and all we can do is keep fighting and move forward. The whole Party and the entire nation must unite more closely around the central leadership and dedicate ourselves to doing solid work. We must display confidence, determination, and an indomitable spirit as we advance towards the Second Centenary Goal.

Notes

[1] Qu Yuan: "The Lament" (Li Sao). Qu Yuan (c. 339-278 BC) was a poet and statesman in the Warring States Period.

[2] Du Fu: "Song of the Thatched Cottage Broken by the Autumn Wind" (Mao Wu Wei Qiu Feng Suo Po Ge). Du Fu (712-770) was a poet of the Tang Dynasty.

[3] Sun Yat-sen: "Declaration for a Military Government", *Selected Works of Sun Yat-sen*, Vol. I, Chin. ed., People's Publishing House, Beijing, 2011, p. 82.

[4] Sima Qian: *Records of the Historian (Shi Ji)*. Sima Qian (c. 145 or 135-? BC) was a historian and writer of the Western Han Dynasty.

[5] *Han Fei Zi*. This is a collection of writings by Han Fei. Han Fei (c. 280-233 BC), also known as Han Fei Zi, was a leading exponent of the Legalist school in the late Warring States Period.

[6] *Huai Nan Zi*. This is a collection of writings by scholars of different schools of philosophy compiled in the Western Han Dynasty under the patronage of Liu An (179-122 BC), prince of Huainan.

Make Solid Progress Towards Common Prosperity[*]

August 17, 2021

Following the launch of reform and opening up in 1978, through a thorough review of both positive and negative experiences, our Party came to a clear understanding that poverty is incompatible with socialism, and began to break conventional institutional constraints, encourage some people and some regions to become prosperous first, and unleash and develop the productive forces.

Since the 18th CPC National Congress held in 2012, the Central Committee has identified the changes in a new stage of development, and given greater weight to achieving common prosperity for all our people. Strong measures have been adopted to promote coordinated development across different regions, ensure and improve people's wellbeing, eradicate absolute poverty, and achieve moderate prosperity, thereby creating favorable conditions for bringing about prosperity for all. Currently, we are in the stage of taking concrete steps towards common prosperity.

Now, we are working towards the Second Centenary Goal – to build China into a modern socialist country that is prosperous, strong, democratic, culturally advanced, harmonious, and beautiful by the centenary of the PRC in 2049. To adapt to the principal challenge facing Chinese society as it evolves, and to meet the growing expectation of the people for a better life and work for happiness for all of our people, we must focus on promoting common prosperity, which will in turn strengthen the foundations of our Party's long-term governance. High-quality development requires a high-caliber

* Part of the speech at the 10th meeting of the Commission for Financial and Economic Affairs under the CPC Central Committee.

workforce. Only by promoting common prosperity, raising urban and rural income levels, and boosting human capital, can we increase total factor productivity and create the driving force for high-quality development. Currently, income inequality has become a glaring problem worldwide. In some countries, the wealth gap is widening and the middle class is shrinking, resulting in social disintegration, political polarization, and a surge of populism. This is a profound lesson. China must prevent polarization between the rich and the poor, promote common prosperity, and ensure social harmony and stability.

At the same time, we must be fully aware that China's development remains strikingly imbalanced and insufficient, as seen in the wide gaps in income distribution between urban and rural areas and between regions. A new revolution in science, technology and industry has significantly boosted the economy, and has had a profound impact on employment and income distribution, including some negative consequences that we must address and resolve.

Achieving common prosperity is a basic requirement of socialism and an important feature of the Chinese path to modernization. The common prosperity that we pursue, both material and cultural, is for all of our people; it is not for a small minority, nor does it imply an absolute equality in income distribution that takes no account of contribution.

Based on thorough research, we should map out phased goals of common prosperity for different development stages:

By 2025, the end of the 14th Five-year Plan period (2021-2025), a solid step will have been taken towards common prosperity, steadily narrowing the gap between people's income and consumption.

By 2035, more substantial progress will have been made in promoting common prosperity, ensuring equal access to basic public services.

By the middle of the 21st century, common prosperity for all will have largely been achieved, narrowing the gap between people's income and consumption to a reasonable level.

To realize the above phased goals, we must lose no time in devising an action plan that contains an effective system of indicators, and a set of evaluation methods suited to China's actual conditions.

In promoting common prosperity, we must uphold the following four principles:

– Encouraging people to pursue prosperity through hard work and innovation. A happy life is earned by hard work; common prosperity is achieved through diligence and ingenuity. We must seek to ensure and improve people's wellbeing through development, and prioritize high-quality development. We will create more inclusive and equitable conditions for all to receive a better education, so as to improve their capacity for development; we will also improve China's human capital, and the professional skills, employability, entrepreneurial competency, and the ability to create wealth through its workforce. We must encourage social mobility, facilitate smooth channels for people to move up the social ladder, and create opportunities for more people to become prosperous. The aim is to create an enabling environment in which everyone participates. We do not want a rat-race, nor do we want a society of layabouts.

– Upholding the basic economic system. As China remains in the primary stage of socialism, we must consolidate and develop the public sector, and at the same time encourage, support and guide development of the non-public sector. We must follow the principle that public ownership plays the dominant role while developing together with other forms of ownership. We should give full play to the key role of the public sector in promoting common prosperity, and at the same time facilitate the sound development of the non-public sector and of people working in this sector. We should encourage part of the population to prosper first and urge these people to guide and help the rest on their way to a better life. We should encourage people to become leaders in pursuing a better life through hard work, bold entrepreneurship, and lawful business operation. Accumulating wealth through dubious means must not be encouraged, and any action that breaks laws or regulations must be punished in accordance with the law.

– Doing everything within our capacity. We must establish a system of sound public policies and a rational distribution system in which everyone enjoys a fair share of benefits. We should adopt more robust and solid measures so that people have a greater sense of gain.

At the same time, we must be aware that there is still a wide development gap between China and the developed countries. We should strike a balance between what is necessary and what is feasible, securing and improving people's wellbeing on the basis of ensuring economic growth and financial sustainability. We will not set unrealistic goals, neither will we make unfulfillable promises. The government cannot take on everything. Instead, it should focus on providing inclusive public services, meeting people's essential needs, and ensuring basic living standards for people in difficulty. Even in the future when China develops further to a higher level and has more financial resources, we still should not set over-ambitious goals, nor should we provide excessive social benefits; otherwise, we will slip into the trap of encouraging idlers by providing excessive welfare.

– Pursuing incremental progress. Common prosperity is a long-term goal. It takes time and is a step-by-step process. It cannot be achieved overnight. We should be fully aware of the long duration, arduous nature, and complexity of this mission. It can neither wait nor be rushed. Some developed countries have been pursuing industrialization for centuries, but have not achieved common prosperity due to institutional and systemic problems; instead they are facing an ever widening gap between the rich and the poor. We must have the patience to do things well, practically, and efficiently, one step at a time. We should work hard on the project of the Zhejiang Demonstration Zone for Common Prosperity Through High-quality Development, encourage all localities to explore feasible and effective approaches to common prosperity in light of their local conditions and their distinctive strengths, sum up their experience, and then steadily roll out their successful experience nationwide.

The overarching principle is to uphold the people-centered development philosophy and promote common prosperity through high-quality development. We must balance efficiency and fairness in income distribution and devise an institutional framework within which distribution, redistribution and third distribution are coordinated and operate in parallel. Efforts should be intensified to improve the role of taxation, social security and transfer payments in adjusting income distribution, particularly for targeted social groups. The proportion of the middle-income group in the entire population should be increased, the low-income group should have their incomes raised, the high-income group should have their incomes reasonably readjusted, and illicit income should be confiscated, so as to form an olive-shaped distribution structure. The goal is to increase social fairness and justice, promote well-rounded development of the individual, and enable the people to make solid progress towards common prosperity.

To achieve this goal, we will take the following measures.

First, pursue more balanced, coordinated and inclusive development. We will quicken our pace in improving the socialist market economy, and seek more balanced, coordinated and inclusive development. We will balance regional development by implementing major regional development strategies and the strategy for coordinated regional development by improving the transfer payment system to narrow regional disparities in terms of per capita fiscal expenditure, and by giving more support to underdeveloped areas. We will coordinate the development of various industries by accelerating the reform of monopolies and by coordinating the development of finance and real estate with the real economy. We will support the development of small and medium-sized enterprises, and create a business ecosystem in which small, medium-sized and large enterprises are interdependent and mutually reinforcing.

Second, enlarge the middle-income group. We will focus on priorities, implement targeted policies, and help more low-income people to join the middle-income group.

University graduates have high prospects of entering the middle-income bracket. We will improve the quality of higher education, ensure that university graduates acquire expertise and useful knowledge, and help them to adapt to the needs of social development as early as possible.

Technicians are an important component of the middle-income group. We will train more skilled personnel, raise the incomes of technicians, and attract more high-caliber people to join their ranks.

Owners of small and medium-sized enterprises and self-employed individuals are major contributors to entrepreneurial growth. We will improve the business environment, cut taxes and fees, and provide more market-oriented financial services, so as to help them to maintain steady business operations and achieve sustained revenue growth.

Rural migrant workers in urban areas constitute a major source of the middle-income group. We will further reform the household registration system, improve access to education for children of migrant workers who have moved with them from rural areas to cities, and enable rural migrant workers to settle and acquire stable employment in cities.

We will raise the incomes of public servants as appropriate, particularly those on the frontline posts at the grassroots level and low-level employees of state-owned enterprises and institutions.

We will increase people's income from property such as urban and rural housing estates, rural land estates, and financial assets.

Third, promote equitable access to basic public services. The low-income group should be the priority in our efforts to achieve common prosperity.

We will increase investment in human capital to cover all social groups, reduce the burden of education costs on families with financial difficulties, and raise the education level of children from low-income households.

We will improve the pension and healthcare security systems by bridging the financial and benefits gaps between working and non-working populations in the city and between urban and rural populations, and by steadily increasing the basic pension level for both urban and rural residents.

We will improve the social assistance system to help those most in need, reduce disparities in assistance standards for urban and rural residents, and steadily increase subsistence allowances for both urban and rural populations to meet their basic needs.

We will improve the housing supply and security systems. Acting on the principle that housing is for living in, not for speculation, we will improve access to both rental and purchased properties, adopt city-specific policies, refine policies for long-term rental housing, increase the supply of government-subsidized rental housing, and ensure housing security for new urban residents.

Fourth, adopt rigorous measures to regulate and adjust high incomes. While protecting legitimate incomes in accordance with the law, we must prevent polarization and eliminate unfair income distribution. We will adjust excessive incomes as appropriate, improve the system of individual income tax, and standardize the management of capital gains. We will actively yet prudently proceed with legislation and reform on property tax through pilot programs. We will improve the regulatory function of excise taxes, and consider expanding their scope. We will better regulate public welfare undertakings and charitable endeavors, improve preferential taxation policies, and encourage high-income individuals and enterprises to do more to give back to society. We will bring excessive incomes under control, strengthen management of income distribution in monopolized industries and SOEs, rectify irregularities in income distribution, and prohibit practices such as raising the incomes of senior executives under the guise of reform. We will prohibit illicit income and prevent people from trading power for money. We will take firm action against anyone who makes illicit gains through insider dealing, stock market manipulation, financial fraud, tax evasion, and so forth.

After years of experimentation, we have developed a complete package of measures to end absolute poverty, but we still need to build up experience on how to achieve prosperity. We must strengthen the protection of property rights and intellectual property rights, and ensure that the pursuit of legitimate wealth is protected. We must firmly oppose unbridled expansion of capital, establish negative lists for access to sensitive fields, and tighten regulation and supervision of monopolies. At the same time, we must mobilize the initiative of entrepreneurs, and promote sound and well-regulated development for all types of capital.

Fifth, promote common cultural prosperity. Bringing prosperity to all is congruous with our goal of promoting well-rounded human development. We must highlight the guiding role of the core socialist values, and strengthen education on patriotism, collectivism, and socialism. By developing public cultural undertakings and improving the public cultural service system, we will continue to meet people's diverse, multilevel and multifaceted demands in the cultural and intellectual sphere. We must also do a better job of guiding public opinion on common prosperity and clear up any confusion on this matter. We should not shy away from challenges while avoiding the rush for quick results, thereby cultivating a public opinion environment favorable to our pursuit of common prosperity.

Sixth, promote common rural prosperity. The most arduous and formidable tasks in promoting common prosperity still lie in rural areas. We must lose no time in pressing ahead with common rural prosperity, but it is inadvisable for us to quantify targets as we did in the poverty alleviation campaign. We will consolidate and build upon the success we have achieved in the fight against poverty. To this end, we will strengthen the monitoring of people at risk of lapsing or relapsing into poverty, and be prepared to take quick action to help them if needed. We will also continue to provide support to counties that have recently shaken off poverty, so as to counter new causes of poverty and prevent any large-scale relapse into poverty. In implementing the rural revitalization strategy, we will accelerate agricultural industrialization, put rural assets to effective use, and increase the property income of rural residents, thereby helping more and more of them to become prosperous through hard work. We will also improve rural infrastructure, rural public services, and the rural living environment.

To sum up, achieving common prosperity for all is a holistic concept similar in nature to realizing moderate prosperity in all respects. Common prosperity is a goal for all of society, and therefore we should not break it up into separate goals for urban and rural areas, or for eastern, central and western regions. Instead, we should adopt an overall perspective. In order to enable 1.4 billion people to realize common prosperity, we must maintain a realistic attitude and make a sustained effort. We cannot make everyone wealthy at the same time, nor bring all regions to the same level of wealth simultaneously. There will be different levels of prosperity among different groups of people and different regions, realized on a different time scale. It should be a dynamic process where consistent efforts result in steady progress.

New Development Stage, Philosophy and Dynamic

A Great Advance Towards National Rejuvenation*

October 29, 2020

Entering the new development stage marks a great advance towards our national rejuvenation. I have said that national rejuvenation has been the greatest dream of the Chinese people since China's modern era began in 1840. Due to foreign invasion and corrupt feudal rule, China missed the opportunity for an industrial revolution, and fell far behind the times. Our nation suffered unprecedented misery.

After the Opium Wars, championed by people of lofty ideals, the Chinese people searched painstakingly for a road to modernization. The Plan for National Reconstruction written by Dr Sun Yat-sen in the late 1910s was China's first blueprint for modernization, but the drive ended in failure as it was simply impossible to modernize a semi-colonial and semi-feudal society.

Over the past hundred years since the founding of the Communist Party of China, all the efforts made by the CPC and by the Chinese people under its leadership have served just one purpose – building China into a strong modern country and realizing national rejuvenation. After the founding of the PRC in 1949, our Party led the people in exploring all possible paths to China's modernization. In his Report on the Work of the Government delivered at the First Session of the First National People's Congress in 1954, Zhou Enlai pointed out, "Unless we establish powerful, modern industry, modern agriculture, modern communications and transport and a modern national defense, we shall neither shake off backwardness and poverty nor attain our revolutionary goals."[1] In 1956, Mao Zedong said, "Our

---

* Part of the speech at the second full assembly of the Fifth Plenary Session of the 19th CPC Central Committee.

people should have an ambitious plan and strive to reverse backwardness in the economy, science and culture within decades and quickly reach the world's advanced level."[2] He also warned that if we failed to achieve this we should be "scoured from the earth". In December 1964, in his Report on the Work of the Government to the First Session of the Third National People's Congress, Zhou proposed a further plan: "We may envisage the development of our economy in two stages beginning with the Third Five-Year Plan. The first stage is to build an independent and relatively comprehensive industrial and economic structure; the second stage is to accomplish the overall modernization of agriculture, industry, national defense and science and technology, so that our economy will be among the front ranks of world economies."[3] Although the plan did not come to full fruition due to the turmoil of the Cultural Revolution, from 1949 to 1978 our Party on the whole succeeded in leading the people in establishing from scratch an independent and relatively complete industrial and economic structure and in safeguarding national sovereignty and security. China made substantial progress in its socialist construction.

After we launched reform and opening up in 1978, Deng Xiaoping proposed a three-step strategic plan for modernization: ensuring that the people would have adequate food and clothing by the end of the 1980s; giving them a moderately prosperous life by the end of the 20th century; increasing the per capita GNP level to that of moderately developed countries and realizing basic modernization by the middle of the 21st century. By the turn of the 21st century, moderate prosperity had largely been achieved. We then introduced the goals of achieving moderate prosperity at a higher level for all by the centenary of the Party in 2021, and in approximately three more decades, achieving basic modernization and turning China into a modern socialist country by the centenary of the PRC in 2049.

Since the 18th CPC National Congress in 2012, socialism with Chinese characteristics has entered a new era, and the Chinese nation has stood up, become better off, and grown in strength. On this foundation, our Party drew up a plan at its 19th National Congress in 2017 to attain the Second Centenary Goal in two stages: realizing basic socialist modernization by 2035, and developing China into a great modern socialist country that is prosperous, strong, democratic, culturally advanced, harmonious and beautiful by the middle of the 21st century.

Turning China into a modern socialist country has been the theme of all 14 five-year plans. Our determination and our resolve to reach this goal have never wavered, despite occasionally straying from our path, and in the face of many unexpected difficulties and setbacks. We have expanded our understanding of this grand program, improved our strategies, and broadened our experience. All of this has paved the way for China's drive to modernization, and laid practical, theoretical and institutional foundations for fully building a modern socialist country in this new development stage.

Notes

[1] Zhou Enlai: "Turning China into a Powerful, Modern, Socialist, Industrialized Country", *Selected Works of Zhou Enlai*, Vol. II, Eng. ed., Foreign Languages Press, Beijing, 1989, p. 142. – *Tr.*

[2] Mao Zedong: "The Purpose of Socialist Revolution Is to Release Productive Forces", *Collected Works of Mao Zedong*, Vol. VII, Chin. ed., People's Publishing House, Beijing, 1999, p. 2.

[3] Zhou Enlai: "Major Tasks for Developing the National Economy", *Selected Works of Zhou Enlai*, Vol. II, Eng. ed., Foreign Languages Press, Beijing, 1989, p. 458. – *Tr.*

Create a New Development Dynamic and Sharpen the Competitive Edge*

October 29, 2020

Go All Out to Create a New Development Dynamic

We have decided to create a double development dynamic with the domestic economy as the mainstay and the domestic economy and international engagement providing mutual reinforcement. This policy decision was made in the context of our current development stage, environment, and changing conditions, and in particular the changes in our comparative strengths. This is a strategic plan tailored to the prevailing situation in China and a vision for the future – a plan that will bring a systemic and profound change to China. We should accelerate the creation of this new development dynamic from an overall and strategic perspective.

In essence, this is also an essential choice we have made in order to adapt to our new development stage and gain a new edge in international cooperation and competition. Before we launched reform and opening up in 1978, the domestic market was the mainstay of our national economy, and imports and exports accounted for only a small share. Later we opened up to the outside world to expand foreign trade and attract more foreign investment. Since we acceded to the World Trade Organization in 2001, we have fully participated in the international division of labor and engaged with the international market. A development dynamic relying on the international

* Part of the speech at the second full assembly of the Fifth Plenary Session of the 19th CPC Central Committee.

market for the supply of resources and sales of products has taken shape. Riding on the waves of economic globalization, this has played a pivotal role in our rapid economic growth and the improvement of our people's lives.

The international financial crisis of 2008 was a watershed in the evolution of our development dynamic. In the face of daunting external crises, we stimulated domestic demand to bolster steady and rapid growth, and made it the main engine of our economy. There has since been a significant increase in the share of domestic market in our economy. After the 18th CPC National Congress in 2012, we continued our policy of expanding domestic demand, and our economic development was driven more by domestic demand, especially by consumption. Our country's trade-to-GDP ratio dropped from a high point of 67 percent in 2006 to nearly 32 percent in 2019; the proportion of the current account surplus in GDP has also fallen from over 10 percent at its peak to around 1 percent at present; the contribution of domestic demand to economic growth has grown to more than 100 percent in seven years. Our policy to create a new development dynamic is based on China's economic conditions and its development trend. It is a practical blueprint.

In the coming years, the dominant position of the domestic market in our economy will become more apparent, and the potential of domestic demand will be further unlocked. In terms of demand, with 1.4 billion people, including a middle-income population of more than 400 million, China's retail sales will soon surpass that of the US, ranking first in the world, and still leaving room for further growth. In terms of supply, our strong production capacity based on the huge domestic market can facilitate the integration and innovation of factors of production worldwide, and maximize the effects of economies of scale and agglomeration. As long as we continue to adapt to changing circumstances and implement precisely-targeted policies, we have all the strengths to create a new development dynamic and gain a new competitive edge.

First, creating the new development dynamic is neither a passive response to pressure nor a stopgap measure, but a proactive move aiming to seize the initiative in development. Looking around, the other major economies are dominated by their domestic demand, with a smooth internal flow of production, distribution, circulation and consumption. China is now the world's second largest economy and largest manufacturing country. The need to adjust the relationship between the domestic economy and international engagement has become increasingly apparent. This was our primary consideration when we put forward this strategy. In the face of growing international instability and uncertainty, we should increase reliance on our domestic market, unleash the potential of domestic demand – which will reduce our exposure to external impacts and the effect of falling foreign demand – and ensure normal functioning of the economy and general stability in society in extreme circumstances.

Second, what we aim to create is an open development dynamic, rather than an enclosed domestic model. Our country is deeply integrated into the global economy. Its economy interacts with and is dependent on the industries of many other countries on a mutual basis. The internal and external markets are interdependent in a relationship of mutual reinforcement. Taking the domestic economy as the mainstay does not mean we run the economy behind closed doors. Instead, we will improve the interaction between domestic and international markets and increase our ability to participate in the allocation of global resources by unlocking the potential of domestic demand, attracting more global resources and factors of production into the domestic market, and taking full advantage of both domestic and international markets and resources. In doing so, we will gain a strategic edge in our opening up. We will not close our doors to the world; we will only open our doors even wider. We must understand the relationship between the domestic economy and the new development dynamic. We will take proactive and effective action to establish new mechanisms for a higher-standard open economy, and open up on a larger scale, across more areas and in greater depth.

Third, the new development dynamic must be built upon a unified national market, not on small and fragmented local markets. The Central Committee's strategy targets the whole country – it does not require localities to create an isolated dynamic within their respective province, city or county. Every area should find its own position and comparative strengths in the domestic economy and the double development dynamic, combine this strategy with other initiatives on regional development, coordinated development between regions, functional zoning, and pilot free trade zones, and reach new heights in reform and opening up. No one should try to build a small but all-inclusive dynamic, or to create regional barriers in the guise of internal economic flow. Areas where conditions permit may explore ways to facilitate the new development dynamic across the country as forerunners.

It is imperative to follow the new development philosophy in creating the new development dynamic. It has been five years since we put forward this philosophy. All sectors have reached agreement on this philosophy, and are applying it to the full in practice. Creating a new development dynamic is essential for applying the new development philosophy, which is determined by both historical trends and present needs. We should press forward in a holistic manner, be forward-looking, plan the broader picture, organize strategies, and implement them as a whole. We need to synergize policies, ensure mutual reinforcement of different sectors, and expand the application of the new development philosophy.

Priorities in Creating the New Development Dynamic

The creation of the new development dynamic is a systemic project. We should strengthen planning and design at the top level, and delegate detailed tasks to lower levels with priorities assigned.

First, accelerating the process of fostering a complete domestic demand system. This is an important foundation for boosting the domestic economy and reinforcing its status as the mainstay of the double development dynamic. Economic activities constitute a dynamic process that rotates and moves in cycles. We should promote deeper reform, strengthen policy guidance, and remove key bottlenecks. To meet domestic demand, we should integrate the strategy of expanding domestic demand with supply-side structural reform, and attune the supply system closer to domestic demand. The goal is to reach an ideal dynamic equilibrium, where demand drives supply and supply in turn creates demand. We need to build a modern logistics system as a key foundation for the double development dynamic, improving both "hardware" and "software", channels and platforms.

Second, expediting greater self-reliance in science and technology. This is the key for China to ensure a smoothly-functioning domestic economy and take further advantage of international markets. We should heighten our sense of responsibility and awareness of crisis, dispense with any illusions, and look reality in the face. We need to make breakthroughs in core technologies in key fields, and remove bottlenecks in major areas. We should rouse the enthusiasm of our people for innovation, educate and attract talent in all fields, give full play to their knowledge and strength, nurture more world-class scientific and technological leaders and innovation teams, and build a reserve force of young scientists who have a competitive edge on the international stage. We should create a favorable environment for scientists and students who have returned from abroad, in which they may live, work, study and conduct R&D in comfort, and place them in suitable posts so that they can fulfill their potential and contribute to the country.

Third, optimizing and upgrading industrial and supply chains. This is urgent if we are to secure the dominance of the domestic economy and increase China's ability in leading international engagement. Manufacturing is critical to our economy and serves as the foundation of all our efforts to strengthen the country. In the fight against Covid-19, our complete manufacturing industry has played a crucial role, which once again proves the significance of the manufacturing sector to the development and security of a country, especially a large country.

Therefore we should prioritize efforts to make our industrial chains more resilient and competitive, and to establish industrial and supply chains that are self-supporting, controllable, safe and highly-efficient. We should thoroughly analyze the industrial and supply chains for key industries, identify and address weak points that are susceptible to risk, design tailored plans and targeted policies for different industries, and gradually improve self-reliance and risk control in industries and fields bearing on national security. We should take strong measures to keep our enterprises well-grounded in the domestic economy, and encourage industries to transfer within the country in an orderly manner, or keep the key elements of the industrial chain in China when they move abroad.

Fourth, modernizing agriculture and rural areas. Economic flow between urban and rural areas is an important element of the domestic economy, and a crucial factor that ensures an appropriate balance between the domestic economy and international engagement. Modernizing agriculture and rural areas is also an important part of building a modern socialist country in all respects, and an essential part of addressing imbalanced and insufficient development. The whole Party should continue to give top priority to matters related to agriculture, rural areas and rural people, and implement the rural revitalization strategy in an all-round way. We need to effectively integrate the consolidation and expansion of poverty elimination results with rural revitalization, further revitalizing all once-impoverished areas, promoting economic and social development, and improving people's lives there. Ensuring a sufficient supply of grain and other major agricultural products is of paramount importance to agriculture, rural areas and rural people. We should never take the issue of food security lightly, and must ensure basic self-sufficiency in grain and absolute security of staple foodstuffs, so that we always have control over our own food supply. We should promote supply-side structural reform of agriculture, optimize the produce mix and distribution of production areas, and reinforce the grain production zones, the protected areas for key agricultural produce, and the areas growing specialty crops.

Fifth, improving quality of life. This is the fundamental purpose of ensuring unimpeded flows in the domestic economy, a key link connecting the domestic economy and international engagement, and a key element of their mutual reinforcement. Satisfying the people's changing demands, improving their wellbeing in all respects, and ensuring a better life for all are the ultimate goals of socialist production. Optimizing the income distribution structure and expanding the middle-income group can strengthen the endogenous momentum of high-quality development, which is a key link in ensuring unimpeded flows in the domestic economy. We should continue with multiple models of distribution with "to each according to their work" as the principal form, increase the proportion of the remuneration for labor in the primary distribution of gross national income, establish a reasonable wage-growth mechanism, and guarantee wages and the rights and interests of laborers. We should continue to expand the middle-income group and pilot ways to increase earnings for middle- and low-income groups, such as through the right of use of land, capital and other factors of production and the right to proceeds from them. Adopting a problem-oriented approach, we must do more to improve the lives and address the concerns of the people, do everything in our capacity to strengthen areas of weakness, and make steady progress towards common prosperity, so that our people will have a greater sense of gain, fulfillment and security.

Sixth, ensuring a security-based development, which is a red line. This is also an important precondition and guarantee for the new development dynamic, and is essential for the smooth flow of the domestic economy. At this plenary session, the Party Central Committee has drawn up a strategic plan for balancing development and security, which is an effective guideline for China's economic and social development in complex circumstances. We should adopt a holistic approach to national security, and strengthen our national security system and capability, placing national interests above everything else, with political security as the foundation and people's safety as the ultimate goal. We need to properly balance opening up and security, build a tight safety net for opening up, and increase our ability to safeguard national security in this environment. Safeguarding people's lives is our top priority, and we must raise our ability to ensure public security. We must do everything possible to ensure that the people live and work in contentment, that society remains stable and orderly, and that our country enjoys enduring peace and stability.

Fully Understand the New Development Stage[*]

January 11, 2021

In order to define the central tasks of current development, and set the guidelines, principles and policies for our work, it is essential to have an accurate understanding of the stage that our Party and the people have reached. This is an important approach our Party has used to move from victory to victory in leading China's revolution, construction and reform.

At the time of the New Democratic Revolution (1919-1949), our Party learned from its arduous efforts that this was a stage that the Chinese revolution would have to traverse. On this basis, it set the tasks, strategies and tactics that enabled it to lead the people to win the Chinese revolution. When the PRC was founded in 1949, our Party was keenly aware that a transitional period would be required to move from new democracy to socialism. It therefore formulated a general guideline for this period, which enabled our country to complete its socialist revolution and evolve smoothly into the period of socialist construction. Following the introduction of the reform and opening-up policy in 1978, the Party reviewed the experience and lessons drawn from socialist development around the world, particularly in China, and concluded that China was in the primary stage of socialism and would remain so for a long time to come. Based on this judgment, it set the basic guideline that led to a phase of reform, opening up, and socialist modernization. Since the 18th CPC National Congress in 2012, the Central Committee has built on the sustained

---

[*] Part of the speech at a study session on implementing the decisions of the Fifth Plenary Session of the 19th CPC Central Committee, attended by principal officials at the provincial and ministerial level.

efforts of our predecessors by pursuing a holistic approach to the Five-sphere Integrated Plan and coordinated implementation of the Four-pronged Comprehensive Strategy. As a result, we have witnessed historic achievements and transformations and brought socialism with Chinese characteristics into a new era.

The 19th CPC Central Committee determined at its Fifth Plenary Session in 2020 that having realized the First Centenary Goal of building a moderately prosperous society in all respects, China would build on this achievement and embark on a new journey towards the Second Centenary Goal of building a modern socialist country in all respects, thus signifying the beginning of a new stage of development. This strategic assessment was based on the following considerations.

From a theoretical standpoint, Marxism embraces both high ideals and practical targets, and insists on the unity between historical necessity and the stage-specific nature of development, in the belief that as human society moves ultimately towards communism, it must pass through certain historical stages along the way. While applying the basic tenets of Marxism to the practical problems of China, our Party came to realize that the development of socialism is a continuous historical process made up of different stages. Between late 1959 and early 1960, Mao Zedong said after reading the Soviet textbook *Political Economy*, "It is possible to divide the period of socialism into two stages: One could be called underdeveloped socialism and one comparatively developed socialism. This latter stage may take even longer than the first."[1] In 1987, Deng Xiaoping stated, "Socialism itself is the first stage of communism, and here in China we are still in the primary stage of socialism – that is, the underdeveloped stage. In everything we do we must proceed from this reality, and all planning must be consistent with it."[2] The new development stage we have now reached is just one part of the primary stage of socialism, but thanks to many decades of hard work, it is a period that marks a new starting point for us.

From a historical standpoint, this new stage will see our Party lead the people in completing the historic transformation from standing up and becoming better off to growing in strength. After its founding in 1921, the CPC united the people and led them through a bitter, 28-year-long struggle to establish the PRC and make the historic transition from the New Democratic Revolution to socialist revolution. After the founding of the PRC, the Party led the people in creatively carrying out a socialist transformation, establishing socialism as China's basic system, and promoting socialist economic and cultural progress on a large scale. The Chinese people stood upright and held firm as they completed the historic transition from socialist revolution to socialist construction. On entering a new historical period, it led the people in launching the great new revolution of reform and opening up, which sparked tremendous enthusiasm, initiative and creativity and opened up the path of socialism with Chinese characteristics. As China made large strides in catching up with the times, it took yet another huge leap forward in the process of socialist modernization and embraced the bright prospects of national rejuvenation. Based on the achievements of the past, we are now writing a new chapter – building China into a modern socialist country in all respects.

In terms of the present reality, we now possess solid material foundations for embarking on a new journey towards an even higher goal. Thanks to the tireless efforts since the founding of the PRC and especially in the past four decades since the launch of reform and opening up, China had scaled new heights in economic development, scientific and technological capability, composite national strength, and better living standards by the end of the 13th Five-year Plan period (2016-2020). China is now the world's second largest economy, the largest industrial nation, the largest trader of goods, and the largest holder of foreign exchange reserves. China's GDP has exceeded RMB100 trillion and stands at over US$10,000 in per capita terms. Permanent urban residents account for over 60 percent of the population, and the middle-income group has grown to over 400 million. Particularly noteworthy are our historic successes in building a moderately prosperous society in all respects and eliminating absolute poverty – a problem that has plagued our nation for thousands of years. These are significant milestones in the process of our socialist modernization; they pave the way as we march towards the Second Centenary Goal in the new development stage.

Shortly after the founding of the PRC, our Party put forward the goal of building a modern socialist country. Over the course of 13 five-year plans, we have laid solid foundations for achieving this goal. The next 30 years make up the development stage in which we will finally complete this great ambition. We have worked out the roadmap and timetable for our development. By 2035, or within three five-year plan periods, we will achieve basic socialist modernization. Then, by the middle of this century, after completing another three five-year plans, China will become a great modern socialist country that is prosperous, strong, democratic, culturally advanced, harmonious and beautiful.

The world today is undergoing change on a scale unseen in a century. The recent international situation could be best described by the word "disorderly", and it appears that this trend will continue for quite some time. The response to the Covid-19 pandemic has highlighted the leadership capabilities and strengths of the social systems of all countries. The fact that time and momentum are on our side gives us reassurance, resolve and confidence.

That said, we must fully recognize that although China remains in an important period of strategic opportunity for development, and will remain so for some time to come, both the opportunities and challenges we face are changing. Though the two are unprecedented in their extent, the opportunities generally outweigh the challenges. The ancient Chinese philosopher Han Fei Zi once said, "We should manage the small and simple things with care so as to avoid difficulties and disasters."[3] All of us in the Party must remain modest, prudent and committed to hard work; we must mobilize all positive factors, unite all available forces, and focus on managing our own affairs well, as we work towards our objectives with all our resolve.

Our task is to build China into a modern socialist country in all respects. Of course, this modernization is tailored to China's realities and carries distinctive Chinese features. At the Fifth Plenary Session, I highlighted five points in particular: China's modernization must cover a massive population, lead to common prosperity, deliver material, cultural and ethical progress, promote harmony between humanity and nature, and proceed along a path of peaceful development. This is the approach China must take. It must be embodied in our principles, policies, strategies, measures and work plans to enable the Party and the Chinese people to work together towards this end.

The new development stage is an important part of socialist development in our country. In 1992, Deng Xiaoping stated, "We have been building socialism for only a few decades and are still in the primary stage. It will take a very long historical period to consolidate and develop the socialist system, and it will require persistent struggle by many generations, a dozen or even several dozens. We can never rest on our oars."[4]

In my opinion, Deng was making this observation from a political perspective. He was pointing out that it would take a fairly long period of hard work to turn China into a modern country based on the weak economic foundations of the time. But he was also emphasizing that we must persevere with China's socialist system from one generation to the next, even after modernization is achieved. We must work continuously to find ways to consolidate and develop socialism, for no solution can last forever once in place.

Mao Zedong once said, "All things have their boundaries. The way things develop is that one stage leads to another, advancing without interruption. But each and every stage has a boundary. To deny that boundary is to deny qualitative changes, full or partial."[5]

The primary stage of socialism is not a static, rigid or stagnant period, nor is it a spontaneous and passive stage that can easily and naturally be passed through. Rather, it is a stage of dynamism, action and promise, one that should always brim with vitality. It develops gradually but ceaselessly, moving from quantitative increases to qualitative leaps. Building a modern socialist China in all respects and realizing basic socialist modernization are essential for China's development in the primary stage of socialism, and essential for China to advance from the primary stage to a higher stage of socialism.

Notes

[1] Mao Zedong: "Talks on Reading the Soviet Textbook *Political Economy* (Excerpts)", *Collected Works of Mao Zedong*, Vol. VIII, Chin. ed., People's Publishing House, Beijing, 1999, p. 116.

[2] Deng Xiaoping: "In Everything We Do We Must Proceed from the Realities of the Primary Stage of Socialism", *Selected Works of Deng Xiaoping*, Vol. III, Eng. ed., Foreign Languages Press, Beijing, 1994, p. 248.

[3] *Han Fei Zi.*

[4] Deng Xiaoping: "Excerpts from Talks Given in Wuchang, Shenzhen, Zhuhai and Shanghai", *Selected Works of Deng Xiaoping*, Vol. III, Eng. ed., Foreign Languages Press, Beijing, 1994, p. 367.

[5] See note 1 above, p. 108.

Apply the New Development Philosophy in Full*

January 11, 2021

To lead the people in exercising governance, we must be clear about what development we want and how to achieve it. On October 29, 2015, at the Fifth Plenary Session of the 18th CPC Central Committee, I stated, "Philosophy is the precursor of action, and likewise, certain developments are led by certain philosophies. Philosophy decides, in a fundamental manner, the success of results. Practice has shown us that as development will undergo changes influenced by the prevailing environment and conditions, development philosophy will change accordingly."

Since the 18th CPC National Congress in 2012, based on a careful assessment of the economic situation, our Party has made timely adjustments to our development philosophy and our way of thinking, which have resulted in historic progress and transformation in the economic development of our country. Here, I would like to mention the most significant of these philosophies.

First, we have followed the people-centered philosophy of development. On November 15, 2012, when the new Standing Committee of the Political Bureau of the 18th CPC Central Committee met with Chinese and foreign journalists, I emphasized our dedication to the goal of meeting the people's aspirations for a better life and to the path of common prosperity. On October 29, 2015, at the Fifth Plenary Session of the 18th CPC Central Committee, I presented the vision of people-centered development. On October 29, 2020, at the

---

* Part of the speech at a study session on implementing the decisions of the Fifth Plenary Session of the 19th CPC Central Committee, attended by principal officials at the provincial and ministerial level.

Fifth Plenary Session of the 19th CPC Central Committee, I further emphasized the need to make substantive progress in promoting common prosperity for all our people.

Second, we have stopped thinking that the GDP growth rate is the sole barometer of success. On December 15, 2012, at the Central Conference on Economic Work, I emphasized that we cannot blindly pursue rapid growth with no regard for objective laws and conditions. On April 25, 2013, at a meeting of the Standing Committee of the Political Bureau, I emphasized that local governments should not take national regulatory growth targets as the baseline for local economic development, nor should they compete with each other to achieve higher growth rates. I highlighted the need to focus on improving the quality and returns of growth, so as to achieve sustained and healthy development, realize genuine rather than inflated GDP growth, and raise economic efficiency, quality and sustainability.

Third, China's economy has entered a period defined by a complex situation. On July 25, 2013, at a meeting of the Standing Committee of the Political Bureau, I noted that our economy was now facing a complex situation which involved a shift in the growth rate, a painful structural adjustment, and a need to absorb the fallout of previous stimulus policies. At the same time, the global economy was also in a period of profound adjustment, which made for a very complex international environment. This required us to gain a proper understanding of the characteristics of China's current development stage and to undertake reforms and adjustments as needed.

Fourth, China's economy has entered a new normal. I pointed this out on December 10, 2013, at the Central Conference on Economic Work. At the same conference on December 9 the following year, I analyzed nine development trends to explain why our economic development had entered a new normal. I made it clear that understanding the new normal, adapting to it, and guiding it would constitute the main theme of China's economic development both at that time and in the period ahead.

Fifth, we have enabled the market to play the decisive role in resource allocation, and the government to better fulfill its functions. I said at the Third Plenary Session of the 18th CPC Central Committee in November 2013 that the market is the most efficient means of allocating resources, and that it is a general economic law that the market decides the allocation of resources, thereby redefining the role of the market in China's economy.

Sixth, we have committed to the idea that lucid waters and lush mountains are invaluable assets. I put forward this concept during a speech at Nazarbayev University in Kazakhstan on September 7, 2013. I explained that developing an eco-civilization and building a beautiful China is a mission of strategic importance, because we want to leave behind a beautiful homeland with blue skies, green fields, and clean waters for our future generations. I reiterated this point during the deliberation session of the Guizhou delegation to the Second Session of the 12th National People's Congress on March 7, 2014.

Seventh, we have applied the new development philosophy. I proposed the idea of innovative, coordinated, green, open and shared development at the Fifth Plenary Session of the 18th CPC Central Committee in October 2015. I explained that under this new philosophy, innovative development focuses on growth drivers; coordinated development aims to solve imbalances; green development highlights harmony between humanity and nature; open development prioritizes interactions between China and the international community; and shared development underpins social equity and justice. I said at the session that the introduction of the new development philosophy marked a profound change with important implications for China's overall development.

Eighth, we have launched supply-side structural reform. At a meeting of the Central Leading Group for Financial and Economic Affairs on November 10, 2015, I called for a greater effort to promote supply-side structural reform. I stated on December 18, 2015, at the Central Conference on Economic Work, that the five priorities in promoting supply-side structural reform were cutting overcapacity, reducing excess inventory, deleveraging, lowering costs, and strengthening areas of weakness. At the same conference on December 19, 2018, I proposed the guidelines of consolidating the gains in the five priority tasks, strengthening the dynamism of micro entities, upgrading industrial chains, and ensuring unimpeded flows in the economy. I pointed out that these guidelines constituted a general requirement for furthering supply-side structural reform and spurring high-quality economic development both at that time and in the period ahead.

Ninth, we have striven to resolve imbalances and insufficiencies in development. At the 19th CPC National Congress in October 2017, I concluded that the principal challenge facing our society had evolved into the gap between imbalanced and insufficient development and the people's growing expectation for a better life. I noted that this represented a historic shift that could affect the whole development prospect.

Tenth, we have worked to deliver high-quality development. At the 19th CPC National Congress, I pointed out that China's economy was transitioning from rapid growth to high-quality development, in order to address the principal challenge now facing our society and implement the new development philosophy.

Eleventh, we have endeavored to modernize our economy. As I said at the 19th CPC National Congress, this is both an urgent requirement for getting us smoothly through this critical transition and a strategic goal for China's development.

Twelfth, we have moved to create a double development dynamic with the domestic economy as the mainstay and the domestic economy and international engagement providing mutual reinforcement. I put forward this strategy on April 10, 2020 at a meeting of the Central Commission for Financial and Economic Affairs.

Thirteenth, we have adopted a holistic approach to development and security. At a group study session of the Political Bureau on May 29, 2015, I emphasized security-based development. On January 18, 2016, at a study session for principal officials at the provincial and ministerial level, I analyzed the risks and challenges we faced in four fields on the path of open development. On January 5, 2018, at a study session for members and alternate members of the newly elected CPC Central Committee and principal officials at the provincial and ministerial level, I listed 16 risks in eight fields that required our full attention. On January 21, 2019, we held a special study session for principal officials at the provincial and ministerial level on worst-case scenario thinking, to forestall and defuse major risks. At the opening ceremony of that study session, I examined major risks in the political, ideological, economic, social, and scientific and technological domains, and in China-US trade friction, in foreign affairs, and within our Party. I also set out clear requirements for preventing and resolving such risks, and emphasized the need to stay keenly alert to "black swan" and "gray rhino" incidents.

In reviewing this course of events, I wish to underline the paramount importance of the new development philosophy among the key theories and concepts on economic and social development that we have put forward since the 18th CPC National Congress. As a systematic framework, the new development philosophy addresses a series of theoretical and practical questions regarding our development goals, drivers, methods and pathways, and defines the key political parameters, including our stance, values, and model and path of development. The whole Party must apply the new development philosophy in full, to the letter and in all fields. To this end, we should adopt the following approaches in its implementation:

First, we need to understand the fundamental aim of the new development philosophy.

As an ancient Chinese statesman observed, "In a country, the people are the most important."[1] The people represent the most solid foundation and the greatest source of strength for our Party in governing the country.

Working for the wellbeing of the people and the rejuvenation of the Chinese nation is the immutable aim of our Party in leading the modernization drive. It is the ultimate goal of all our work, and also the root and essence of the new development philosophy. We will gain a sound understanding of development and modernization only if we follow a people-centered approach and adhere to the principle that development is for the people and by the people, and that its benefits are shared by the people.

The Soviet Union was the world's first socialist country and once enjoyed spectacular success. Ultimately, however, it collapsed. One main reason for its failure was that the Communist Party of the Soviet Union became detached from the people and turned into a group of privileged bureaucrats who only served their own interests. Even in a modernized country, if the party in power turns its back on the people, it will imperil the fruits of modernization.

Realizing common prosperity is more than an economic goal. It is a major political issue that bears on the foundations of our Party's governance. We must not allow the gap between rich and poor to get any wider – where the poor keep getting poorer while the rich continue to grow richer. We cannot permit the wealth gap to become an unbridgeable gulf. Of course, we must pursue common prosperity in a progressive manner, giving full consideration to what is necessary and what is possible and adhering to the laws governing economic and social development.

At the same time, however, we cannot afford to just sit around and wait. We must be proactive about narrowing the gaps between regions, between urban and rural areas, and between rich and poor people. We should promote all-round social progress and well-rounded personal development, advocate social equity and justice, and ensure that development offers greater benefits to all the people in a fair way. We should see that our people have a stronger sense of gain, fulfillment and security, and make them feel that common prosperity is not an empty slogan, but a concrete fact that they can see and feel for themselves.

Second, we need to stay problem-oriented in implementing the new development philosophy.

Today, China stands at a new starting point in development, which requires us to employ a problem-oriented approach so that we can apply the new development philosophy with greater precision.

We need to effectively address imbalances and insufficiencies in order to improve the quality of our development. For example, many obstacles are impeding our progress towards greater self-reliance in science and technology, which is essential to China's survival and development. Another problem is how to narrow the wide development gap between urban and rural areas and between regions. The answer calls for extensive and in-depth research into many new issues. In particular, we need to intensify our research, and come up with clear ideas about how to manage disparities and restructuring in regional development, accelerated population migration across regions, and a lower desire among rural residents to settle in cities.

There is a broad consensus about promoting a green transformation in every aspect of economic and social development. However, our energy system is still heavily reliant on coal and other fossil fuels, which puts a great strain on our efforts to realize a green and low-carbon transformation in our production models and ways of life. The targets of achieving peak carbon dioxide emissions by 2030 and carbon neutrality by 2060 are formidable.

Given the backlash against economic globalization and the complex and volatile international environment, we need to strike a good balance between strengthening self-reliance and pursuing openness and cooperation, between participating in the international division of labor and safeguarding national security, and between introducing foreign investment and conducting security reviews, so that China can open wider to the outside world without prejudice to its national security.

In short, at the new development stage, we need to expand our understanding of the new development philosophy, so that we can take more targeted and more concrete measures that will truly deliver high-quality development.

Third, we need to be mindful of potential risks.

"Prior planning prevents pitfalls and proper preparation preempts perils."[2] As the principal challenge in our society has changed and the global balance of power is shifting, China will have to contend with more internal and external risks. We must be more aware of potential dangers, have plans in place to counter worst-case scenarios, and prepare for more complex and graver challenges.

The Central Committee prioritized issues of security in its Recommendations for Formulating the 14th Five-Year Plan for Economic and Social Development and Long-Range Objectives Through the Year 2035. It advises that we ensure security in all areas and throughout the process of China's development. If our security foundations are unstable, our development will be precarious. We should uphold political security, the safety of the people, and the interests of the nation as an indivisible whole. We must have the courage and capacity to meet challenges, and build up our strength to deter threats.

We should prevent drastic fluctuations in the macro economy and avoid excessive foreign investment inflows or outflows in the capital market. We must ensure the security of food, energy, and key resources, as well as the stability and security of industrial and supply chains. We need to prevent the disorderly expansion and unchecked growth of capital, and ensure eco-security and workplace safety. We should guard against the risk of large-scale job losses, improve public health security, and effectively prevent and handle incidents of social disturbance.

In strengthening the institutional framework for safeguarding national security, we should draw on the experience of other countries, work out how to establish appropriate safeguards where necessary, and identify effective solutions for a range of national security issues.

Notes

[1] Fang Xuanling *et al.*: *Book of Jin (Jin Shu)*. Fang Xuanling (579-648) was a scholar and statesman of the Tang Dynasty.

[2] Liu Xiang: *Garden of Stories (Shuo Yuan)*. Liu Xiang (77-6 BC) was an economist and writer of the Western Han Dynasty.

Move Faster to Create a
New Development Dynamic[*]

January 11, 2021

The Recommendations for Formulating the 14th Five-Year Plan for Economic and Social Development and Long-Range Objectives Through the Year 2035 defined the creation of a new development dynamic with the domestic economy as the mainstay and the domestic economy and international engagement providing mutual reinforcement. This major strategy concerns our country's overall development interests and must be thoroughly understood and actively implemented.

In recent years, we have witnessed a backlash against economic globalization and profound changes affecting the international economy. The Covid-19 pandemic exacerbated opposition to globalization, and many countries have now become more inward-looking. During the epidemic, I visited several provinces to gain an in-depth understanding of their measures to contain the virus and the problems in reopening the economy. During my visit to Zhejiang Province, I found that global industrial and supply chains had been partially disrupted due to the pandemic. This had directly impacted the domestic economy. Many companies were forced to suspend operations because they could not bring in the raw materials and personnel they needed or send their goods overseas. I realized just how much things had changed; the environment and the conditions that had facilitated large-scale imports and exports were no longer in place.

* Part of the speech at a study session on implementing the decisions of the Fifth Plenary Session of the 19th CPC Central Committee, attended by principal officials at the provincial and ministerial level.

Given these new circumstances, we needed to come up with new thinking to steer development. Accordingly, in April last year I proposed that we create a double development dynamic. At the Fifth Plenary Session of the 19th CPC Central Committee in October 2020, we adopted comprehensive measures to launch this strategy. The establishment of the new development dynamic is a strategic and proactive step for taking the initiative in development, a major historic mission that must be fulfilled in the new development stage, and an important measure for applying the new development philosophy.

As a socialist country with a large population and a vast market, China is certain to encounter various pressures and challenges in the process of modernization, the likes of which no other country has ever experienced. In 1936, Mao Zedong made an observation that still holds true for us even today. He said, "No matter how complicated, grave and harsh the circumstances, what a military leader needs most of all is the ability to function independently in organizing and employing the forces under his command. He may often be forced into a passive position by the enemy, but the important thing is to regain the initiative quickly. Failure to do so spells defeat." "The initiative is not something imaginary but is concrete and material."[1]

If we can, through our own efforts, ensure that the flows of the domestic economy remain unimpeded, we can effectively shield ourselves from harm. We will then have the vigor and vitality not only to survive but to thrive in the most volatile international situations, making it impossible for anyone to keep us down or to back us into a corner. We must speed up our efforts to create the new development dynamic, so that we will be better able to survive, compete, and maintain sustainable development, whatever challenges or difficulties we encounter, whether anticipated or not. This way, we can ensure the course of national rejuvenation is never delayed or interrupted.

In practice, there are some misunderstandings that we need to guard against.

Firstly, some people tend to speak only about the first part, that is, the domestic economy as the mainstay of the new development dynamic, and call for China to sharply narrow its opening to the outside world.

Secondly, some others speak only of the latter part, or the mutual reinforcement between the domestic economy and international engagement, and still subscribe to the old dynamic of large-scale imports and exports with both ends of the economic process – markets and resources – being located abroad, despite the changes to the international landscape.

Thirdly, sticking to one's own line and focusing only on one's own sphere of interest is also a mistake. Some are neglecting the building of a unified national market with a nationwide economic flow, preferring instead to focus on their own local or regional market.

Fourthly, some have equated unimpeded economic flow with smooth logistics and are focused only on this basic level of circulation.

Fifthly, in resolving technological bottlenecks, some people want to do everything themselves, which results in redundancy, or heedless of unfavorable conditions such as a weak industrial base, they tend to carry out extravagant projects that will ultimately fail.

Sixthly, in working to boost domestic demand and expand the domestic market, some people have once again resorted to blind lending to expand investment, and over-stimulating consumption, or even have reverted to energy-intensive and high-emission projects.

Seventhly, some are concentrating on demand-side management at the expense of supply-side structural reform, making it impossible to achieve a higher-level, dynamic equilibrium in which supply promotes demand.

Eighthly, some think that the new development dynamic is a matter for the economic and technology departments and hardly concerns them.

All of these mindsets are inadequate or even erroneous; we must guard against them and rectify them should they arise.

The key to building a new development dynamic is to ensure unimpeded economic flow, as is the case in traditional Chinese medicine, one must remove blockages to stimulate the free flow of vital energy and maintain the body's balance. Economic activity requires the integration of various production factors at all stages, from production through distribution and circulation to consumption, in order to realize a smooth economic cycle. Under normal circumstances, this will lead to greater material production, greater social wealth, greater wellbeing for the people, and greater national strength, giving rise to an upward spiral of development. When obstructions and breakdowns occur, economic flow is disrupted. From a macroeconomic perspective, the economic growth rate drops, unemployment rises, risks arise, and the balance of payments falls into disequilibrium. At the microeconomic level, it leads to problems such as overcapacity, declining enterprise returns, and falling personal incomes.

In the present stage of China's development, the most important task in ensuring smooth economic flow is maintaining effective operations on the supply side. If we have a strong capacity for effective supply we can clear obstructions, resolve bottlenecks, create jobs, and provide incomes, which will increase our capacity to create demand. To this end, we must treat further supply-side structural reform as our main task and continue to carry out the priority tasks of cutting overcapacity, reducing excess inventory, deleveraging, lowering costs, and strengthening areas of weakness. We must comprehensively improve and upgrade the industrial structure, increase our capacity for innovation, our competitiveness, and our overall strength, boost the resilience of the supply system, and ensure that inputs produce higher-quality outputs with greater efficiency, so as to achieve a dynamic economic equilibrium at a high level.

I have said that the essence of the new development dynamic is realizing a high level of self-reliance. The environment for our economic development is changing, particularly with respect to our comparative advantages in production factors. As labor costs are rising and the carrying capacity of our resources and environment have reached a limit, the production function formula of the past is no longer sustainable, and science and technology are becoming more and more important on all fronts. In these circumstances, it is important to put more emphasis on home-grown innovation. As a result, the Recommendations present two major measures – promoting scientific and technological innovation, and removing bottlenecks in industry.

We must understand that these issues are vital to the survival and development of our nation. We should comprehensively strengthen planning for scientific and technological innovation to bring together superior resources, and implement a competitive mechanism to award research projects in order to promote strong and steady progress in innovation. We must better align the chains of innovation and industry, and draw up roadmaps, timetables and systems of responsibility. Where appropriate, relevant departments and local governments should play the leading role in this effort. Where it is appropriate for enterprises to take the lead, governments should give them their full support. State-owned enterprises directly administered by the central government and other state-owned enterprises must have the courage to shoulder their responsibilities and take the lead in making themselves the source of original technologies and the leaders of the modern industrial chain.

In today's world, markets are the scarcest resource. China's market is thus a huge advantage for our country. We must make full use of this factor and steadily consolidate it to make it a strong pillar of the new development dynamic. Expanding domestic demand is not a temporary policy to cope with financial risks and external shocks, nor is it about unleashing a deluge of strong stimulus policies or increasing government investment. Rather, it is about establishing an effective institutional framework to boost domestic demand based on our country's actual economic status, moving to tap the potential of demand, working faster to build a complete demand system, strengthening demand-side management, and expanding consumer spending while also upgrading the level of consumption, so that the development of our vast domestic market becomes a sustainable process.

To create a new development dynamic and pursue high-standard opening up, we require a robust domestic economic flow and stable economic fundamentals. On this base, we can create a strong pull for global production factors and resources, the ability to hold our own amid intense international competition, and powerful momentum for the allocation of global resources. We should continue to expand opening up based on the flow of production factors such as goods, services, capital and talent, and steadily expand institutional opening up with regard to rules, regulations, management and standards. We should ensure that China's domestic economy plays a stronger role in guiding the double development dynamic, and foster new strengths for China's participation in international economic cooperation and competition. We should work to harness international engagement as a means for improving the efficiency and level of the domestic economy and the quality and allocation of our production factors. Through competition in the international market we will boost the competitiveness of our export products and services, and promote industrial transformation and upgrading to increase China's influence in global industry chains, supply chains, and innovation chains. Chinese enterprises now have interests that extend to many countries around the world. This requires that we pay more attention to understanding international affairs and carrying out thorough studies on countries that are our stakeholders, trading partners, and investment destinations, in order to establish a clear picture of potential benefits and risks.

To sum up, the requirements to enter a new development stage, apply a new development philosophy, and build a new development dynamic are determined by the theoretical, historical and practical logic of our country's economic and social development. These three elements are closely interrelated. Our entry into the new development stage clarifies the historic juncture that national development has reached, the new development philosophy makes clear the guiding principles behind our modernization drive, and the new development dynamic elucidates the path that will take us to economic modernization. An understanding of the new development stage will provide us with the practical basis for applying the new development philosophy and creating a new development dynamic. The new development philosophy will provide us with a guide for understanding the new development stage and creating a new development dynamic. Creating a new development dynamic is a strategic choice in terms of our response to the opportunities and challenges in the new development stage and our implementation of the new development philosophy.

Notes

[1] Mao Zedong: "Problems of Strategy in China's Revolutionary War", *Selected Works of Mao Zedong*, Vol. I, Eng. ed., Foreign Languages Press, Beijing, 1965, p. 234.

At a Va minority village in Qingshui Township, Tengchong City, on the first day of his visit to Yunnan Province to extend Chinese New Year greetings to people of various ethnic groups, January 19-21, 2020.

Chatting with officers and soldiers from a border defense battalion, during his inspection visit to the troops stationed in Yunnan Province, January 19, 2020.

Hearing reports on the coronavirus response and making corresponding plans, particularly on patient treatment, when presiding over a meeting of the Standing Committee of the Political Bureau of the 19th CPC Central Committee, January 25, 2020.

Watching treatment of patients infected with the coronavirus on the monitoring screen and speaking to medical staff on duty via video link at Beijing Ditan Hospital affiliated with Capital Medical University, during his inspection tour to review the epidemic response in Beijing, February 10, 2020.

Greeting residents under home quarantine in Donghu Xincheng Community during his inspection tour to review epidemic prevention and control measures in Wuhan City, Hubei Province, March 10, 2020.

Talking to tea farmers at a demonstration park of the Nüwa-Phoenix modern tea plantation in Jiangjiaping Village, Pingli County, on the second day of his visit to Shaanxi Province, April 20-23, 2020.

Examining preservation work on the Yungang Grottoes, a historical and cultural heritage site in Datong City, on the first day of his visit to Shanxi Province, May 11-12, 2020.

Meeting model workers and representatives of Masteel Group, China Baowu, in Maanshan City, on the second day of his visit to Anhui Province, August 18-21, 2020.

Meeting with recipients of national medals and honorary titles, and representatives of model individuals and groups, before addressing the national gathering to commend exemplary service in the fight against Covid-19 in the Great Hall of the People, Beijing, September 8, 2020.

Walking with teachers and pupils of Diyipian Primary School in Wenming Yao Township, Rucheng County, on the first day of his visit to Hunan Province, September 16-18, 2020.

Placing a flower basket before the bronze statue of Deng Xiaoping at Lianhuashan Park in Shenzhen City, Guangdong Province, October 14, 2020. The same day, Xi addressed a grand gathering to celebrate the 40th anniversary of the establishment of the Shenzhen Special Economic Zone.

Delivering a speech at the Fifth Plenary Session of the 19th CPC Central Committee held in Beijing from October 26 to 29, 2020.

Meeting venue staff, athletes and coaches at the National Alpine Skiing Center in Beijing's Yanqing District, January 18, 2021. Xi visited Beijing and Hebei and presided over a briefing on preparations for the Beijing 2022 Winter Olympics and Paralympics, January 18-20.

Extending Chinese New Year greetings to people of all ethnic groups, Hong Kong, Macao and Taiwan compatriots, and overseas Chinese, in the public square of Huawu Village in Xinren Miao Township, Qianxi County, on the first day of his visit to Guizhou Province, February 3-5, 2021.

Delivering a speech at the preparatory meeting for the education campaign on CPC history in Beijing, February 20, 2021.

Meeting with representatives of model individuals and groups, including relatives of those who died on duty in the battle against poverty, before addressing the national conference to review the fight against poverty in the Great Hall of the People, Beijing, February 25, 2021.

Talking to staff of the memorial hall in Quanzhou County, Guilin City, dedicated to the Battle of the Xiangjiang River during the Long March in the 1930s, on the first day of his visit to Guangxi Zhuang Autonomous Region, April 25-27, 2021.

Retaking the oath of admission to the Party after a visit to the exhibition "Aspiration and Mission" at the Museum of the Communist Party of China, along with Li Keqiang (4th right, 2nd row), Li Zhanshu (3rd left, 2nd row), Wang Yang (3rd right, 2nd row), Wang Huning (2nd left, 2nd row), Zhao Leji (2nd right, 2nd row), Han Zheng (1st left, 2nd row), Wang Qishan (1st right, 2nd row) and other Party leaders and officials, June 18, 2021.

Speaking from the Beijing Aerospace Control Center with Shenzhou-12 *astronauts Nie Haisheng (2nd right), Liu Boming (1st right), and Tang Hongbo (3rd right) on board the* Tianhe *core module of China's space station, June 23, 2021.*

Entering the Great Hall of the People together with July 1 Medal recipients for the award ceremony in celebration of the centenary of the CPC, June 29, 2021.

Delivering a speech at the ceremony marking the centenary of the CPC in Tian'anmen Square, Beijing, July 1, 2021.

Greeted by local people upon arrival at Nyingchi Mainling Airport for a visit to the Tibet Autonomous Region on the occasion of the 70th anniversary of Tibet's peaceful liberation, July 21-23, 2021.

Chatting with farmers in the fields in Gaoxigou Village, Mizhi County, on the first day of his visit to Yulin City, Shaanxi Province, September 13-14, 2021.

Delivering a speech at the meeting marking the 110th anniversary of the Revolution of 1911 at the Great Hall of the People, Beijing, October 9, 2021.

At the estuary of the Yellow River in Dongying City, Shandong Province, October 20, 2021. Two days later, Xi chaired and addressed the forum on eco-conservation and high-quality development of the Yellow River Basin in Shandong's Jinan City.

At the Sixth Plenary Session of the 19th CPC Central Committee, along with Li Keqiang (3rd right), Li Zhanshu (3rd left), Wang Yang (2nd right), Wang Huning (2nd left), Zhao Leji (1st right), and Han Zheng (1st left). The session was held in Beijing from November 8 to 11, 2021.

Meeting with Carrie Lam Cheng Yuet-ngor, chief executive of the Hong Kong Special Administrative Region, who came to Beijing to deliver her work report at Zhongnanhai, December 22, 2021.

Meeting with Ho Iat Seng, chief executive of the Macao Special Administrative Region, who came to Beijing to deliver his work report at Zhongnanhai, December 22, 2021.

Delivering a New Year message to welcome in 2022 through China Media Group and the internet, December 31, 2021.

On a video call from the Joint Operations Command Center with infantry battalions and engineer, medical and helicopter units on overseas peacekeeping missions, during his inspection visit to the PLA Central Theater Command, January 28, 2022.

Greeting residents at Maona Village, Wuzhishan City, on the second day of his visit to Hainan Province, April 10-13, 2022.

A discussion with students in a moral and political education class at Renmin University of China, Beijing, April 25, 2022.

High-Quality Development

Foster New Opportunities and Open Up New Horizons[*]

May 23, 2020

We need to take a comprehensive, dialectical and long-term view of the current economic situation, develop new opportunities in the midst of crisis, and open up new prospects in the midst of change. We need to tap China's potential and role as the world's largest market, clarify the strategic direction of supply-side structural reform, maintain the basic trend of steady and long-term economic growth, and consolidate the fundamental position of agriculture. We will stabilize the Six Fronts – employment, finance, foreign trade, inbound investment, domestic investment, and market expectations, and guarantee the Six Priorities – jobs, daily living needs, food and energy security, industrial and supply chains, the operation of market players, and the smooth functioning of grassroots government.

We will also ensure that all our policies and plans are implemented, and that the goals and tasks of securing a decisive victory in building a moderately prosperous society in all respects and in eradicating absolute poverty are accomplished. This will enable the Chinese economy to brave the waves and forge ahead.

We should make a rational analysis of where we are now, be mindful of the overriding trend towards development, and view current difficulties, risks and challenges from a comprehensive, dialectic and long-term perspective. The whole of society, and market entities in particular, should be encouraged to be confident and maintain

---

[*] Main points of the speech at a joint panel discussion of CPPCC National Committee members from the economic circles during the Third Session of the 13th CPPCC National Committee.

209

the momentum in driving the steady and long-term growth of the Chinese economy.

This is a pivotal period for transforming our growth model, improving our economic structure, and fostering new drivers of growth. The prospects for economic development are promising, but we are also confronted with difficulties and challenges brought about by a lattice of structural, institutional and cyclical problems and the impact of the Covid-19 epidemic. It can be seen that China's economy is coming under great pressure.

We also have to face a deep recession in the global economy, a sharp contraction in international trade and investment, turbulence in international financial markets, restrictions on international exchanges, countercurrents in economic globalization, rampant protectionism and unilateralism in some countries, and rising geopolitical risks. This means we have to pursue our development in a more unstable and uncertain world.

It is important to note that the basic features of the Chinese economy remain unchanged: It has great potential, deep resilience, ample room for maneuver, and multiple policy tools. China has the world's largest and most complete industrial system, strong production and support capacity, more than 100 million market players, more than 170 million people with higher education or professional skills, and 1.4 billion consumers, including a middle-income group of over 400 million, forming a super-large domestic market.

China is making great headway in new industrialization, informatization, urbanization, and agricultural modernization, with huge potential for investment. Its basic socialist economic system – public ownership playing the dominant role while developing together with other forms of ownership, multiple models of distribution with "to each according to their work" as the principal form, and a socialist market economy – is conducive to stimulating the vitality of market entities, unleashing and developing productive forces, promoting efficiency and equity, and achieving common prosperity.

In the future, satisfying domestic demand will be the starting point and goal of development. We will establish a complete system of domestic demand, promote innovation in science and technology and other fields, and accelerate the development of strategic emerging industries such as the digital economy, intelligent manufacturing, life sciences, health, and new materials, so as to foster new growth poles. In order to cultivate new strengths for China's participation in international cooperation and competition, we need to ensure smooth production, distribution, circulation and consumption, and gradually form a double development dynamic with the domestic economy as the mainstay and the domestic economy and international engagement providing mutual reinforcement.

Protectionism is on the rise in today's world, but we need to stand on the right side of history. We should uphold multilateralism and democracy in international relations, pursue development in a spirit of open and win-win cooperation, strive to make economic globalization open, inclusive, balanced and beneficial to all, and foster an open world economy. At the same time, we need to adopt a vision of safe development with the appropriate systems and mechanisms in place, shore up points of weakness, safeguard the security of industrial and supply chains, and guard against and defuse major risks.

Promote Integrated, High-Quality Development
of the Yangtze River Delta*

August 20, 2020

We should fully recognize the position and role of the Yangtze River Delta in our country's economic and social development. Given the new situation and new requirements for integrated development in this region, we need to be both goal- and problem-oriented, and do hard and solid work on key tasks to achieve concrete results in the Delta.

Since the launch of the strategy for promoting integrated development of the Yangtze River Delta more than a year ago, people in Jiangsu, Zhejiang and Anhui provinces and Shanghai Municipality – regions which make up the Delta – together with those of the competent government departments, have worked hard to implement the decisions and plans of the CPC Central Committee and secured remarkable results.

First, you have gained a good understanding of the strategy of the CPC Central Committee and pursued the integrated development of the Yangtze River Delta as a part of the overall national strategy for regional development. You are clear about the region's strategic position as a vibrant growth pole for the country, and you are striving to turn it into a model of high-quality development, a pioneer area in realizing basic modernization, a demonstration area for integrated regional development, and a new pacesetter of reform and opening up.

Second, you have adopted innovative approaches and made breakthroughs in key sectors and areas to accelerate integrated development of the Delta.

---

* Major points of the speech at a forum on advancing the integrated development of the Yangtze River Delta.

Third, you have achieved preliminary results in implementing the strategy. Key pillars of the planned policy framework have been put into place, and the multitiered work mechanism has started to function. Both the integration mechanism and interconnected infrastructure have played their roles in Covid-19 epidemic prevention and control as well as in reopening the economy.

In general, a new dynamic driving the integrated development of the Yangtze River Delta is taking shape. This shows the decisions and plans of the CPC Central Committee are sound and they are being rigorously implemented.

To further the integrated development of the Yangtze River Delta in the face of significant and complex challenges, people must be clear about the position and role of the Delta in China's economic and social development.

First, the region should be the first to form a new development dynamic. As the global market is shrinking, we should concentrate our efforts on running our own affairs well. China is a massive market; we should lose no time in creating a double development dynamic with the domestic economy as the mainstay and the domestic economy and international engagement providing mutual reinforcement. The region should leverage its strengths, such as a wealth of talent, advanced science and technology, an advanced manufacturing industry, largely complete industrial and supply chains, and huge market potential, and explore ways to create a new development dynamic.

Second, the region should become a trailblazer in promoting innovative development in China's science, technology and industry. As a new revolution in science, technology and industry gathers pace, China urgently needs to boost its capacity for scientific and technological innovation. Shanghai and the other parts of the region should not only produce quality products, but also become a source of advanced technologies to support high-quality development of the whole country.

Third, the region should move faster to make itself a pacesetter of reform and opening up. In recent years, economic globalization has encountered headwinds. The more this is the case, the harder we should work to promote and spearhead economic globalization, and build a global community of shared future. The Yangtze River Delta has always been at the forefront of China's reform and opening up. It should improve its business environment by following world-class standards and attract talent and companies from home and abroad with an open, efficient, innovative and enabling environment. It should promote trade and investment facilitation, and become an important bridge between the international and domestic markets.

Integration and high quality are two pillars underpinning the development strategy of the Delta. An integrated approach should be taken to break local administrative barriers, strengthen policy coordination, and enable the smooth flow of production factors in more sectors. This will raise the comparative advantages of various areas of the region, ensure a well-balanced division of labor, and pool more resources to form a stronger synergy. And this will enable the region to achieve high-quality development.

First, you should promote high-quality economic development in the Yangtze River Delta. You in Jiangsu, Zhejiang, Anhui and Shanghai should implement the policies of the CPC Central Committee while carrying out regular epidemic prevention and control. And you should lead the country in stabilizing the Six Fronts – employment, finance, foreign trade, inbound investment, domestic investment, and market expectations. You should also lead the country in guaranteeing the Six Priorities – jobs, daily living needs, food and energy security, industrial and supply chains, the operation of market players, and the smooth functioning of grassroots government. You should ensure that various support measures cover all those working on the ground and directly benefit market players, while financial capital should support manufacturing and micro, small and medium-sized enterprises on a priority basis. You should fully leverage the strengths of the digital economy, speed up industrial transformation enabled by digital and smart technology, and improve the stable performance and competitiveness of industrial and supply chains. You should accelerate the construction of major projects and release potential effective demand for investment.

Second, you should step up scientific and technological research. You must keep yourselves well positioned in innovation and development. You in Jiangsu, Zhejiang, Anhui and Shanghai should pool your strengths in science and technology and focus on key areas and major fields including integrated circuits, biomedicine and artificial intelligence, so as to achieve early breakthroughs. Micro, small and medium-sized technology companies should be able to get the support they need to grow themselves.

Third, you should boost quality development of cities in the Yangtze River Delta. Built and developed many years ago, many cities and towns in the region have old districts and face a pressing need for urban renewal. This involves the vital interests of the general public and is important for long-term urban development. No matter how difficult the problem is, you must find a solution to it. But you must not simply engage in large-scale demolition and construction. You should protect urban history, culture and landscapes, and avoid constructing faceless buildings and cities. You should resolutely stop speculation in real estate under the name of urban renewal. You should firmly implement the principle that houses are for living in and not for speculative investment, and put in place a long-term mechanism to ensure steady and sound development of the real estate market.

Fourth, you should speed up high-quality development of underdeveloped regions. An important goal of integration is to address imbalanced development between different regions. Gaps in development also mean potential for development. The competent government departments should take more targeted measures for underdeveloped regions to help them keep pace with the Yangtze River Delta in pursuing integrated, high-quality development. As a Chinese saying goes, "The sea is vast because it embraces many rivers." Gaps do exist in economic and natural conditions between different regions, such as those between cities and villages, between plains and mountains, and between industrial areas and eco-environmental protection areas. You should not address these gaps in a simplistic or inflexible way. To solve imbalanced development, you should follow economic and objective laws, tailor measures to local conditions, provide differentiated guidance, see differences for what they are, and avoid applying a one-size-fits-all approach.

Fifth, you should advance the high-standard reform and opening up of Pudong. This year marks the 30th anniversary of Pudong's reform and opening up. You should support Pudong's pioneering reform of its system to improve coordination and performance, promote its high-standard institutional opening up and its ability to allocate its resources globally, and upgrade its modern urban governance. Try out new things in these fields and create new experience. This is of strategic significance to Shanghai, to the integrated, high-quality development of the Yangtze River Delta, and to socialist modernization in China. The newly launched Lingang Special Area of China (Shanghai) Pilot Free Trade Zone should be run well, and it should play its full role as a trailblazer of reform. Shanghai will be further developed as an international financial center to support the high-quality economic development of the Yangtze River Delta and the rest of China.

Sixth, you should consolidate the foundations for the green development of the Yangtze River Delta. As the flagship of the Yangtze River Economic Belt, the Delta should take the lead in both economic development and eco-environmental protection. Priority should be given to the protection and restoration of the eco-environment of the Yangtze River, and measures must be taken to resolve serious environmental problems such as the treatment of urban sewage and garbage, chemical pollution, agricultural non-point source pollution, pollution from ships and tailings ponds. Urban and rural organic waste should be better treated and utilized in areas around the Taihu Lake, and a full range of supporting measures should be taken to set an example for eco-environmental protection through the treatment and utilization of organic waste in both the Yangtze River Delta and the rest of China.

The Yangtze River fishing ban is important to the whole country and future generations. Provinces and cities along the river and the competent government departments should strengthen overall planning and coordination, refine policies and measures, specify responsibilities for all those involved, and ensure the livelihoods of former fishermen. You should strengthen law enforcement and supervision, take firm action on illegal fishing, and see that the fishing ban is rigorously enforced.

Seventh, you should expand basic public services in the region. In the course of pursuing regional integration, you should work for the benefit of the people of the region, solve their problems, and guarantee their livelihoods. You in Jiangsu, Zhejiang, Anhui and Shanghai should make the best use of experience drawn from the Covid-19 response, take advantage of the Yangtze River Delta cooperation mechanism to establish an emergency response system that manages public health and other emergencies, and keep a good stock of medical supplies. You should plan and implement a phased policy of basic medical insurance, and unify the drug catalogue, diagnosis and treatment, and standards of medical facilities. A social security card should be issued to residents in the region to access all public services, and there should be equal access to transport, tourist attractions, and cultural activities across the region. You should also shore up weak links in grassroots governance and strengthen capacity to resist natural disasters.

Efforts should be made to reinforce the Party's ability and resolve to steer the course, make overall plans, devise policies, and promote reform, so as to provide a strong political guarantee for the integrated development of the Yangtze River Delta. In the course of implementing the integrated development strategy, you need to identify and cultivate the best talent and give them opportunities to shine. Political commitment and integrity must be the primary criteria for selecting officials to ensure they are trustworthy and reliable. You should improve the management of officials to ensure the capable are promoted, the excellent rewarded, the mediocre demoted, and the incompetent dismissed.

An official-rotating mechanism commensurate with the integrated development of the region should be established. Standards and procedures in Party organizations in all enterprises should be improved to give play to their supporting roles in decision-making, market development, technological innovation, and improving performance. This will enable Party organizations to use their political and organizational strengths to help business grow. You should recruit more Party members from non-public economic entities, train them and manage them well, and guide them to play an exemplary role as pacesetters.

The integrated development of the Yangtze River Delta cannot be achieved overnight. People should remain patient and think long term, and also act with a sense of urgency. The leading group should steer the course and ensure that the decisions and plans of the CPC Central Committee are fully implemented. All of you in Jiangsu, Zhejiang, Anhui and Shanghai and in the competent government departments should shoulder your responsibilities, move proactively and make bold breakthroughs in accordance with the decisions and plans of the CPC Central Committee. You should make implementation plans for pursuing integrated development of the Yangtze River Delta during the 14th Five-year Plan period (2021-2025), and continue to deliver fruitful outcomes.

Address Problems Related to Agriculture, Rural Areas and Rural People in the New Development Stage*

December 28, 2020

I have often said that leading officials should concentrate on the overall work of the Party and the country. At this important juncture, as we move towards the Second Centenary Goal, as elimination of absolute poverty has been accomplished, and as Covid-19 is exacerbating global turbulence and provoking change, we need to consolidate and expand our achievements in poverty elimination, comprehensively promote rural revitalization, and speed up agricultural and rural modernization. This is a major issue of overarching importance that requires attention from the whole Party.

– The rejuvenation of the Chinese nation calls for rural revitalization.

Agriculture has been the foundation of our country since ancient times. China created a great and time-honored agricultural civilization that led the world for a long time. Looking back on history, if agriculture was prosperous and peasants led a contented life, the country would be unified and society in order. If agriculture was unproductive and peasants led a hard life, the country would be divided and society would be in turmoil.

After 1840, China suffered from foreign invasions, which led to desolation in the countryside and destitution for the people.

Soon after its founding in 1921, our Party realized that the fundamental issue in the Chinese revolution was the peasants. It began to see

---

* Part of the speech at the Central Conference on Rural Work.

the welfare of the peasants as a priority and devoted itself to freeing them from political oppression and economic exploitation.

During the Great Revolution (1924-1927), Mao Zedong pointed out that the peasants were the largest and most loyal ally of the Chinese proletariat, thus issues related to peasants were key to the national revolution. When meeting with American writer Edgar Snow in Yan'an in 1936, he observed that whoever won the support of the peasants would win China, and whoever solved the land problem would win the support of the peasants.

During the New Democratic Revolution (1919-1949), our Party led the peasants in fighting local tyrants and distributed land to them, and through arduous armed struggle, hundreds of millions of peasants were liberated.

After the founding of the PRC in 1949, our Party launched a series of new initiatives to organize farmers, restore order, and revive production.

Under the leadership of the Party, farmers took the lead in embracing reform and opening up in 1978. By constantly unleashing and developing productive forces and promoting all-round progress in rural areas, they made a historic leap from lacking adequate food and clothing to enjoying moderate prosperity in all respects.

Since the 18th CPC National Congress in 2012, solving problems related to agriculture, rural areas and rural people has been a top priority in the work of the whole Party, and poverty elimination a landmark project in building a moderately prosperous society in all respects. We have organized the largest and most determined campaign against poverty in human history, which has benefited the largest number of people. We have launched the rural revitalization strategy, and achieved historic change and transformation in agriculture and rural areas.

Our country's overall agricultural production capacity has increased visibly, and its grain output has exceeded 650 million tonnes for the past six years. The per capita income of farmers has more than doubled compared with 2010, their lives have significantly improved, and the countryside has been transformed. Extraordinary changes have taken place in poverty-stricken areas, and we have achieved historic success in eliminating the absolute poverty that has plagued the Chinese nation for thousands of years.

All of this has contributed to our success in building a moderately prosperous society in all respects, and laid a solid foundation for building China into a modern socialist country. These achievements are the result of a concerted effort on the part of the whole Party and the whole country.

As has long been said, "Agriculture is the foundation of a country and the top priority in governance."[1] "Attaching importance to agricultural development is the fundamental plan of the country."[2] History and our experience show that only when agriculture is stable can a country enjoy peace. We should view agriculture, rural areas and rural people from a broad historical perspective. Only with this perspective can we better understand our Party, our country, and our nation. In building a modern socialist country in an all-round way and realizing the rejuvenation of the Chinese nation, the most arduous and onerous tasks are to be found in rural areas, where the broadest and most profound foundations are set.

Despite the progress we have achieved in issues of agriculture, rural areas and rural people, the foundations of our agriculture are not yet solid. There are still wide gaps in development and incomes between urban and rural areas and between regions. Our major social problems are still exemplified by the urban-rural imbalance caused by insufficient rural development. With only three five-year plan periods between now and 2035, we need to act quickly. We need to define agricultural and rural modernization, conduct rational analysis and in-depth studies, and set the goals and tasks to be accomplished by 2035 and by the middle of this century. The priority at this stage is to formulate the agricultural and rural development plan for the 14th Five-year Plan period.

– The world is undergoing change on a scale unseen in a century. Stability in agricultural production and solid foundations for agriculture, rural progress and the wellbeing of rural people will serve as ballast in our dealing with change and seeking future development.

Only with progress in issues related to agriculture, rural areas and rural people can China, a huge country with a population of 1.4 billion, secure the initiative in overall development. At present, the international environment is becoming increasingly complex, with more instability and uncertainties. The Covid-19 pandemic is exerting a far-reaching impact, economic globalization is facing counter-currents, and the world is undergoing turbulence and change. We must have a clear understanding of the situation and be prepared for prolonged endeavors.

I have repeatedly emphasized the need to run our own affairs well. One of them is to focus on agricultural production and deal with uncertainties in the external environment with the certainty of stable domestic production and supply.

To cope with risks and challenges, we must stabilize not only agriculture but also rural areas. When the economy wobbles, it is migrant workers who bear the brunt. When the international financial crisis broke out in 2008, more than 20 million migrant workers lost their jobs and returned to their rural homes. This year, due to the impact of Covid-19 and the international economic downturn, nearly 30 million migrant workers either stayed at home or returned to their hometowns from cities. The key reason why our society has remained stable in adversity is that farmers still have their land and houses back home, which means they have land to farm, food to eat, and work to do if they return home. Even if they do not return to the cities, they still feel secure. It will take us a long time to build a modern socialist country in an all-round way. Before these migrant workers are fully settled in cities, we should not rush to sever their links with the countryside. Instead, they should have the choice of either living in cities or in the countryside. This is why China's urbanization is unique. It also gives us room for maneuver and a particular advantage in addressing risks and challenges.

Building the new development dynamic is a strategic measure

that China has taken to respond to world changes. It is also a strategic move to adapt to changes in its own development stage and to seize the initiative. We have focused our strategy on expanding domestic demand. To achieve this, we must fully tap the vast potential of the countryside. The comprehensive modernization of areas that are home to hundreds of millions of rural residents will unleash huge demand for consumption and investment. The economic flow between urban and rural areas is an inherent part of the domestic economy, and is also key to ensuring a healthy balance between the domestic economy and international engagement in the double development dynamic.

The whole Party must be fully aware of the importance and urgency of addressing problems related to agriculture, rural areas and rural people in the new development stage, and address these problems as a top priority in the work of our Party. We need to mobilize the whole Party and society to promote rural revitalization, ensure high-quality and efficient development of agriculture, make rural areas more livable and suitable for business, and ensure that rural people lead a better life.

Notes

[1] Sima Qian: *Records of the Historian (Shi Ji).*
[2] Fang Xuanling *et al.*: *Book of Jin (Jin Shu).*

Strive for Greater Strength and Self-Reliance in Science and Technology*

May 28, 2021

In today's world, change on a scale unseen in a century is unfolding rapidly. The international environment is complex, the world economy has remained sluggish, global industrial and supply chains are being reshaped, and instability and uncertainty are on the rise. The Covid-19 pandemic is having a far-reaching impact, and support for deglobalization, unilateralism and protectionism is surging.

Against this backdrop, scientific and technological innovation has become one of the main fields of international strategic competition, and the contest in key sci-tech areas is fierce. Therefore, we must maintain an acute sense of potential risks and challenges, and be well-prepared in both mind and action.

At present, a new revolution in science, technology and industry is in rapid progress. The paradigms of scientific research are undergoing profound change; interdisciplinary integration is expanding steadily; and sci-tech advances are rapidly translating into economic and social development.

Scientific and technological innovation has greatly advanced the frontiers of global research in macro fields, including the revolution of celestial bodies, the evolution of galaxies, and the origin of the universe, and in micro fields, including gene editing, particle structures, and quantum control.

* Part of the speech at the joint session of the 20th Meeting of the Members of the Chinese Academy of Sciences, the 15th Meeting of the Members of the Chinese Academy of Engineering, and the 10th National Congress of the China Association for Science and Technology.

Scientific and technological innovation has significantly increased the depth of human knowledge, with deep space exploration becoming a key field, and deep sea and deep earth exploration extending humanity's understanding of nature.

Scientific and technological innovation has accelerated exponentially, with emerging technologies represented by information technology and artificial intelligence at the forefront, expanding the limits of time, space, and human cognition, and ushering in an era of intelligent interconnection of everything, featuring a ternary integration of man, computer and object.

Basic and applied research in biological sciences is making rapid progress. The precision of scientific and technological innovation has increased remarkably, with research on biomacromolecules and genes having entered the stage of precise control. While bringing benefits to humanity, the transition from understanding and transforming to synthesizing and designing life also gives rise to ethical issues.

Through years of endeavor, our country's overall strength in science and technology has improved substantially. We therefore have a solid foundation, and are fully confident in our ability to seize the opportunities offered by the new revolution in science, technology and industry to achieve greater results.

Meanwhile, we should also note that China still needs to strengthen its capacity for original innovation, raise its overall innovation efficiency, and better integrate and allocate its innovation resources. To effectively underpin development in science and technology, China has to increase the return on its investment, optimize the talent structure, reform its research evaluation system, and improve the ecosystems for innovation. Many of these deficiencies are long-standing, and it will require a considerable effort to resolve them.

The 19th CPC National Congress set the strategic goal that China will become a global leader in innovation by 2035. The Fifth Plenary Session of the 19th CPC Central Committee stated that we should uphold the core role of innovation in our country's modernization drive and take greater strength and self-reliance in science and technology as a strategic support for national development.

To ground our efforts in the new development stage, apply our new development philosophy, foster the new development dynamic, and promote high-quality development, we must further implement our strategies for invigorating China through science and education, making China a talent-strong country, and driving development through innovation. We must also improve the national innovation system and achieve more self-reliance to become a pioneer in science and technology.

First, we should devote more effort to original and pioneering research and make breakthroughs in core technologies in key fields. A country can thrive only when it is strong in science and technology.

Reinforcing basic research is essential to building greater strength and self-reliance in science and technology, and to transforming the unknown into knowledge, and uncertainty into certainty. We should expedite the preparation of a 10-year action plan for basic research. We should be bold in the extent of our reach and highlight originality. In furthering our exploration into the evolution of the universe, the nature of consciousness, the structure of matter, and the origin of life, we seek to extend our understanding of nature and open new realms of knowledge.

Basic research should be oriented towards applications and breaking through bottlenecks. It should identify research questions from the practical problems facing economic growth, social development, and national security, and grasp the basic theories and principles of technological barriers. We should increase and optimize fiscal spending on basic research, offer tax incentives for enterprises to invest in basic research, and encourage social organizations and individuals to fund basic research through multiple channels – including making donations and establishing foundations – to form stable mechanisms for sustainable funding.

Major science and technology programs should focus on solving the most pressing problems. To meet the urgent and long-term needs of the country, we should devote attention to core technologies in key fields, including oil and gas, basic materials, high-end chips, industrial software, crop seeds, equipment for scientific experiments, and chemicals, and look to achieve breakthroughs in core technologies in medicines, medical devices and equipment, and vaccines.

In basic and core areas bearing on China's overall development and national security, we should focus on frontier fields such as artificial intelligence, quantum information, integrated circuits, advanced manufacturing, life and health, brain science, bio-breeding, aerospace technology, and deep earth and deep space explorations. We should make forward-looking research and development plans for expanding our strategic technology reserves, so as to give us the technological and industrial edge in the future. We need to improve fiscal investment in science and technology, and give priority to key sectors of strategic importance.

The integration of innovation and industrial chains hinges on the status of enterprises as the main players in innovation. We should motivate enterprises to innovate by giving them incentives and facilitating their transformation. We should challenge them to formulate questions and find answers through collaboration on key projects and integrated research and development. We should encourage innovation consortia established by leading enterprises with the support of universities and research institutions and the collaboration of all parties involved. Our aim is to develop an efficient and powerful supply system of generic technologies, and accelerate progress in applying and commercializing advances in science and technology.

Modern engineering and technical sciences are an indispensable bridge between theoretical science and industrial development, and play a key role in science and technology. We should strengthen interdisciplinary research in modern engineering and technical sciences, to drive the development of basic science and engineering technology and form a complete framework of modern science and technology.

Second, we should increase our country's strategic capacity in science and technology and improve the overall efficiency of the national innovation system. National strategic capacity in science and technology is the focus of international competition among scientific and technological powers. As important components, national laboratories, national scientific research institutions, high-quality research universities, and leading science and technology enterprises should take on the mission of reinforcing China's sci-tech self-reliance and strength.

National laboratories should target global scientific and technological frontiers, serve the economy, meet major national needs, and strive to improve people's lives and health. They should follow global trends in science and technology, adapt to the missions set by our country's strategies for national development, and seek major research advances of strategic and critical importance. Together with key national laboratories they should form a national laboratory system with Chinese features.

State research institutions should be guided by national strategic needs, and devote their energy to solving major scientific and technological issues that hinder overall national development and affect long-term national interests. They should move faster to build themselves into sources of original innovation and make breakthroughs in core technologies in key fields.

High-quality research universities should better integrate their efforts in developing science and technology as the primary productive forces, in cultivating talent as the primary resource, and in strengthening innovation as the primary driver of development. They should make good use of their strengths in basic research and interdisciplinary integration to become the main force in basic research and a vital force for major scientific and technological breakthroughs. They need to better align the development of research universities with national strategic goals and tasks, and make greater efforts in researching basic and frontier fields and seeking breakthroughs in key technologies. They should build disciplinary, academic, and discourse systems with salient Chinese features, style and ethos, and contribute to the cultivation of more outstanding talent.

Leading science and technology enterprises should leverage their strengths in market orientation, integrated innovation, and organizational resources. They should open a channel through which science and technology can boost corporate, industrial and economic development. They should be the initiators in gathering and integrating innovation resources and forming innovation bases featuring intensive cross-sector collaboration. They should engage in the research and development of key generic industrial technologies, the application and commercialization of scientific and technological advances, and resource-sharing services. They should promote the comprehensive allocation of projects, facilities, personnel and funds for key sectors, improve the basic capacity of our country's industries, and modernize its industrial chains.

Provincial governments should produce well-designed plans for sci-tech innovation based on their respective strengths and industrial needs. They should support eligible localities in building comprehensive national science centers or regional scientific and technological innovation centers, and help turn these centers into global hubs for scientific innovation in frontier fields, technological innovation in emerging industries, and sci-tech innovation in other sectors.

Third, we should advance the reform of scientific and technological systems and form basic institutions supporting all-round innovation. We should leverage the strengths of the socialist market economy to improve the system of concentrating national resources to accomplish major undertakings. As the organizer of major scientific and technological innovations, the state should support strategic science plans and programs that have good prospects even if they involve considerable risks and challenges, and take a long time to produce results.

We should reinforce systematic planning, organization and cross-sector integration. The strength of the government, the market, and society should be pooled to give us an edge in future development. We should better combine a well-functioning market with a competent government, assign to the market the decisive role in resource allocation, and guide the allocation of innovation resources through market demand, so as to create a powerful synergy for sci-tech innovation.

We should focus on reforming the system for evaluating research. Evaluation should be directed towards quality, performance and contribution as the core indicators, in order to fully and accurately reflect the originality of research results, the impact of their application, and their actual contribution to economic and social development.

In terms of research project evaluation, we should establish a system that is in line with the norms of research activities and differentiates exploratory research and task-oriented research, and a mechanism for evaluating projects on which a consensus is not yet achieved.

In terms of talent evaluation, we should discard the approach that overemphasizes research papers, academic titles, educational backgrounds, and awards, establish new standards, and expedite a new system that values innovation, ability and contribution as main indicators. We should support public research institutions in piloting more flexible remuneration systems. We should address the concerns of professionals engaged in basic, cutting-edge, and public welfare research and provide for their needs, so that they can concentrate on their research without worry.

In reforming science and technology management, we should not simply build on the existing systems and mechanisms; we also need to streamline them. We should be bolder in transforming the functions of management authorities in science and technology. According to their defined responsibilities for strategy, reform, planning and services, these authorities should improve their work practices, raise their capabilities, and reduce direct intervention in the allocation of funds and materials and in the approval of projects. They should strengthen planning and policy guidance, give more decision-making autonomy to research institutions, grant scientists more freedom to choose research pathways and use funds, and free research institutions and their staff from institutional red tape.

Heroes are not defined by their origins. Likewise, innovators must not be defined by their backgrounds. We should reform the approval, organization and management of major scientific and technological projects, and adopt open competition mechanisms for selecting the best candidates to undertake key research projects and multi-team research mechanisms for finding the best pathways and achieving optimal results.

We must identify real questions and form targeted research projects, make genuine efforts to answer these questions, and allow leading professionals in science and technology who possess the will, capacity, and determination to do solid work to take charge of projects. We should implement a project management system where chief technologists lead implementation, a project funding system that allows greater flexibility and discretion in the use of funds, and a commitment system to uphold research integrity and ethics. We should remove seniority and other barriers to ensure that all capable scientists and technologists have the opportunity to display their talent.

Fourth, we should build an open innovation ecosystem and participate in global science and technology governance. Science and technology respond to the call of the times and have a global impact; they belong to all of humanity. We must coordinate development and security, plan and promote innovation with a global vision, and take active measures to become an integral part of the global innovation network. We should focus on issues such as climate change and human health and boost joint research and development with researchers in other countries. We should design and initiate international Big Science plans and projects and establish globally-oriented scientific research funds.

While science and technology are instrumental in national development, they can also create risks. We should be able to foresee social risks, ethical challenges, and potential conflicts with existing rules brought by sci-tech developments, and we must improve relevant laws and regulations, ethical review provisions, and supervision frameworks accordingly. We should participate to the full in global science and technology governance, contribute Chinese wisdom, and shape a philosophy of technology for good purposes, so that science and technology better serve human wellbeing, and enable China's science and technology industry to contribute more to building a global community of shared future.

Fifth, we should foster innovation vitality in talented people from all fields, and build China into a global leader in terms of talent resources. A global science and technology power must be able to attract, retain, and make best use of competent professionals from across the world. In the final analysis, China must rely on capable innovative talent to realize greater strength and self-reliance in science and technology.

The cultivation of innovative talent is crucial to the long-term development of any country. Competition in today's world is essentially competition in talent and education. Therefore, we must strengthen our own education and training systems and nurture the spirit of science, innovation, and critical thinking. We should reinforce the training of young talent, strive to produce top-notch scientific and technological talent with global influence, keep and support innovative teams, and nurture more first-class scientists and technicians.

We must know that our education system is capable of producing masters of science and technology. We must foster a social climate of respecting science, knowledge, hard work, talent, and creativity, and inspire more young people to pursue science and innovation.

"A tall and luxuriant Chinese parasol tree attracts golden phoenixes." We should build science and innovation centers that gather outstanding talent from all over the world, and improve our policies concerning high-end and specialized talent coming to work, conduct research, and engage in exchanges in China.

Innovation in science and technology requires a sustained investment of time and energy. In 1961 the central authorities set a provision to ensure that researchers should not be distracted to do things not related to their research. Time is a prerequisite for innovation. We should establish a mechanism that enables scientists and technologists to devote most of their energy to research, development and innovation. No loss will occur if researchers attend fewer non-essential social events. We must free them from meaningless public relations activities, from unnecessary reviews and appraisals, and from excessive formalities and bureaucracy.

Expand and Strengthen the Digital Economy*

October 18, 2021

In recent years, innovation in technologies like the internet, big data, cloud computing, artificial intelligence and blockchain has been accelerating. It now permeates every field and the whole process of economic and social development. Countries are competing to formulate strategies and roll out incentive policies to develop the digital economy. Its unprecedented speed, coverage and influence have made it a vital force in reorganizing global factor resources, reshaping the global economic structure, and changing the landscape of global competition.

I have always attached importance to digital technology and the digital economy. When working in Fujian Province in the year 2000 I proposed building a Digital Fujian, and in 2003 during my tenure in Zhejiang Province, I again made a plan to build a Digital Zhejiang. Since the 18th CPC National Congress in 2012, I have emphasized on many occasions the importance of the digital economy. For example:

At the 36th group study session of the Political Bureau of the 18th CPC Central Committee in 2016, I emphasized the importance of expanding and strengthening our digital economy to open up new space for economic development.

At the 2016 G20 Summit in Hangzhou, I was the first to propose that we should develop the digital economy, which was widely welcomed by participating state leaders and entrepreneurs.

At the second group study session of the Political Bureau of the 19th CPC Central Committee in 2017, I said we must move faster to

* Main part of the speech at the 34th group study session of the Political Bureau of the 19th CPC Central Committee.

build a digital China, develop a data-driven digital economy, and integrate the digital economy with the real economy.

At the Central Conference on Economic Work in 2018, I emphasized the need to speed up the construction of the infrastructure for 5G, artificial intelligence, and the industrial internet.

In my congratulatory letter to the 2021 World Internet Conference Wuzhen Summit, I pointed out that for people of all countries to benefit from digitalization, we must stimulate the vitality of the digital economy, increase the efficiency of digital government, optimize the environment of the digital society, set up a digital cooperation model, and build a digital security shield.

Since the 18th CPC National Congress, the Central Committee has given high priority to developing the digital economy, making it a national strategy. The 18th CPC Central Committee decided at its Fifth Plenary Session in 2015 to implement the national big data strategy and the strategy of building China into a cyberpower, expand space for the cyber economy, integrate the development of the internet with economic and social progress, and support internet-based innovation.

The 19th CPC National Congress in 2017 proposed to further the integration of the internet, big data and artificial intelligence with the real economy, and build a digital China and a smart society. At its Fifth Plenary Session in 2020, the 19th CPC Central Committee emphasized once again the need to develop the digital economy, advance the digital industry and the digital transformation of traditional industries, fully integrate the digital economy with the real economy, and develop digital industry clusters with an international competitive edge.

We have unveiled the Outline for Implementing the National Cyber Development Strategy, and the Outline for the Digital Economy Development Strategy, promoting the digital economy at the national level.

Our digital economy has witnessed rapid growth and remarkable progress over the years. According to the data report from the 2021 Global Digital Economy Conference, China ranked second in the world in scale, a position it has maintained for several years. Digital technology and the digital economy have played an important role in the fight against Covid-19 and the resumption of normal work and life since the onset of the epidemic.

In the meantime, we must be aware that when compared with countries with stronger digital capacity, our digital economy is not competitive enough, despite its wide coverage and rapid growth. In addition, some unhealthy and unacceptable tendencies are emerging that require our attention. They must be resolutely addressed and reversed as they have violated laws and regulations, affected the sound development of our digital economy, and posed a threat to national economic and financial security.

All factors considered, developing the digital economy is of vital importance since it creates a strategic opportunity for a new revolution in science, technology and industry.

First, the sound growth of the digital economy helps to build a new development dynamic, which is designed mainly to inject momentum into growth and ensure a smooth economic flow. Digital technology and the digital economy can drive a rapid flow of resources and production factors and speed up the integration of various market entities, helping them rebuild organizational structures, realize development across different fields, break space-time limitations, and extend their industrial chains, which will boost domestic and international economic flows.

Second, the sound growth of the digital economy helps to build a modern economy. Data, a new type of production factor, exerts significant influence upon the transformation of traditional production models. Highly innovative, penetrable and extensive in coverage, the digital economy is not only a new growth driver, but also a pivot for transforming and upgrading traditional industries. It can become an important engine in building a modern economy.

Third, the sound growth of the digital economy gives China an edge in international competition. In this new era, digital technology and the digital economy are critical factors for the new revolution in science, technology and industry, and will be key to a new round of international competition. We must seize the opportunity and gain an edge in future development.

Looking forward, we should take into consideration both the domestic and international situation, and both development and security, with a view to achieving the overall goal of national rejuvenation against a backdrop of global change on a scale unseen in a century. We should fully exploit our advantages in massive data and the diverse scenarios where it is applicable, and further integrate digital technology with the real economy. We should empower traditional industries to transform and upgrade, foster new industries and business forms and models, and improve, expand, and strengthen our digital economy.

First, we will intensify efforts to make breakthroughs in core technologies in key fields. We should maximize our strengths in the socialist system, in the new framework of pooling nationwide effort and resources for major missions, and in the super big market. We will improve our R&D ability in basic digital technologies and achieve breakthroughs in core technologies. We must achieve a high level of independence and the capacity for self-improvement, and keep the development of the digital economy securely in our own hands.

Second, we will accelerate the construction of new infrastructure. We should make strategic plans and move faster to build a high-speed, ubiquitous and comprehensive digital information infrastructure that is smart and agile, green and low-carbon, and reliable and controllable, that integrates space with earth networks and cloud computing with communications net, and that focuses on the 5G network, the national system of integrated data centers, and the national industrial internet. This will help unclog the information arteries for economic and social development. We should go all out to scale up the industrialization and extensive application of the digital information technology. We will develop large software enterprises with international influence, support them in making breakthroughs in key software, help them expand and grow, and increase our capacity for technological innovation and supply capabilities in key software.

Third, we will integrate the digital economy with the real economy. We must follow the development trends of digitalization, networking and smart technology, and advance digital transformation of the manufacturing industry, service sector, and agriculture. We should transform traditional industries thoroughly with new internet technology, improve the total-factor productivity, and release the full potential of digital technology in amplifying and doubling economic growth. We should make further efforts to integrate the internet, big data, and artificial intelligence with industry, and develop single-product manufacturing champions and specialized manufacturers with new, unique and competitive products. This requires us to be practical and take a differentiated approach, rather than digitalize enterprises for the sake of digitalization.

Fourth, we will develop the digital industry in key fields. We must focus on strategic frontiers and leading technologies, and aim at major technological breakthroughs and development demands. We should increase the competitiveness of key links in industrial chains, improve the supply chain in major industries, and accelerate the upgrading of products and services. Attention should be given to key technologies such as integrated circuits, new display technology, communications devices, and intelligent hardware. We will reinforce our strengths and shore up weak points, develop a group of large enterprises with international competitiveness and leading enterprises capable of shaping their respective industry chains, and build independent and controllable industrial ecosystems. We need to boost cluster development and build world-class digital industry clusters.

Fifth, we will regulate the development of the digital economy. To this end we should put equal emphasis on both sound development and regulation, and make them mutually complementary. We must build a comprehensive, multilevel and all-dimensional supervisory system with improved market access and a mechanism for fair competition review and regulation in place. This will bring every step and every aspect of the operation under oversight, closing loopholes and improving efficiency in supervision. We must correct and regulate conduct and practices that undermine the people's interests and hinder fair competition, and protect against platform monopolies and runaway expansion of capital. We must investigate and punish monopolistic conduct and unfair competition in accordance with the law. We should protect the legitimate rights and interests of platform employees and consumers, and strengthen tax supervision and inspection.

Sixth, we will strengthen governance of the digital economy. We must improve laws, regulations, policies, and the institutional framework, and modernize the governance system and capacity for the digital economy. We should rationalize the division of responsibilities between the department in charge and the department for supervision, and ensure their smooth cooperation. We should improve supervisory technologies and methods and bring every step in innovation, production, operation and investment under supervision and governance. We should clearly define the major responsibilities and obligations of platform enterprises, and build an industry self-discipline mechanism. Scrutiny by the public and the media and through public opinion should be integrated to create synergy. We should improve the national security system, with a focus on building capacity and mechanisms for pre-warning, and prevention and control of safety risks in the digital economy, to ensure that core technologies, important industries, essential facilities, strategic resources, major science and technology projects, and leading enterprises are secure and controllable. We should double our efforts in theoretical research in the digital economy.

Seventh, we will actively participate in international cooperation in the digital economy. We must follow up on developments and take timely action while actively participating in negotiations on the digital economy in international organizations. We will carry out bilateral and multilateral cooperation in governance of the digital economy, maintain and improve multilateral governance mechanisms, offer our proposals in a timely manner, and make our voice heard.

The digital economy bears on the overall development of the

country. We must take into consideration our needs and possibilities in top-level design and in building the institutional framework. We must put more effort into research and assessment of the situation, and seize the initiative by grasping opportunities. Leading officials at all levels must improve their professional competence, thinking and capacity to develop the digital economy, and raise their security awareness so that they may help the digital economy better serve and integrate with the new development dynamic. We should also improve the digital literacy and skills of the general public and the nation as a whole, to lay a solid foundation for the development of our digital economy.

Key Issues in the New Development Stage[*]

December 8, 2021

In the new development stage, our country is experiencing a profound level of change in its domestic and external environment and faces many new matters of consequence. We should understand them fully. Here I want to emphasize the following:

First, we must understand our strategic goal of common prosperity and know how to make it happen.

"A country is truly prosperous only when its people are prosperous."[1] The creation and distribution of wealth is a critical issue faced by all countries. In some Western countries, growing social wealth is accompanied by polarization and a persistent wealth gap. In Latin America, the disparity in distribution is significant in some low-income countries.

Under socialism, our expectation is that the country will progressively unleash and develop the productive forces, create and accumulate social wealth, and at the same time prevent polarization and make more substantive progress in promoting well-rounded human development and common prosperity for all. We used to practice inflexible egalitarianism when the level of average income was low in our country. After we launched reform and opening up in 1978, some people and regions took the lead in achieving prosperity, and the income gap in the country grew quickly. Some people have amassed wealth by dubious means, and this can pose threats and challenges to healthy economic and social development.

Common prosperity is an essential requirement of socialism with Chinese characteristics. How can we achieve this goal? We are

---

* Part of the speech at the Central Conference on Economic Work.

charting a path forward. First, we should make the "cake" of social wealth bigger through the concerted efforts of all our people; then we should properly handle the relationship between growth and distribution by institutional means so as to share the cake fairly. This will take a long time, and we should create the conditions, improve the relevant institutions, and take steady steps towards this goal.

In promoting high-quality development we should prioritize employment, which is pivotal to people's wellbeing. Economic growth should play a bigger part in boosting employment and providing more and better employment opportunities. We should support the development of micro, small and medium-sized enterprises and their role as main job providers. We must draw lessons from some Western countries where the real economy has been sidelined by the virtual economy. We should continue to make the real economy stronger to create more high-quality jobs. We should invest more in human capital, raise the quality of education, and strengthen vocational education and skills training. This will help us to improve the quality of the workforce, adapt to the need for high-quality development, and prevent the risk of large-scale unemployment.

We should make greater use of the functions and roles of distribution. We should properly handle the relationship between efficiency and equity and put in place a basic institutional framework in which distribution, redistribution and third distribution coordinate with and complement each other. Distribution according to work should continue as the mainstay, and we should increase the share of work remuneration in primary distribution and improve distribution based on factors of production.

We should ensure the adjusting role of redistribution and make it more targeted by better leveraging taxation, social security, and transfer payments. We should bring into play the role of third distribution, and guide and support enterprises and social groups with both the will and the capacity to participate actively in public welfare and charity undertakings, but we will not allow charitable donations to be coerced by means of moral blackmail.

We should improve our system of policies and institutions on public services. In pursuing common prosperity, we must not resort to welfarism. In the past, some countries embraced populism, and pampered a large number of lazy people who were given something for nothing. Consequently, the fiscal burden became too heavy, and they were caught in the middle-income trap. Once welfare has gone up, there is no way to bring it back down again. Welfarism beyond the means of the state is unsustainable and will inevitably have severe economic and political consequences. We should respect the principle of doing what we can to the best of our ability, focus on improving public services, provide basic public services in a targeted manner in education, health care, elderly care, housing, and other fields that concern the people the most, and ensure subsistence for those in difficulty. We should not set expectations too high or make unrealistic commitments.

Second, we must understand the nature of capital and how it works.

Karl Marx and Frederick Engels did not envisage the possibility of a market economy under socialism. Thus they could not anticipate how socialist countries should treat capital. Though Vladimir Lenin and Joseph Stalin led socialist development in the Soviet Union under a highly centralized planned economy they did not encounter significant problems caused by capital.

Creating the socialist market economy has been one of our Party's great achievements. As we develop our socialist market economy, it is to be expected that various types of capital will become involved. Although capital in a socialist economy is inherently different in many respects from that in a capitalist economy, they both have a natural tendency to pursue profit. "It is wealth that binds the people of a country together, and it is the law that governs the wealth of a country."[2] We need to explore how to boost the positive contribution of capital in the socialist market economy while keeping its negative effects under control. Due to inexperience and a lack of regulation in recent years, disorderly capital expansion, cynical manipulation of the capital market, and the pursuit of exorbitant profits became apparent in some areas of our economy. This requires us to regulate capital, draw on its strengths, and manage its deficiencies. We must not allow financial magnates to act unscrupulously. Meanwhile, we should ensure that capital functions properly as a production factor. This is a major political and economic issue that must be addressed.

In our work, we should do a good job in the following:

We must set up "traffic lights" for capital flows. Traffic on the road needs to be controlled with traffic lights. Likewise, capital also needs to be regulated. No capital of any type can be allowed to run out of control.

We must prevent unchecked growth of capital and combat monopolies, exorbitant profits, sky-high prices, destructive speculation, and unfair competition.

We must reinforce effective regulation of capital in accordance with the law. The socialist market economy is law-based, and capital must operate in accordance with the law. Curbing the disorderly expansion of capital is not intended to deny its worth, but to ensure its orderly growth. To regulate capital, we should strictly enforce the relevant laws and regulations and improve those that are incomplete.

We must support the healthy growth of capital through regulation and guidance. We should uphold and improve the basic socialist economic system, and remain committed to consolidating and developing the public sector and to encouraging, supporting and guiding the non-public sector. We should promote healthy development in the non-public sector and of all those working in the sector.

Third, we must understand how to ensure the supply of primary products.

Guaranteeing the supply of primary products is a major strategic issue for a large country like ours. We should strengthen strategic planning and make timely adjustments when necessary to ensure that supplies are secure.

We should give priority to resource conservation. "Utilized with restraint, resources will be abundant; otherwise, they will be scarce."[3]

We should implement a comprehensive resource conservation strategy and promote conservation campaigns in all fields.

In manufacturing, we should promote efficient, economical use and recycling of resources, reduce energy and material consumption per unit of product, accelerate technological transformation, and raise productive efficiency.

In consumption, we should heighten public awareness of conservation and encourage simple, moderate, green and low-carbon ways of life. We should oppose waste, extravagance, and excessive consumption, continue the "Clear Your Plate" and other campaigns that aim to reduce food waste, and launch initiatives to make Party and government institutions more conservation-conscious, families and residential communities more environmentally conscious, and transport and commutes more eco-friendly.

We should increase our capacity in domestic production and supply of resources. We should invest more effort in exploring for resources, carry out a new round of strategic mineral prospecting, and better develop and conserve marine and mineral resources. We must hold to the principle of producing and supplying key energy resources at home, make use of the buttressing role of state-owned enterprises (SOEs), and speed up the development and application of advanced technologies for oil and gas exploitation. We should improve the national system for strategic reserves to ensure supply during critical periods. We should promote domestic waste sorting and recycling, increase the utilization of solid waste, and move faster to establish an overall waste recycling system.

We should secure our supply of resources from overseas. We should fully utilize domestic and international markets and resources in a mutually beneficial way. While guarding against investment risks, we should strengthen cooperation with energy producing countries and increase our holdings and access to high-quality resources overseas.

Here, I would like to draw your special attention to the issue of agricultural products supply and security. The latest national land survey shows that the area of arable land in our country is still falling. In some places, basic cropland is no longer used for growing grain crops, but for fruit trees or other high value-added crops. I have consistently emphasized that we in China must always have control over our own food supply and that we should mainly rely on domestic food supplies. We should continue to prioritize increasing overall agricultural production capacity, creating high-quality cropland, revitalizing our seed industry, and upgrading agricultural machinery and equipment. We must guarantee reasonable returns for grain farmers, ensure absolute security in staple foods and basic self-sufficiency in grains, and raise our production capacity and self-sufficiency rate in soybeans and other oil crops.

Fourth, we must understand how to prevent and defuse major risks.

Since the 1990s, our country has dealt effectively with the 1997 Asian financial crisis, the 2008 international financial crisis, and the Covid-19 pandemic. Currently, we see many potential risks in our economy and finance, but for the most part they are manageable.

We should have plans in place for worst-case scenarios. A 13th-century Chinese scholar said, "We must nip troubles in the bud and eliminate illnesses at their earliest stage."[4] We should give full play to Party leadership and other strengths of Chinese socialism, be quick and sharp in perceiving potential risks, identify problems early and correct them while they are nascent, and preempt major risks and crises.

Recently, we have defused the risks of shadow banking and those in internet finance. However, we need to note that new risks keep emerging. "Black swan" and "gray rhino" events occur from time to time. There are several important causes of these phenomena:

The first is a long-term cumulative effect. Our economy is still facing a complex situation which involves a shift in the growth rate, a painful structural adjustment, and a need to absorb the fallout of previous stimulus policies. Risks from earlier stages remain to be resolved.

The second is insufficient regulatory capacity and institutional deficiencies. There is serious negligence in supervision of corporate governance in financial institutions, and financial regulatory capabilities fall short of actual needs. The management of local government debt is slack. Some local governments raise funds in an illegal and clandestine manner, leading to rising debts.

The third is irrational borrowing. Some large enterprises have been impulsive and irrational in diversifying their business, relying too much on financial leverage. As a result, an excessive amount of industrial capital passes from the real economy into the financial sector. Some shareholders and *de facto* controllers run financial enterprises in ways that violate laws and regulations. These enterprises are controlled by insiders and manipulated by large shareholders, who engage in financial fraud and misappropriation of funds.

The fourth is corruption and collusion between officials and businesspeople. Some government officials and heads of financial institutions commit dereliction of duty or engage in corruption; they line their pockets with public funds and cause huge losses to the country.

The fifth is the changing economic cycle. A slowing growth rate has exposed various hidden risks. The possibility of systemic risks triggered by local risks is rising. The risk posed by insolvency is high.

As our next step, we should continue to properly handle risks in accordance with the principles of maintaining overall stability, ensuring coordination, applying differentiated measures, and defusing risks through targeted efforts.

We must improve the legal framework of the financial sector in accordance with laws and regulations, and establish a system for regularly updating the law.

Responsibilities should be clearly defined, and we should ensure that local Party committees and governments address the need to maintain social stability and mitigate or eliminate risks in the areas under their jurisdiction. We should urge financial regulatory departments, authorities in charge of specific sectors, and discipline inspection and supervision commissions to fulfill their respective responsibilities for dealing with risks. We should ensure that enterprises assume the principal responsibility for working out feasible plans to address their own risks.

We should strengthen our regulatory capacity, upgrade our regulation technology, strengthen areas of weakness, and build a competent contingent of financial regulatory officials.

We should ensure sufficient resources, and move faster to set up a financial stability fund, give play to the role of the deposit insurance system and the protection funds of industries in risk disposal. We will consider and formulate policies that facilitate mergers and acquisitions of financial institutions and support their efforts to deal with nonperforming assets.

Local governments should take action to put idle assets to use and eliminate related risks. Enterprise shareholders should be the first to bear risks and losses, to the full value of their equity if necessary.

All parties in the financial sector should cooperate extensively, and establish an integrated risk-response mechanism with adequate authorization and coordination, to improve the sector's capacity for dealing with risks through cross-market and cross-industry coordination.

We should pay special attention to the risks in some real estate developments. Local governments must shoulder their responsibilities, strengthen regulation, forestall systemic risks, and maintain healthy and steady development of the real estate market.

Fifth, we must understand how to achieve peak carbon dioxide emissions by 2030 and carbon neutrality by 2060.

The Party's central leadership gave careful consideration before deciding to pursue these goals as a key national strategy. It is our solemn commitment to the international community and an essential requirement for promoting high-quality development.

Yet some problems have become apparent recently. Some local authorities have attempted to fast track energy-intensive and high-emission projects ahead of the carbon peak; some have imposed uniform restrictions and launched impulsive or arbitrary carbon reduction actions; some have even resorted to power rationing. None of this conforms to the requirements of the central authorities.

Green and low-carbon development is a complex and long-term project involving the full-scale transition of economic and social development. Adjusting the energy mix and the industrial structure cannot be accomplished overnight or without consideration of our realities. If the phaseout of conventional energy is not accompanied by a substitution with safe and reliable new energy, it will have an impact on economic development and social stability. Reducing pollution and carbon emissions is integral to economic restructuring. We need to establish the new before getting rid of the old and make holistic plans.

At the ninth meeting of the Central Commission for Financial and Economic Affairs, I outlined our agenda for realizing peak carbon and carbon neutrality and highlighted the principles that we should follow – to coordinate efforts nationwide, prioritize conservation, give play to the role of both the government and the market, ensure smooth domestic and international supply, and prevent risks. The central authorities have issued guidelines for achieving peak carbon and carbon neutrality and approved an action plan for the former.

While we must be resolute in pursuing our carbon goals, we should also be aware that they cannot be realized overnight. Therefore, we must make steady progress, striving to reach these goals step by step.

We must base our policies and actions on our national conditions, recognizing the fact that coal has long been our primary source of energy. We must take this into consideration when pursuing our peak carbon goal. While promoting the clean and efficient use of coal, we should expedite the adaptation of coal-fired power plants to fluctuating demand, develop renewable energy, promote an optimal combination of coal and new energy, and increase our new energy accommodation capacity.

We must make every effort to achieve breakthroughs in green and low-carbon technologies and to promote and apply advanced technologies.

We should be more objective in the assessment of carbon control work, improve the system for dual control over the volume and intensity of energy use, create conditions for a subsequent transition to dual control over the volume and intensity of carbon emissions, and accelerate the formation of a mechanism providing incentives and disincentives in order to reduce pollutants and carbon emissions. All local authorities and relevant departments should take a holistic approach to their work on these controls and on the peak carbon and carbon neutrality goals, and avoid a simplistic tasking of every lower level with targeted quotas.

We must ensure the nation's energy supply, balance multiple goals, and increase energy supply via more channels. Large enterprises, and SOEs in particular, should take the lead in guaranteeing supply and maintaining stable prices. Serious incidents like extensive power cuts will not be accepted.

We should promote the energy revolution, push forward reform in energy use, supply, technology, and institutions, strengthen international cooperation, and build up our strength in energy.

Notes

[1] Zhong Hui: *My Humble Views* (*Chu Rao Lun*). Zhong Hui (225-264) was a general in the Three Kingdoms Period.

[2] Wang Anshi: "An Essay on Wall Inscriptions at the Vice Finance Minister's Office" (Du Zhi Fu Shi Ting Bi Ti Ming Ji). Wang Anshi (1021-1086) was a thinker, writer and statesman of the Northern Song Dynasty.

[3] Zhang Juzheng: "Memorial to the Throne on Current Affairs" (Lun Shi Zheng Shu). Zhang Juzheng (1525-1582) was a statesman of the Ming Dynasty.

[4] He Tan: *Xichou's Sayings* (*Xi Chou Chang Yan*). He Tan (dates unknown), also known as Xichou, was a scholar and official of the Southern Song Dynasty (1127-1279).

Guide and Regulate the Capital Market[*]

April 29, 2022

Capital is a key factor of production in the socialist market economy, and we should regulate and guide the use of capital within this context. This is an economic as well as a political issue of both practical and theoretical significance. It concerns the basic socialist economic system, the fundamental state policy of reform and opening up, high-quality development, common prosperity, national security, and social stability. Therefore, we must have a deeper understanding of all types of capital and their functions, ensure their healthy growth through regulation and guidance, and promote their constructive role as a key factor of production.

Throughout our Party's 100-year history, we have upheld the basic tenets of Marxism, increased our understanding of how capital functions, and explored guidelines and policies for regulating and guiding healthy capital growth in light of the actual conditions of our country and major tasks in different stages of development.

After the launch of reform and opening up at the Third Plenary Session of the 11th CPC Central Committee in 1978, we broke free from a restrictive mindset on ownership and came to realize that capital, as a major factor of production, can serve as a tool for the market to allocate resources and an effective means to grow the economy. We realized that a socialist country can use all types of capital to promote economic and social development. Step by step we established the basic socialist economic system and introduced the socialist market economy in which various forms of ownership develop together with public ownership playing the dominant role and multiple forms of

---

* Main points of the speech at the 38th group study session of the Political Bureau of the 19th CPC Central Committee.

distribution coexist, observing "to each according to their work" as the principal form. We remained committed to consolidating and developing the public sector, and at the same time to encouraging, supporting and guiding development of the non-public sector.

Since the 18th CPC National Congress in 2012, we have improved the basic socialist economic system, and established the two above-mentioned commitments as a fundamental strategy for upholding and developing socialism with Chinese characteristics in the new era, and as a major guideline for the Party and the country. We have launched comprehensive reform, highlighting the decisive role of the market in the allocation of resources and an effective role of the government in creating a more enabling market and legal environment for all types of capital to grow. We have redoubled our effort to control monopolies in order to prevent disorderly expansion of capital, forestall potential risks, and protect fair competition in the market. We have guarded against and defused financial risks, and checked the tendency of moving from real economy to virtual economy, with a focus on mitigating the risks of non-performing assets and asset bubbles. We have opened wider to the outside world, and are working to create a double development dynamic with the domestic economy as the mainstay and the domestic economy and international engagement providing mutual reinforcement, so as to build an open economy of higher standards. We have learned more about the nature and role of capital and the law of capital circulation, and developed a greater capacity to govern the operation of capital.

Over more than 40 years of reform and opening up, capital and other factors of production such as land, labor, technology and data have jointly contributed to the prosperity of the socialist market economy. We must recognize the positive role of all types of capital. At present, there are various forms of capital in our country, including state-owned capital, collective capital, private capital, foreign capital, and mixed capital. Capital is expanding in size and operating at a faster speed. Market players are diversifying and international capital is pouring into Chinese market.

We must uphold Party leadership and the socialist system, and keep to the correct political direction. We must take a problem-oriented approach, develop systems thinking, and take account of current realities to plan for the future. We must prevent unchecked growth of capital while encouraging investment, and adopt differentiated policy measures as appropriate. We must strike a balance between development and security, between efficiency and fairness, between vitality and order, and between domestic and international markets. We must boost the vigor of all types of capital, including non-public capital, and maximize the role of capital in promoting scientific and technological progress, growing the market economy, adding convenience to daily life, and increasing our participation in international competition. We must ensure that capital always serves the interests of the people and the country, and contributes to comprehensive socialist modernization and national rejuvenation.

We should strengthen theoretical research on capital in the new era. How to ensure its healthy growth through regulation and guidance has become a key topic of theoretical and practical importance in Marxist political economics. We should review both our successes and failures in handling capital since the founding of the PRC in 1949, and particularly since the launch of reform and opening up. We should probe deeper into theories on capital in the context of the socialist market economy, and guide practice with sound theories. In this way, we can facilitate an orderly growth of all types of capital, and leverage their role in boosting productive forces, creating wealth, and improving people's wellbeing.

We should understand all types of capital in our country and their role from a historical, developmental and dialectical perspective. In the socialist market economy, capital is an important means of gathering and allocating factors of production and boosting productive forces. Therefore, we must allow capital to play an active role in this regard. Yet we must be aware that capital is profit-driven in nature, and, if unregulated and unconstrained, will cause immeasurable damage to the economy and society. In this new development stage, we should practice the new development philosophy, foster a new development dynamic, and propel high-quality development. To this end, we must properly handle the relationships between various forms of capital, clearly define their respective nature and role, and ensure their healthy growth through regulation and guidance.

We should properly manage the operation of capital and distribution of gains. The socialist nature of our country determines that we must adopt multiple forms of distribution with "to each according to their work" as the principal form, and implement the principle of putting people first in social distribution. We should make economic development benefit more people and ensure fairness in primary distribution. While supporting capital growth and value addition in the process of social distribution, we should, more importantly, respect the underlying principle of "to each according to their work". Development is for the people and by the people, and its benefits should be shared by the people. In this way, we will remain committed to the path towards common prosperity.

We should continue to reform the capital market. We should further improve the fundamental institutions of domestic capital market, and better leverage its role to create greater space for the growth of all types of capital. We should improve the system of property rights protection, fully implement relevant policies and policy reviews to ensure fair competition, and remove market barriers, providing all types of capital with equal access to orderly competition and fair opportunities to participate. We should improve the institutions of the open economy, pursue high-standard opening up, and facilitate investment. With an enabling market environment, we will be able to attract more international capital to our country for investment and business growth. We should support and encourage domestic capital and enterprises to go global.

We should regulate and guide the growth of capital. We should set up "traffic lights" for capital flows by improving relevant laws, and developing a complete and cohesive framework of well-conceived rules and systems. To protect property rights, respect contracts, unify the market, and ensure equal exchange, fair competition and effective regulation, we should enact, amend, repeal or interpret relevant laws and regulations to address prominent problems. We should maintain strict controls on capital market access, improve relevant institutions, and make the negative list for market access more precise and appropriate. We should improve the rules for capital operations. We must strengthen regulation and law enforcement against monopolies and unfair competition, and punish abuses of a dominant market position and other illegal activities in accordance with the law. We should advocate a healthy culture of credibility and integrity, and encourage players in the capital market to practice the core socialist values, uphold business ethics, and fulfill their social responsibilities.

We should promote comprehensive and effective governance of capital operations. We should document successful experiences, identify market trends, and enable innovation. We should make our governance more targeted, rational and effective. We should devise a whole-process capital governance system that ensures ex ante guidance, in-process safeguards, and ex-post regulation. We should further institutional reforms, and exercise accurate and sound regulation in accordance with the law, in a fair manner, and at the source. We should fully enforce accountability, adopt new approaches and overcome weaknesses, and modernize our capital regulation capacity and system. Regarding the regulatory responsibilities that are not explicitly stipulated in laws, we should remain faithful to the principle that whoever exercises the power of approval or the administrative authority performs capital regulation. We should strengthen capital regulation by local governments, and ensure that their responsibilities are fulfilled to the letter. We should improve the collaboration mechanisms for industry governance and for comprehensive governance, and reinforce coordinated multi-agency regulation in the areas of industries, finance, foreign investment, competition and security. We should accurately identify the key areas and targets that may cause systemic risks, exercise capital governance with more foresight and agility, and identify and resolve risks as early as possible.

We should combat capital-related corruption. We must maintain a tough stance against corruption, strike hard at profit-driven abuses of power, and punish corruption behind disorderly expansion of capital and platform monopolies.

One of the Party's main economic tasks is to ensure the healthy growth of capital through regulation and guidance. Party committees and Party leadership groups at all levels must think and act in accordance with the decisions and plans of the Central Committee, perform their responsibilities, and improve their capabilities in capital governance. They must promote policies more widely, properly guide market expectations, and preempt systemic risk by all means.

Further Reform and Opening Up

Focus All Reform Efforts on Creating a New Development Dynamic[*]

September 1, 2020

We must move faster to create a double development dynamic with the domestic economy as the mainstay and the domestic economy and international engagement providing mutual reinforcement. This is a strategic decision made in the context of the stage, environment and conditions of China's development, and a systematic and in-depth reform of overall importance. We must continue to make full and good use of reform as a powerful instrument, and press ahead with resolve. The focus of our work is to uphold and improve the socialist system with Chinese characteristics, and to modernize China's system and capacity for governance. To this end, we will promote in-depth reform and high-standard opening up, which will provide stronger impetus for building the new development dynamic.

To create this dynamic, we have institutional strengths and a firm foundation based on reform. Since the Party's 18th National Congress in 2012, we have launched a series of major reform measures to implement the new development philosophy, promote high-quality development, and pursue greater opening up, and we have achieved a range of theoretical, institutional and practical outcomes. To make good use of these, we must redouble our efforts, quicken our pace, and tackle deeper-seated problems, so that further reform will deliver substantial results. In brief, we must focus all reform efforts on creating the new development dynamic.

But this will not come easily, as we currently face many new problems.

---

[*] Main points of the speech at the 15th meeting of the Central Commission for Further Reform.

Therefore, with the necessity of reform in mind, we must balance short-term response and medium- to long-term development. We need to formulate a sound strategy, and at the same time make the right moves in key areas of reform. We should accelerate reform programs that increase the efficiency of resource allocation, improve the quality and benefits of development, and mobilize all sectors of society. We must focus on key problems, integrate and coordinate various reform measures for greater efficiency, and remove bottlenecks in policy coordination for overall impact. We should integrate the pursuit of the new development dynamic with the strategy of coordinated regional development and the program of pilot free trade zones, so that regions with the right conditions can pioneer new models of development and become the new drivers of reform and opening up. We need to be forward-looking in our research on reform so as to identify the factors that change the nature of related problems. Always innovative and enterprising, we should follow the right direction and become more proactive and effective in tackling uncertainties. Accordingly, we must be well-prepared, leave more room for policy adjustment, and make our institutions more responsive.

Work Together to Boost Global Trade in Services[*]

September 4, 2020

China International Fair for Trade in Services (CIFTIS) is a large exhibition and trading platform dedicated to trade in services. This comprehensive, state-level event has a global reach and has been held six times since 2012. We hope that this year's CIFTIS, whose theme is "Global Services, Shared Prosperity", will present an opportunity and serve as a platform and a bridge for people from across the world to fully showcase new progress and breakthroughs in services trade, and share in new technologies and the benefits of human progress. We hope that through in-depth exchanges and closer cooperation, you delegates participating in the event will contribute your wisdom and energy to expanding cooperation on trade and investment in services and invigorating economic and social development.

Our world is going through change on a scale unseen in a century, and the Covid-19 pandemic is accelerating this process. There is a backlash against economic globalization; protectionism and unilateralism are on the rise; the world economy is stagnating; international trade and investment have slumped. Such are the unprecedented challenges and tests that humanity faces.

That said, let us not forget that a new revolution in science, technology and industry in recent years has spurred a boom in digital technologies, led to deeper industrial integration, and allowed the service economy to flourish. During this pandemic certain services have become widely used: telemedicine, e-learning, sharing platforms, cooperative office systems, and cross-border e-commerce, to name

---

* Part of the speech at the Global Trade in Services Summit of the 2020 China International Fair for Trade in Services.

just a few. They have played an important part in ensuring economic stability in all countries and promoting international cooperation against Covid-19. Going forward, open cooperation in the services sector is becoming an increasingly important driver of development.

Here, I would like to take this opportunity to share with you three proposals:

First, let us work together to foster an open and inclusive environment for cooperation.

A review of human history shows that the global economy thrives in openness and withers in seclusion. The services sector is unique as it is asset-light but heavy in soft factors of production. As such, it requires more than other sectors an open, transparent, inclusive and nondiscriminatory environment, to allow businesses to grow. It calls for the concerted efforts of all countries to reduce border and behind-the-border barriers constraining the flow of production factors, and promote cross-border connectivity. China will remain steadfast in opening up wider to the world. We will continue to work on a negative list system for managing cross-border trade in services. We will develop open platforms to pilot innovative development in services trade. We will further ease market access for the services sector and increase imports of quality services. To meet the actual need for growing trade in services, China will promote greater harmonization of rules for the services sector at multilateral and regional levels, and work for continued improvements in global economic governance and more inclusive global economic growth.

Second, let us work together to unleash the power of innovation in driving cooperation.

We need to adapt to the trend towards digital-driven, internet-based and smart growth, jointly eliminate the "digital divide", and advance the digitalization of trade in services. China will continue to build bases for exporting particular services and develop new business forms and models in services trade. China will work with other countries to strengthen macro policy coordination, accelerate international cooperation in the digital sector, step up intellectual property protection, and facilitate the vibrant growth of the digital economy and the sharing economy. Our efforts will generate renewed dynamism in the global economy.

Third, let us work together to promote mutually beneficial cooperation.

In this age of economic globalization, countries share a new level of economic interdependency and interlinked interests. To treat each other with sincerity and pursue shared benefits holds the key to state-to-state relations in today's world. Countries need to forge greater synergy in growing their trade in services, try to find new ways and identify more areas of cooperation, and look for the widest possible convergence of interests in development so as to steadily make the "pie" bigger. China will make full use of CIFTIS and other platforms, such as the China International Import Expo, to promote policy exchange and experience sharing, and foster diverse partnerships with foreign governments, international organizations, business associations, and enterprises. China supports the establishment of a global alliance for trade in services. We hope to see more tangible results from our practical cooperation, so that people in different countries will all benefit from growing trade in services.

To better leverage Beijing's role in spearheading the opening up of China's services sector, we will support the city in developing a national demonstration zone for greater openness in the services sector. It will enable Beijing to take bigger, bolder steps, and gain more experience that can be replicated and scaled up. We will also support Beijing in setting up a pilot free trade zone directed towards scientific and technological innovation, an open services sector, and the digital economy. It will serve as a platform for higher-standard opening up and coordinated development of the Beijing-Tianjin-Hebei Region, and create new and broader horizons for reform and opening up.

Raise Reform and Opening Up
to a Higher Level*

October 14 and November 12, 2020

I

The current situation calls for new responsibilities and new actions. The special economic zones (SEZs) must uphold socialism with Chinese characteristics, implement the Five-sphere Integrated Plan and the Four-pronged Comprehensive Strategy, apply the new development philosophy, promote high-quality growth, and foster the new development dynamic in the new development stage which China has entered. The SEZs must press ahead non-stop with reform and opening up at a higher level to achieve new progress, and must contribute more to delivering the Second Centenary Goal, that is, building China into a modern socialist country that is prosperous, strong, democratic, culturally advanced, harmonious and beautiful by the centenary of the People's Republic of China in 2049.

Looking to Shenzhen for further reform and opening up and innovative development, the Party Central Committee issued guidelines last August on supporting Shenzhen in building a demonstration pilot zone for socialism with Chinese characteristics, with a comprehensive plan to achieve the goal. Shenzhen must succeed in building this pilot zone, thereby exemplifying what a model city in a strong and modern socialist country will be like. It should strengthen its capacity to implement the new development philosophy, create a new dynamic for deeper reform and broader opening up on all fronts, contribute to

---

* Excerpts from two speeches made on October 14 and November 12, 2020.

development in the Guangdong-Hong Kong-Macao Greater Bay Area to enrich the practice of the One Country, Two Systems policy, and lead the country in achieving socialist modernization. All this is the historic mission assigned by the Party Central Committee to Shenzhen in the new era.

(from the speech at a grand gathering to celebrate the 40th anniversary of the establishment of the Shenzhen Special Economic Zone, October 14, 2020)

II

On the new journey forward, the role and mission of Pudong will be determined with reference to the overall plans for revitalizing the Chinese nation, and in the context of global change on a scale unseen in a century. It will also be weighed against the drive to create a double development dynamic with the domestic economy as the mainstay and the domestic economy and international engagement providing mutual reinforcement. We should accurately identify and wisely respond to changes, proactively seek opportunities, and seize the initiative in crises.

The CPC Central Committee is formulating Guidelines on Making Pudong New Area a Pioneering Zone in Socialist Modernization Through High-Standard Reform and Opening Up, and will assign the area new major tasks for reform and opening up. Pudong should seize this opportunity to achieve robust development. Following the guiding principles of the 19th CPC National Congress and the second, third, fourth and fifth plenary sessions of the 19th CPC Central Committee, Pudong should implement the new development philosophy and create the new development dynamic based on a sound understanding of the new development stage. Guided by the underlying principle of pursuing progress while ensuring stability, Pudong is expected to take on the most arduous and difficult tasks. You should strive to become a pacesetter for higher-level reform and opening up, a forerunner of comprehensive socialist modernization, and a model to exemplify our confidence in the path, theory, system and culture of socialism with Chinese characteristics, displaying more vividly China's philosophy, values, and development path to the world.

(from the speech at a grand gathering to celebrate the 30th anniversary of the development and opening up of Shanghai's Pudong New Area, November 12, 2020)

Greater Breakthroughs for Reform in the New Development Stage[*]

December 30, 2020

Since the Third Plenary Session of the 18th CPC Central Committee in 2013, the central leadership has shown unprecedented resolve and made unprecedented efforts. It has broken free from the fetters of old thinking and ideas, broken through the barriers of vested interests, and broken down institutional obstacles.

Responding proactively to the risks and challenges arising from a changing external environment, we have launched another wave of sweeping reform. We have made progress in fulfilling the tasks and goals set at the plenary session, established basic systems and frameworks in all areas, and systematically overhauled or restructured many of these areas in a drive for historic transformation. A solid foundation has been laid for a well-conceived, procedure-based and effective framework to ensure that all our systems are more mature and better-defined. Great successes of historic significance have been achieved in furthering reform. Pressing ahead with confidence, we will forge a strong synergy of reform and work even harder to ensure that reform achieves greater breakthroughs and successes in the new development stage.

Over the past years, we have put forward a series of new theories, adopted a range of major measures, and made a number of important breakthroughs. All of this is revolutionary, bringing about groundbreaking change of historic significance, in which reform and opening up advances all undertakings of the Party and the state.

---

[*] Main points of the speech at the 17th meeting of the Central Commission for Further Reform.

First, this represents a profound change in thinking and theory. We have continued to use new theory to guide innovations in reform, and summarized past experience to enrich and develop our theory. We have devised a number of groundbreaking, strategic and guiding concepts in terms of general goals, focus, priority tasks and reform measures, to provide an answer to a series of theoretical and practical questions, such as why overall and deeper reform is necessary in the new era, and how to further reform in an all-round way.

Second, it represents a profound change in organization. We have strengthened the Party's centralized, unified leadership over all-round reform, and driven it forward with a holistic view and systems thinking. From laying the groundwork in the initial stage, through building momentum on all fronts in the intermediate stage, to strengthening systems integration, coordination and efficiency at the present stage, we have done away with institutional barriers, obstructive mechanisms, and problems impeding policy innovation in various areas in a steady, forceful and orderly manner. With clear targets, strategic plans and effective measures, we have removed bottlenecks and achieved a historic change from local pilots to systemic, coordinated and deeper reform across the board.

Third, it represents a profound change in state and governance systems. We have always taken the improvement of systems as the general goal of further reform. We must continue to improve our system framework, consolidate our fundamental systems, improve our basic systems, and upgrade important systems. These endeavors have played an important role in the fight against Covid-19, the completion of a moderately prosperous society in all respects, the final victory over absolute poverty, the implementation of the 13th Five-year Plan, and the economic work of the whole year. Institutional reform is obviously essential to these successes. Reviewing the scale and depth of our reforms, and the progress on all undertakings of the Party and the state, we can say that these achievements have been in keeping with the times and have satisfied our practical needs.

Fourth, it represents a profound change involving the people's extensive participation. We promote reform with the people at the center. We uphold Party leadership while respecting the people's creativity. As if we were crossing a river by feeling for stones, we explore each step forward while improving top-level design; we launch pilot programs while advancing reform on all fronts. Focusing on the most pressing and immediate problems that concern the people the most, we have implemented reforms in key fields, giving our people a stronger sense of gain, fulfillment and security. Championing reform and innovation, our society is progressing with vitality.

However, reform is still confronted by many complex conflicts and problems. Although we have surmounted many formidable obstacles, still there are tough ones to be overcome.

We should combine our efforts to continue reform with our work towards achieving the overall goals of the Party and the state, and employ innovative and pioneering reforms in such strategic tasks as implementing the new development philosophy, creating the double development dynamic, and promoting high-quality development.

We should combine our efforts to further reform with our work on institutional integration. We should focus on fundamental and leading reform measures, strengthen alignment and coherence among institutional innovations, and increase the comprehensive efficacy of reform.

We should integrate reform with preventing and defusing major risks. We should conduct in-depth analysis and assessment of situations and tasks, and conduct reform measures at the right moment, in a suitable form, and at an appropriate pace, in a bid to achieve solid and sustainable results.

We should combine our efforts to stimulate innovation with our drive to pool our strengths, boost incentive mechanisms, and fully mobilize all sectors to use their initiative and creativity, promote reform in all fields, and open up new vistas in the new development stage.

Let China's Openness Benefit the World[*]

November 4, 2021

Your Excellencies Heads of State and Government,
Your Excellencies Heads of International Organizations,
Your Excellencies Heads of Delegations,
Distinguished guests,
Ladies and gentlemen,
Friends,

Good evening.

As the Fourth China International Import Expo (CIIE) opens today, it gives me great pleasure to join you online in this virtual meeting. At the outset, on behalf of the Chinese government and people and also in my own name, I would like to extend a warm welcome to our distinguished guests, and cordial greetings and best wishes to our friends old and new.

China always honors its words with actions. The measures for further opening up I announced at the Third CIIE have largely been implemented. The negative list for cross-border trade in services at the Hainan Free Trade Port has been released, steady progress is being made in reform and innovation in pilot free trade zones, foreign investment access continues to expand, the business environment continues to improve, negotiations on the China-EU Comprehensive Agreement on Investment have been concluded, and China is among the first to have completed domestic ratification of the Regional Comprehensive Economic Partnership. China has overcome the impact of Covid-19 to achieve exceptional growth in foreign trade. As the only major

---

[*] Keynote speech at the opening ceremony of the Fourth China International Import Expo.

270

economy to register positive growth of trade in goods last year, China has made an important contribution to keeping global industrial and supply chains stable and boosting world economic recovery.

Ladies and gentlemen,

Friends,

As we speak, the world is experiencing the combined impact of major changes and a pandemic, both on a scale unseen in a century. Unilateralism and protectionism are on the rise, and economic globalization is facing headwinds. Studies show a steady decline of the World Openness Index over the past decade and a weakening of global support for opening up, which are causes for great concern. For a boat to sail upstream, it must forge ahead; otherwise the current will drive it backward. We must have an accurate perspective of the trends in economic globalization, and support countries around the world in opening up wider while rejecting unilateralism and protectionism. This is vital if we are to take humanity to a better future.

Opening up is the hallmark of contemporary China. This year marks the 20th anniversary of China's accession to the World Trade Organization (WTO). Over the last two decades, China has fully delivered on its accession commitments. Its overall tariff rate has been cut from 15.3 percent to 7.4 percent, lower than the 9.8 percent accession commitment. The central government has reviewed and revised over 2,300 laws and regulations, and local governments over 190,000 items, which has helped to unleash market and social vitality.

Since the start of Covid-19, China has provided to the international community some 350 billion masks, over 4 billion protective suits, over 6 billion testing kits, and over 1.6 billion doses of vaccine. China has actively promoted international cooperation against the pandemic, and supported waiving intellectual property rights on vaccines for developing countries. These are the concrete actions China has taken to honor our commitments and fulfill our responsibilities.

Over the past 20 years, China's economy has grown from the 6th to the 2nd largest in the world, trade in goods from 6th to 1st, and trade in services from 11th to 2nd. China has led developing countries in the use of foreign investment, and its outbound direct investment has risen from 26th to 1st. The past 20 years have seen a China that is expanding reform and pursuing all-round opening up, a China that is seizing opportunities and rising to challenges, and a China that is stepping up to its responsibilities and benefiting the whole world.

Since joining the WTO, China has continued to open wider to the world, thus generating a new wave of domestic development while injecting fresh impetus into the global economy.

China's development and progress since its WTO accession 20 years ago is the result of much hard work and great tenacity on the part of the Chinese people under the robust leadership of the CPC. It is also the result of China's proactive steps to strengthen international cooperation and pursue win-win cooperation.

On this occasion, I wish to express my heartfelt thanks to all Chinese and foreign friends from different social sectors for taking part in and witnessing this historic process and for supporting China's opening up and development.

Ladies and gentlemen,

Friends,

An ancient Chinese once observed: "One can tell the inside of a thing by observing its outside and see future developments by reviewing the past."[1] For any country or nation to thrive, it must follow the logic of history and develop in line with the trend of the times. We in China will not lose our resolve to open wider at a high standard; we will not lose our determination to share development opportunities with the rest of the world; we will not lose our commitment to economic globalization that is more open, inclusive, balanced and beneficial to all.

First, China will safeguard true multilateralism.

The multilateral trading system with the WTO at its core is the cornerstone of international trade. Right now, the multilateral trading system is under threat. China supports WTO reform in the right direction. We support the inclusive development of the multilateral trading system, as well as the legitimate rights and interests of the developing members. China will take an active and open attitude in negotiations on issues such as the digital economy, trade and the environment, industrial subsidies, and state-owned enterprises, and we will uphold the position of the multilateral trading system as the main channel for international rule-setting and safeguard the stability of global industrial and supply chains.

Second, China will share market opportunities with the rest of the world.

China has a population of over 1.4 billion and a middle-income group of more than 400 million people. Our annual imports of goods and services are valued at around US$2.5 trillion. All this offers an enormous market. Going forward, China will lay more emphasis on expanding imports, and pursue balanced development of trade.

China will open more demonstration zones for promotion of imports and innovation in trade, optimize the catalogue of retail imports via cross-border e-commerce, encourage the on-site processing of imported goods from trading between border residents, and increase imports from neighboring countries. China will better integrate its domestic and foreign trade, develop some of its major cities into international consumption hubs, promote Silk Road e-commerce, establish modern logistics systems, and build additional capacity in cross-border logistics.

Third, China will promote high-standard opening up.

It will further reduce the negative list for foreign investment, and expand the opening of telecommunications, health care and other services in an orderly fashion. We will revise and enlarge the encouraged industry catalogue to guide more foreign investment towards sectors such as advanced manufacturing, modern services, high and new technology, energy conservation, and environmental protection, and towards the central, western and northeastern regions.

China will conduct stress tests for high-standard opening up in pilot free trade zones and the Hainan Free Trade Port, and will release a negative list for cross-border trade in services in the pilot free trade zones. China will engage in extensive international cooperation on green and low-carbon development and the digital economy, and work continuously for its accession to the Comprehensive and Progressive

Agreement for Trans-Pacific Partnership and the Digital Economy Partnership Agreement.

Fourth, China will uphold the common interests of the world.

It will take an active part in cooperation within the United Nations, the WTO, the G20, APEC, the Shanghai Cooperation Organization and other institutions, and encourage wider discussions on such issues as trade and investment, the digital economy, and green and low-carbon development. China will support fair global distribution of vaccines and other key medical supplies, and unimpeded trade in these public goods.

China will promote high-quality Belt and Road cooperation to provide development opportunities and deliver real benefits to more countries and people. China will actively join in global efforts to tackle climate change and safeguard food and energy security, and provide more assistance to fellow developing countries within the framework of South-South cooperation.

Ladies and gentlemen,

Friends,

As a Qing-dynasty scholar said, "The going may be tough when one walks alone, but it gets easier when people walk together."[2] As the pandemic continues to wreak havoc and the global economy faces a rocky recovery, it is all the more important that the world joins together to pull us through this difficult time. China stands ready to work with all countries to build an open world economy, so that the spring breeze of openness will bring warmth to all parts of the world.

Thank you.

Notes

[1] *Lie Zi*. This is a Taoist classic attributed to Lie Yukou. Lie Yukou (dates unknown), also known as Lie Zi, was a Taoist thinker and writer in the Warring States Period (475-221 BC).

[2] Wei Yuan: *Essays by Wei Yuan* (*Mo Gu*). Wei Yuan (1794-1857) was a thinker and writer of the Qing Dynasty.

Whole-Process People's Democracy

Heighten the Sense of National Identity and Improve the Party's Work on Ethnic Affairs in the New Era*

August 27, 2021

It is imperative to accurately understand and fully implement our Party's guidelines on ethnic affairs, and strengthen and improve this work in the new era, with the goal of reinforcing the sense of the Chinese nation as one community. We need to take a Chinese approach to ethnic issues, build a cultural home shared by the Chinese nation, enhance interactions, exchanges and integration among all ethnic groups, accelerate modernization in areas with large ethnic minority populations, strengthen law-based governance of ethnic affairs, and prevent and resolve major risks and hidden threats in ethnic affairs. We should improve the quality of our ethnic work in the new era, and mobilize the whole Party and all the people to work together for the Second Centenary Goal of building China into a great modern socialist country in all respects.

The history of our Party shows that our greatest achievement in ethnic work is that we have adopted a Chinese approach to ethnic issues. Since the policy of reform and opening up was introduced in 1978, particularly since the 18th CPC National Congress in 2012, the Party has emphasized that the Chinese nation is one family and one single community and that we should heighten this shared identity. We have consistently implemented the Party's theories and policies concerning ethnic groups while adapting to the changing times. Thus, we have gained valuable experience in properly understanding and

---

* Main points of the speech at the Central Conference on Ethnic Affairs.

handling ethnic issues. The Party has established a set of important principles on strengthening and improving ethnic work, which can be summarized as follows:

First, we must make national rejuvenation our principal goal, understand the historic significance of ethnic work in the new era from the strategic perspective of national rejuvenation, and take a holistic approach to planning and advancing it to serve the purpose.

Second, we must make it a major task for the new era to motivate all ethnic groups to build China into a modern socialist country in all respects, and ensure all ethnic groups strive in unity to achieve shared prosperity and common development.

Third, with a focus on heightening the sense of national identity, we must cultivate in all ethnic groups a growing sense of identity with the home country, the Chinese nation, the Chinese culture, the Communist Party of China, and Chinese socialism, and continue to build the Chinese nation into a strong community.

Fourth, we must develop a good understanding of the history of our nation and strengthen the sense of identity with and pride in the Chinese nation.

Fifth, we must uphold the equality of all ethnic groups, and see to it that they are the masters of the country and participate in the management of state affairs, and that their legitimate rights and interests are protected.

Sixth, we must uphold the unity of the Chinese nation and ensure all ethnic groups remain closely united like the seeds of a pomegranate.

Seventh, we must uphold and improve the system of regional ethnic autonomy, ensure the effective implementation of the Central Committee's policies and decisions, and of state laws and regulations, and support ethnic groups in their economic development and all-round improvement towards common prosperity.

Eighth, we must build a cultural home shared by the Chinese nation, creating a strong bond among all ethnic groups and inspiring them to move forward in unity and interdependence.

Ninth, we must promote interactions, exchanges and integration among all ethnic groups, and reinforce their affinity and unity in terms of ideals, convictions, mindset and culture, so that they will support each other like brothers and sisters.

Tenth, we must manage ethnic affairs in accordance with the law and actively modernize our system and capacity for handling ethnic affairs.

Eleventh, we must resolutely safeguard our national sovereignty, security, and development interests, and encourage, through education and guidance, all ethnic groups to carry forward the patriotic tradition and consciously safeguard the unity of the country, national security and social stability.

Twelfth, we must uphold the Party's leadership over work related to ethnic affairs, and increase our ability and performance in handling ethnic affairs.

These important ideas come from our Party's theoretical and practical work with ethnic communities, and constitute a set of fundamental principles governing ethnic work in the new era. The whole Party must understand them thoroughly and implement them in full and to the letter.

In the new era the Party's top priority in managing ethnic affairs is to reinforce our sense of national identity. This is to help people of all ethnic groups develop an awareness of the Chinese nation as one community of shared future, in which everyone shares the rough times and the smooth together.

Having a stronger sense of national identity is essential to defending the fundamental interests of all ethnic groups. Only with this sense rooted in our mind can we build a solid cultural Great Wall for safeguarding national unity and ethnic solidarity, pool efforts of all ethnic groups to defend national security and maintain social stability, and effectively combat infiltration of extremist and separatist ideas and subversion. This is the only way for people to fulfill their expectation for a better life, and to realize, protect and develop the fundamental interests of all ethnic groups.

This sense of national identity is essential to realizing national

rejuvenation. Only with this sense rooted in our mind can we effectively address any risks and challenges that may arise in ethnic affairs
on our journey towards national rejuvenation, and guarantee the long-
term prosperity and stability of the Party and the country.

This sense of national identity is essential to consolidating and
developing socialist ethnic relations based on equality, solidarity,
mutual aid, and harmony. Only with this sense rooted in our mind
can people of all ethnic groups develop a strong sense of belonging
to the Chinese nation. Only then can we lay a solid foundation for
closer ethnic relations, and make the Chinese nation a more cohesive
community of shared future.

This sense of national identity is essential to making new advances
in the Party's work related to ethnic affairs. We should adapt to the
changing times and improve our ethnic work by balancing commonality and diversity and by accommodating ethnic and regional factors,
with a view to increasing commonality. Only by so doing can we
manage ethnic affairs properly and efficiently and deliver concrete
results.

To manage ethnic affairs innovatively, we must continue to apply
measures that have been proved to be sound and adjust those which
are outdated, to better protect the legitimate rights and interests of all
ethnic groups.

We need to properly understand the relationship between
commonality and diversity that exist among ethnic people. One of
the important principles in managing ethnic affairs is to promote
commonalities on the one hand, and accommodate differences on the
other.

We need to properly understand the relationship between the
sense of national identity and that of ethnic identity. It is necessary
to guide people of all ethnic groups to always put the interests of
the Chinese nation first. Ethnic identity should be subordinate and
subscribe to the sense of national identity. However, while ensuring
the overall interests of the Chinese nation, we must ensure the specific interests of each ethnic group. Both Han chauvinism and regional

ethnic chauvinism are detrimental to the building of the Chinese nation as one community.

We need to properly understand the relationship between Chinese culture and cultures of individual ethnic groups. The fine cultures of the latter constitute an integral part of the former. Chinese culture is like the trunk of a tree, while individual ethnic cultures are branches and leaves; only when the roots are deep and the trunk is strong can the branches and leaves grow well.

We need to properly understand the relationship between material needs and cultural life. Our reform and development should serve the goals of reinforcing the sense of national identity, safeguarding unity, opposing division, improving the wellbeing of the people, and gathering extensive support so as to make our nation a strong community.

Reinforcing our sense of national identity is the fundamental principle for our work concerning ethnic affairs in the new era, and the focus of all activities in this regard.

We should build a cultural home shared by the whole Chinese nation. While studying the history of the CPC, the PRC, reform and opening up, and the development of socialism, we need to work on two specific fronts. One, we must sum up our Party's century-long experience in ethnic affairs, and further study the important ideas on strengthening and improving this work. Two, we must strengthen education on modern civilization by pressing forward with initiatives to improve social conduct and ethical standards, and foster a new generation well tuned to the new era. We will guide people of all ethnic groups to upgrade their vision and ideas, and modernize their cultural pursuits and lifestyle.

We should popularize the standard spoken and written Chinese language, while at the same time protecting the spoken and written languages of all ethnic groups as well as their rights to study and use their own languages.

We will work to lead all ethnic groups towards socialist modernization.

We need to improve differentiated policies to support regional development and promote further reform and opening up in ethnic minority areas, so that they will build greater capacity for self-development. Based on such factors as their natural resources, development conditions, and comparative strengths, ethnic minority areas need to find the best sector to start the reform and the right point for concerted effort. From there they should apply themselves to understanding and taking advantage of the new development stage, implementing the new development philosophy, integrating into the new development dynamic, achieving quality development, and promoting common prosperity.

We need to increase support for infrastructure construction and industrial restructuring in ethnic minority areas, optimize overall plans for social and economic development and eco-environmental progress there, and ensure that the people of all ethnic groups have a greater sense of gain, fulfillment and security.

We need to help all ethnic minority areas to effectively consolidate the results of poverty alleviation in tandem with rural revitalization, to achieve more efficient and higher-quality development of agriculture and animal husbandry, to build the countryside into a pleasant place to live and work, and to provide farmers and herdsmen with a prosperous and happy life.

We need to improve the policies for developing and opening up border regions, and advance the campaigns aimed at ensuring their stability, reviving their economy, and bringing prosperity to their inhabitants.

We should promote interactions, exchanges and integration among all ethnic groups. It is essential that we give full consideration to the specific conditions of different ethnic groups and regions, coordinate urban and rural construction planning and allocation of public service resources, improve relevant policies and measures, foster a favorable social atmosphere, and gradually realize an all-round integration of all ethnic groups in terms of space, culture, economy, society and ethos. We should initiate innovative and meaningful activities in multiple forms to promote unity and progress for all ethnic groups. We should put in place a mechanism for regular education on strengthening the sense of national identity, incorporate it into the education of officials, Party members and all citizens, and make it a society-wide education and communication program.

We will modernize our system and capacity for governing ethnic affairs. We should create and implement differentiated policies to address specific problems or concerns in specific regions in light of the local conditions and needs of specific ethnic groups and based on the principle of fairness and justice. These policies should be targeted and should respect regional differences. We must protect the lawful rights and interests of all ethnic groups, properly handle cases or incidents involving ethnic factors, combat all kinds of criminal act in accordance with the law, and ensure equality of all before the law.

We must resolutely protect against major risks and hidden threats in ethnic affairs. We must defend our ideological positions, actively and prudently handle political issues involving ethnic factors, and constantly work to eliminate harmful influences calling for ethnic separatism and inciting religious extremism. We should strengthen international cooperation against terrorism, and effectively conduct the anti-terrorism work in cooperation with key countries and regions, international organizations, and ethnic minority Chinese overseas.

Stronger and better overall leadership by the Party is the fundamental political guarantee of success in work related to ethnic affairs in the new era. Party committees at all levels should strengthen their commitment to the Four Consciousnesses, the Four-sphere Confidence, and the Two Upholds. They should constantly strengthen their political acumen, understanding and capacity to deliver, always keep in mind the fundamental interests of the country, and conscientiously fulfill their principal responsibilities. We should ensure the leadership of the Party in handling all matters concerning ethnic affairs. A mechanism for the Party's ethnic work in the new era will be put in place in which the government manages ethnic affairs under the leadership of the Party committee in accordance with the law, with the united front department of the Party playing a coordinative role, the ethnic affairs department of the government taking up the responsibility for ethnic affairs with due diligence, all other Party and government departments acting in concert, and the whole society being involved.

We should strengthen the primary-level offices for ethnic affairs and their staffing to ensure that they function properly and ethnic affairs are effectively handled. We will build a team of competent public servants in ethnic minority areas in accordance with the qualification requirements for public servants in the new era, and ensure that the management of ethnic affairs at all levels is in the hands of those who unswervingly uphold the centralized, unified leadership of the Party, take a firm stance on major issues of principle, act decisively to reinforce the sense of national identity, and show genuine compassion and care for all ethnic groups. We must ensure that the leadership at all levels is in the hands of officials who are loyal, honest and responsible. It is of critical importance that attention and care are given to public servants working on the front line of disadvantaged regions. We must attract more competent personnel into this work. We should pay special attention to the training and selection of ethnic minority people, trust them fully and assign important posts to those outstanding ones with a firm political stance and the courage to shoulder responsibilities.

We need to strengthen the government at the primary level in ethnic minority areas, so that the Party's theories and policies concerning ethnic groups are correctly understood and fully implemented at the grassroots.

Uphold and Improve the People's Congress System*

October 13, 2021

The people's congress system operates under the leadership of the CPC and in conformity with the basic tenets of Marxist theory of the state. It is designed to support the state system of people's democratic dictatorship and effectively ensures that China advances along the path of socialism.

Under this system, all power of the state belongs to the people to guarantee their status as masters of the country. The system also ensures the Party's leadership status, the people's principal position, and law-based governance, thereby bringing an end to the cycle of rise and fall characteristic of the imperial dynasties in Chinese history.

Under this system, major political relationships that are essential to the nation's future are properly managed, all social undertakings advance under the effective and unified organization of the state, national unity and ethnic solidarity remain strong, and vigor, stability and order prevail in the country's political life.

Since the 18th CPC National Congress in 2012, the Central Committee has implemented a national rejuvenation strategy against a backdrop of global change on a scale unseen in a century. Taking into account the strategic requirements to uphold and improve Party leadership and consolidate the system of socialism with Chinese characteristics, it has continued to break new ground in the theory and practice of the people's congress system and proposed a new vision, new thinking, and new requirements, which are focused on the following:

First, we must uphold CPC leadership.

* Part of the speech at the Central Conference on the Work of People's Congresses.

We must uphold the core role of the Party in exercising overall leadership and coordinating the efforts of all sides, uphold the authority of the Party Central Committee and its centralized, unified leadership, and ensure that the Party's theories, guidelines, principles, policies, decisions and plans are fully and effectively implemented in the work of the state. We should provide support to agencies of state power and ensure that they carry out their work in accordance with the Constitution and the law, and in an active, independent, and coordinated manner. We must strengthen and improve Party leadership, turn the Party's views into the will of the state through legal procedures, ensure that candidates recommended by Party organizations will become leaders of agencies of state power, exercise Party leadership over the country and society through agencies of state power, and maintain the authority of both the Party and the state and the solidarity within the Party and across the country.

Second, we must provide institutional safeguards to ensure that the people run the country.

We must remain committed to a people-centered approach, uphold the principle that all power of the state belongs to the people, and support and ensure the people's exercise of state power through people's congresses. We should improve democracy, create more forms of democracy, expand channels for democracy, and ensure the people's equal right to participation in governance and in development, so as to promote a whole-process people's democracy that is broader, fuller, and more robust.

Third, we must ensure that every dimension of governance is law-based.

We must follow a path and develop a system of socialist rule of law with Chinese characteristics and build a socialist country under the rule of law. We should carry forward the spirit of socialist rule of law, advance all undertakings and initiatives of the country in accordance with the Constitution and the law, safeguard social equity and justice, respect and protect human rights, and bring all the work of the country under the rule of law.

Fourth, we must uphold democratic centralism.

We must ensure that the people exercise state power in a unified manner through people's congresses, that people's congresses at all levels are formed through democratic elections, and that they are accountable to the people and subject to their oversight. Administrative, supervisory, adjudicatory, and prosecuting offices at all levels must be created by people's congresses, and be accountable to them and subject to their oversight. There must be an appropriate division of work as well as mutual coordination between decision-making, executive, and oversight powers. State agencies must exercise their powers and perform their duties within the scope of their statutory authority and procedures. Local authorities must demonstrate their initiative and enthusiasm under the unified leadership of the Party Central Committee, and all undertakings must advance under the unified and effective organization of the state.

Fifth, we must keep to the path of socialist political development with Chinese characteristics.

It is essential that we uphold the unity of Party leadership, the people's status as masters of the country, and law-based governance of the country. Of these, Party leadership is of the paramount importance. The system of people's congresses is a fundamental political system established to guarantee the implementation of these principles. It enables the Party to lead the people to govern the country effectively and in accordance with the law. We can draw on the political achievements of other societies, but we should never copy any Western political system.

Sixth, we must modernize our system and capacity for governance.

The people's congress system is an important component of the system of socialism with Chinese characteristics and of China's system of governance. We must uphold and improve the institutional framework under which the people run the country. We should continue to improve the institutions, standards, and procedures of socialist democracy and translate our institutional strengths into effective governance.

The world today is undergoing change on a scale unseen in a century. Competition in terms of systems is an important aspect of competition in composite national strength, and a well-founded system enables a country to seize the strategic initiative. History and our experience have shown that a country cannot remain stable and strong without a strong system. At its 18th and 19th national congresses, the Party created overall plans for strengthening the system of people's congresses and for improving the work of people's congresses. On our new journey towards a modern socialist country in all respects, we must firmly uphold the people's congress system while improving it in pace with the times, so as to strengthen and improve the work of people's congresses in the new era.

First, we should ensure the full implementation of the Constitution and safeguard its authority and sanctity.

Ancient Chinese believed that "law is the scale of a state and the ethical benchmark for a society."[1] As China's fundamental law, the Constitution embodies the concentrated will of the Party and the people, and it has supreme legal status, supreme legal authority, and supreme legal effect. I have emphasized on many occasions that to uphold the authority of the Constitution is to uphold the authority of the common will of the Party and the people, to safeguard the inviolability of the Constitution is to safeguard the inviolability of the common will of the Party and the people, and to secure the implementation of the Constitution is to secure the fundamental interests of the people. All the people of China and all state agencies, armed forces, political parties, social organizations, enterprises, and public institutions must take the Constitution as their fundamental code of conduct, treat the Constitution as sacrosanct, and ensure its implementation. No organization or individual has the right to act beyond the Constitution and the law. Any act in violation of the Constitution and the law must be investigated and rectified.

To ensure law-based governance of the country, we must first ensure governance based on the Constitution; to ensure law-based exercise of state power, we must first ensure exercise of state power based on the Constitution. To ensure Constitution-based national governance and exercise of state power, we must remain committed to upholding the leadership position of the CPC, upholding the people's democratic dictatorship as our state system, and upholding the people's congress system as our system of state power, all of which are enshrined in our Constitution.

Full implementation of the Constitution is the primary task in building our socialist country under the rule of law, and it is also essential for upholding and improving the people's congress system. We must take the Constitution as our fundamental code of conduct and build a sound, effective and complete institutional framework to ensure the implementation of the Constitution. We must reinforce constitutional oversight, promote the spirit of the Constitution, and safeguard the authority and sanctity of the Constitution.

Our Party leads the people in enacting and enforcing the Constitution and the law, and it must act within the scope of the Constitution and the law. People's congresses, governments, supervision commissions, courts, and procuratorates at all levels should work in strict accordance with the Constitution and the law and perform their duties in a proactive, independent and coordinated manner.

The National People's Congress (NPC) and its Standing Committee should improve the legal system pertaining to the Constitution and ensure that the systems, principles and rules established by the Constitution are fully implemented. They should strengthen oversight and inspection of the implementation of the Constitution and the law, improve constitutionality review, and the recording and review of rules, regulations, and other normative documents, and resolutely correct constitutional and legal violations. They should implement procedures and mechanisms for constitutional interpretation and actively attend to concerns about constitutional issues.

The NPC and its Standing Committee should improve the legal system under which the central government exercises overall jurisdiction over the special administrative regions in accordance with the Constitution and the regions' basic laws, refine the regions' systems and mechanisms related to the implementation of the Constitution and their basic laws, and maintain constitutional order and the rule of law in the regions as established by the Constitution and their basic laws.

Local people's congresses at all levels and their standing committees must exercise their functions and powers in accordance with the law, and ensure that the Constitution and the law are observed and implemented within their respective administrative regions, maintaining consistency in laws and regulations across the country.

Second, we should improve the socialist legal system with Chinese characteristics, developing and ensuring good governance with sound laws.

"If good laws are established under Heaven, then there will be order under Heaven; if good laws are established in a state, then there will be order in that state."[2] A socialist legal system with Chinese characteristics has taken shape. This comes from the leadership of our Party and the hard work of all quarters over the decades following the launch of reform and opening up in 1978. This is a remarkable achievement in the history of the rule of law. That said, we must be clear that the times are changing and practice is evolving, which calls for an improved legal system. Our legal system must improve in step with the times.

We must strengthen the Party's centralized, unified leadership over legislative work. We will improve the legislative framework under which Party committees provide overall guidance, people's congresses play a leading role, governments offer support, and all parties concerned are involved. We should better align decision-making for reform and development with legislative decision-making, and improve the rule of law through further reform while ensuring reform and innovation in all fields through improved rule of law, so as to provide a legal basis for national development and major reforms. We must advance the rule of law in domestic and foreign affairs in a coordinated manner, balance development and security imperatives, and develop a system of laws for extraterritorial application. We must use legal means to meet challenges, forestall risks, and safeguard national sovereignty, security, and development interests. We should apply systems thinking and enact, revise, repeal, interpret, and codify laws in a coordinated way. We should also work towards an all-round improvement of state laws, administrative regulations, supervision regulations, and local regulations.

As the national legislature, the NPC and its Standing Committee should speed up the pace of legislative work while ensuring quality. They should make legislation more systematic, integrated and coordinated and the legal system more complete, consistent and authoritative. They should strengthen legislation concerning key and emerging sectors and China's overseas activities. With a focus on imbuing legislation with the core socialist values, they should work to improve laws and systems that are urgently needed in national governance and that are essential for meeting the people's growing expectation for a better life. Codification work should be continued in legislative areas where conditions are mature.

Good laws are a prerequisite for good governance. An ancient Chinese philosopher said, "The law does not fall from the sky or grow from the earth; it manifests from among the people and reflects their will."[3]

Focusing on improving the quality of legislation, the NPC and its Standing Committee should play their role as leaders in legislative work. They should follow objective laws, abide by the principle of serving the people and relying on them, and act in line with their statutory authority and procedures as they advance law-based legislation that is more professional and democratic. They should adopt diverse forms of legislation and make it more targeted, applicable, and practicable. In order to secure the quality of regulations and rules, they must make sure that administrative regulations, supervision regulations, and departmental rules are formulated in strict accordance with their statutory authority and procedures.

Local people's congresses with legislative powers must strictly remain within their scope of legislative power. They must enact local legislation with a focus on implementing the Party Central Committee's major policies, decisions and plans and on solving practical problems.

Third, people's congresses should fully exercise their powers granted by the Constitution and carry out appropriate, effective and law-based oversight.

The power of all state agencies and their staff is subject to oversight and checks. This is an important principle of the people's congress system as well as a basic requirement of its institutional design. We should give better play to the important role of people's congresses in the oversight of the Party and the state to ensure that power is exercised under public oversight, in broad daylight, within an institutional cage, and under the reins of the rule of law.

People's congresses at all levels and their standing committees should make use of their oversight powers granted by the Constitution and the law, and exercise appropriate, effective, and law-based oversight. They should uphold the uniformity, sanctity and authority of the law and make sure that laws and regulations are effectively implemented and that administrative, supervisory, adjudicatory, and prosecuting powers are properly exercised in accordance with the law.

In our country's political system, people's congresses play the role of overseeing the work of governments, supervision commissions, courts, and procuratorates at the same level, and they coordinate the work of all state agencies to create synergies. People's congresses should concentrate on pursuing their central task, serving the overall national interests, giving priority to key areas, focusing on the decisions and plans of the Party Central Committee, and delivering on the people's aspirations and expectations. They should work hard to facilitate the resolution of prominent issues and problems that hinder economic and social development. They should employ various statutory oversight methods, strengthen oversight of the implementation of laws and regulations, and ensure that all state agencies perform their duties and functions within the scope stipulated by the Constitution and the law.

We should improve the system of oversight by people's congresses and develop sound mechanisms and methods for their oversight of law enforcement and judicial work. Governments, supervision commissions, courts, and procuratorates at all levels must strictly implement the laws, regulations, resolutions and decisions made by people's congresses and their standing committees at the same level, report on their work in accordance with the law, and readily accept oversight from people's congresses.

Fourth, people's congresses should give full play to the role of their deputies, and see that deputies respond to the calls of the people.

"Conforming to the will of the people is the key to governance."[4] The key to the great vitality and strengths of the people's congress system lies in the fact that it is deeply rooted in the people. All state agencies and their staff must foster a strong sense of service to the people, put the people above all else, maintain close ties with them, listen to their opinions and suggestions, accept their oversight, and work hard to serve them. People's congresses should ensure that their deputies reach out to the public on a greater variety of issues and in more diversified ways, broaden their channels of contact, actively respond to public concerns, better engage with the people, gain a good knowledge of their conditions, gather their ideas, and improve their wellbeing. Standing committees of people's congresses at all levels should build up deputies' capacity to do their job, and provide support and safeguards for them to fulfill their duties in accordance with the law, and showcase their role in manifesting the people's principal status as masters of the country.

Shouldering the honorable duties entrusted by the people, deputies to people's congresses should faithfully represent the will and interests of the people and participate in the exercise of state power in accordance with the law. Deputies should maintain a firm political stance, fulfill their political responsibilities, improve their thinking and conduct, set a good example in abiding by the Constitution and the law, and act with political acumen.

They should use their distinctive strengths of coming from among the people and being rooted in the people, forge closer ties with them, and serve as a bridge through which the Party and the government maintain contact with the people. They should do their best to mobilize positive factors and mitigate negative ones and conduct themselves in ways that befit their role as people's congress deputies in the new era.

Fifth, people's congresses should be clearly aware of their identity as political institutions and intensify self-improvement.

People's congresses and their standing committees at all levels must be deeply conscious of the need to maintain political commitment, think in terms of the general picture, follow the core leadership of the CPC Central Committee, and act in accordance with its requirements. They must stay confident in the path, theory, system and culture of socialism with Chinese characteristics, uphold the core position of the general secretary on the CPC Central Committee and in the Party as a whole, and uphold the authority of the Central Committee and its centralized, unified leadership. They must continuously strengthen their political acumen, understanding and capacity to deliver.

They should improve themselves in all respects and always serve as political institutions that conscientiously uphold Party leadership and ensure the running of the country by the people, as working institutions that fully perform duties and functions conferred by the Constitution and the law, and as representative institutions that always maintain close ties with the people.

People's congresses should improve the composition of their standing committees and special committees and build work teams that are politically committed, willingly serve the people, hold the rule of law in awe, promote democracy, and work with diligence and a strong sense of responsibility. They should strengthen discipline, improve conduct, perform statutory duties, follow statutory procedures, and guard against favoring form over substance and excessive bureaucracy, so as to make their work more effective.

Sixth, we should strengthen the Party's overall leadership over the work of people's congresses.

The people's congress system is an important institutional vehicle for the Party to exercise leadership over agencies of state power, and it is also an important medium through which the Party fully promotes democracy and implements its mass line in the exercise of state power. Party committees at all levels should give priority to the work of people's congresses, improve the systems of Party leadership over the work of people's congresses, hear work reports from Party leadership groups of people's congress standing committees on a regular basis, and study and resolve major issues in the work of people's congresses.

We should support people's congresses and their standing committees in performing duties and exercising powers in accordance with the law. We should guide and urge governments, supervision commissions, courts, and procuratorates to readily accept the oversight of people's congresses. We should strengthen the leadership teams of people's congress standing committees and the work teams of people's congresses, and promote job rotation between people's congresses, Party and government departments, and judicial offices. The Party's organization, communication, and other departments at all levels should coordinate and cooperate with relevant departments of people's congresses to create powerful synergies for advancing the work of people's congresses in the new era. Party leadership groups of people's congress standing committees at all levels should earnestly implement the systems of Party leadership and ensure that they fulfill their principal responsibilities for full and strict Party self-governance.

Notes

[1] Wu Jing: *Governance of the Zhenguan Period (Zhen Guan Zheng Yao)*. Wu Jing (670-749) was a historian and official of the Tang Dynasty.

[2] Wang Anshi: "The Duke of Zhou" (Zhou Gong).

[3] *Shen Zi*. This is a book written by Shen Dao. Shen Dao (c. 395-c. 315 BC), also known as Shen Zi, was a scholar of the Legalist school in the Warring States Period.

[4] Cheng Yi: "A Reply to an Imperial Edict in the Name of Lü Huishu" (Dai Lü Hui Shu Ying Zhao Shu). Cheng Yi (1033-1107) was a philosopher and educator of the Northern Song Dynasty.

Whole-Process People's Democracy: The Most Extensive, Genuine and Effective Socialist Democracy*

October 13, 2021

Democracy is a shared human value and an ideal that has always been cherished by the CPC and the Chinese people. To translate the concepts and values of democracy into effective institutions and concrete actions, we need to adopt appropriate systems, mechanisms, ways and means. To do this we have to combine theory and practice, form and content, past experience and current reality.

As I have said, the best way to evaluate whether a country's political system is democratic and effective is to observe whether the succession of its leaders is orderly and law-based, whether the people can manage state and social affairs and economic and cultural undertakings in accordance with the law, whether the public can express their needs through open channels, whether all sectors of society can effectively participate in the country's political affairs, whether the country's decision-making can be conducted in a rational and democratic manner, whether people in all sectors can enter the state leadership and administrative systems by way of fair competition, whether the governing party can lead state affairs in accordance with the Constitution and the law, and whether the exercise of power is subject to effective checks and oversight.

Democracy is not an ornament to be put on display, but an instrument for addressing the issues that concern the people. Whether a country is democratic depends on whether its people are truly the

---

* Part of the speech at the Central Conference on the Work of People's Congresses.

masters of the country, and whether the people have the right to vote, and more importantly, the right to participate extensively in governance of the country; it depends on what promises they are given during elections, and more importantly, how many of these promises are delivered after elections; it depends on what kind of political procedures and rules are set through state systems and laws, and more importantly, whether these systems and laws are truly enforced; it depends on whether the rules and procedures for the exercise of power are democratic, and more importantly, whether the exercise of power is genuinely subject to public oversight and checks. If the people are only addressed in order to solicit votes and then are left out in the cold, if they must listen to grandiose election slogans but have no voice when the elections are over, or if they are wooed by candidates during election campaigns only to be cast aside afterwards, this is not true democracy.

In sum, democracy is the right of the people of all countries, not the prerogative of a few nations. Whether a country is democratic should be judged by its own people, not by a handful of meddlesome outsiders. In the international community, whether a country is democratic should be judged by community consensus, not by a few self-appointed judges. There is no uniform or single model of democracy; it comes in many forms. It is undemocratic in itself to measure the world's diverse political systems against a single criterion, or to view the colorful political civilizations of humanity from a single perspective.

The Communist Party of China has always upheld people's democracy and has always adhered to the following basic ideas:

First, people's democracy is the lifeblood of socialism; without democracy, there would be no socialism, socialist modernization, or national rejuvenation.

Second, the running of the country by the people is the essence and heart of socialist democracy. The very purpose of developing socialist democracy is to give full expression to the will of the people, protect their rights and interests, spark their creativity, and provide an institutional framework to ensure that the people are the masters of the country.

Third, the Chinese socialist path of political development is the right path, as it conforms to China's national conditions and secures the position of the people as masters of the country. It is the logical outcome of history, theory, and practice based on the strenuous efforts of the Chinese people since the 1840s. It is a requisite for maintaining the very nature of our Party and fulfilling its fundamental mission.

Fourth, China's socialist democracy takes two important forms: One, the people exercise rights by means of elections and voting, and two, people from all sectors of society are consulted extensively in order to reach the widest possible consensus on matters of common concern before major decisions are made. These are the institutional features and strengths of China's socialist democracy.

Fifth, the key to developing China's socialist democracy is to fully leverage its features and strengths. As we continue to advance socialist democracy with soundly-designed institutions, standards and procedures, we can provide better institutional safeguards for our Party and country's prosperity and long-term stability.

Deng Xiaoping once said, "The democracy in capitalist societies is bourgeois democracy – in fact, it is the democracy of monopoly capitalists. It is no more than a system of multiparty elections, separation of judicial, executive and legislative powers and a bicameral legislature. Ours is the system of the people's congresses and people's democracy under the leadership of the Communist Party; we cannot adopt the practice of the West. The greatest advantage of the socialist system is that when the central leadership makes a decision, it is promptly implemented without interference from any other quarters."[1]

Since its 18th National Congress in 2012, our Party has advanced whole-process people's democracy as a key concept on the basis of a profound understanding of the rules governing the development of democracy. Whole-process people's democracy in China is a complete system with supporting mechanisms and procedures, and fully-fledged civil participation. China's state system is the system under the people's democratic dictatorship led by the working class and based on the alliance of workers and farmers. Its system of state power is the system of people's congresses, and its basic political systems include the system of multiparty cooperation and political consultation under the leadership of the CPC, the system of regional ethnic autonomy, and the system of community-level self-governance. Building on these systems, China has consolidated and developed the broadest possible patriotic united front. It has formed a comprehensive, extensive and well-coordinated set of institutions that make it possible for the people to be genuine masters of our country, and it has put in place diverse, open channels for people to practice democracy in an orderly manner. This allows all the people to engage in law-based democratic elections, consultations, decision-making, management and oversight and to manage state, economic, cultural and social affairs in various ways and forms in accordance with the law.

Whole-process people's democracy in China integrates process-oriented democracy with results-oriented democracy, procedural democracy with substantive democracy, direct democracy with indirect democracy, and people's democracy with the will of the state. It is a democracy that covers all aspects of the democratic process and all sectors of society. It is the broadest, most genuine, and most effective socialist democracy. We should continue to advance whole-process people's democracy, so that in concrete and tangible ways the principle of the people as masters of the country is reflected in our Party's governance policies and measures, in all aspects and at all levels of the work of Party and state agencies, and in our efforts to realize the people's aspirations for a better life.

The people's congress system is an important institutional vehicle for realizing whole-process people's democracy in China. Under CPC leadership, we should continue to expand orderly political participation by the people, strengthen legal protection for human rights, and ensure that the people enjoy extensive rights and freedoms as prescribed by law. We should ensure that the people can exercise their lawful right to elect people's congress deputies through democratic elections, that the people's rights to information, participation, expression, and oversight are implemented in every aspect of the work of people's congresses, and that the people's voice can be heard at every step in the process of making, executing and scrutinizing the decisions of the Party and the state.

We should improve the outreach platforms and vehicles of people's congresses through which the general public can express opinions, we should refine working mechanisms for soliciting public comments and collecting ideas from the people, and we should advance consultation through people's congresses and consultation on legislative issues, in an effort to protect the fundamental interests of the people by taking into account all aspects of social conditions and public sentiment. We should reinforce our study and public promotion of Chinese socialist democracy and the people's congress system, elucidate the features and strengths of China's political system, and share our story of democracy.

Upholding and improving the people's congress system is the common responsibility of the whole of the Party and society. The Party and the entire Chinese nation should stay confident in the system of socialism with Chinese characteristics, continue to uphold and improve the people's congress system, continue to consolidate and enhance political vitality, stability and unity, and contribute China's wisdom to political progress for all.

Notes

[1] Deng Xiaoping: "We Shall Speed Up Reform", *Selected Works of Deng Xiaoping*, Vol. III, Eng. ed., Foreign Languages Press, Beijing, 1994, pp. 237-238.

Religions in China Should Conform to China's Realities*

December 3, 2021

We should fully implement the Party's theory on religious affairs in the new era, and its basic policies on religious affairs and freedom of religious belief. Religions in China should conform to China's realities, and we should guide religions to be compatible with socialist society. We should help religious groups strengthen their self-management. We should improve the law-based management of religious affairs, and bring about new advances in our religious work. We should encourage religious believers to join in the national endeavor to develop China into a great modern socialist country in all respects and realize the Chinese Dream of national rejuvenation.

The Party Central Committee has attached great importance to religious affairs since the 18th CPC National Congress in 2012. Party committees at all levels have implemented the decisions of the Central Committee and performed well in managing religious affairs. Our Party's basic policy on religious affairs has been fully implemented, the relevant systems and mechanisms have been further improved, the related legal and policy framework has been strengthened, and both religious leaders and believers are increasingly aware of the need to learn, respect, observe and apply the law. Religions in China have thus become more compatible with China's realities.

Religious groups are patriotic, and value our national interests. They respect the law and science and care about public wellbeing. They are committed to China, the Chinese nation, and the Chinese culture, and they support the CPC and socialism with Chinese characteristics.

* Main points of the speech at the National Conference on Religious Affairs.

The Central Committee has put forward a set of new guidelines and measures on religious work since 2012. It has answered major theoretical and practical questions on how to view religion, how to deal with religious issues, and how to properly handle religious affairs in the new era. We must have a keen understanding of the importance of religious affairs in the work of the Party and the state, strengthen leadership, continue to practice and develop a socialist theory on religion with Chinese characteristics, and follow the Party's basic policy on religious affairs. We must act on the principle that religions in China should conform to China's realities, rally all religious believers around the Party and the government, foster positive and healthy relations among religions, support religious groups in self-improvement, and strengthen the law-based management of religious affairs.

We should fully, accurately and faithfully implement the Party's policy on freedom of religious belief, respect people's religious beliefs, manage religious affairs in accordance with the law, adhere to the principle of religious groups managing their own affairs independently, and see to it that religion is compatible with socialist society.

The Party's work related to religious affairs calls for engaging with the people. Both religious believers and non-believers share our fundamental political and economic interests, and both are the public foundation of our Party's governance. We should respect believers' freedom of religious belief, do all we can to stay engaged with them, and patiently address their concerns.

Religious groups serve as a bridge between the Party and the government and religious leaders and believers. We should support them and help them in their operation; we should respect them and see that they play their role in managing their own affairs.

We should make sure that religions in China conform to China's realities and observe the core socialist values. We should encourage religious leaders and believers to remain committed to our country, the Chinese nation, and the Chinese culture, and to support the CPC, and socialism with Chinese characteristics. We should carry out activities in the religious community to strengthen its commitment to patriotism, collectivism and socialism and help religious believers to learn more about the history of the CPC, the PRC, reform and opening up, and the development of socialism. Religious leaders and believers should be guided to cultivate and apply the core socialist values, and esteem Chinese culture. We should uphold a holistic approach to national security and the principle of religious groups managing their own affairs independently, and carry out related work accordingly. We should strengthen the management of religious affairs online, and effectively address major problems that impair the healthy development of religion in China.

We should support and guide the religious community to improve its self-education, self-management and self-discipline. The religious community should exercise full and strict self-management. It should take the lead in abiding by China's laws and regulations and urge believers to practice self-cultivation in order to achieve greater attainment.

Religious organizations should improve themselves and strengthen democratic oversight over members of their leadership. We should promote law-based management of religious affairs in all respects, and carry out an extensive program to raise awareness of the law.

Religious activities should be conducted within the scope prescribed by China's laws and regulations. Such activities should not impair the health of citizens, disrupt public order, erode moral values, or interfere with educational, judicial and government affairs as well as public life.

We should train Party and government officials engaged in religious work so that they will have a good command of the Marxist view on religion, have a good knowledge of religious affairs, and be able to communicate effectively with religious believers. These officials should study the Marxist view on religion, the Party's theory and policies on religious affairs, and increase their knowledge on religion, so as to raise their capacity to provide guidance.

We should see that religious leaders are politically reliable, excel in religious teachings, have morals and integrity, and can respond to challenges at critical times.

We should see that those who conduct research on religion have a firm belief in the Marxist view on religion, maintain academic integrity, and are eager to explore new ground; and we should strengthen the discipline of Marxist studies on religion.

We should improve the systems and mechanisms of religious work and create a model of religious affairs management featuring leadership by Party committees, government management, public participation, and self-discipline. We should properly handle major issues involving religious affairs, lay solid foundations, and make continued efforts to deliver long-term benefits.

Ensure Long-Term Multiparty Cooperation
Led by the CPC*

January 29, 2022

This year, the CPC will hold its 20th National Congress, which is a major political event for the Party and the country. All our work will be planned and carried out in preparation for the congress, to ensure its success and implement its guiding principles. We must uphold and improve the system of CPC-led multiparty cooperation and political consultation, consolidate and develop the broadest possible patriotic united front, promote whole-process people's democracy, strive to achieve great unity and solidarity, and pool as much strength as possible for our collective endeavors.

I hope you will hold to the right political direction and keep in line with the CPC Central Committee in thinking, action and political commitment. Through in-depth research, you will be able to offer constructive advice and proposals, so as to make consultation among the political parties more effective. It is important to guide members of your organizations effectively in terms of political thinking and understanding, improve their ability to discern between right and wrong, and ensure that they take a firm stance, and build and pass on positivity.

This year, the other eight political parties and the All-China Federation of Industry and Commerce will elect new leaderships at the central and provincial levels. It is necessary to ensure a smooth transition of leadership, consolidate consensus, and carry forward the great tradition of multiparty cooperation, underpinned by patrio-

---

* Main points of the speech when celebrating the Spring Festival with prominent non-CPC individuals.

tism, dedication, earnest cooperation, devotion to the people, and working together with the CPC with one heart. You should pass on your predecessors' political convictions, upright conduct, and close bond with the CPC, to ensure that CPC-led multiparty cooperation is sustained through generations. A sound approach should be applied to appointing officials, with high standards for candidates in terms of political reliability and incorruptibility. By scrutinizing their ideals and beliefs, political quality and moral character, you can be sure that those you select are trustworthy and responsible, and enjoy popular support.

Speaking to the political parties, I hope you will stick to your goals and principles for participating in state governance. It is vital to increase your ability to understand the political landscape, participate in the deliberation and administration of state affairs, exercise leadership, cooperate with others, address your own problems, and achieve new successes. It is crucial to update your theoretical and political training and make it more targeted and effective, to consolidate the foundations of our concerted efforts. You can improve your institutions by turning successful experiences and practices into rules and norms. You can conduct in-depth theoretical research, review your experience gained as political parties participating in state governance, and turn your insights into institutional practices.

The All-China Federation of Industry and Commerce should strengthen its grassroots organizations, reform and build up its chambers of commerce, and improve its services to promote healthy growth of the non-public sector of the economy, help those working in this sector to achieve success, and raise the quality and efficiency of the work of the federation.

Follow the Chinese Path of Comprehensive Progress in Human Rights*

February 25, 2022

Throughout its century-old history, the CPC has led the people in a tireless effort to realize, respect, protect and develop human rights. At a time when China has embarked on a new journey towards social-ist modernization in all respects, as described in the Second Centenary Goal to be realized in 2049, we must fully appreciate the importance and urgency of promoting human rights, attach greater importance to respecting and protecting human rights, and adhere to the Chinese path in this cause to deliver better results.

Respecting and protecting human rights is an ongoing quest of China's Communists. Since its founding in 1921, the CPC has always committed itself to national salvation, democracy, and human rights in China. In successive periods of history, from the New Democratic Revolution, through socialist revolution and construction, to reform and opening up and socialist modernization, the CPC has never deviated from its original aspiration and founding mission – to seek happiness for the Chinese people and to revitalize the Chinese nation. The Party has led the people to resounding victories in revolution, construction and reform. Today, the people of China have become the masters of our own country, our society and our future. Our rights to subsistence and development and other basic rights are well protected and keep progressing.

Since the 18th CPC National Congress in 2012, the Party has prioritized human rights as an important aspect of national gover-

---

* Main points of the speech at the 37th group study session of the Political Bureau of the 19th CPC Central Committee.

nance and achieved historic progress.

We have realized the First Centenary Goal of building a moderately prosperous society in all respects and, for the first time, eliminated extreme poverty, laying a more solid material foundation for advancing human rights in our country.

To ensure that our people enjoy fuller and more extensive democratic rights, we have put in place whole-process people's democracy and legal protection for human rights, and defended social fairness and justice.

We have promoted fuller and higher-quality employment, established the world's largest education, social security and healthcare systems, and remarkably improved the living environment of our people.

Under the principle that nothing is more precious than people's lives, we have effectively responded to the Covid-19 pandemic and protected lives and health to the largest extent.

We have fully implemented the Party's policies on ethnic affairs and religion, maintaining that all ethnic groups are equal, respecting all religious beliefs, and protecting the lawful rights and interests of all ethnic groups.

We have continued reform of the judicial system, launched the Peaceful China Initiative, strengthened the rule of law, carried out education and rectification campaigns among judicial, prosecuting and public security agencies in a bid to improve their conduct, and taken resolute action against criminal gangs and organized crime, and illegal and criminal activities, to ensure lasting social stability and protect lives and property.

China is the only major country that has formulated and implemented four successive national human rights action plans. We have taken an active part in global governance on human rights, and contributed Chinese solutions to worldwide progress in human rights.

In promoting human rights in China, we have integrated the Marxist outlook with China's actual conditions and traditional culture, reviewed the successful experience of our Party in respecting and protecting human rights, and learned from the outstanding achievements of other civilizations. This has enabled us to chart a course of human rights protection that follows the tide of the times and suits China's realities. In this process, we have adopted the following six principles:

First, uphold the leadership of the CPC. It is the CPC and the socialist system that have defined the socialist nature of human rights in China and ensured the status of the people as masters of the country. On this basis we are able to ensure that all our people enjoy human rights equally, promote comprehensive progress in all categories of human rights, and realize, protect and develop the fundamental interests of the greatest possible number of the people.

Second, respect and ensure the principal status of the people. "For the people" is the distinguishing feature of the Chinese path of human rights protection. We safeguard the people's democratic rights, stimulate their enthusiasm, initiative and creativity, and enable them to become the dominant participants in, contributors to, and beneficiaries of our progress in human rights. We have made concrete efforts to promote the well-rounded development of the individual and to achieve substantial progress in common prosperity.

Third, proceed from China's realities. We have applied the principle of universality of human rights in the context of our national conditions, propelled progress in accordance with the people's demands, and ensured that they enjoy full, extensive, genuine, concrete and effective human rights in accordance with the law.

Fourth, focus on basic human rights, primarily the rights to subsistence and development. Subsistence is the foundation of all human rights. Living a life of contentment is the ultimate human right. We have implemented the new development philosophy in full, to the letter and in all fields. We have adopted the vision of people-centered development, upholding the principle that development is for the people and by the people, and the people share the benefits. We have stepped up efforts to achieve higher-quality development that is more efficient, equitable, sustainable and secure. During the process, we have striven to give the people a greater and more sustainable sense of gain, fulfillment and security.

Fifth, protect human rights in accordance with the law. Under the principle that everyone is equal before the law, we have strengthened human rights protection throughout the process of legislation, judicature, enforcement and observance of the law. We have accelerated improvement of the legal system featuring equal rights, equal opportunities, and fair rules for all. We have protected the citizens' personal rights, property rights, and right to dignity, their basic political rights to engage in democratic elections, consultations, decision-making, management, and oversight, and their economic, cultural, social and environmental rights. We have made consistent efforts to strengthen legal protection for human rights.

Sixth, take an active part in global governance on human rights. We have championed the common values of humanity, practiced multilateralism in the real sense, participated in reforming and developing the global governance system on issues including human rights, and contributed to building a global community of shared future.

The above six principles, drawn from our practical experience, are the defining features of China's human rights protection. We must do a better job in implementing these principles in the future.

We will promote comprehensive progress in human rights, follow the Chinese path in advancing this cause, respond to the people's expectation for a better, higher-quality life, and meet their growing demand for rights in all respects. We will ensure coordinated development of the economy, democracy, the rule of law, ethics, culture, fairness, justice, social governance, and environmental protection. We will ensure all-round improvements in employment, income distribution, education, social security, health care, housing, old-age care and childcare. We will strengthen human rights protection in the process of advancing material, political, cultural, ethical, social and eco-environmental progress.

We will strengthen legal protection for human rights and further the reform of related legal institutions. We will provide legal guarantees that cover the whole process, every link and every dimension of human rights protection, including legislation, judicature, enforcement and observance of the law, so that the people can see that justice is served in every law, every law enforcement action, and every judicial case. We will systematically address legal issues of major concern to the public, handle their appeals equitably in accordance with the law, and eliminate acts of judicial injustice that fail the people and damage their interests. We will, in strict accordance with the law and Party discipline, investigate and punish any act infringing upon the legitimate rights of the people, and any act against public interests, and hold the perpetrators accountable.

We will promote our understanding of human rights, carry out an extensive educational campaign among the people to raise their awareness, and create a healthy atmosphere of respecting and protecting human rights. We will disseminate information on human rights, particularly among young people, and incorporate both the Marxist perspective and the Chinese outlook on human rights into the national education system. We will strengthen training in human rights for public servants, particularly those at the grassroots. We will leverage the strengths of people's organizations in protecting the rights and interests of specific groups such as women, children, the elderly and people with disabilities. We will extract original ideas from our experience in advancing human rights, and develop systems of academic research, disciplines and discourse. We will establish and improve think tanks and research centers on human rights protection, and train human rights professionals who are proficient in theory, strong in academic research, familiar with international rules, and skilled in international communication.

We will contribute to global governance on human rights, advocating the common values of humanity, and embracing the principles of equality, mutual trust, inclusiveness, mutual learning, win-win cooperation, and common development. The aim is to promote greater fairness, justice, reason, and inclusivity in global governance on human rights. We will take an active part in UN human rights affairs, carry out extensive exchanges and cooperation with other countries, particularly developing countries, on human rights protection, and play a constructive role in this cause.

Human rights are concrete, rooted in history, and based on current realities. We cannot mouth empty words on human rights regardless of the social and political conditions and the historical and cultural traditions of a country. In evaluating the status of human rights in a given country, one cannot apply the standards of other countries. Adopting double standards or using human rights as a political tool to interfere in the internal affairs of other countries is even more unacceptable. We must be proactive in telling China's stories of human rights protection, with concrete examples, and present our ideas in a more engaging way to influence more people.

Party committees and Party leadership groups at all levels must take on their responsibilities for promoting human rights, strengthen leadership, and take active measures to effectively implement China's National Human Rights Action Plan. Officials at all levels, particularly leading officials, must conscientiously study both the Marxist perspective and the Chinese outlook on human rights, strive to better understand the concept of human rights, build our confidence, and do a still better job in respecting and protecting human rights. All provincial authorities, central departments, and sectors of society must raise their awareness of respecting and safeguarding human rights and forge a synergy in advancing this cause.

Give of Your Best in National Rejuvenation[*]

May 10, 2022

Realizing the Chinese Dream of national rejuvenation is a relay race through time, in which you young people should give of your best in running your leg. Young people have always been entrusted with historic responsibilities. For China's youth in the new era, the timing is ideal to do great things since you have a vast stage to display your talents, and brighter prospects than ever before of realizing your dreams. At the ceremony marking the centenary of the Communist Party of China on July 1, 2021, representatives from the Communist Youth League and the Young Pioneers declared their commitment to building a strong country. This is what is expected of China's youth in the new era – a commitment that must be shared by all members of the Party's youth organization.

On the new journey ahead, there is a major topic that needs to be addressed by China's youth movement, and in work relating to youth – how to better unite, organize and mobilize young people in the nation's endeavor to achieve the Second Centenary Goal and realize the Chinese Dream. The Communist Youth League must reinforce its leadership, organization and services, unite its members and other young people, and help them grow into models of the new era who have ideals, the courage to assume responsibilities, the stamina to endure hardship, and the resolve to work hard. In this way, young people will add to the momentum for national rejuvenation with their energy and creativity, and build a better China with their ingenuity and perseverance.

---

* Part of the speech at a meeting marking the centenary of the Communist Youth League of China.

Here I would like to share some of my expectations of the Youth League.

First, I hope that the Youth League will continue to prepare the young people for the cause of the Party and remain a school that helps youth raise their political awareness.

Only those who aim high will scale the heights and look afar, and only those with a global vision will achieve great things. In the prime of youth, you need to have lofty ideals and convictions. By including the word "communist" in the name of the Youth League, the Party hopes that its youth organization will always occupy the high ground of ideals and beliefs, equip young people with the Party's theories, inspire them with the Party's original aspiration and founding mission, guide them forward under the Party's glorious banner, and shape them with the Party's fine conduct.

Young Chinese in the new era are more confident and capable of self-improvement, and think more critically. But when you come under the influence of diverse ideas, it is inevitable that you may become confused about matters such as ideals and reality, doctrines and practical issues, egoism and altruism, personal interests and the common good, and China and the world. More pertinent, meticulous education and guidance are needed to help young people observe society with a keen eye, think about life with a sober mind, and create the future through your wisdom.

The Youth League is a school for young people to learn through practice about socialism with Chinese characteristics and about communism. It should help you to set lofty goals at an early age, and to build trust in the Party, confidence in Chinese socialism, and faith in Marxism through political and theoretical education adapted to the nature and character of young people. The Youth League should be guided by a vitally important goal – making sure that the cause of our Party is carried forward from generation to generation. It should focus on the fundamental task of preparing our youth to contribute to and carry forward the socialist cause. It should help our young people to become more assured, proud, and confident in their identity as Chinese by tempering themselves in both thought and deed, so that the cause of the Party will be carried on for generations to come.

Second, I hope that the Youth League will fulfill its responsibilities and remain a vanguard in organizing China's youth to march forward into the future.

Hard work paints a bright backdrop for a young life, and action is the best way for young people to hone their skills. Taking on responsibilities and showing commitment are what brighten the years of one's youth. Young people are always pioneers who are most passionate about innovation and most motivated to innovate. The cause of the Party and the people would not have advanced without the endeavor and dedication of generations of young aspirants. Only when you people align your passion and vigor with the cause of the Party and the people, can you display your brilliance and apply your energy to the full.

Young people are the most vigorous and enterprising, and the least conservative group in society, who possess endless power to change the world and society for the better. The Youth League should unite its members and other young people and lead them in driving the new era. Young people should heed the call of the Party and the people, bear in mind the country's most fundamental interests, and fulfill your missions. Set your goals, distinguish yourselves, and be successful in the new era. Pursue the great ideals and drive the great cause. Your hard work should be invested where the Party and the people need it most.

Third, I hope that the Youth League will attend to the interests of China's youth and remain the strongest bond between them and the Party.

The Youth League is a people's organization under the leadership of our Party, as well as an organization that belongs to the young. The greatest strength of the organization lies in its extensive network at the grassroots that allows it to stay close to young people. It should focus on its central task of serving young people and carry out its political duty of consolidating and expanding their support for the

Party's governance. It should be a go-between, letting the Party know young people's aspirations, and communicating the Party's concern and support for young people. The Youth League should make every effort to benefit young people, solve their difficulties, think from their perspective, respond to their concerns, and make full use of the resources and channels provided by the Party to offer them tangible support. In this way, China's youth will genuinely feel that the Party is always close by and ready to help.

Fourth, I hope that the Youth League has the courage to reform itself and remain a progressive organization that closely follows the Party and stays at the forefront of the times.

The Youth League must answer two major questions of fundamental importance: What kind of organization should it be, and how should it become that organization? "A fixed system is not able to respond to myriad changes, a single road will not lead to multiple destinations, and a sword lost in a river will not be found by leaving a mark on the boat."[1] Only through bold self-reform can the Youth League keep pace with the times, with young people's development, and with innovative trends.

The Youth League should ensure the Party's overall leadership throughout the process of its work in all areas, follow the Chinese socialist path of developing people's organizations, focus on the goal of maintaining and strengthening its political commitment, its pioneering nature, and its connection with the people, and continue its self-reform. It should develop a keen understanding of young people and, in the context of the evolving patterns of their work and life, explore new approaches and models for its grassroots organizations. It should lead youth and student federations in promoting patriotism and socialism, and continue to consolidate and expand the patriotic united front among the young. The Youth League should also learn from the Party's experience and best practices in strict self-governance and apply them to its own self-improvement. It should do so in a strict, rigorous, and practical manner and in a spirit of reform and innovation. Through comprehensive self-improvement and setting high standards, the Youth League will always be an enterprising organization that reflects the spirit of the times.

There is a line in an ancient Chinese poem: "One must experience everything in life for oneself; every step counts on the path to a wider world."[2] Striving for progress is the most precious characteristic of youth, and also what our Party and the people expect of you most.

In the new era, Youth League members should be role models in upholding lofty ideals and firm beliefs. Take the lead in studying Marxist theory, remain committed to communism as your ultimate ideal and socialism with Chinese characteristics as your shared mission, conscientiously practice the core socialist values, and always love your country. Play an exemplary role in attentive study and bold innovation, commit to your profession to improve your abilities and strive for excellence, and try your best to become reliable workers and pioneers of your trade.

You should be brave and adept in confronting adversity, lead the way in rising to challenges and tackling tough problems, and stand up for yourselves in the face of pressure, danger or threat. Be models of diligence and dedication, stand on the side of the people, be realistic, pragmatic and down-to-earth, be the first to accept hardship and the last to seek comfort, and be willing to forgo the limelight in your work. Set an example in pursuing virtue, observing a strict code of conduct, and upholding political integrity and public and personal morals. Abide by discipline and the law, and fulfill your obligations as members of the Youth League. All League members should receive political training, strive to increase your political awareness and be tempered by political experience. On this basis, you should draw closer to Party organizations, set it as your goal to become a qualified Party member, and take pride in achieving that goal.

For many years, office-bearers of the Youth League have carried forward fine traditions, diligently performed your duties, and made a significant contribution to the Party's work related to youth. Always maintain your loyalty and political commitment to the Party, pursue noble ideals, and remain clear-minded and strong-hearted. Be like fresh air in the workplace – clean and upbeat. Consciously follow the mass line and firmly uphold the correct mass viewpoint. Maintain close ties with young people, be their friends rather than their superiors, and work more for their benefit and less for yourselves. Develop a responsible and practical approach to work, and walk the walk rather than talking the talk. You must be willing to work at the grass-roots where conditions may be harsh, and have the courage to bear hardship, take on difficult tasks, shoulder heavy responsibilities, and even confront danger. Be clean, upright, honest and hard-working. Cultivate your moral compass, remain honest and self-disciplined, and think, speak and act prudently. Build up your resolve, perseverance and self-control, be upright and righteous, always bear the public good in mind, and remain untainted by malpractice.

Revolutionaries are always full of vigor and vitality. Today, a hundred years on from its founding, the CPC is still in its prime, and remains as determined as ever to achieve lasting greatness for the Chinese nation. Quoting Engels, Lenin once said, "We are the party of the future, and the future belongs to the youth. We are a party of innovators, and it is always the youth that most eagerly follows innovators. We are a party that is waging a self-sacrificing struggle against the old rottenness, and youth is always the first to undertake a self-sacrificing struggle."[3] Both history and our experience show that the CPC is a political party that has always maintained its youthful energy, a party that is worthy of young people's trust, and a party that is worth following.

On the quest to realize national rejuvenation, the Party is the vanguard, the Youth League is the spearhead, and the Young Pioneers are the reserve force. Joining the Young Pioneers, the Youth League, and then the Party makes up the "trilogy of life" for aspirational young people. The Party has kept its gates open to all young people and will continue to welcome them to add fresh blood to the Party. The Youth League must perform its political duty of guiding the Young Pioneers. It must standardize and strengthen the mechanisms by which the Pioneers recommend outstanding members to the

League, and the League recommends outstanding members to the Party. It must ensure a smooth process for developing members from the Pioneers to the League, and from the League to the Party. Party organizations at all levels must attach great importance to the training and admission of outstanding young people and should focus in particular on cultivating and admitting outstanding League members into the Party, so as to ensure that our socialist country never changes its nature.

One of the founders of the CPC, Li Dazhao once said, "Young people are the soul of a country."[4] The Party's work relating to young people has been and always will be of strategic importance. Party committees and Party leadership groups at all levels must invest great efforts in understanding the growth of young people and the times they have grown up in, devote great energy to work relating to young people, and serve wholeheartedly as their confidants and their guides.

Party organizations at all levels must implement the systems and mechanisms for strengthening the Youth League as part of their effort to strengthen the Party. They must study and resolve major issues regarding the League on a regular basis, attend to League office-bearers and set higher expectations for them, and support the League in creatively carrying out its initiatives in accordance with the principles governing the development of people's organizations.

Notes

[1] Ge Hong: *The Master Who Embraces Simplicity* (*Bao Pu Zi*). Ge Hong (c. 281-341), also known as Bao Pu Zi, was an official of the Eastern Jin Dynasty.

[2] Fan Peng: "The Wang Clan's Nengyuan Tower" (Wang Shi Neng Yuan Lou). Fan Peng (1272-1330) was a poet and official of the Yuan Dynasty.

[3] V. I. Lenin: "The Crisis of Menshevism", *V. I. Lenin: Collected Works*, Vol. 11, Eng. ed., Progress Publishers, Moscow, 1972, p. 354.

[4] Li Dazhao: "The Mission of the Morning Bell – Create a Youthful China", *Collected Works of Li Dazhao*, Vol. 1, Chin. ed., People's Publishing House, Beijing, 2013, pp. 332-333. Li Dazhao (1889-1927) was a pioneer in acquiring and disseminating Marxism and one of the founders of the CPC.

Socialist Rule of Law

Implement the Civil Code in Earnest[*]

May 29, 2020

The Civil Code has an important place in China's socialist system of laws. It is a basic law that consolidates governance foundations, meets public expectations, and brings long-term benefits. It is of great significance in advancing law-based governance and building a socialist country under the rule of law, in growing the socialist market economy and reinforcing the basic socialist economic system, in pursuing people-centered development, in protecting the people's rights and interests in accordance with the law, in promoting human rights, and in modernizing the state system and capacity for governance.

The Civil Code is an integration of the civil laws that have been enacted over the past 70 years since the founding of the PRC. It has drawn on the essence of the 5,000-year-old Chinese legal tradition, as well as the achievements of other civilizations in the rule of law. It is in accord with the socialist nature of our country, the wishes and interests of our people, and the requirements of contemporary development. It highlights equal protection of people's rights and interests concerning life, health, property, transactions, happiness and dignity. It carries distinctive Chinese features, guides practice, and has strong contemporary relevance. To implement the Civil Code in earnest, we must focus on the following.

First, we must raise public awareness of the significance of the Civil Code. It must be made clear that the implementation of the Civil Code is essential to protecting the people's rights and interests and achieving people-centered development. The Civil Code

* Part of the speech at the 20th group study session of the Political Bureau of the 19th CPC Central Committee.

regulates personal relationships and property relationships among natural persons, legal persons, and other parties. These are the most common social and economic relations, which manifest themselves in all aspects of social and economic activity, and are integral to people's life and work and the development of all sectors. Only when the Civil Code is well implemented can the people's rights and interests be effectively protected, and social order and harmony be maintained.

It must be made clear that the implementation of the Civil Code is essential to growing the socialist market economy and strengthening the basic socialist economic system. The Civil Code has codified China's major institutional achievements in the socialist market economy and the socialist rule of law in the past decades. As it regulates the economy as well as the property relationships and transactional relationships essential to economic activities, the Civil Code is of great significance in upholding and improving the basic socialist economic system and boosting the socialist market economy.

It must be made clear that the implementation of the Civil Code is essential to improving our Party's capacity for governance. The Civil Code is an important institutional vehicle for law-based governance. Many of its stipulations are directly related to state agencies, and to the rights, interests and obligations of citizens and legal persons. In performing duties and exercising power, state agencies must be very clear about the scope and boundaries of their activities. Party and state agencies at all levels must respect the stipulations of the Civil Code, and must not infringe upon the lawful civil rights of any individual, including personal rights and property rights. Furthermore, relevant government agencies, supervisory offices and judicial departments must function in accordance with the law to protect civil rights from being violated and to promote order and harmony in civil relations. The effective implementation of the Civil Code is an important index for evaluating the performance of all levels of Party and state agencies in serving the people.

Second, we must improve civil legislation. The promulgation and implementation of the Civil Code does not mean that all problems in civil laws have been resolved once and for all; on the contrary, many issues need to be tested and studied in practice, and the laws need to be further refined, supplemented and supported by relevant statutes. Relevant state agencies must meet the changing needs of reform and opening up and socialist modernization, and thereby improve laws and regulations related to the Civil Code. By summarizing experience, we need to constantly amend the laws and regulations related to the Civil Code and judicial interpretations. As to administrative regulations that are inconsistent with the stipulations and principles of the Civil Code, we must amend or revoke them without delay. We will issue judicial interpretations to clarify the provisions of the Civil Code and the legal grounds of its application, so that it can remain both consistent and adaptive.

"The law must be adaptive to the changing times, so that social order and stability are maintained."[1] As social and economic relationships keep changing along with social and economic progress, new problems will always emerge during the implementation of the Civil Code. In the fight against Covid-19, we have seen new technologies, new industries, and new forms of businesses emerge, and our ways of life, work and socializing have changed accordingly, which prompt new subjects for civil legislation. We must focus on solving problems and adapt ourselves to technological progress, striving to constantly improve the Civil Code based on our experience.

Third, we must strengthen the enforcement of the Civil Code. We must see that law is enforced in a strict, procedure-based, impartial and non-abusive way, and we must raise public confidence in the judiciary. This is an effective means to assert the authority of the Civil Code. Governments at all levels must ensure the effective implementation of the Civil Code, as a major channel for building law-based government. The Civil Code must serve as a key yardstick for administrative decision-making, administration and scrutiny. The government must never violate the law in making decisions that curtail or damage the lawful rights and interests of citizens, legal persons and other organizations, or expand their obligations.

Government activities must abide by the law, whether in administrative licensing, penalty, coercion, expropriation, charges, inspection, or adjudication. The government must improve its capacity and performance in law-based administration, and punish any acts or individuals that harm the lawful rights and interests of the public.

Civil cases are most directly and closely connected with public rights and interests. Upholding impartial administration of justice, judicial departments at all levels must increase their capacity and efficiency for adjudicating civil cases. The delivery of civil justice must be improved, particularly in terms of the quality of case handling and public confidence in the judiciary. We must improve the judicial interpretation of other civil laws to ensure their consistency with the stipulations and principles in the Civil Code and to adopt unified application standards of all civil laws. We must improve adjudication of civil cases and provide better oversight and guidance, particularly concerning the protection of property rights, right to dignity, intellectual property rights, and the eco-environment, and respond to public concerns in a timely manner. We must improve prosecuting work regarding civil cases, strengthen supervision of judicial activities, provide unimpeded channels for judicial remedy, and prevent intervention in civil and economic disputes on the pretext of handling criminal cases, so as to protect the lawful rights and interests of citizens, legal persons and other organizations.

The Civil Code is a very specialized law. In applying the Code, we should bring into full play the role of lawyers and law firms. These professionals and professional organizations should help people to realize and protect their lawful rights and interests. At the same time, we must leverage diverse mechanisms for resolving disputes, such as people's mediation and commercial arbitration, and improve legal aid and judicial remedies. The engagement of non-governmental entities and grassroots organizations in solving civil disputes will also facilitate the implementation of the Civil Code.

Fourth, we must popularize the Civil Code nationwide. The Civil Code is composed of 1,260 articles in 7 books, with a total of over

100,000 Chinese characters. In China's whole legal system it is the biggest in size and the most complex in structure, with the largest number of articles. To implement the Civil Code properly, we must ensure it is widely understood and well received by the public. We will popularize the Civil Code nationwide, as part of our legal education campaign during the 14th Five-year Plan period (2021-2025). We will raise public awareness that the Civil Code is a law to protect their rights and interests, as well as a set of norms that all members of society must observe. We will help them develop an awareness of abiding by the law, looking to the law when running into problems, and relying on the law to resolve problems. We will include the Civil Code into the national education system, and strengthen education among young people.

The Civil Code contains a large number of terms that require accurate interpretation. We need to fully comprehend the essence and key points of the General Part and the six books on specific topics. In so doing, we can convey its underlying principles of equality, free will, fairness and good faith. We need to explain clearly its basic stipulations of ensuring the equal legal status of all parties in civil activities, protecting property rights, facilitating transactions, protecting human dignity, promoting family harmony, and identifying tort liability, and in the process give an accurate interpretation of the new stipulations, new concepts and new principles in the Civil Code.

Fifth, we must improve theoretical research on our civil law system. Since reform and opening up was launched in 1978, China has achieved notable progress in theoretical research on civil law and the relevant discourse system. However, this theoretical progress is not working in parallel with our legal acts that keep changing with the passing of time. We must persist in making the theory of Chinese socialist rule of law our guidance and proceed from realities, to improve theoretical research on the civil law system. We must move faster to build a theoretical system and a discourse on civil laws that display the socialist nature of our country, carry distinctive Chinese features, guide practice, and remain responsive to the times. These systems will provide theoretical support for implementing the Civil Code and developing our civil legal instruments.

Party and state agencies at all levels must take the lead in publicizing the Civil Code, facilitating and guaranteeing its full, effective implementation, and strengthening inspection and supervision. Leading officials at all levels must set a good example in studying, observing and upholding the Civil Code. We must improve our capacity and performance in using the Civil Code to protect the people's rights and interests, in resolving problems and disputes, and in promoting social harmony and stability.

Notes

[1] *Han Fei Zi.*

Provide Sound Legal Guarantees for Socialist Modernization*

November 16, 2020

After the 18th CPC National Congress in 2012, the Central Committee set the goal of comprehensively advancing the rule of law, and included it in the Four-pronged Comprehensive Strategy. In 2014, the Fourth Plenary Session of the 18th CPC Central Committee took up the issue and adopted the Resolution on Major Issues Concerning Comprehensively Advancing the Rule of Law in China. After the 19th CPC National Congress in 2017, the Central Committee established the Commission for Law-based Governance and made a series of decisions and plans on advancing law-based governance from an overall and strategic perspective, leading to historic changes and achievements in developing socialist rule of law in China.

We have laid down in China's Constitution that leadership by the Communist Party of China is the defining feature of socialism with Chinese characteristics. We have strengthened the systems for ensuring that the CPC provides guidance for legislation, guarantees law enforcement, supports judicial justice, and plays an exemplary role in abiding by the law, making the Party's leadership over law-based governance more effective. We have improved the top-level design and built legislative, enforcement, supervisory, and supporting systems for the rule of law, as well as a sound system of Party regulations, forming an overall framework of law-based governance. We have improved legislation in key areas, expanded reform in the domain of law-based governance, and taken further steps in building a law-based government. We have also established state supervision institutions, reformed

* Part of the speech at the Central Conference on Law-based Governance.

the judicial system, raised public legal awareness, run the military in accordance with the law, and striven to build a strong contingent of professionals devoted to the rule of law. We have resolutely upheld social fairness and justice, and rectified a number of unjust cases. All this has contributed to progress in practicing law-based governance.

Now and for the foreseeable future, to advance law-based governance, we must implement the decisions made at the 19th CPC National Congress and the second, third, fourth and fifth plenary sessions of the 19th CPC Central Committee. We need to focus on the general goal of establishing a system of socialist rule of law with Chinese characteristics and building a socialist country under the rule of law. We must ensure the Party's leadership, the people's position as masters of the country, and law-based governance. By addressing prominent problems related to the rule of law, we will keep to the path of socialist rule of law with Chinese characteristics and modernize China's governance system and capacity in accordance with the law. In doing so, we aim to provide sound legal guarantees for building China into a modern socialist country and realizing the Chinese Dream of national rejuvenation. To this end, solid efforts should be made in the following areas.

First, uphold overall Party leadership in law-based governance.

Party leadership is the fundamental guarantee for comprehensive law-based governance in our country. The CPC is the world's largest ruling party and governs the world's most populous country. How can it exercise state power and govern the country well? How can it mobilize 1.4 billion Chinese people to build a modern socialist country? These are critical questions that always deserve our full attention.

History is the best textbook; it can teach us knowledge and prudence. While leading the drive towards socialist rule of law, the Party has accumulated successful experiences and drawn painful lessons. Especially during the 10-year turmoil of the Cultural Revolution (1966-1976), China's legal system was devastated, at heavy cost to the Party and the people. After the Cultural Revolution, Deng Xiaoping regarded strengthening the legal system as an issue of great

importance to the future of our Party and our country. He emphasized that "we must strengthen our legal system. Democracy has to be
institutionalized and written into law"[1].

A review of previous successes and failures indicates that the
more complex the international and domestic environment, and the
more difficulties we face in reform, opening up and socialist modernization, the more we need to use law-based thinking and approaches
to consolidate our Party's governing status and improve its exercise of
power and capacity for governance, so as to ensure enduring stability
in our Party and our country.

All Party members must be clearly aware that promoting law-
based governance will strengthen and improve the Party's leadership
rather than weakening it. We should institutionalize Party leadership
over law-based governance, codify rules for the exercise of leadership
by the Party, and ensure effective implementation of the Party's guidelines, principles and policies through strengthening the rule of law. We
should combine law-based governance of the country and rule-based
governance of the Party, ensuring that the Party governs the country
in accordance with the Constitution and the law, and practices self-
governance pursuant to Party rules and regulations.

I addressed the question of whether the Party is above the law
on several occasions in 2015, including the time when I heard the
reports of the Party leadership groups of the Supreme People's Court
and the Supreme People's Procuratorate at a meeting of the Standing
Committee of the Political Bureau of the CPC Central Committee,
and when I attended the opening ceremony of a study session for
principal officials at the provincial and ministerial level on implementing the decisions of the Fourth Plenary Session of the 18th CPC
Central Committee on advancing law-based governance.

I have made it clear that this question itself is problematic and is
a political trap. We must leave no room for confusion, but answer the
question clearly: Party leadership and law-based governance are not in
conflict but inherently coherent. Our country's laws embody the will
of the Party and the people, and our Party acts in accordance with

the law, which manifests an inseparable relationship between the two. All Party members should keep in mind that Party leadership is the soul of our country's socialist rule of law and the biggest difference between Chinese and Western rule of law. Without Party leadership, we would be unable to promote law-based governance and build a socialist country under the rule of law.

We do not consider the question to be relevant because the Party is seen as one integral whole exercising leadership in national governance as the country's ruling party. Every Party and government organization and every official must abide by the Constitution and the law. Certain matters should be submitted to Party committees for decision, but that does not mean they can override the law or interfere with enforcement to cover up illegal deeds; instead, they must honor their responsibility, and ensure political and procedural integrity. We should keep in mind that there is a clear boundary here.

Second, uphold a people-centered approach.

The people are the broadest and most solid foundation for comprehensive law-based governance, which must rely on and benefit the people. We must represent the people's interests, reflect their wishes, protect their rights and interests, and improve their wellbeing throughout the process of law-based governance in all sectors. Moreover, we must ensure that the people, under the leadership of the Party, are able to administer state affairs and manage economic, cultural and social affairs through various channels and in various ways, and ensure that they enjoy extensive rights and freedoms and fulfill due obligations in accordance with the law.

The ultimate goal of law-based governance is to protect the people's lawful rights and interests. Alongside China's sustained economic and social development and steady improvement of living standards, the people's demands continue to grow with respect to democracy, rule of law, justice, fairness, security, and environmental protection, among others. In this context, we should actively respond to their new demands and expectations, and adopt a solution-oriented approach to achieving our goal. We should employ dialectical thinking, see the broader picture, and systematically study and address major concerns of the people in the domain of law-based governance. In this way, we strive to increase their sense of gain, fulfillment and security, and safeguard their wellbeing through the rule of law.

Third, uphold the rule of law under socialism with Chinese characteristics.

I once said that in essence, our path of Chinese socialist law-based governance is an embodiment of Chinese socialism in the domain of rule of law, our theory of Chinese socialist rule of law is a fruit of the theory of Chinese socialism in the rule of law, and our system of Chinese socialist rule of law is a legal manifestation of the Chinese socialist system. On the one hand, based on the present situation, we need to use law-based thinking and approaches to solve deep-seated problems hindering economic and social development; on the other hand, looking into the future, we need to lay the foundations for the rule of law, give full play to the power of the rule of law, and gather momentum for advancing the rule of law, so as to build more mature and well-defined systems and provide long-term institutional guarantee for developing the cause of the Party and the state.

Since ancient times, China has formed a legal system that occupies a unique place in the history of world legal systems, and has fostered a profound legal culture. Traditional Chinese law took shape in the Qin Dynasty (221-206 BC) and gradually matured in the Sui (581-618) and Tang (618-907) dynasties, best represented by the book *Tang Code with Commentaries* compiled in the seventh century. The influence of traditional Chinese law declined after the late Qing Dynasty (1616-1911).

Unlike legal systems such as Continental law, Anglo-American law, and Islamic law, traditional Chinese law was formed against a historical background unique to China. It testifies to the great creativity of the Chinese nation and the cultural profundity of China's legal tradition. It epitomizes the ethos and wisdom of the Chinese nation and contains many excellent ideas and concepts worth passing on. These include the governance strategy of enforcing public discipline through the application of both morality and law, the people-centered concept that the people are the foundation of a state and only when the foundation is solid will the state be stable, the wish for social harmony without lawsuits, the idea of prudence that prioritizes moral enlightenment over legal punishment, the concept of equality that advocates passing judgment in accordance with the law and ensures that the punishment fits the crime, and the principle of leniency towards widowers, widows, orphans, childless couples, the elderly, children, women, and people with disabilities. All of these shed light on the wisdom of China's traditional legal culture.

In modern times, some attempted to clone Western rule of law in China, but all such efforts ended in failure. History and reality have told us that while we can learn and benefit from foreign experience in the rule of law, we can only consolidate the legal foundations for building China into a modern socialist country and realizing the rejuvenation of the Chinese nation by carrying forward the Chinese legal tradition and by exploring a path of rule of law best suited to our country in the process of revolution, construction and reform.

It must be noted that in the drive to advance law-based governance, under no circumstances should we try to duplicate the models and practices of other countries or adopt such Western models as "constitutionalism", "separation of powers", and "judicial independence". Practice has proved that our country's current political system and legal framework suit our own national context and realities, and have remarkable strengths. We must maintain confidence, faith and resolve on this point. The facts have helped the Chinese people to grow in confidence.

Since the coronavirus hit China, we have upheld the general principles of strengthening confidence and solidarity and taking science-based and targeted measures. On February 5, at a crucial moment in the fight against the virus, I presided over the third meeting of the Commission for Law-based Governance to make arrangements for advancing epidemic prevention and control in accordance with the law. I laid particular emphasis on the fact that the greater the challenges we face in the battle against the epidemic, the greater the need to uphold law-based approaches and coordinate the implementation of all prevention and control measures in line with the law. All provincial authorities and central departments have done their best in legislation, judicature, public legal education, and law enforcement and observance. They have rigorously implemented measures such as partial lockdown, isolation of the infected, traffic restrictions, and disposal of infected corpses in accordance with statutory mandates and procedures. They have taken resolute action against offenses hindering epidemic prevention and control, and defused epidemic-related disputes in accordance with the law. These measures have provided legal guarantees for realizing strategic success in epidemic prevention and control.

Fourth, uphold Constitution-based governance and exercise of state power.

The Constitution is the fundamental law of China and has the supreme legal authority. Our Party leads the people in enacting and enforcing the Constitution and the law, and it must act within the confines of the Constitution and the law. All the people, as well as all state agencies, armed forces, political parties, social organizations, enterprises, and public institutions must regard the Constitution as their basic code of conduct and perform their duty of upholding the authority of the Constitution and ensuring that its provisions are observed. No organization or individual will be permitted to enjoy any special privilege that places them above the Constitution and the law, and all acts in violation of the Constitution or the law must be punished.

The Fourth Plenary Session of the 18th CPC Central Committee stated that in pursuing law-based governance, we must first uphold Constitution-based governance, and that in pursuing law-based exercise of state power, we must first uphold Constitution-based exercise of state power. Our Constitution-based governance and exercise of state power are essentially different from the "constitutionalism" of the West, and we should treat them as such. To uphold Constitution-based governance and exercise of state power, we must resolutely uphold the CPC's status as the governing party, the people's democratic dictatorship as the governing system, and the system of people's congresses as the governing structure, which are stipulated in the Constitution.

Maintaining the unity of law across the country is a serious political issue. China is a unitary country, so it is essential to maintain consistency in laws and regulations across the country. In 2015, the Legislation Law was amended, granting local legislative powers to all cities with districts. Since then, progress has been made in local legislation. Despite a positive overall situation, problems such as violation of laws and substandard legislation still exist in some regions, with far-reaching consequences.

We will strengthen implementation and oversight of the Constitution, and address questions of constitutionality. All regulations and normative documents that violate the Constitution and the law must be rectified or revoked. Moreover, local legislation should be formulated in the light of actual needs. There is no need for anything more than is necessary to address a relevant issue. If five articles will suffice for a particular issue, construct a five-article regulation. Do not try to make things grandiose and intimidating. The key lies in fully understanding the Central Committee's guiding principles and solving pressing problems based on local realities.

Fifth, uphold the rule of law in modernizing the state system and capacity for governance.

The rule of law is a key pillar for the state governance system and capacity. Only through comprehensively advancing law-based governance can we ensure that our state governance system is systematic, coordinated, and procedure-based and can forge the widest possible consensus in society.

Over the seven decades since the founding of the PRC, our country has maintained rapid economic growth and lasting social stability, an achievement remarkable by any standards. This is closely related to our ongoing efforts to advance socialist rule of law.

In the battle against Covid-19, we resolved to coordinate epidemic prevention and control with economic and social development under the rule of law, maintaining overall social stability and reopening the economy in an orderly manner. This represents a major strategic success in our response to Covid-19. China is expected to be the only major economy with positive growth this year.

As we advance our great struggle, great project, great cause, and great dream in a coordinated way, and build our country into a modern socialist country, we should particularly value and promote the rule of law and enable it to play a greater role in consolidating foundations, stabilizing expectations, and bringing long-term benefits. We should also address major challenges, defuse major risks, overcome major obstacles, and solve major problems in accordance with the law.

Sixth, develop a system of socialist rule of law with Chinese characteristics.

This system is the focus of the drive to advance law-based governance. We should expedite the establishment of a complete system of laws, a highly effective enforcement system, a stringent supervision system, an effective supporting system, and a sound system of intra-Party regulations. We should also integrate the rule of law with the rule of virtue so that they complement and reinforce each other.

As an ancient Chinese scholar observed, "A country that is not ruled by law will descend into chaos; a country that sticks to outdated laws will fall into decline."[2] We must improve China's socialist system of laws to make it well-defined, systematic, unified and authoritative.

Since the 18th CPC National Congress in 2012, the National People's Congress and its Standing Committee have adopted an amendment to the Constitution, enacted 48 laws, made 203 revisions to laws, issued 9 legal interpretations, and passed 79 decisions on legal issues and other matters of great importance. Currently, we have 282 laws in effect, 608 administrative regulations, and more than 12,000 local regulations.

The Civil Code sets a good example for codification of laws in other areas. We should draw on our experience in formulating the

Civil Code, and advance the codification of laws in fields where conditions mature. We should study how to enrich lawmaking forms. We need both substantial legislation and short, quickly-formulated and effective laws and regulations. We should make legislation more targeted, practical and operational.

We need to step up legislation in key areas such as national security, technological innovation, public health, biosafety and biosecurity, eco-civilization, risk management, and law-based governance of foreign-related matters. We need to improve laws that are urgently required by state governance and necessary for meeting the growing expectation of the people for a better life, while filling in gaps and remedying weak points. The rapid development of new technologies and applications such as the digital economy, internet finance, artificial intelligence, big data, and cloud computing has fostered many new business forms and models. However, relevant legislation still lags behind and creates lacunae. Cybercrime has become one of the major threats to China's political, cyber, social and economic security.

Seventh, pursue coordinated progress in law-based governance, exercise of state power, and government administration, and integrate the rule of law for the country, the government, and society.

Comprehensive law-based governance is a great systematic endeavor. Therefore, we must formulate integrated plans and pursue this goal in a more systematic, holistic and coordinated way. Law-based governance, exercise of state power, and government administration form an indivisible whole, the key to which is that the Party must keep its commitment to law-based governance and that governments at all levels must administer in accordance with the law. A law-based country, government, and society are mutually reinforcing. A law-based country is the goal of developing the rule of law; a law-based government is the key in building a law-based country; a law-based society is the foundation for building a law-based country.

I have emphasized on many occasions that building a law-based government is our principal task, and it is the main force of the drive to advance law-based governance, and plays an exemplary and leading role for building a law-based country and society. We need to first make breakthroughs in this regard. At present, some tough challenges are yet to be overcome in building a law-based government, including the lack of a strong commitment to law-based government administration, and a tendency to go through the motions in the legal review of administrative decisions.

We also need to lay down the rules and define the boundaries for the exercise of administrative power, standardize the procedures for administrative decision-making, and improve the mechanism for building a trustworthy government under the rule of law, so as to increase our ability to administer in accordance with the law. Based on the characteristics of the new development stage, focusing on high-quality development and the new development dynamic, we need to expedite the transformation of government functions, move faster to create a market-oriented, law-based and internationalized business environment, break sectoral monopolies and local protectionism, and remove barriers hindering economic flows, so as to form a unified, orderly, fair and rule-based national market.

Administrative law enforcement involves diverse areas and requires arduous efforts. It connects the government with the people and directly affects the people's trust in the Party and the government and their confidence in the rule of law. We need to improve the credibility of the judiciary, and promote strict, procedure-based, impartial and non-abusive law enforcement. In recent years, notable progress has been made in resolving problems such as irregularities and malpractices in law enforcement. Meanwhile, cursory and one-size-fits-all enforcement occurs occasionally in some areas, and neglect of duty is still a vexatious problem.

We emphasize strict law enforcement rather than brutal, excessive enforcement of the law with the goal of forcing violators to treat the law with awe and respect. We would prefer to see that the law is enforced with both rigor and compassion. We need to build a mechanism for coordinating and overseeing administrative law enforcement that covers provincial, city, county and township levels, and strengthen all-round, whole-process oversight to improve the quality of law enforcement.

Ensuring the observance of law by all is a fundamental requirement for building a law-based society. Public legal education needs to keep up with the times and calls for targeted, effective measures. We must implement a responsibility system in which law enforcement departments are responsible for providing legal education to the public, and in particular to young people, and constantly increase the public's awareness and understanding of the rule of law, thereby making it a social norm and a basic principle. We need to reinforce law-based governance and foster a sound social environment in which members of society conduct their business in accordance with the law, turn to the law when they need assistance, and rely on the law to solve problems and disputes.

As an ancient Chinese physician noted, "Remove health risks before they emerge and treat ailments before they are serious, thus preventing illnesses before they arise."[3] To develop the rule of law we must prioritize prevention and defuse potential risks while treating symptoms and solving existing problems. Our country's national conditions determine that China should not rely on litigation as the first and last resort. Considering that the country has a population of 1.4 billion, it would create an intolerable burden for the judicial system if every dispute, large or small, were to be brought to court. We need to direct more legal resources to providing public guidance and mediating conflicts, improve preventive legal systems, and maintain and develop the Fengqiao model in the new era. We also need to integrate mechanisms for preventing, mediating and settling social disputes, and attach greater importance to work at the grassroots level. We should give full play to the role of community-level governance based on collaboration, participation, and common interests, and modernize municipal social governance, with the goal of maintaining social harmony and stability.

Eighth, ensure sound lawmaking, strict law enforcement, impartial administration of justice, and the observance of law by all. We must continue to carry forward reform in the domain of rule of law in order to solve prominent conflicts and problems in devising, enforcing, applying and observing the law.

Fairness and justice are the soul and lifeline of the judicature. We should carry out comprehensive and integrated reform of judicial accountability and strengthen regulation and supervision over judicial bodies. We should improve category-based management of judicial personnel and ensure their occupational security. We should regulate the exercise of judicial power and increase the quality and efficiency of case handling.

We should improve the law-based system for ensuring social fairness and justice, and make sure that fairness and justice are served in every judicial case. We should also continue improving the public interest litigation system and effectively safeguard public interests.

Since the 18th CPC National Congress, the Central Committee has rolled out major reform measures for improving the institutions and mechanisms by which discipline inspection and supervision departments, courts, and public security, prosecuting and judicial administrative bodies fulfill their respective functions and work closely together while exercising mutual checking in the exercise of investigative, prosecuting, judicial and enforcement powers. We must work hard to implement these measures to produce concrete results.

A raft of judicial corruption cases have emerged in recent years. This reveals that checks and supervision on the exercise of power remain inadequate. Through bribery, some have got away with their crimes, with dozens of judicial, prosecuting and public security officials speaking on their behalf and green-lighting their conduct, rendering the supervision system toothless. We must accelerate the creation of an effective and procedure-based system to regulate and supervise the exercise of power. We must resolutely break down the support networks, cut the profit chains, and eliminate the underhanded activities, and close the "hidden doors" – loopholes through which those who engage in corruption or commit crimes escape punishment.

In January 2018, we launched a three-year nationwide campaign against criminal gangs and organized crime. The campaign cracked down on criminal gangs and their protective umbrellas and support networks, and removed a number of corrupted members within our ranks. The number of gang-related organizations hunted down in these three years matched the total number of the previous 10 years, and this had a significant deterrent effect. We must continue to take lawful action against crimes that disrupt the social order. In particular, we must continue the campaign against criminal gangs and organized crime, and continue to fight gangland forces and their protectors on an ongoing basis, so as to ensure peace and stability in both urban and rural areas and provide the people with a secure and peaceful life.

Ninth, take a coordinated approach to the rule of law at home and in matters involving foreign parties.

The rule of law is an integral part of a country's core competitiveness. At present, the world is experiencing an accelerating rate of change on a scale unseen in a century. Although peace and development remain the underlying theme of our times, the international landscape is experiencing growing instability and uncertainty, and the Covid-19 pandemic has had a widespread and far-reaching impact. As our country continues to develop, it is moving closer to the center stage of the world. We should accelerate our efforts to create a strategic framework for the rule of law in foreign-related matters, pursue coordinated progress in both domestic and international governance, and better safeguard our country's sovereignty, security and development interests. We must build a sound system of laws and regulations on foreign-related matters, and increase law enforcement and judicial efficiency in this regard. We should encourage Chinese enterprises and citizens who go abroad to abide by local laws, regulations, customs and practices, and to protect their own legitimate rights and interests with laws and rules. We also need to foster world-class arbitral institutions and law firms, and achieve greater results in serving and supporting the rule of law in matters involving foreign parties.

We need to resolutely safeguard the international system with the United Nations at its core and the international order with international law as its foundation, and uphold the basic principles of international law and the basic norms of international relations based on the purposes and principles of the UN Charter. We must propose plans to reform international rules and mechanisms that are unjust, unreasonable and against positive international trends, so as to promote reform in global governance and contribute to building a global community of shared future.

Tenth, develop a force of high-caliber legal personnel with moral integrity and professional competence.

To advance law-based governance, first and foremost we must build a highly competent team of legal professionals. We must strengthen education in our ideals and convictions, carry out in-depth education on the core socialist values and socialist rule of law, train judicial personnel to be more politically aware, consistent, specialized and professional in their conduct, and ensure that they are loyal to the Party, the country, the people, and the law.

We must employ stricter standards and higher requirements in the management of legal professionals. Some judicial personnel and law enforcers fail to maintain integrity in exercising their power. They take bribes, abuse the law for personal gain, and manipulate cases for money, power, and personal favors, severely undermining the authority of the rule of law. We must formulate and improve stringent rules, discipline and regulations, and use these institutions to regulate key officials, critical areas and core projects. We must weed out those who take bribes, violate the law, and are disloyal and dishonest to the Party, and we must combat corruption in law enforcement and the judicature.

A recently launched pilot program aiming to strengthen education and regulation of judicial, prosecuting and public security officers has identified some rotten apples and held them accountable. The initial results have been acclaimed by the public. We should consolidate and expand the results of the pilot program, and show zero tolerance for corruption. We should be strict with ourselves, and remove all irregularities whatever the pain.

Legal service providers play an important role in law-based governance. They perform their duties well on the whole, but there are also many problems to be addressed. Some legal professionals are obsessed with money and renown. They engage in misconduct and dishonest activities, damaging the reputation of their profession. A small number are disloyal in their political commitment and even denigrate our country's political and legal systems.

Upholding CPC leadership and socialist rule of law must be the fundamental requirement for legal professionals. Through better education, management and guidance, we should enable them to keep to the right political orientation, perform their duties with moral integrity and in accordance with laws and regulations, honor their social responsibilities, and contribute to building China into a socialist country under the rule of law. We should advance the reform and development of law schools, and improve the quality of legal education. We should also strengthen foreign-related legal education, with the focus on training personnel for foreign-related law enforcement, judicature, and legal services, and cultivating and recommending legal professionals for international organizations, so as to better serve the overall work in foreign affairs.

Eleventh, make sure that leading officials, though small in number, play a key role in implementing the rule of law.

It is leading officials who exercise the governing power of the Party and the legislative, administrative, supervisory and judicial powers of the state. Therefore, they are key to comprehensive law-based governance. Leading officials at all levels must implement the decisions and plans of the CPC Central Committee on law-based governance. They must take the lead in upholding the rule of law and respecting the law, and in understanding and having a good mastery of the law. They must strive to become more adept at applying law-based thinking and approaches to expand reform, promote development, resolve problems, maintain stability, and defuse risks. They must set a good example in upholding, studying, observing and applying the law. Understanding the rule of law and being able to fulfill duties in accordance with the law must be important criteria for evaluating the performance of officials. Upholding, studying, observing and applying the law must be a prerequisite and a conscious action for officials.

Comrades,

We must uphold the Party's centralized, unified leadership over law-based governance. Party committees and governments at all levels should strengthen leadership in promoting the rule of law, and exercise leadership over major plans, key tasks, and priority programs to ensure their full implementation. We must implement the decisions of the Fifth Plenary Session of the 19th CPC Central Committee, and simultaneously plan, arrange, and push forward economic and social development and the rule of law during the 14th Five-year Plan period (2021-2025).

The CPC Central Committee will soon issue outlines for building a law-based country and society, and a new outline for building a law-based government will be promulgated. Party committees and governments at all levels should take concrete measures to implement these outlines. Departments in all sectors should heighten their awareness of the rule of law, act in strict accordance with the law, and strengthen the role of rule of law on all fronts. Legal and judicial departments must perform their duties in full. The Office of the Commission for Law-based Governance should fulfill its duties in planning, coordination, supervision, inspection and implementation, and promote timely identification and resolution of problems in the process. We must do all we can to avoid the practices of favoring form over substance and bureaucratism, and deliver solid results in all tasks related to law-based governance.

The drive to comprehensively advance law-based governance marks a profound change in China's state governance. We must guide the drive with sound theories, reinforce theoretical reflection, and find theoretical answers to a critical question of our times: How should we advance law-based governance? With constant progress in combining theory and practice, we should review our Party's innovative theories concerning the rule of law in the new era, and apply these theories to better guide law-based governance in all respects.

Notes

[1] Deng Xiaoping: "Emancipate the Mind, Seek Truth from Facts and Unite as One in Looking to the Future", *Selected Works of Deng Xiaoping*, Vol. II, Eng. ed., Foreign Languages Press, Beijing, 1995, p. 156.

[2] *Shen Zi.*

[3] Ge Hong: *The Master Who Embraces Simplicity (Bao Pu Zi).*

Develop the System of Socialist Rule of Law with Chinese Characteristics*

December 6, 2021

I have emphasized on many occasions that respect for the law contributes to the prosperity of a nation and the rise of a country. As China is now at a crucial stage for national rejuvenation and the world is experiencing an accelerating rate of change on a scale unseen in a century, we face formidable tasks in advancing reform, promoting development, maintaining stability, and further opening up. It is essential that the rule of law plays its role in consolidating the foundations, stabilizing public expectations, and pursuing long-term interests.

Domestically, we are moving towards the Second Centenary Goal of building a modern socialist country. In this new development stage we are working to implement the new development philosophy, create a new development dynamic, and pursue high-quality development. We will meet the people's growing demands for democracy, the rule of law, equity, justice, security, and a good environment. We will improve people's quality of life and promote common prosperity. All these endeavors raise new and higher requirements for the rule of law. We must improve our capacity and performance in law-based governance across the board and provide firm legal support for realizing the Second Centenary Goal.

In a volatile world, international competition is increasingly manifesting the contention between systems, rules and laws. This requires us to strengthen the laws and regulations concerning foreign-related matters, and improve the efficacy of law enforcement and the judicature, so as to

* Part of the speech at the 35th group study session of the Political Bureau of the 19th CPC Central Committee.

firmly safeguard our national sovereignty, security, and development interests.

In developing a system of Chinese socialist rule of law, we need to plan according to our needs and adopt a holistic approach. At present and in the near future, we should concentrate on the following tasks.

First, follow the right direction.

I have emphasized that the key to law-based governance lies in the right direction and effective political guarantees. Specifically, it means we must uphold the Party's leadership and the system of Chinese socialism, and put into practice the theory of socialist rule of law with Chinese characteristics. The system of socialist rule of law with Chinese characteristics is an important component of Chinese socialism. We must always keep this in mind, and be fully committed to our path of socialist rule of law. We must properly handle the relationships between political governance and the rule of law, between reform and the rule of law, between the rule of law and the rule of virtue, and between law-based governance of the country and rule-based governance of the Party.

We must be clear-headed and take a firm stance on upholding overall leadership by the Party and the principle of the people as masters of the country. Staying true to our commitment to the people-centered philosophy, we will continue to rely on the people to develop the rule of law in their interests and for their benefit and protection. In the whole process of developing the system of socialist rule of law, we must represent the people's interests, reflect their wishes, protect their rights and interests, and improve their wellbeing. This system must be based on China's culture and conditions and solve its problems. We must not be misled by erroneous Western ideas.

Second, speed up legislation in key areas.

As an ancient Chinese thinker said, "Sound laws for the whole world lead to peace and order under Heaven, and sound laws for a country lead to peace and order in this country."[1] We need to strengthen legislation on national security, scientific and technological innovation, public health, biosafety and biosecurity, the eco-environment, and risk prevention. We should step up legislative efforts to make laws regulating the development of the digital economy, internet finance, artificial intelligence, big data, and cloud computing. And we need to improve laws and regulations that are urgently needed for state governance and are essential for satisfying the people's growing expectation for a better life. Rule-based governance of the Party provides a political guarantee for the cause of our Party and country, and state laws and Party regulations should complement each other.

Work will be done to strengthen legislation on social matters of public concern affecting people's wellbeing. Improvements will be made to laws to close loopholes and strengthen weak areas in supervision, to address problems of strong public concern, such as telecom and online fraud, new types of drug abuse, and those in the entertainment industry – fanatical celebrity cults, unregulated fan misconduct and exploitation, and dual contracts for tax evasion. There will be no tolerance with regard to these issues.

In recent years, the disorderly expansion of capital has become a salient problem. Unconstrained growth of the platform economy and the digital economy in the absence of adequate regulation has given rise to many problems in some sectors. Therefore, the Anti-Monopoly Law and the Anti-Unfair Competition Law need to be revised quickly, and relevant laws and regulations should be improved at a faster pace.

Mao Zedong said, "Constitution-making is a matter of science."[2] Focusing on the quality of legislation, we will conduct legislative work in a well-conceived manner, through a democratic process and in accordance with the law. We need to coordinate the promulgation, revision, abolition, interpretation, and compilation of laws to improve the efficiency of legislation and ensure that our legislation is systematic, holistic and synergetic. Ensuring consistency and coherence in the legal system is a serious political matter. Legislative bodies and relevant departments at all levels should follow legislative procedures, act strictly within the limits of their powers, and refrain from making laws beyond their authority or producing duplicated or ill-conceived legislation. They should do everything possible to effectively prevent departmental interests and local protectionism from interfering with legislative work.

"The most difficult thing about law is not legislation but law enforcement."[3] In advancing the rule of law, what is most important and also most difficult is to ensure that laws are enforced strictly, properly and impartially, and that everybody observes the law. It is imperative that we turn legislation on paper into law enforcement and compliance in action. Efforts will be made to guarantee that everyone is equal before the law, to safeguard the consistency, dignity and authority of the legal system, and to call to account anyone who violates the Constitution or other laws. Party organizations and leading officials at all levels must unswervingly support judicial bodies in independently exercising judicial power in accordance with the law. They should never abuse their power of office to interfere in the administration of justice or meddle in cases.

Third, further reform in the rule of law.

Some prominent problems in this domain are attributable to inadequate reform.

We will advance comprehensive and integrated reform of the judicial system and develop an impartial, efficient and authoritative socialist judicial system, so that our people can see equity and justice served in every piece of legislation, in every law enforcement decision, and in each judicial case.

We will improve the legal system to ensure social equity and justice, refine the public interest litigation system, the mechanisms for law enforcement, the exercise of supervision power and administration of justice, and strengthen checks and oversight concerning such powers.

We will move faster to establish a complete, procedure-based, and effective system of constraints to strengthen oversight over legislative, judicial, supervisory and law enforcement powers. We must improve the mechanisms under which discipline inspection and supervision departments, courts, and public security, prosecuting, and judicial administrative bodies perform their respective duties, while investigation, prosecuting, judicial, and enforcement powers are mutual restraints. This will ensure that the entire process of law enforcement and administration of justice is conducted under effective restraint and supervision.

We must strengthen overall planning and improve the training system of legal personnel. We should move faster to develop a corps of socialist legal professionals, including lawyers, notaries, judicial authenticators, arbitrators and mediators, who remain loyal to the Party, the country, the people, and the law.

We will further reform the management system of judicial and law enforcement personnel, and strengthen management, education and training of legal professionals. We will advance education and regulation of judicial, prosecuting and public security personnel, continue to combat corruption in law enforcement and administration of justice in accordance with the law, and take resolute action against criminal gangs and organized crime on a regular basis.

It should be noted that reform of the system of rule of law, which is of great political significance and bears on the implementation of policies, must follow the correct political direction and uphold fundamental principles. Never should anyone defer to the Western legal system or copy Western practices in the name of reform.

Fourth, apply legal means in international matters.

Since the 18th CPC National Congress in 2012, we have coordinated our efforts in the rule of law in both domestic and international matters. Our capacity to defend the interests of the people and the country with legal means has grown remarkably.

We must continue to coordinate our efforts in this field at home and abroad. Prioritizing areas with urgent needs, we will strengthen foreign-related legislation, improve laws and regulations against sanctions, interference, and abuse of long-arm jurisdiction, and establish a legal system applicable beyond our borders. We should make cooperation in law enforcement and judicial activities an important topic on the agenda of bilateral and multilateral relations, and extend the security chain for protecting our overseas interests. We should train more professionals in foreign-related legal affairs.

Fifth, strengthen theoretical research and public education on the rule of law.

We have formed new concepts and measures on law-based governance of the country by summing up China's experience in practicing the socialist rule of law, carrying forward the quintessence of Chinese legal culture, and drawing on international achievements in promoting the rule of law. At the Central Conference on Law-based Governance held in November 2020, I consolidated these concepts and measures into 11 points that we must continue to implement.[4]

We must strengthen research on the original concepts, principles, domains and theories of the rule of law in China, and build a Chinese system of academic disciplines, research and discourse for the science of law.

We will introduce the thought on Chinese socialist rule of law for the new era into textbooks and the classroom of all law disciplines, so as to train more competent legal professionals with firm ideals and convictions, love for our country, and solid legal knowledge.

It is necessary to strengthen political guidance for lawyers, so that they consciously comply with the basic requirements for the profession, including supporting our Party's leadership status and socialist rule of law, and they meet the expectations of the Party and the people.

To ensure observance of the law by all is a fundamental task. We will fully implement a responsibility program in which law enforcement departments are responsible for raising public awareness of the law.

Leading officials at all levels should set examples in respecting, studying, observing and applying the law, while at the same time guiding the people to observe the law and look to the law for solutions to problems whenever they arise.

We need to sum up China's experience in developing and practicing the rule of law, elucidate our traditional culture in this area with stories and examples, and increase the international influence of our legal system and theories of the rule of law so that we can have a stronger voice on the global stage.

Notes

[1] See note 2, p. 250.

[2] Mao Zedong: "On the Draft Constitution of the People's Republic of China", *Collected Works of Mao Zedong*, Vol. VI, Chin. ed., People's Publishing House, Beijing, 1999, p. 330.

[3] Zhang Juzheng: "Memorial to the Emperor on the Performance Evaluation of Officials" (Qing Ji Cha Zhang Zou Sui Shi Kao Cheng Yi Xiu Shi Zheng Shu).

[4] See "Provide Sound Legal Guarantees for Socialist Modernization", pp. 329-346.

Advanced Socialist Culture

Give Greater Prominence to Cultural Development*

September 22, 2020

Building socialism with Chinese characteristics is a great undertaking defined by progress in all areas and endeavors. There can be no socialist modernization without a thriving socialist culture.

Since the 18th CPC National Congress in 2012, we have raised cultural development to new heights. We have included confidence in our culture as part of the Four-sphere Confidence in Chinese socialism, along with confidence in our path, theory and system. We have reaffirmed the guiding position of Marxism in the ideological domain, which is fundamental to all systems of socialism with Chinese characteristics. We have highlighted the promotion of the core socialist values as an imperative in upholding and developing Chinese socialism in the new era.

Recent years have witnessed historic achievements and shifts in our cultural development. This is the result of our continued efforts to clear up confusion and misunderstandings and innovate on the basis of what has worked in the past. All this has provided tremendous strength for upholding and developing Chinese socialism in the new era and for breaking new ground in all undertakings of the Party and the state.

I have emphasized on many occasions that we should have unwavering confidence in our culture and promote the creative transformation and development of traditional Chinese culture. We should carry forward revolutionary culture and foster an advanced socialist culture, so as to add new luster to Chinese culture and build China into a

---

* Part of the speech at a meeting with experts and representatives from education, culture, health and sports sectors.

country with a strong socialist culture.

Culture is an important factor in advancing the Five-sphere Integrated Plan and the Four-pronged Comprehensive Strategy. It is a fulcrum for high-quality development, an important element of our efforts to meet the people's growing expectation for a better life, and a source of strength in overcoming risks and challenges on our way ahead. During the 14th Five-year Plan period (2021-2025), we will give greater prominence to cultural development and strive for practical results.

We should uphold the guiding position of Marxism in the ideological field, base our efforts on Chinese culture, and continue to guide cultural development with the core socialist values. We should promote socialist cultural and ethical progress, and develop cultural undertakings and industries with a focus on our mission to uphold socialism, rally public support, foster a new generation with sound values and ethics, develop Chinese culture, and present a positive image of China. We will continue to reinforce China's soft power, increase the influence of Chinese culture, and leverage the role of culture in building social norms, educating the people, serving society, and promoting development.

A sense of civic duty and pride is a key attribute of any modern country. Strengthening social norms and civil conduct will be a major task in building a great socialist culture, and we will make sustained efforts to pursue cultural progress. Ideas, attitudes, civilized customs and norms of conduct must be fostered to meet the requirements of the new era.

We should study and gain a deeper understanding of our Party's innovative theories and promote regular education campaigns on ideals and convictions. We should strengthen education on the history of the CPC, the PRC, reform and opening up, and the development of socialism, and education on patriotism, collectivism and socialism. Through this education, we can help the people to build greater confidence in the path, theory, system and culture of Chinese socialism, and promote unity of thinking and spirit among all Chinese people.

We need to study the origin and characteristics of Chinese civilization and culture, and form a comprehensive system of ideas rooted in Chinese culture. We will continue to raise the people's moral, ethical, and cultural standards, and encourage them to take part in voluntary service. We will build an honest society, and promote a sound environment on the internet. We should advocate hard work and thrift, resolutely oppose extravagance and waste, and create a social atmosphere in which thrift is honorable and waste is shameful.

Developing cultural undertakings is the best way to meet the people's cultural needs and protect their cultural rights and interests. Ensuring that our culture serves the people and socialism, and keeping to the principle of letting a hundred flowers blossom and a hundred schools of thought contend, we should comprehensively build up the press and publishing, radio, film and television, literature and art, philosophy and social sciences, and help them to flourish and prosper.

We must improve public cultural services so that our people can enjoy a richer cultural life of higher quality. We will integrate public cultural services between urban and rural areas to narrow the current gap by optimizing the allocation of cultural resources, improving the rural cultural infrastructure network, and increasing the total supply of public cultural services in rural areas.

What matters most in judging the quality and level of development of the cultural industry is not its economic returns, but whether it can provide more cultural products to meet the needs of the people and empower them. We should continue to give top priority to social benefits and integrate this with economic returns, further reform the cultural system, improve plans and policies for the cultural industry, and expand the supply of quality cultural products.

While following the trend of digitalization and transformation of traditional industries with digital technologies, we should develop new types of cultural business, transform and upgrade traditional cultural enterprises, and improve the quality, efficiency and core competitiveness of the cultural industry.

In accordance with China's major regional development strategies, we should analyze the rules governing the development of the cultural industry and its resource factors, and foster a new development model for the industry. The cultural and tourist industries are inseparable. We should enrich tourism with culture and promote cultural prosperity through tourism to facilitate integrated development, so that people can appreciate culture and cultivate their minds while enjoying the beauty of nature.

Promote Traditional Culture and Increase Cultural Confidence*

September 28, 2020

I have made it clear on many occasions that cultural confidence is a broader, deeper, and more essential confidence, and it represents a more fundamental, more profound, and long-lasting force. China has firm confidence in its path, theory and system. This is essentially a confidence in its culture based on more than 5,000 years of civilization.

Archeological work is a significant cultural undertaking, highly important in both a social and political sense. As our fight against skepticism towards and distortion of Chinese history and culture will continue for a long time to come, we must pay more attention to archeological research and let historical facts speak for themselves. This will provide strong support for our efforts to carry forward the best of traditional Chinese culture and increase our cultural confidence. To this end, we must:

First, explore the unknown and reveal the truth.

Much of our ancient history is yet to be discovered, and will require a lot of hard work in our archeological research. For example, the lack of adequate written records leaves a noticeable gap in the history of the Xia Dynasty (c. 2070-1600 BC). This highlights the importance of archeology in documenting an accurate account of this period. Archeologists must solve the mysteries over the Three Sovereigns and Five Emperors, and other pre-Xia figures: Are they mythological or historical?

* Part of the speech at the 23rd group study session of the Political Bureau of the 19th CPC Central Committee.

We should ensure the smooth implementation of projects such as "Comprehensive Research into the Origins of the Chinese Civilization and Its Early Development" and "Archeological Finds in China". We need a better survey of our archeological heritage and better research on applicable policies, and we need to improve overall planning for archeological work. We should make proper arrangements for archeological research into major historical issues and pool our resources in pursuit of new breakthroughs.

Second, strive for new progress in archeological excavation, and in documenting and interpreting the findings.

Archeologists should work closely with researchers from other fields – economics, law, politics, culture, society, eco-environment, science and technology, and medicine – to study artifacts and ruins, and make an interpretive analysis of these material remains. They need to give a clearer and more comprehensive explanation of the origins and evolution of Chinese civilization and its contribution to humanity. Archeologists should draw on the latest research findings on history and update information on China's ancient past to provide the public with more complete and accurate information.

Third, bring historical and cultural heritage under proper protection.

As the evidence-bearers of our history, archeological sites and relics must be well protected. We will put in place a sound system for managing historical and cultural heritage and resources, and build a national database of cultural relics. We will strengthen the overall guidance of departments and institutions involved in cataloging relics and disseminating that information; we will intensify the technical support they need and guide their public engagement.

While prioritizing the protection of historical and cultural heritage, we need to make best use of it in providing public cultural services and meeting the people's intellectual and cultural needs.

We need to improve mechanisms for protecting immovable cultural relics and incorporate the tasks of protection and management into the overall planning and use of our territorial space. We need to design systems and support policies under which archeological work is carried out before land transfer. This means that land which might contain historical or cultural relics cannot be used for any other purposes before archeological investigation, fieldwork and excavation have been carried out.

We must draw lessons from the cases of serious damage to cultural relics at home and abroad, supervise relevant departments in fulfilling their responsibilities, take more measures to address hidden risks, and improve our ability to protect historical and cultural heritage. We must strengthen law enforcement and supervision, standardize the procedures for reporting misconduct related to the protection of historical and cultural relics, and fight against related crimes.

Fourth, build up our capacity for archeological research and develop relevant disciplines.

We must apply dialectical and historical materialism, and undertake in-depth theoretical research to specific ends, for example to establish historically accurate criteria for defining a civilization, especially the Chinese civilization. We will develop a Chinese approach to archeology with our own features, style and ethos, and give China more influence and a stronger voice in archeology on the international stage.

We will use new technology-based approaches and tools to find and analyze artifacts and to protect historical and cultural heritage. We will proactively cultivate and expand our archeological talent base, so that more young enthusiasts will be attracted to this work and devote themselves to this field now and in the future.

Spread Traditional Chinese Culture from a Marxist Standpoint*

March 22, 2021

During my inspection tour in Shandong, I made a special trip to the Confucius Temple and his family mansion in Qufu. Now I have arrived in Wuyishan City, and I must therefore come and visit the park commemorating Zhu Xi[1].

As we have opted for the path of socialism with Chinese characteristics, we must adapt Marxism to the Chinese context. If there were no 5,000-year Chinese civilization, how could we build anything with what we describe today as "Chinese characteristics"? And if it were not for these characteristics, how could we have successfully embarked on the path to "socialism with Chinese characteristics"?

That is why we should value the cream of our civilization, and explore its depths. We should carry forward the best of traditional Chinese culture from a Marxist standpoint and with a Marxist viewpoint and methodology, and stick to the path of Chinese socialism.

Notes

[1] Zhu Xi (1130-1200) was a neo-Confucian philosopher and educator of the Southern Song Dynasty.

---

* Part of the speech at the Zhu Xi Park in Wuyishan City during a visit to Fujian Province.

Present an Accurate, Multidimensional and Panoramic Image of China[*]

May 31, 2021

To strengthen our international communication capacity, it is important to tell genuine and engaging stories, make our voice heard, and present an accurate, multidimensional and panoramic image of China. We should be fully aware of the importance and necessity of strengthening international communication in the new era, and aim to have a stronger voice in the world that is compatible with China's overall national strength and international status. We can thereby create an environment where public opinion outside China is positive towards our reform, development and stability – this will contribute to building a global community of shared future.

Our Party has always attached great importance to international communication. Since the 18th CPC National Congress in 2012, we have devised new forms of international communication based on the best of our traditions, improved our domestic and international systems, established media clusters with international influence, and continued to promote the global outreach of Chinese culture.

We have presented an effective discourse to an international audience, and put in place a basic framework for international communication that is wide-ranging and multidimensional, and involves multiple players. China's voice is much better heard, and its international influence has increased significantly. At the same time, we are faced with a new situation and new tasks.

To meet these challenges, we should strengthen top-level design

* Main points of the speech at the 30th group study session of the Political Bureau of the 19th CPC Central Committee.

and overall planning, and establish strategy for our international discourse with distinctive Chinese features. The strategy will focus on how to shape international public opinion by making our communication more effective, our culture more attractive, our image more positive, and our narrative more powerful in the global arena.

We should move faster to establish our own discourse and narrative, interpret China's practice with China's theory, and enrich China's theory with China's practice. We should create new concepts, domains and expressions that are accessible to an international audience, and present panoramic and distinctive stories of China and its culture. We need to let the audience of other countries know more about the CPC, and help them understand that our Party truly works in the interests of the Chinese people and what are the reasons for the success of our Party, of Marxism and of Chinese socialism.

We should conduct in-depth studies from a range of perspectives – politics, economics, culture, social affairs, and the eco-environment – focusing on China's spirit, values and strengths, so as to provide academic and theoretical support for our international communication.

We must promote Chinese culture beyond our national borders, advocating common values, sharing our ideas, and increasing mutual understanding, to let the world know more about our culture and how it embodies Chinese spirit and wisdom. We need to strike the right tone, be open, confident, and modest, and present a true image of China as a country worthy of friendship, trust and respect.

China's ideas, visions and solutions should be better communicated to the international community. China is moving closer to the center stage of the world. We have both the capacity and the duty to play a bigger role in global affairs, to work together with other countries in solving the common problems of humanity, and to make a greater contribution to the world.

We will champion the cause of building a global community of shared future and share with the world our approach to development, civilization, security, human rights, the eco-environment, international order, and global governance, based on our successful experience and a history dating back more than 5,000 years. We will continue to advocate multilateralism and oppose unilateralism and hegemonism. We will work closely with the international community to shape a new international order that is fairer and more equitable, and to build a new model of international relations. We need to make best use of countless vivid and inspiring examples to illustrate that China's development is its greatest contribution to the world in its own right and offers a Chinese approach to resolving problems confronting humanity.

We should carry out cultural and people-to-people exchanges with other countries in all forms and through all channels to promote mutual understanding and friendship. We will innovate our systems and mechanisms to turn our institutional, organizational and human resource strengths into strengths in communication. We need to better leverage the role of prominent experts and make their voices heard through platforms and channels such as major international conferences, forums and mainstream foreign media. All provincial authorities and central departments should make use of their unique features and strengths to present a vivid, colorful and multidimensional image of China.

We need to make our international discourse more effective and see that our communicators are competent and can adapt to the needs of international communication in the new era. We will step up theoretical research to better understand the rules governing international communication. We will establish a system for international communication, and improve our communication skills. To make our stories and voice more engaging and relevant, we must adopt an approach tailored to global, regional or specific audiences, and adapted to different regions, countries or groups of people. We need to make more friends, unite more people, and win more support. We need to expand the circle of friends who understand and have a positive view of China, and will speak up for China on the international stage. We must adopt the appropriate tactics and techniques to make our voice better heard on major issues.

Party committees and Party leadership groups at all levels should take capacity building for international communication as one of their key responsibilities. They should reinforce their organization and leadership and see that adequate funds are available and practical issues are solved to ensure that progress is made. Leading officials at all levels should personally engage in international communication; principal officials mandated for the job should be personally involved. They should receive training in international communication, and Party organizations at all levels should help create an atmosphere where all participants conscientiously uphold the dignity and image of the Party and the country. Party schools (academies of governance) should incorporate international communication skills in their curriculum. Colleges and universities should strengthen the development of academic disciplines related to international communication, train a corps of professionals, and undertake relevant theoretical research.

Build a Better Cyberspace[*]

November 19, 2021

As an important element of civilized social conduct in the new era, a sound cyber culture will contribute to China's growing strength in cyberspace.

In recent years, by reinforcing cyber governance, China has enriched and improved online content and achieved notable results in promoting civility, decency and desirable practices and trends online.

We need to coordinate development and governance, and online and offline efforts, and bring together all positive forces for the common good. Party committees and governments at all levels must shoulder their responsibilities, and internet platforms, social organizations and netizens need to play an active role in promoting civility in running and using the internet. Let us shape cyberspace with healthy practices and build a better cyberspace together.

---

* Main part of the congratulatory letter to the First China Internet Civilization Conference.

Create New Prospects for Chinese Literature and Art*

December 14, 2021

A country will thrive only if its culture thrives, and a nation will be strong only if its culture is strong. China today is a nation of magnificent landscapes and open-hearted people, with a great future ahead. This era provides a huge and broad stage for our literature and art to thrive. It is incumbent on Chinese writers and artists to build the strongest possible socialist culture in our country. Take this responsibility on your shoulders and you can accomplish a great deal.

As writers and artists, you must have a deeper understanding of and greater confidence in our culture. Act with a stronger sense of purpose and mission to contribute to a culture that serves the people and socialism. Respond to the call to let a hundred flowers blossom and a hundred schools of thought contend, and press ahead with the creative transformation and development of our fine traditional culture, upholding socialism, rallying public support, fostering a new generation with sound values and ethics, and building a better national image. Take on the great responsibility of nourishing the roots and forging the soul of our nation, and accomplish new feats in your literary and artistic creations based on our fine cultural traditions.

To this end, you should yourselves meet higher standards of virtue and moral integrity through self-cultivation. We expect you to produce more edifying works to encourage the people to improve themselves and embrace higher virtues and ethics, so as to create new prospects

* Part of the speech at the opening ceremony of the 11th National Congress of China Federation of Literary and Art Circles and the 10th National Congress of China Writers Association.

for Chinese literature and art, and add new luster to Chinese culture. This will provide a powerful force to guide values, strengthen cultural cohesion, and motivate the people to contribute to the achievement of the Second Centenary Goal and the realization of the Chinese Dream of national rejuvenation.

Here, I would like to share with you some of my expectations.

First, I hope that as writers and artists you will champion the cause of national rejuvenation and invest your enthusiasm in showcasing the spectacular achievements of the Chinese nation on the new journey towards rejuvenation in the new era.

National rejuvenation has been the greatest dream of the Chinese people in the modern era. Over the past century the CPC has adapted the basic tenets of Marxism to China's realities and its fine traditional culture, united the people across the country, and led them in writing a magnificent chapter in the history of human progress – the most brilliant in the millennia-long history of the Chinese nation. China's rejuvenation has become an irreversible historic process. We are closer to, more confident in, and more capable of achieving the goal than ever before. But we must be prepared to work harder than ever to get there.

Culture is the lifeblood of a nation, while literature and art sound the clarion call of the times. An ancient Chinese once said, "Literature is the channel by which ideas are disseminated."[1] As Chinese socialism has entered a new era and China has embarked on the new journey towards a modern socialist country, you writers and artists should firmly grasp the contemporary theme of national rejuvenation and closely integrate your life and artistic goals with the future of our country, the destiny of our nation, and the aspirations of our people. Your literary and artistic creations should record the history of national rejuvenation and portray the people's endeavors on the journey, helping to boost this great undertaking, consolidate its foundations, shape the national spirit, and forge the soul of the nation.

Over the past 100 years, the CPC has led the Chinese people through a tenacious struggle to success in China's transformation from standing up, becoming better off, and growing in strength, through its great leap forward from lagging behind to catching up with the times, and to steering current and future trends. In this process it has created an epic in the history of humanity.

As writers and artists, you need to see things from a broader perspective so as to develop an accurate understanding of the underlying trends of history and our times. A perfect command of the overall situation is as powerful as a million-strong army.

Your literary and artistic works should reflect the tremendous changes in the millennia-long history of the Chinese nation and China's historic achievements over the past hundred years. In them, you should advocate the national spirit with patriotism at its core and the spirit of our times with reform and innovation at its core, and champion the great founding spirit of the CPC and China's underlying values.

For the Chinese people, the new era of socialism with Chinese characteristics is one of overcoming new trials and challenges, creating a bright future and striving for a better life. There is a saying, "From a mountain top you will enjoy a broader outlook; down by the riverside you will enjoy a pleasant prospect."[2] Writers and artists need to keep pace with the times, and feel the pulse of art from the heartbeat of our era. Your literary and artistic creations should embrace the great struggle of hundreds of millions of people and depict their rich and colorful life. You need to draw inspiration for your subject matter from the changing times, from China's advances, and from the call of the people. You should reveal the beauty of China's history, landscapes and culture, showcase the people's dedication, creativity and attainments, and present the prevailing features of the new era in every respect.

Second, I hope that you will stand firmly on the side of the people and create an enduring epic about the people. Fundamentally, socialist literature and art are from the people, for the people, and of the people. The people make the progress and prosperity of Chinese literature and art possible. You should take a people-centered approach, putting the people first. Their satisfaction should be the highest standard against which to judge the quality of your literary and artistic works. You should create more excellent works that meet the people's cultural aspirations, build up their cultural strength, and let the flowers of art and literature forever blossom for the people.

People are the creators of history and of this era. Their individual struggles are bright chapters telling of their zeal for making history; when put together, they will form a shining epic. People are the wellspring of literature and art and an inexhaustible source of nourishment and inspiration. They offer a world of subjects that literature and art can build on. Literary and artistic works should sing the praises of the people's efforts to make history, of all those who have contributed to national rejuvenation, and most of all of the heroes who have sacrificed their lives for others.

Mao Dun once said, "A writer of novels must not only have extensive life experience but also a well-trained mind, to be able to examine and understand complex social phenomena."[3] The Russian writer Leo Tolstoy observed, "Art is not a handicraft; it is the transmission of the feelings that the artist has experienced."[4] Life is the people, and the people are life. People are genuine and down-to-earth; they should neither be portrayed as fictional caricatures, nor be ridiculed for fun; they must be treated with respect. Only by engaging deeply with the people to understand their resilience in weal and woe can you gain an insight into the nature of life, feel the pulse of the times, and appreciate the aspirations of the people. Only in this way can you create thought-provoking works that have enduring appeal. The people should be the heroes in your works, and you need to think and feel the way the people are thinking and feeling and stay close to the people, showing empathy and opening your heart. You need to embrace the new era and enjoy the brilliance of life together with the people, and sing for them and for our era.

Literature and art excel in images, and the classical images of literature and art became the hallmark of the era they represent. All aspirational and capable writers and artists should increase their ability to study and understand life, constantly exploring new phenomena and people who represent the spirit of our age. Literature and art should come from life and transcend it. You should create more images that are fascinating, appealing and moving, with a style that integrates realism and romanticism, leaving as your legacy memorable artistic classics for future ages.

"Writing is about expressing ideas through the optimal use of words."[5] Works that encourage the pursuit of excellence and extol virtues and beauty can sound the clarion call of the times. Perfect goodness makes perfect beauty. Writers and artists should carry on China's fine literary and artistic tradition of pursuing excellence and goodness, and promote the core socialist values through vivid language and images. You need to present what shows strength, morality and warmth, advocate what is healthy, and discard what is coarse. You are encouraged to create more excellent works from a fresh perspective that are thought-provoking and eloquent, in order to cultivate people's aesthetic values and enrich their cultural life.

Third, I hope you will continue to innovate on the basis of what has succeeded in the past, and open up new horizons for literature and art with masterpieces that reflect the times we live in. It is through works that we evaluate the literary and artistic achievements of an era or the value of a writer or an artist. So, you should do your best to innovate and produce great works that do justice to our great nation and to this great era.

Through the ages, the most outstanding works of literature and art have invariably been those that best combine ideas and artistic expression. As a Chinese philosopher once put it, "A good and well-constructed argument makes one feel upright and righteous; only by feeling upright and righteous can one be eloquent and articulate; only with articulate eloquence can one create well-structured and meaningful writing."[6]

No work will have a soul and spread far and wide unless it is infused with the value of beauty and its theme and art form complement each other. As writers and artists, you should take quality as the lifeblood of your works and be strict in selection of content and meticulous in your artistic creation. You should think profoundly, strive to add more artistic and cultural value to your works, and make them a source of the people's cultural strength.

Personal style is essential to literature and art. The writer Liu Qing said, "Those engaged in writing will become real writers only when they stop imitating others"[7]; and "literature of each era has its own style"[8]. You writers and artists need to respect and learn from your predecessors, but beyond that, you should have the ambition to outshine them. Have the courage to force yourselves towards a higher realm of creation by resisting the temptation to plagiarize, follow the fashion, or ride on the coattails of others.

China's extensive and profound civilization embodies the distinctive traits of the Chinese nation. It underpins contemporary Chinese literature and art and provides valuable resources and inspiration for literary and artistic creation. Chinese culture always advocates the practice of "collecting even incomplete articles and essays from previous generations, and gathering even heritage that may have been neglected or ignored by our forebears"[9]. To sustain its vitality, Chinese writers and artists should try to tap into the ideas, humanism and ethics of traditional Chinese culture, integrate artistic creativity with Chinese cultural values, and combine traditional and modern aesthetics. It is not the way of inheritance to hold fast to established conventions and follow the old ways; neither should it be called innovation to sever links with tradition purely to create a novelty. You need to properly handle the relationship between legacy and innovation, by learning from the past but not in a rigid manner, and by innovating but not breaking entirely with the past, so that China's fine traditions can serve as a major source of innovation in literature and art.

Today, different forms of art are interconnected and different forms of expression converge. New technologies, including the internet, big data and artificial intelligence, have given birth to new forms of literary and artistic expression and expanded the space for creation. That said, we must understand that all techniques and methods are means to serve the content. While science and technology progress and innovation can help to update forms of artistic expression and rendition, life remains the essential source of inspiration for all literary and artistic works if they are to achieve depth and richness. New technologies and new methods should be employed as appropriate to stimulate creativity and inspiration, enrich cultural value, and express ideas and emotions, so as to make works broader and more meaningful.

Fourth, I hope you writers and artists will put your heart and soul into telling Chinese stories, and present China as a country worthy of friendship, trust and respect. As the Chinese people have always been firm champions of the common good of humanity, contemporary Chinese literature and art should always have the whole world in its sights. Writers and artists should have the confidence and ambition to carry on our traditional culture while developing it to reflect what is new in the world, and should produce more outstanding works that highlight Chinese aesthetics, spread contemporary Chinese values, and reflect the common values pursued by all of humanity.

People of different countries, though vastly different in their circumstances and prospects, share the same unremitting desire for a better life and face the same unyielding struggle to better their lot. These are themes that readily strike a chord. Marx once said, "What the nations have done as nations, they have done for human society."[10] We, the Chinese people, during our most arduous and bitter struggles, have applied our indomitable will and resolve along with unprecedented wisdom and strength to forge a path of socialism with Chinese characteristics. We have created two wonders – rapid economic development and long-term social stability. We have created a new model for human progress, and dramatically increased China's soft power. The international community deserves to be given a true picture of China's development path and its successes, and to understand the transformation in Chinese people's lives and thinking.

Literature and art facilitate communication and connect souls. You should root yourselves firmly in China's earth to tell stories about China. With broader vision and greater confidence you should select the subjects that best represent the spirit of China, and make more images of Chinese culture widely known to the world. You should strive to present a lively and multidimensional China, and contribute to the building of a global community of shared future.

The cultural identity of a nation is often embodied in the national character of its literature and art. Writers and artists should keep Chinese culture in mind when communicating with other writers and artists around the world. It is important to attend to the artistic content and forms of the Chinese nation, inheriting and bequeathing the traditions of national folk literature and art by expanding their genres, forms and styles, and establishing the Chinese style in the world's literary and artistic canon.

Fifth, I hope that writers and artists will keep to the right path and realize your life's worth by pursuing both moral integrity and artistic success. As a Qing scholar said: "A cultivated person of noble and lofty aspirations can produce succinct and vigorous expressions of profound thoughts."[11] Literature and art must serve to cultivate virtue and nurture the mind. Be mindful of the connection between individual virtue, your social images, and the social impact of your works. Hold to the ideal, strive to be upright, promote integrity, and win a reputation for yourselves with your moral excellence and great works.

Those who undertake the mission of cultivating virtue and nurturing the mind must cultivate and nurture themselves first. Timeless classics are often the products of writers and artists who are open-minded, knowledgeable, talented and upright, and whose integrity can be read from the quality of their work. As an ancient writer said, "Writings, if useful to society, are never enough even if there are more than a hundred of them; while if useless, one single page is far too many."[12]

Artistic creation is a painstaking process. Excellence can never be reached overnight, but requires concentration, devotion, and sustained effort. There is no future for those who want to take shortcuts to quick results and superficial success, for those who dream of overnight fame and worldly wealth. Literature and art should be popular but not vulgar; they must be close to life but must never be the source or advocate of negative social influences; they must be innovative but should never descend into absurdity. It is not wrong for literature and art to pursue material success, but they cannot be all about money and must not become slaves to the market. Creation comes from heart and soul, good performance relies on ability, positive social image emerges from hard work, financial success depends on quality, and fame rests on moral integrity and artistic attainments. Humor in poor taste, sensationalism, reckless indulgence, and insatiable desire for wealth will only do harm to literature and art. You must work with profound respect, devote yourselves wholeheartedly to your profession, and work diligently to hone your skills and achieve genuine fame.

Self-improvement can never be an entirely personal matter for writers and artists. The moral standards of the literary and art sector will influence the cultural environment and society. Writers and artists are prominent forces in society; your every move will have an impact on the public. You must cherish that influence and take the social impact of your works into serious consideration. A writer or artist who does not have moral integrity will be rejected by the people and the times. Those who do not respect themselves will not win respect from others. Take your social responsibilities seriously, abide by the law, support public order, and uphold good morals. Guard against the temptations of mammonism, hedonism, and extreme selfish interests, and remain upright and incorruptible. Keep in mind the famous lines: "Holding my head high in defiance of the enemy's attacks, bowing my head low in obedience to the people."[13] Exalt the true, the good, and the beautiful while rejecting the false, the evil, and the ugly. The positive should be acknowledged and praised openly, while the negative should be resisted and condemned without hesitation. Promote healthy trends and good morals, create a positive image of the literary and art sector, and foster a clean cultural environment that values self-esteem and mutual learning.

Notes

[1] Li Han: "Preface to *Collected Works of Han Yu*" (*Chang Li Xian Sheng Ji* Xu). Li Han (dates unknown) was an official of the Tang Dynasty, and a student and son-in-law of Han Yu (768-824), one of China's finest prose writers.

[2] Hong Yingming: *Tending the Roots of Wisdom* (*Cai Gen Tan*). Hong Yingming (dates unknown) was a philosopher of the Ming Dynasty (1368-1644).

[3] Mao Dun: "My Retrospect", *Complete Works of Mao Dun*, Vol. 19, Chin. ed., People's Publishing House, Beijing, 1991, p. 406. Mao Dun (1896-1981) was a well-known novelist and left-wing activist.

[4] Leo Tolstoy: *What Is Art?*

[5] Liu Xie: *Carving a Dragon with a Literary Mind* (*Wen Xin Diao Long*). Liu Xie (c. 465-532) was a literary critic during the Southern Dynasties.

[6] Li Ao: "A Replying Letter to Zhu Zaiyan" (Da Zhu Zai Yan Shu). Li Ao (772-841) was a philosopher and prose writer of the Tang Dynasty.

[7] "A Collection of Liu Qing's Short Notes", sorted by Liu Kefeng, daughter of Liu Qing.

[8] Liu Qing: "Life Is the Foundation of Literary Creation", *Collected Works of Liu Qing*, Vol. 4, Chin. ed., People's Literature Publishing House, Beijing, 2005, p. 332.

[9] Lu Ji: *The Art of Writing* (*Wen Fu*). Lu Ji (261-303) was a writer and calligrapher of the Western Jin Dynasty.

[10] Karl Marx: "Draft of an Article on Friedrich List's Book *Das Nationale System der Politischen Oekonomie*", *Karl Marx & Frederick Engels: Collected Works*, Vol. 4, Eng. ed., Lawrence & Wishart, 2010, p. 281.

[11] Ye Xie: *On the Origin of Poetry* (*Yuan Shi*). Ye Xie (1627-1703) was a poet and poetry critic of the Qing Dynasty.

[12] Wang Chong: *Discourses Weighed in the Balance* (*Lun Heng*).

[13] Lu Xun: "Self-Mockery", *Complete Works of Lu Xun*, Vol. VII, Chin. ed., People's Literature Publishing House, Beijing, 2005, p. 151. Lu Xun (1881-1936) was a man of letters, thinker and revolutionary, and one of the founders of modern Chinese literature.

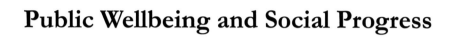

Public Wellbeing and Social Progress

Build a Strong Public Health System[*]

June 2, 2020

Since the 18th CPC National Congress in 2012, the Central Committee has made clear the Party's working guidelines for public health in the new era, and reaffirmed its responsibility to provide safe, effective, convenient and affordable public health services and basic medical care. We contained and responded effectively to the outbreaks of such epidemics as the H1N1 flu in 2009, H7N9 bird flu in 2013, and Ebola hemorrhagic fever in 2014. The incidence of major epidemics has fallen remarkably in China.

At the Fourth Plenary Session of the 19th CPC Central Committee in 2019, the Party proposed to strengthen the institutional guarantee for improving public health. It was decided that one of the important goals and tasks for modernizing China's governance system and capacity would be to strengthen the system of public health services, and address major emerging infectious diseases (EIDs) in a timely and meticulous manner. Special emphasis was laid on preventing and controlling serious epidemic diseases and steadily developing the system of public health services. In the course of achieving the Two Centenary Goals, public health has always been and will continue to be one of the foundations of all undertakings. It is inextricably linked with our country's overall development strategy and plays a strong supporting role.

The fight against Covid-19 has proved that China's public health service system, medical care system, medical security system, and medicine supply system, and the system of prevention and control and emergency response to major epidemics are effective on the

---

[*] Part of the speech at a meeting with experts and scholars.

whole, but there are weak links. Some of these problems can be attributed to shortcomings in our systems and mechanisms, some to poor policy enforcement, and some to the limits of our development to date. Only by building a strong public health system, improving the early warning and response mechanisms, reinforcing our capacity for prevention, control, and treatment, and creating a tight-knit network of forceful protective measures, can we guarantee the people's health. Based on your views and proposals, I would like to elaborate on the following points:

First, we should reform the disease prevention and control (DPC) system. Prevention is the most efficient and economical strategy for health. The DPC system is an important guarantee, protecting and safeguarding public health, and maintaining social and economic stability. In the fight against Covid-19, our public health system has played a significant role, but has exposed some deficiencies, such as insufficient capacity, inflexible mechanisms, inadequate impetus, and disconnects between prevention and treatment measures. These are long-standing problems, and it is time to resolve them once and for all. Efforts should be directed towards more precise and effective prevention, with further reform to coordinate systems and mechanisms, define functions and boundaries, and improve professional competence.

We should put in place a reliable funding mechanism for public health, and improve DPC facilities and public health service programs.

We must optimize the functional structure of DPC institutions. We need to establish a DPC system that is mainly composed of DPC centers at the national, provincial, city and county levels and specialized DPC institutions, that relies on the support of medical institutions with primary medical and health institutions serving as the first DPC line, that is characterized by civil-military integration in medicine and health services, and that gives equal weight to prevention and treatment. We need to set up mechanisms with clearly defined responsibilities for each level of management from top to the bottom and with effective coordination among them.

We should improve the capacity building of national DPC institutions, update their technology, expertise and talent reserve, and strengthen their leading role in protecting public health. We need to improve coordination between DPC institutions and urban and rural communities, and strengthen the role of town and township health centers and community health service centers in epidemic prevention, so as to consolidate the foundations for joint prevention and control at the grassroots.

We should initiate a mechanism for increasing collaboration between hospitals and disease control agencies, in which personnel, information, and resources are shared, and oversight and regulation operate as mutual restraints.

We should cultivate high-caliber DPC professionals, develop mechanisms for their training and management that are adaptive to the modern DPC system, and introduce measures to ensure grassroots DPC institutions are always well-staffed.

We should develop a number of first-class public health academies, and focus on the training of professionals specialized in pathogen identification, epidemic trend analysis, research on the patterns of epidemic transmission, field epidemiology, and laboratory testing.

Second, we should strengthen the capacity for monitoring, early warning, and emergency response. After the SARS epidemic in 2003, China established mandated online reporting of cases of infectious diseases, and has seen a notable improvement in the facilities and equipment of DPC institutions.

We should strengthen monitoring and early warning as the top priority for improving the public health system, as detection holds the key to the policy of early detection, reporting, quarantine and treatment.

We need to put in place a better monitoring system for epidemic outbreaks and public health emergencies, as well as for diseases with unknown causes and abnormal health incidents, and improve the sensitivity and accuracy of assessment and monitoring. We should build smart early warning mechanisms through multi-point triggers, improve the multi-channel monitoring and early warning mechanism, and increase the capacity for real-time comprehensive analysis and assessment.

The network of laboratory testing for epidemic diseases must be improved. Public health institutions and medical institutions must coordinate their efforts in epidemic monitoring to ensure early detection, early reporting, and early treatment at grassroots institutions.

We should improve contingency plans for public health emergency response, and organize response teams at various levels and in various categories, with plans and staff covering outbreak assessment, epidemiological investigation, medical treatment, laboratory testing, community guidance, and deployment of supplies.

Grassroots medical staff should receive response training and drilling to expand their knowledge and raise their skill level in providing early treatment. Education on public health emergency response should be provided to increase the public's awareness and their capacity for disease prevention and self and mutual medical aid.

Party committees and governments at all levels should establish working mechanisms for regular analysis and planning on the prevention and control of major epidemics. They should improve coordination among different levels for concerted, interdepartmental, and cross-region anti-epidemic measures that are applicable for both normal circumstances and emergencies, and they should see to it that instructions are given clearly and executed systematically, smoothly and effectively.

Third, we should improve the system for medical treatment during major epidemics. Treatment of Covid-19 patients is a challenging test for our nation's medical services, developed over the past 40 years since the launch of reform and opening up. It also tests the results of building key medical specialties that have developed over the past 20 years, and the reform of the medicine and healthcare system that has unfolded over the past 10 years.

China has put the people first in its Covid-19 response, because we know nothing is more precious than people's lives. We have mobilized medical resources across the country on a scale never seen before. Not a single infected person is left unattended; not a single confirmed patient is left untreated. From newborns to centenarians, all have been treated to the best of our ability. There is not a single case of lack of treatment due to affordability.

Almost all the 42,000 medical workers of the 346 medical teams from across the country who rushed to Hubei Province for emergency relief work were from public hospitals. Experience has proved that a treatment system that is dominated by the government, that serves the public interest, and that is underpinned by public hospitals provides an important guarantee for effective response to major epidemics. Therefore, public hospitals must develop stronger capacity for the treatment of infectious diseases, and general hospitals must enact higher standards for prevention and control facilities, so that we have a greater reserve for emergency medical treatment. With these measures in place, we will raise China's system and capacity for fighting major epidemics to a higher level.

Medical resources should be rationally distributed. We should coordinate emergency response efforts by medical institutions in terms of mobilization, regional cooperation, and personnel deployment, to shore up weak points and be prepared for both normal circumstances and emergencies.

We need to put in place a sound, graded, multilevel, and referral-based treatment network for infectious diseases and other serious epidemic threats. We should improve the three-tiered urban-rural medical service network with the focus on urban communities and rural villages, border and port cities, county-level hospitals, and traditional Chinese medicine (TCM) hospitals.

We will further develop national and regional medical centers to provide more effective treatment of serious epidemic diseases. We must redouble our effort to develop disciplines related to the treatment of diseases during major epidemics, particularly intensive care medicine, respiratory medicine, anesthesiology, and other urgently-needed disciplines. We must enact policies and measures to recruit more high-caliber medical workers to the profession of epidemic prevention and control.

Fourth, we should further implement public health campaigns. The campaigns, which began in the 1950s with an emphasis on sanitation and personal hygiene, represent a successful case of our Party's application of the mass line to boosting public health. We must summarize our successful experience in Covid-19 prevention and control, and integrate new concepts with new approaches to drive this campaign. The focus of our work should shift from public sanitation governance to comprehensive public health management, targeting widespread and long-lasting issues concerning public health.

We must comprehensively improve the living environment, public health infrastructure, and urban and rural environmental sanitation, and honor model cities and towns in public health.

We should encourage positive, healthy and green lifestyles, popularize health knowledge, and promote healthy dietary trends. Good habits in daily life, such as wearing masks when going out, sorting garbage, maintaining social distancing, using individual serving dishes and serving chopsticks, and making clinical appointments online, should be promoted.

We should include public health in all government policies, apply the philosophy of full life-cycle health management to the whole process and every link of urban planning, construction, and management, and move faster to build a public health system adapted to rapid urbanization and high population density.

Party committees and governments at all levels must put the public health campaign high on their agenda, ensure its implementation through rational organizational structure, appropriate adjustment in functions and responsibilities, adequate staffing, and proper funding, and explore more effective ways of public mobilization.

Fifth, we should exploit the strengths of TCM in the prevention and control of major epidemics. The clinical approach to combining Chinese and Western medicine and therapies has been a success as well as a point to be noted in the fight against Covid-19. This manifests the inheritance and innovative development of the best of our TCM heritage. Over five millennia, the Chinese nation has pulled through numerous health crises thanks to TCM; in the fight against disease, many TCM classics have been written and handed down, including *Treatise on Febrile and Miscellaneous Diseases*[1], *Treatise on Differentiation* and *Treatment of Epidemic Febrile Diseases*[2], and *Treatise on Epidemic Febrile Diseases*[3]. The Three TCM Drugs and Three Herbal Formulas selected for the clinical treatment of Covid-19 in China derived exactly from TCM classics.

We should strengthen research and clinical trials, summarize TCM theory in epidemic prevention and control and the best clinical practices, and carry out intensive R&D for breakthroughs. We should explain the therapeutic effect of TCM, by adopting modern assessment tools and drawing on ancient experience at the same time.

We should delve deeper into and analyze TCM classics, create a number of TCM research platforms, and reform the mechanisms for TCM review and approval, to encourage the R&D of new medicines and boost the TCM industry.

We should improve the TCM service system and raise the capacity of TCM hospitals in emergency response and treatment. Training of TCM professionals should be strengthened in order to build a highly capable TCM team for epidemic prevention and control at the national level.

We must probe into the institutional problems in the administration of TCM, strengthen the leadership over and management of its development, and promote complementary and coordinated development between TCM and Western medicine.

Sixth, we should improve laws and regulations on public health. Since its victory over SARS in 2003, China has revised the Law on the Prevention and Treatment of Infectious Diseases, and enacted the Emergency Response Law and the Regulations on Response to Public Health Emergencies along with contingency plans. These laws and regulations constitute the legal basis for responding to epidemics but some of their stipulations are incoherent or inconsistent with each other.

We need to further amend the Law on the Prevention and Treatment of Infectious Diseases and promulgate a law on the response to public health emergencies to meet new demands, and strengthen law enforcement mechanisms for epidemic prevention and control, with clearly defined powers and responsibilities and standardized procedures for effective enforcement. All of these will help improve legislation on the measures against emerging epidemic diseases, and define the functions and responsibilities of central and local authorities, of the government and its functional departments, and of administrative organs and professional institutions.

We need to raise public awareness of laws and regulations on public health security and on epidemic prevention and control, so that all members of society act in accordance with the law in this regard.

Seventh, we should leverage the essential role of science and technology in the prevention and control of epidemics. I have always emphasized that science and technology are effective weapons for fighting epidemics. Humanity's victories over major disasters and pandemics could not have been possible without scientific progress and technological innovation.

In the early stage of the Covid-19 epidemic, China's research institutions acted together in etiological investigation and pathogen identification. It took us only eight days to identify the pathogen of this "viral pneumonia of unknown cause" as a novel coronavirus. It took us only 16 days to optimize the nucleic acid test kits, enabling the screening of suspected cases on a large scale. We acted promptly in selecting a number of effective medicines and therapeutic regimens. We expedited the development of vaccines through multiple approaches and made them available for clinical trial. All these efforts have laid solid ground for China's fight against Covid-19.

Major scientific and technological achievements in life security and biosafety are treasures of the country and must be kept in our own hands.

We must increase science and technology input in public health endeavors: improving the systems for epidemic prevention and control and for key public health R&D that are applicable for both normal circumstances and emergencies; intensifying efforts to make breakthroughs in core technologies; increasing funding for the prevention and control of epidemics; addressing defects in such areas as life sciences, biotechnology, medicine and health care, and medical equipment at a faster pace.

Currently, we must leverage our institutional advantage of being able to pool nationwide resources and strive to become the first developer of Covid-19 vaccines, so as to keep ourselves well-positioned strategically.

Moreover, we need to extend institutional reform for the development of science and technology talent, and improve the mechanisms for discovering, training and motivating leading scientists with strategic vision and innovative technology talent, so that more outstanding professionals will engage in scientific research and have the opportunity to demonstrate their outstanding capabilities.

Eighth, we should strengthen international exchanges and cooperation on public health. Since the Covid-19 epidemic broke out, China, which is committed to building a global community of shared future, has been actively fulfilling its international obligations through close cooperation with the WHO and other countries. China has shared its successful experience with the rest of the world concerning case reporting, virus identification, and control measures. China has, to the best of its ability, offered material and technological assistance to more than 100 countries and international organizations, honoring its responsibilities as a major country.

In responding to Covid-19, we must have plans in place for worst-case scenarios. We must maintain our strategic resolve, stay firmly on track, meet challenges head-on, adopt effective approaches, and unite all the forces at our disposal.

At the 73rd World Health Assembly in 2020, I explained, in my video speech, China's vision and proposals on fighting Covid-19, and announced five policy measures, which were widely welcomed by the international community. The final agreements reached at the Assembly conform to China's position as well as the shared aspirations of most countries.

Covid-19 is still raging around the world. China will continue to perform its international obligations, play its role as the world's biggest supplier of protective materials, participate in the formulation of relevant international guides, norms, and standards, and share its solutions and experience. In doing so, China will exert a greater impact on and have a greater say in the global health governance system as we work with other countries to build a global community of health for all.

Notes

[1] *Treatise on Febrile and Miscellaneous Diseases (Shang Han Za Bing Lun)* was composed by Zhang Zhongjing (c. 150-219) of the Eastern Han Dynasty. – *Tr.*

[2] *Treatise on Differentiation and Treatment of Epidemic Febrile Diseases (Wen Bing Tiao Bian)* was composed by Wu Tang (1758-1836) of the Qing Dynasty. – *Tr.*

[3] *Treatise on Epidemic Febrile Diseases (Wen Re Lun)* was compiled by Ye Gui (1666-1745) of the Qing Dynasty. – *Tr.*

Optimize Social Governance Based on Collaboration, Participation and Common Interests[*]

August 24, 2020

Experience has shown us that development brings problems, and they are equally numerous before and after. The social structure of our country is undergoing profound change. The internet has reshaped human interaction. Social norms, attitudes and behaviors have changed too.

During the 14th Five-year Plan period (2021-2025), we will have to thoroughly study the following issues and take steps to address them:

- how to adapt to profound change in social structure, relationships, attitudes and behaviors;
- how to realize fuller and higher-quality employment;
- how to improve the social security system to realize full coverage and sustainability;
- how to strengthen public health and disease control;
- how to promote long-term balanced population growth;
- how to strengthen social governance, resolve social conflicts, and maintain stability.

Modernity is built on a balance between order and dynamism. We must optimize social governance based on collaboration, participation, and common interests, synergize government efforts with public self-regulation and community-level self-governance, and build a community of social governance in which everyone fulfills their responsibilities and shares in the benefits.

We must develop and adopt new approaches to grassroots social governance, and energize all the "cells" of society. Conflicts and

* Part of the speech at a meeting with experts from economic and social sectors.

disputes should be resolved when they first arise so that harmony and stability can be maintained at the grassroots. Greater emphasis should be placed on upholding social equity and justice and promoting well-rounded individual development and comprehensive social progress.

Accelerate Educational Modernization and Prepare a New Generation for National Rejuvenation*

September 22, 2020

We will foster a new generation capable of shouldering the mission of national rejuvenation. Education is a matter of great significance to the country and the Party. It has been a top priority of the Central Committee since the 18th CPC National Congress in 2012. We have held the National Education Conference and released a new guideline – China Educational Modernization 2035. We have strengthened moral and political education in schools of all types and at all levels, advanced comprehensive reforms in education, and made curriculum content a matter of national responsibility. Fundamental changes are taking place.

In the coming 14th Five-year Plan period (2021-2025), education will be one of the top missions of the Party and the state. We will fully implement the Party's education policy, give priority to education, cultivate talent for the Party and the country, and develop education that satisfies the demands of the people. In accelerating the modernization of education we will foster a new generation and prepare them for the mission of national rejuvenation. We will keep to the socialist path in education, take the fostering of values and moral integrity as the fundamental goal of education, and make education play its role in encouraging students to foster and apply the core socialist values. We will further reform and innovate school courses on moral standards and political philosophy, strengthen and improve physical and aesthetic

---

* Part of the speech at a meeting with experts and representatives from education, culture, health and sports sectors.

education, and expand programs on basic life and work skills. We will develop well-rounded education, promote equal access to education, and ensure the all-round development of students in terms of morality, intellectual ability, physical fitness, aesthetic sensibility and work skills. In our school education we will foster patriotism, a sense of social responsibility, a pioneering spirit, and the ability to put ideas into practice.

Human resources are an important support for the new development dynamic. We will optimize the structure of disciplines and programs, and the training of personnel to meet the needs of the new development dynamic. We will improve the mechanism to promote lifelong learning for all, and build a more flexible lifelong learning system with richer resources and easier access. We will intensify efforts to develop vocational education and training, improve workers' skills and increase their incomes, expand the middle-income group through fuller and higher-quality employment, and release the potential in domestic demand.

Improving our capacity for independent innovation and our ability to make quick breakthroughs in core technologies in key fields is essential to fostering the new development dynamic. Our colleges and universities should take on the responsibility for releasing their potential in basic research and scientific and technological innovation, respond to China's strategic needs, and make faster breakthroughs in core technologies, particularly in bottleneck technologies that have been withheld from us. We will support institutions of higher learning that aim to become first-rate universities or develop first-class disciplines in strengthening scientific and technological innovation and building research facilities that serve this purpose. We will foster synergy of enterprises, universities, and research institutes. We will further reform the training of highly competent staff for colleges and universities, so as to have a contingent of high-caliber teachers and nurture a greater number of outstanding staff. To serve regional development strategies, we will optimize the distribution of educational resources across regions and accelerate the creation of an education model. We must move faster to integrate education across the country, and create an environment in which the eastern region, the central region and the western region progress together in educational development. This will enable education to play a bigger role in regional development strategies.

We will continue to implement comprehensive, systematic, holistic and coordinated reforms in education. We will introduce and implement the Overall Plan for Further Reform on Education Evaluation in the New Era, and ensure that it succeeds in building a world-class evaluation system grounded in China's realities. We must review the experience of booming online education since the outbreak of Covid-19, and use information technology to update educational concepts and reform teaching models. We must open the education sector wider to the outside world, optimize global cooperation in education, and strengthen international exchanges and cooperation in science and technology at higher levels. At the same time, we must maintain our principles and keep to the correct political orientation.

Develop Quality and Sustainable Social Security*

February 26, 2021

Today, at the 28th group study session of the Political Bureau, we will discuss the topic of building a social security system that covers the entire population. To achieve the goals set for the 14th Five-year Plan period (2021-2025), we will analyze the current status of our social security system and its problems, and lay out a plan for ensuring future quality and sustainable development.

Social security is a system for ensuring people's basic needs, improving their wellbeing, and safeguarding social equity. It is an important institutional framework for social and economic progress, and for allowing the people to share the fruits of reform and development. As a social safety net, an income distribution regulator, and an economic shock absorber, it is of overarching importance to national stability and governance.

Our Party has always attached great importance to social security and people's wellbeing. At its Second National Congress in 1922, the CPC proposed to improve workers' benefits through measures such as providing factory insurance and protecting the unemployed. The Labor Law of the Chinese Soviet Republic, promulgated in 1931 when the soviet government was seated in Ruijin, Jiangxi Province, had a special chapter on social security. In 1951, shortly after the PRC was founded, the central government enacted the Regulations of the People's Republic of China on Labor Insurance, in accordance with the stipulation on introducing a labor insurance system in the Common Program of the Chinese People's Political Consultative

---

* Speech at the 28th group study session of the Political Bureau of the 19th CPC Central Committee.

Conference. Since reform and opening up began in 1978, we have made steady and significant progress in developing the social security system as a pillar for improving people's lives.

Since the Party's 18th National Congress in 2012, the Central Committee has brought social security to the top of its agenda to ensure faster progress. At the meetings of the Political Bureau and of its standing committee, and meetings of the Central Commission for Further Reform, plans for reforming basic pension schemes and guidelines for deeper reform of medical insurance have been discussed and reviewed, to form the top-level design for improving the social security system and to make reform more systematic, holistic and coordinated.

We have unified the basic pension schemes for rural and non-working urban residents, merged the pension schemes for staff of government offices, public institutions and enterprises, and established a regulatory system for the central government to balance pension funding for enterprise employees across provinces.

We have integrated the basic medical insurance system for non-working urban residents and the new rural cooperative medical care system to form the basic medical insurance for rural and non-working urban residents. We have introduced critical illness insurance for rural and non-working urban residents and formed the National Healthcare Security Administration.

We have extended social insurance coverage across the whole population, reduced social insurance contributions, and transferred state capital to replenish social security funds. We have developed social welfare undertakings to care for the elderly and children and to help people with disabilities. With institutional support in place, all citizens, whether they are rural or urban residents and regardless of their region, gender and occupation, can feel secure when they get old, fall ill, lose their job, suffer a work-related injury or disability, or fall into poverty.

A complete social security system has taken shape. Social insurance is the mainstay while social assistance, social welfare, and benefits and services are provided for eligible groups. With basic medical insurance covering 1.36 billion people and basic pension schemes covering nearly 1 billion people, China has the world's largest social security net. This has laid solid foundations for a better life, provided strong support for eliminating extreme poverty, and facilitated efforts to achieve all-round moderate prosperity and the First Centenary Goal on schedule.

While celebrating our achievements, we need to be aware that as the principal challenge facing our society has changed and urbanization, population aging, and employment diversification accelerate, the weaknesses in our social security net are becoming more apparent, and these call for our attention and action. The main weak points are:

- unsatisfactory transition between different social security arrangements due to incomplete integration;
- failure to cover all migrant workers, those in flexible employment, and those engaged in new forms of business;
- the over-reliance on basic social security services initiated and managed by the government and the inadequate provision of supplementary insurance by market players and the private sector;
- pressure on balancing regional social security receipts and payments due to lack of high-level coordination;
- differential benefits for urban and rural residents, between regions, and between groups;
- the gap between social security services and people's needs;
- insufficient social security funding in some places.

At the Fifth Plenary Session of the 19th CPC Central Committee in 2020, a blueprint was drawn up for China's development in the next 5 to 15 years, aiming for more tangible progress towards common prosperity. Social security directly concerns the people's most immediate interests. We need to strengthen income redistribution as a tool of mutual assistance, include more people in the social security net, and provide them with reliable and satisfactory services. To meet people's diverse needs, we need to develop a fair, unified, sustainable, and multitiered social security system that covers both urban and rural areas and forms a tight-knit safety net for the entire population.

First, we should build a social security system with Chinese characteristics. It is natural that different countries have different social security systems, as they differ in level of development, social conditions, and culture. Learning from foreign experience does not mean mechanically copying their models, but exploring and creating a distinctively Chinese social safety net based on the conditions in our country.

Leveraging the strengths of CPC leadership and our socialist system, we have been able to pool resources from around the country to develop social security in a solid and steady manner. Following a people-centered approach and the principle of common prosperity in developing social security, we have focused on improving people's wellbeing and upholding social equity, so that all our people can enjoy the benefits of reform and development in a fairer way. We are strengthening the institutional network for social security to become an inclusive, multitiered, and sustainable system that ensures basic living needs. Adapting the system to the needs of the times, we have addressed problems and broken through institutional barriers by means of reform and innovation. Seeking truth from facts and doing all we can within our capacity, we have based improvements in social security on sustainable economic and financial growth – always respecting our realities and never transcending our stage of development. These successful experiences must be continually enriched and applied in future work.

Second, we should be forward-looking in planning for social security during the 14th Five-year Plan period and beyond. The outline for developing social security during the 14th Five-year Plan period, passed at the Fifth Plenary Session of the 19th CPC Central Committee, should be incorporated into our overall planning and implemented in full.

We should apply systems thinking and understand the requirements to implement the new development philosophy and create a new development dynamic in the new development stage. Furthermore, social security should proceed in the context of the Five-sphere Integrated Plan and the Four-pronged Comprehensive Strategy. This requires strategic thinking, commitment to meeting people's expectation for a better life, and alignment with the goals of well-rounded individual development and common prosperity. It should sustain progress in providing better access to childcare, education, employment, medical services, elderly care, housing, and social assistance.

To be better prepared for new social security challenges and to be able to take preemptive action against risks, we should remain alert and analyze the trends of population aging, growing average life expectancy, the increase in years of schooling, and changes in the workforce structure for the next 5, 15 and 30 years. We should employ an international perspective, and draw lessons and insights from the past and present practices of other countries. In particular, we should avoid the blind pursuit of better welfare that has led some countries into the middle-income trap, and the provision of excessive social welfare that has caused the loss of dynamism in some societies. We must always remember that the economy and social security are like water and a boat – shallow water allows for a small boat, and deeper water allows for a larger boat. If this rule is not respected the boat may be swamped, or run aground.

Third, we should extend social security reform. Our reform in social security is targeting greater integration and efficiency. It calls for improved planning and coordination between different elements of social security and between social security and other related sectors, so that reform in all areas builds a strong synergy. We should focus on the people's most immediate concerns in social security, and remove the obstacles hindering its development.

We will establish a multi-pillar, multitiered old-age pension system, improve the mechanisms for adjusting funding and benefits for basic pension and medical insurance, and expand the coverage of enterprise annuities. Third-pillar pension plans will be developed under regulation, and commercial health insurance will be promoted to meet the people's diverse needs. Basic medical insurance, unemployment insurance, and work-related injury insurance will be brought under unified management at the provincial level, and the respective powers and expenditure responsibilities of central and local governments will be further clarified.

Social assistance for rural residents should be planned as part of the rural revitalization strategy, and the system for social assistance in rural areas should be improved by putting in place measures for providing regular assistance. Improvements to social security should be made to cover all migrant workers, those in flexible employment, and those engaged in new forms of business. Similarly, improvements should be made in providing support and services for veterans, care and services for the elderly, and social assistance and welfare benefits for orphans and those with disabilities.

After we introduced the central regulatory system for pension funding in 2018, RMB176.8 billion was transferred last year alone from the more developed eastern regions to the less developed central and western regions and provinces with old industrial bases. This has mitigated the structural imbalance in social security funding between regions, and ensured pensions are paid on time and in full. To end the regional imbalance in social security, basic pension premiums should be brought under unified management at the national level as soon as possible. This conforms to the law of large numbers and constitutes a prerequisite for creating a new development dynamic.

China is now faced with greater pressure from rising medical insurance expenditure due to a rapidly aging population, the growing prevalence of chronic diseases among the elderly, and advances in medicine, which has made more previously untreatable diseases treatable and controllable. We should continue to connect and coordinate reforms in medical treatment, medical insurance, and medicine supply[1], and improve the mechanisms for adjusting funding and benefits for basic medical insurance. Further reform will be carried out in government bulk purchase of medicines and medical consumables and in the payment methods of basic medical insurance. The pricing mechanism for medicines and medical services will be improved, and the basic medical insurance funds will operate with greater efficiency.

In recent years, many developed countries and emerging economies with aging populations have introduced reform plans to raise the statutory retirement age. Not all their plans have gone well, and some have experienced setbacks. In China, we should set the right direction, tempo and intensity, strengthen guidance of public opinion, and build a broad consensus to maximize the synergy for achieving this reform.

Fourth, we should advance law-based governance in social security. Social security should be strengthened in legislation, law enforcement, judicature, and law observance. Its healthy development should be guided by the rule of law.

Legislation on social insurance, assistance, and welfare should be enacted or revised. For individuals, employers, governments, and other sectors of society, their legitimate rights and interests in social security should be guaranteed, and they should also fulfill their statutory obligations and responsibilities.

Supervision of social security funds should be improved in accordance with the law, to defuse operational risks and ensure that the funds remain secure. There will be zero tolerance for insurance fraud or embezzlement of social security funds, and every coin from the funds, as well as social aid and charity, will be guarded and put to good use.

Fifth, we should take a more targeted approach to social security management. Aiming for high efficiency in social security governance, improvements should be made to the management and services network at the central, provincial, city, county, and township/sub-district levels, with greater attention to the precision of management and the quality of services.

As population flows increase and people change their jobs more frequently, social insurance registration, transfer, and renewal should be updated accordingly. We will optimize the mechanism for accurately identifying the recipients of social assistance and welfare benefits, and ensure that our social security net provides everyone with the insurance, assistance, and services to which they are entitled.

The unified national platform for social security services should be upgraded to enable better handling of social security matters online by incorporating internet, big data, and cloud computing technologies. Traditional services should be provided in the same measure to ensure ease of access for the elderly, people with disabilities, and other groups with special needs.

Sixth, we should leverage the positive role of social security in our Covid-19 response. Since the coronavirus struck last year, social security has made a major contribution to effective epidemic prevention and control in the all-out people's war on the virus, and to our success in achieving moderate prosperity and eradicating extreme poverty in China.

As the virus continues to spread around the globe, we still face grave challenges in preventing inbound cases and domestic resurgence; here social security can offer help in containing the virus and stabilizing economic and social development. When the situation improves, reductions or exemptions of social security contributions and other temporary relief measures should be withdrawn progressively in coordination with similar measures in other areas.

We should improve the social security response to major emergencies based on our successes in Covid-19 prevention and control, and mitigate conventional and foreseeable risks such as illness and death as well as exceptional challenges that are hard to foresee.

Lastly, I would like to emphasize the importance of building a social security system with unified standards throughout the country. When social security had just been established, local governments were encouraged to innovate and try new approaches. As the social security system has developed and expanded, top-level design should now be followed to ensure unified management.

Mandatory institutional requirements must be executed, and operations should be brought under strict management and supervision. All localities must have the broader picture in mind and enforce institutional reform as instructed; no unauthorized local alterations can be allowed. There can be regional differences in social security standards for some time, but the goal of achieving a unified system is not open to debate. No one is allowed to deviate from this principle or go their own way.

Party committees and governments at all levels should gain a deeper understanding of how important social security is and how it works, coordinate all efforts to implement the decisions, plans and reform measures formulated by the Party Central Committee, and make steady progress in building a social security network for all our people.

Notes

[1] This refers to a people-centered approach to public health, by making reforms in medical treatment, medical insurance, and medicine supply more holistic, systematic and coordinated through legal, administrative and market means. It aims to boost public health and medical services, improve the multilevel medical security system, and regulate the supply of medicine and medical consumables. The sound allocation of medical resources will ensure public access to quality, efficient and affordable basic medical and health services.

Carry Forward the Spirit of the Beijing Winter Olympics and Paralympics and Build China into a Strong Sporting Nation*

April 8, 2022

A great cause nurtures a great spirit, and a great spirit promotes a great cause. All of you involved in the Beijing 2022 Olympic and Paralympic Winter Games cherished this opportunity. Throughout the process of bidding, organizing and hosting the Games, you have fostered a spirit of the Beijing Winter Olympics and Paralympics – having a broad vision, staying confident and open, rising to the occasion, pursuing excellence, and creating a better future together.

By having a broad vision, you have kept the interests of our country at heart and aimed high. You regarded the preparation and hosting of the Games as an important national mission, and you saw it as your duty to win glory for China and as an honor to make your contribution. You took on great responsibilities, united as one, and strove for excellence for our country and the people.

By staying confident and open, you have been graceful, open and accommodating. You have remained confident in the path, theory, system, and culture of socialism with Chinese characteristics. You have creatively presented China's rich and profound cultural heritage. You have demonstrated the visions of the ancient Chinese civilization in a style of simplicity. You have demonstrated the sincerity and friendship of the Chinese people with your hospitality. And you have promoted mutual understanding and friendship among different

---

* Part of the speech at a meeting to review the Beijing 2022 Olympic and Paralympic Winter Games and commend outstanding individuals and groups.

peoples through sports exchanges.

By rising to the occasion, you have worked hard, persevered, and maintained high morale in the face of daunting challenges and met them head-on.

By pursuing excellence, you have been dedicated and meticulous in all preparations. You stuck to the highest standards, met the most demanding requirements, refined every plan and measure, sought perfection, and achieved one success after another.

By endeavoring to create a better future together, you have worked in coordination, interaction and cooperation. You responded to the Beijing Olympic and Paralympic motto "Together for a Shared Future" and the new Olympic motto "Faster, Higher, Stronger – Together", and, with the future of China and the wider world in mind, you called on all of humanity to build a global community of shared future.

Seven years of meticulous preparation ensured the success of the Games, and now we are ready to move to the next stage. The Beijing 2022 Winter Olympics and Paralympics are a landmark event held at a crucial time as all of us in the Party and the country are striving towards the Second Centenary Goal of building a modern socialist country. As we forge ahead, we should make the most of the legacy of the Games.

The Games have left us not only with venues and facilities, but even more importantly, cultural heritage and a talent pool. These are all valuable assets; we must exploit them, convert them into new drivers for development, and use them to the full.

We will strengthen strategic planning and make better use of sports venues and facilities to make ice and snow sports more popular. We will develop the winter economy, hold a range of ice and snow sports activities, and encourage public participation.

We will fully tap into the cultural legacy of the Games to boost confidence in Chinese culture, make China's voice heard around the globe, and tell China's stories in an engaging way.

We will stay true to humanitarianism, respect and safeguard human rights, and improve social security for people with disabilities and the systems of care and services. We will promote all-round development of programs for people with disabilities, and encourage and support them in making sustained efforts for self-improvement. As a vision-impaired athlete said at the Games, "I cannot see the world, but I want the world to see me."

We will promote throughout society volunteerism, characterized by dedication, friendship, mutual support, and pursuit of excellence; and we will fully leverage the role of volunteers in promoting social progress.

We will carry forward the Olympic spirit, turn the Games into an opportunity for promoting peace and development, and contribute China's vision and strength to human progress.

Our success in hosting the Games has stimulated enthusiasm for sports among hundreds of millions of Chinese and energized China's sports development. We will endeavor to build up the physique and improve the physical fitness and the quality of life of the whole nation. We will fully leverage the important role of sports in advancing well-rounded development of the person. We will continue to boost reform and innovation in promoting sports. We will strengthen research and development in sports science and technology. We will improve public fitness programs and encourage the public and in particular the young people to keep fit through sports. We will promote China's overall strength and performance in sports, increase its international competitiveness, and redouble our efforts to build China into a strong sporting nation.

We have realized our dream of hosting the Winter Olympics and Paralympics, and we are now continuing our journey towards the future. Let us rally even more closely around the Party Central Committee; let us be inspired by the spirit of the Beijing Winter Olympics and Paralympics; let us forge ahead with greater resolve and confidence to realize the Second Centenary Goal and the Chinese Dream of national rejuvenation.

Harmony Between Humanity
and Nature

Build an Eco-Civilization for Sustainable Development[*]

April 10, 2020

We must ensure harmony between humanity and nature.

I have consistently emphasized that humanity and nature form a community of life. As human beings, we must respect nature, follow its ways, and protect it. Our Covid-19 response has made us more keenly aware that building an eco-civilization is vital to our nation's sustainable development, and our plan of economic and social progress must be based on harmony between humanity and nature.

Engels made it clear long ago: "Let us not, however, flatter ourselves overmuch on account of our human victories over nature. For each such victory nature takes its revenge on us."[1] Since the First Industrial Revolution, people have continuously improved their ability to exploit nature, but overdevelopment has led to a reduction in biodiversity, and forced wild animals to migrate, increasing transmission of the pathogens they carry as they do so. Since the beginning of this century, humans have suffered from a marked increase in the incidence of new infectious diseases worldwide, including SARS, avian influenza, MERS, Ebola, and now Covid-19. Only by maintaining a balance between humanity and nature and in our ecosystems can we protect human health. We must understand fully how humanity and nature form a community of life and step up efforts on all fronts to build an eco-civilization. We must always prioritize eco-environmental progress.

More and more human activities are pushing at the boundaries of

* Part of the speech at the seventh meeting of the Commission for Financial and Economic Affairs under the CPC Central Committee.

ecosystems and testing their limits. We must defend these boundaries, both tangible and intangible, to ensure harmony between humanity and nature. We need to improve planning regarding our territorial space, implement our functional zoning strategy, and draw up red lines for ecological conservation. We should accelerate efforts to establish a system of nature reserves, improve biodiversity protection networks, and set reasonable spatial limits for economic and social activities.

Notes

[1] Frederick Engels: "Dialectics of Nature", *Karl Marx & Frederick Engels: Collected Works*, Vol. 25, Eng. ed., Lawrence & Wishart Electric Book, 2010, pp. 460-461.

Yangtze River Economic Belt:
A Showcase for Green Development*

November 14, 2020

We will implement the guidelines of the 19th CPC National Congress in 2017 and the second, third, fourth and fifth plenary sessions of the 19th CPC Central Committee held in the three years that followed. To write a new chapter in green development that gives priority to eco-environmental conservation, we will act on the new development philosophy and promote high-quality development of the Yangtze River Economic Belt (YREB). This will set a new example of coordinated development among regions, raise opening up to new and higher levels, build new strengths in innovation-driven development, and create a new example of harmony between humanity and nature. The goal is to make the YREB a showcase for China's green development prioritizing eco-environmental conservation, a major artery boosting domestic and global economic flows, and an important leader in high-quality economic development.

In the past five years, under the leadership of the CPC Central Committee, provinces and cities along the Yangtze River have worked with unprecedented intensity and on a grand scale to improve their eco-environment and accelerate their transformation to green and low-carbon economic and social development. The result has been huge progress in eco-environmental protection in the YREB, and historic successes have been achieved in economic and social development. The YREB region has generally enjoyed steady economic growth under an optimized structure. Local living standards have

---

* Main points of the speech at a forum on the development of the Yangtze River Economic Belt.

significantly improved, and economic growth has been achieved together with improvements in environmental protection. In particular, since the beginning of this year, provinces and cities along the river have responded effectively to the sudden outbreak of the coronavirus epidemic by balancing epidemic prevention and control with economic and social development, and have effectively offset the impact of major floods and the worsening external environment, playing a prominent role in making China the first major economy to return to positive growth.

The YREB represents a major policy decision on the part of the CPC Central Committee. It is an important strategy with a bearing on China's overall development. The 19th CPC Central Committee detailed specific requirements for the YREB initiative in the proposals adopted at its Fifth Plenary Session earlier this year. The YREB covers 11 provinces and cities along the river, and spans the east, center, and west of China, accounting for half of the country's population and economic output. It is of critical importance to the national eco-environment and has huge development potential. This has determined that it should play a key role in implementing the new development philosophy, creating a new development dynamic, and promoting high-quality development.

Protection and restoration of the eco-environment should be strengthened. We must take a holistic and systematic view of the ecosystem and the Yangtze River Basin, identify the root causes of existing problems, carry out systematic protection and restoration, and avoid any resort to stopgap measures. We must make coordinated efforts to manage such eco-elements as mountains, rivers, forests, farmland, lakes and grasslands, promote interaction and cooperation in the upper, middle and lower reaches of the river, and strengthen the coordination of all relevant measures. At the same time we need to focus on overall progress. While making breakthroughs in key areas, we need to strengthen systematic and holistic measures to prevent imbalanced development and guard against the tendency of attending to one matter while losing sight of others.

Conditional on the strictest eco-environmental protection, we will improve the efficiency of resource utilization, accelerate green and low-carbon development, and strive to build green development pilot zones where humanity and nature coexist in harmony.

Top priority must be given to restoring the eco-environment of the Yangtze River, and a new system for comprehensive control must be established. To improve the eco-environment of the river and the eco-functions of its waters, and to secure the quality and stability of the ecosystems, we should take into consideration multiple factors and their interactions, including the aquatic environment, the aquatic ecosystem, water resources, water security, water culture and the coast-line. We must implement coordinated management and control of the upper, middle and lower reaches of the Yangtze River, its banks, trunk streams and tributaries, and the rivers, lakes and reservoirs in the basin.

We must strengthen territorial space control and negative list management, enforce red lines for ecological conservation, continue to carry out projects for eco-environmental restoration and pollution control, and keep the ecosystems of the Yangtze River natural and intact. We need to step up efforts to establish mechanisms to realize the market value of green products, so that environmental protection and restoration efforts receive reasonable returns and those who damage the environment pay the price. We will improve the systems for monitoring and early warning of water disasters, for disaster prevention and control, and for emergency rescue and relief. We will make comprehensive efforts to improve river courses and reinforce embankments, so as to build the Yangtze River into a tranquil river that does not burst its banks.

Achieve Modernization Based on Harmony Between Humanity and Nature[*]

April 30, 2021

Today we gather here for the 29th group study session of the Political Bureau of the CPC Central Committee. The theme of this session is strengthening our efforts in building an eco-civilization in the new era. Since the 18th CPC National Congress held in 2012, the Political Bureau has had two group study sessions on subjects related to building an eco-civilization. This is the third.

The goals of the session are to take on the new tasks and meet the new requirements that we face in building an eco-civilization in this new development stage, applying the new development philosophy, and creating a new development dynamic, to analyze the new developments in building an eco-civilization, and to achieve modernization characterized by harmonious coexistence between humanity and nature.

Since the 18th CPC National Congress, we have strengthened the Party's leadership in all our efforts to build an eco-civilization, and made a series of strategic plans to prioritize these efforts in our overall work. Pursuing eco-environmental progress is one of the five core tasks in the Five-sphere Integrated Plan; ensuring harmony between humanity and nature is a fundamental principle for upholding and developing socialism with Chinese characteristics in the new era; promoting green development is a defining feature of our new development philosophy; preventing and controlling pollution is the target of our three critical battles along with fighting major risks and

* Speech at the 29th group study session of the Political Bureau of the 19th CPC Central Committee.

poverty; building a beautiful China is an integral part of our goal of making China a great modern socialist country by the middle of the century.

All these fully embody our understanding of the importance of building an eco-civilization and affirm the status of eco-environmental progress in the overall development of the Party and the state.

With unprecedented determination and effort, we have taken a host of actions of fundamental, groundbreaking and long-term significance: comprehensively strengthening the building of an eco-civilization, planning in a systematic manner the reform of the institutions for developing an eco-civilization, and taking a holistic approach to managing mountains, rivers, forests, farmlands, lakes, grasslands and deserts. Our achievements are unprecedented, and historic progress has been made in our understanding and approach in building an eco-civilization.

I have given instructions and directives on typical cases such as the environmental damage to the Qilian Mountains in Gansu Province, the illegal construction of villas at the northern foot of the Qinling Mountains in Shaanxi Province, and the illegal mining activities in the Muli Coalfield in Qinghai Province. Local authorities have investigated and held accountable the people who abused their power and committed dereliction of duty.

Over the past nine years, solid steps have been taken to build a beautiful China: Blue skies are returning; the country's vegetation coverage has grown; a green economy is developing rapidly; energy and material consumption has been reduced; heavy smog has been contained; the number of black and foul water bodies has fallen; cities and rural areas have become more livable. The entire Party and the whole of society have come to a realization that clear waters and green mountains are invaluable assets and have acted upon this understanding.

According to satellite data from the National Aeronautics and Space Administration of the United States, from 2000 to 2017, China contributed about a quarter of the newly-added vegetation area across the whole planet. Our country has taken the lead in global climate change talks. It has been an active proponent in the signing, effecting and implementation of the Paris Agreement. China has announced the goals of achieving peak carbon dioxide emissions by 2030 and carbon neutrality by 2060. Our country has won widespread approval for its achievements in building an eco-civilization.

Eco-environmental protection and economic development constitute a dialectical unity and are complementary. Through building an eco-civilization and promoting green, low-carbon and circular development, we can meet people's growing demands for a beautiful eco-environment, achieve higher-quality development that is more efficient, equitable, sustainable and secure, and create a model of sound development featuring increased production, higher living standards, and healthy ecosystems.

The restoration and improvement of the eco-environment is a process demanding a long and arduous effort. It cannot be accomplished at one stroke; instead it requires perseverance and solid work. Currently, our country still faces many problems and challenges in building an eco-civilization. The foundations for eco-environmental stability and progress are not solid enough, and the turning point from quantitative to qualitative change is yet to come. The quality of the eco-environment still falls well short of the people's expectation for a better life, of the goal of building a beautiful China, and of the requirements for forming a new development dynamic, promoting high-quality development, and building a modern socialist country.

Restructuring our country's industry will take time. At present, traditional industries still account for a large proportion of our economy; strategic emerging industries and high-tech industries have not become the dominant driver for economic growth; there has not yet been a fundamental change in energy structure; the root causes of pollution in key regions and sectors have not been addressed; the tasks of achieving peak carbon dioxide emissions and carbon neutrality remain daunting; the limiting effect of resources and the environment on development is growing.

Green and low-carbon development is an international trend, and the green economy has become a critical area in global industrial competition. Some Western countries have taken every opportunity to vilify China on environmental matters and constantly make this an issue. This shows that major countries are in fierce contention on the eco-environmental front.

At the Fifth Plenary Session of the 19th CPC Central Committee held in late October 2020, I emphasized that China's socialist modernization has many distinctive features. One of these is that it is a modernization characterized by harmonious coexistence between humanity and nature – a modernization that synchronizes material progress and eco-environmental progress.

During the 14th Five-year Plan period (2021-2025), in its efforts to build an eco-civilization, our country has entered a crucial stage in which the country makes carbon reduction a strategic priority, builds synergy between reducing pollution and bringing down carbon dioxide emissions, pushes for a complete green transition in socio-economic development, and strives for quantitative-to-qualitative improvement of the eco-environment.

We must apply the new development philosophy in full, to the letter and in all fields of our work, maintain strategic resolve, and plan economic and social development with the goal in mind of achieving harmony between humanity and nature.

Implementing our fundamental national policy of conserving resources and protecting the environment, and acting on the principles of prioritizing conservation and protection and letting nature restore itself, we will develop spatial configurations, industrial structures, production models, and ways of life that are resource-saving and environment-friendly.

We need to make coordinated efforts to control pollution, protect ecosystems, tackle climate change, and ensure continuous improvement of the eco-environment, so as to achieve a modernization characterized by harmonious coexistence between humanity and nature.

First, we must persevere in promoting green and low-carbon development.

I have emphasized several times that eco-environmental problems are essentially the consequences of our development model and way of life. Establishing a sound economic structure that facilitates green, low-carbon and circular development, and promoting a thorough transition towards eco-friendly economic and social development are the fundamental solutions to China's eco-environmental problems.

On March 15, I chaired the ninth meeting of the Commission for Financial and Economic Affairs under the CPC Central Committee, at which the basic approach to achieving peak carbon dioxide emissions and carbon neutrality was studied and major measures were planned.

We must focus on forming a synergy between reducing pollution and bringing down carbon dioxide emissions to promote a comprehensive transformation towards environment-friendly economic and social development, and expedite the structural adjustment of industries, energy, transport and land use.

We must strengthen territorial planning and land use regulation, observe the boundaries for basic cropland, for protected ecosystems, and for urban development, implement a strategy of functional zoning, draw red lines for ecological conservation and rigorously defend them.

We should address resource problems by focusing on utilization, and promote total volume management, sound allocation, comprehensive conservation, and recycling, to raise the utilization efficiency of all kinds of resources.

Taking industrial structural adjustment as the key, we must accelerate the development of strategic emerging industries, high-tech industries, and modern service industries, and promote clean, low-carbon, safe and efficient use of energy, to continuously reduce carbon intensity.

To solve the problem of insufficient scientific and technological support for green and low-carbon development, we must make greater efforts to research carbon capture, utilization and storage, zero-carbon industrial process reengineering, and facilitate the application of innovation achievements in green and low-carbon technologies.

We should develop green finance to buttress innovation in green technology.

I have emphasized time and again that reducing carbon dioxide emissions and tackling climate change are an active rather than a passive choice. Achieving peak carbon dioxide emissions and carbon neutrality are solemn commitments that our country has made to the world. They require a broad and profound economic and social transformation. Achieving them will be no easy task.

Currently, some central departments and local governments still have a strong tendency to launch energy-intensive and high-emission projects. At the study session in January on implementing the decisions of the Fifth Plenary Session of the 19th CPC Central Committee, attended by principal officials at the provincial and ministerial level, I particularly emphasized that we must avoid eight misunderstandings. One of them is giving the green light to energy-intensive and high-emission projects under the pretext of boosting domestic demand and expanding the domestic market.

Relevant central departments and local governments must be strict in giving approval and put a stop to projects that do not meet the standards. In the spirit of "leaving our mark in the steel we grasp and our print on the stone we tread", Party committees and governments at all levels should work out clear timetables, roadmaps and work plans, and ensure that economic and social development is based on resource-efficient, green, and low-carbon transformation.

Second, we must fight a tough battle against pollution.

Now, people have higher expectations for the quality of the eco-environment and a lower level of tolerance for problems in this regard. We must concentrate our efforts on resolving prominent eco-environmental problems that directly affect people's lives, and ensure that people truly feel the improvement of the eco-environment.

We must control pollution in a targeted, well-conceived and law-based manner, maintaining the intensity and expanding the scope of our efforts to improve the quality of air, water and soil. We should strengthen coordinated control of different pollutants, especially fine particles and ozone, and coordinated control measures of different regions, with the goal of largely eliminating severe air pollution.

We should coordinate the management of water resources, the water environment, and water ecosystems. Pollution prevention and control and ecological protection for rivers, lakes and reservoirs should be strengthened, our bays should be clean and beautiful, safety of drinking water should be guaranteed, and black and fetid water bodies in cities should be eliminated.

We must press ahead with soil pollution prevention and control, and effectively manage the risk of pollution of farmland and land for construction. We should sort, reduce and recycle garbage, make a greater effort to control plastic pollution, and collect and dispose of hazardous waste and medical waste. We should take more solid steps to prevent and control heavy metal pollution, and attach importance to controlling pollutants of new types. We should extend pollution control to towns and rural areas, and intensify the prevention and control of non-point source agricultural pollution to notably improve rural living environments.

Third, we should improve the quality and stability of ecosystems.

This is not only an essential requirement for increasing the supply of high-quality ecological products, but also an important means to mitigate and adapt to the adverse impact of climate change. "Vegetation is a valuable asset of a country."[1] A good eco-environment itself holds economic and social value. We should adopt a holistic approach to improving ecosystems, promote the integrated conservation and restoration of mountains, rivers, forests, farmlands, lakes, grasslands and deserts, and lay greater emphasis on taking comprehensive and systematic measures to deal with problems by addressing their root causes.

We should create a framework of protected areas with a focus on national parks, and improve the supervision system for protected areas and for ecological conservation red lines.

A sound mechanism for realizing the market value of green products should be established to ensure that those who protect and restore the eco-environment get reasonable rewards and those who damage it pay a corresponding price.

We should promote the comprehensive treatment of desertification, stony desertification, and soil erosion, and carry out large-scale greening programs. We should promote the rehabilitation of grasslands, forests, rivers, and lakes, enforce the 10-year ban on fishing in the Yangtze River, and improve the systems of crop rotation and fallowing.

We need to carry out major biodiversity conservation projects, strengthen regulation and control over alien species, and work to ensure the success of the 15th meeting of the Conference of the Parties to the Convention on Biological Diversity.

Fourth, we should actively promote global sustainable development.

To protect the eco-environment and address climate change is a challenge for all of humanity. Guided by the vision of building a global community of shared future, we should actively participate in global environmental governance, and increase international cooperation in climate change response, marine pollution control, and biodiversity conservation, among others. We should earnestly implement international conventions, actively undertake environmental governance obligations commensurate with China's national conditions, development stage and ability, and provide more public products for the world.

We should continue to boost our institutional rights, achieve a balance between obligations and rights, and demonstrate that China is a responsible major country.

China should play a leading role as a large developing country, strengthen South-South cooperation and cooperation with neighboring countries, provide financial and technical support within its means for other developing countries to help them improve their environmental governance capacity, and work together with them to build a green Belt and Road.

China is committed to the principles of equity, common but differentiated responsibilities, and respective capabilities. It firmly upholds multilateralism, effectively responds to the attempts of some Western countries to corral its progress, and resolutely safeguards its development interests.

Fifth, we must modernize our national governance system and capacity in the eco-environmental field.

We must improve a modern environmental governance system that is led by Party committees, guided by the government, and supported by enterprises as the main players, in which social organizations and the general public are active participants, and we must form systems and mechanisms for integrated planning, implementation and performance assessment.

We should make in-depth efforts to advance the reform of the system for developing an eco-civilization, strengthen legal and policy support for green development, and improve the property rights system and the laws and regulations relating to natural resources and assets.

We must improve the management of the binding targets for environmental protection, energy conservation and emissions reduction, and establish a sound and stable fiscal investment mechanism. A pollutant permit system should be implemented across the country to encourage the trading of pollutant discharge rights, energy use rights, water use rights and carbon emissions rights. A sound risk management mechanism will also be put in place.

We should make great efforts to promote eco-environmental progress, increase citizens' awareness of resource conservation, environmental protection, and a healthy ecosystem, encourage simple, moderate, green, and low-carbon ways of life, and transform the initiative to build a beautiful China into conscious action by all.

On May 18, 2018, at the National Conference on Eco-environmental Protection, I pointed out that China has entered a critical period in which it is under heavy pressure and faces a series of heavy tasks in building an eco-civilization. It is a period of tough challenges for the provision of more high-quality eco-friendly products to meet people's growing demand for a beautiful eco-environment; but it is also a window of opportunity when conditions are right and the country has the ability to solve prominent eco-environmental problems.

Party committees and governments at all levels must strengthen their political acumen, understanding and capacity to deliver. Bearing in mind the priorities of the state, they should shoulder the responsibility of building an eco-civilization, strictly implement the central authorities' policies, and ensure that the decisions and plans of the Central Committee on the eco-environment are carried out effectively.

Notes

[1] *Guan Zi.*

Let the Yellow River Serve the Nation[*]

We should have a clear understanding of major issues of eco-environmental protection and high-quality development in the Yellow River Basin, based on a rational analysis of its current situation. We must be pragmatic and committed to this goal, and make every effort to deliver tangible results during the 14th Five-year Plan period (2021-2025), to ensure the Yellow River always serves the nation.

Since the CPC Central Committee formulated the national strategy for eco-conservation and high-quality development of the Yellow River Basin, we have done a lot of work to address relevant problems, such as putting in place a framework for the protection and governance of the river, tackling eco-environmental problems, and protecting and restoring ecosystems. We have improved the basin's governance system and made new progress in its high-quality development. However, we must recognize that some prominent problems still exist. We must focus on solving these problems and continue to step up our efforts.

Provinces and autonomous regions along the Yellow River must fully implement the national strategy, and be committed to a path of modernization that prioritizes eco-environmental conservation and pursues green development.

First, we must have a correct attitude towards assessing officials' performance and an accurate understanding of the relationship between protection and development. Focusing on well-coordinated

* Main points of the speech at a forum on further eco-conservation and high-quality development of the Yellow River Basin.

environmental conservation, we should improve the eco-environment of the Yellow River Basin by addressing environmental problems, intensifying efforts to conserve water and control water use, and protecting and restoring ecosystems. We must make sure that red lines for ecological conservation are never crossed in our activities of development along the Yellow River, and that utilization of resources, particularly water resources, is within their bearing capacity. Strict measures should be adopted to guarantee high-quality development with greater efficiency.

Second, we should coordinate development and security to improve risk prevention and response. We should give high priority to risks in water security, and advocate water conservation throughout society. We must pay careful attention to the complex and far-reaching influence of global climate change, respond proactively in the interests of security, and improve all-round disaster prevention and control to guarantee the safety of the people.

Third, we should improve strategic thinking and apply systems thinking to the whole process of environmental protection and high-quality development. We should balance the relationship between the whole and the part, always having the broader picture in mind and giving priority to the overall interests on major issues. We should handle the relationship between the present and the future properly, be far-sighted, and avoid the mindset of seeking quick success or instant benefits.

Fourth, we will be committed to green and low-carbon development, and work hard for better quality, higher efficiency, and more robust drivers in economic growth in the Yellow River Basin. Measures should be put into effect, in both supply and demand, for dual control over the volume and intensity of energy use. Strict pre-launch scrutiny should be applied to energy-intensive and high-emission projects. Adjustments to energy production should be made in a timely and orderly manner, and outdated production facilities and technologies with high carbon emissions should be phased out. Efforts should be redoubled to ensure stability in the supply of coal and electricity and the order of the economy and society.

The 14th Five-year Plan period is critical to eco-conservation and high-quality development in the Yellow River Basin. The following tasks must be completed as soon as possible to make new progress.

First, we should move faster to build a defense line against natural disasters. To be prepared for major floods and other serious natural disasters in the future, we must lose no time in strengthening weaknesses in early warning and monitoring exposed by previous experiences, and identify and address any shortcomings in infrastructure. We should ramp up efforts to build urban flood control and drainage systems as well as disaster prevention and mitigation facilities, and bring elements such as urban eco-spaces and spillways under strict protection.

Second, we must make plans for population distribution, land use, and urban and industrial development in accordance with the water resources available. To develop in an economical and efficient way, we will ensure water security, efficient use of water resources, and a tangible improvement in water ecology. We must economize on water resources through strict and refined management, and implement innovative trading measures for water rights and wastewater discharge permits by applying fiscal leverage and pricing mechanisms to improve water conservation.

Third, we should do our best to improve eco-environmental protection and governance. We should focus on maintaining the integrity of the natural ecosystem of headwaters, protect every element of the unique ecosystems of plateaus and alpine regions, and take steps to help nature to recover and regenerate. It is imperative that we stop soil erosion and desertification in the upper and middle reaches of the Yellow River, and take comprehensive measures to improve the entire river basin. We should clean up the watercourses and mudflats in the lower reaches, and increase biodiversity in the Yellow River Delta.

Fourth, we should accelerate our effort to build a new framework for the protection and use of land resources. Key eco-environmental functional zones should receive a higher level of transfer payment, so that they can focus their attention on protection and properly develop eco-industries. To develop modern agriculture, we should focus on water conservation, apply advanced technologies, and develop dry farming and high-standard farmland for better economic returns. City clusters and metropolitan areas must seek intensive and efficient development rather than blind expansion.

Fifth, we should take solid steps towards high-quality development. It is important that we stay creative and innovative, and improve coordination between innovation and industrial chains. We will press ahead with the energy revolution to ensure stable supply, strengthen connectivity between the Yellow River regions and coastal areas and regions along the Yangtze River, prioritize new-generation infrastructure, and expand effective investment.

The Central Committee has made overall plans for eco-environmental protection and high-quality development in the Yellow River Basin. It is essential to reach agreement, build up confidence, and take concerted actions. We should continue the working mechanism whereby the central leadership makes overall plans, provincial-level governments take overall responsibility, and city and county governments ensure implementation, with all sides acting proactively and fulfilling their respective duties. It is also necessary to stimulate the enthusiasm of major market players and various social forces.

Since late July, some places in the Yellow River Basin have been hit by unprecedented floods. Local governments in the affected areas must take a serious approach to post-disaster recovery and reconstruction. A particular effort must be directed to helping those affected by floods, to ensure their livelihoods and basic living needs and to get them back to work. The situation dictates that relevant authorities take targeted measures to redress the impact of autumn floods and focus on autumn and winter seed sowing. With winter approaching, all regions concerned must make early preparations and work out contingency plans to ensure stable supplies of electricity and heating, and protect people from cold in the winter.

Peak Carbon and Carbon Neutrality: An Extensive and Profound Transformation*

January 24, 2022

Achieving the goals of peak carbon dioxide emissions by 2030 and carbon neutrality by 2060 is essential to the new development philosophy. It is key to building a new development dynamic and promoting high-quality development; it represents a strategic decision the Party Central Committee has made by taking into account the situation both at home and abroad. We must conduct an in-depth analysis of the challenges and the tasks and fully understand the urgency and arduous nature of the work. We need to define priorities, make sure that they are understood by all, and ensure effective implementation of the decisions and plans of the Party Central Committee.

Since the 18th CPC National Congress in 2012, the Central Committee has put the new development philosophy in action, pursuing green and low-carbon development that prioritizes environmental protection. Marked progress has been made in powering the transition towards a green economy and society. We have established a sound economic structure that facilitates green, low-carbon, and circular development, adjusted the structure of industry and energy, launched the national carbon trading market, announced a halt to new coal-fired power plants overseas, accelerated the creation of a policy framework for peak carbon dioxide emissions and carbon neutrality, and actively participated in international negotiations on climate change.

All these efforts have demonstrated China's sense of responsibility as a major country.

---

* Main points of the speech at the 36th group study session of the Political Bureau of the 19th CPC Central Committee.

We pursue the goals of peak carbon dioxide emissions and carbon neutrality not under compulsion but of our own accord. As we have entered a new stage of development, there is a serious need to achieve these goals, which will help to ease constraints imposed by resources and the environment and realize sustainable development. We must embrace technological advances, promote transformation and upgrading of the economic structure, meet the people's growing expectation for a beautiful eco-environment, and promote harmony between humanity and nature. All of this derives from the need to take on our responsibility as a major country and build a global community of shared future.

In short, we must fully understand the importance of peak carbon dioxide emissions and carbon neutrality, and increase our confidence in meeting these goals.

Realizing these two goals is an extensive and profound transformation; it will not be an easy task. We must improve our capacity for strategic thinking, apply systems thinking from beginning to end, and properly deal with four relationships.

First, development and emissions reduction. Cutting emissions does not mean decreasing industrial activity, or zero emissions. Rather, it is a commitment to green and low-carbon development which prioritizes eco-environmental conservation and drives a green transition with booming economic development. We need to make sound plans for cutting carbon dioxide emissions while ensuring energy security, food security, industrial and supply chain security, and the normal life of the people.

Second, the whole and the part. On the one hand, we must make concerted efforts across the country to ensure synergy generated by greater integration and coordination of policies and measures. On the other hand, we need to do research and determine the correct way to adjust the industrial structure of different regions and build action plans for peak carbon dioxide emissions and carbon neutrality based on a full consideration of the regional distribution of resources and industrial specialization rather than imposing uniform requirements.

Third, long-term goals and short-term objectives. We must stay grounded in today's realities and address each specific problem until small victories add up into big ones. We also need to think in the long term. Instead of pursuing quick success and instant benefits, we should get the pace and intensity right in cutting carbon emissions, and work towards the goal with a pragmatic and progressive approach.

Fourth, the government and the market. We should lay equal emphasis on both to better leverage the role of a well-functioning government and an efficient market, and put in place sound incentive and restraint mechanisms.

All in all, this work requires us to pool strengths across the country, prioritize conservation, leverage the role of the government and the market, coordinate efforts on the domestic and international fronts, and guard against risks. We must make better use of our institutional strengths, rich resources, potential in technology, and market vitality, and we must move faster to build an industrial structure, production model, way of life, and spatial configuration that are resource-sparing and environment-friendly.

First, strengthening overall planning and coordination. Achieving peak carbon dioxide emissions and carbon neutrality will be integrated into the overall plans for promoting eco-environmental progress and economic and social development. Reducing carbon emissions and mitigating pollution should operate in parallel with expanding green transition and promoting economic growth. We will speed up the roll-out of relevant plans, initiatives, and support measures; we will implement 10 actions for achieving peak carbon dioxide emissions[1] and strengthen policy coordination. Local authorities and central departments should maintain the broadest perspective, set the right pace for peak carbon, and clarify responsibilities, tasks and deadlines while advancing the work in a steady and orderly manner.

Second, advancing the energy revolution. Taking into account the energy-resource endowment of our country, we will introduce overall planning and adopt the method of establishing the new before abolishing the old — safe and reliable new energy must be secured in the first place before traditional energy is phased out.

We will step up efforts to build a new energy supply and accommodation system based on large wind and photovoltaic (PV) power plants, supported by clean, efficient, advanced, and energy-saving coal power stations in areas surrounding those plants, and carried by steady, safe, and reliable UHV transmission and transformation lines.

We will resolutely control consumption of fossil fuels – particularly coal – by reducing coal use and replacing it with alternative energy resources in an orderly manner. We will upgrade coal-fired power plants to conserve energy and reduce carbon emissions, and make them more flexible in operation and more efficient for heating.

We will strengthen the foundations for domestic energy production, ensure coal supply security, maintain the stable growth of production capacity of crude oil and natural gas, increase the reserve capacity of coal, gas and oil, and promote large-scale application of advanced energy storage technology.

We will give higher priority to new energy and clean energy, and work for the active and orderly development of energy from such sources as light, silicon, hydrogen, and other types of renewable energy. We need to promote deeper integration of energy technology with modern information, new materials, and advanced manufacturing technologies, and explore new approaches to energy production and consumption. We will increase the scale and accelerate the profitable development of new energy such as wind, solar, biomass, geothermal, ocean and hydrogen. We will coordinate hydropower development and eco-environmental protection, and develop nuclear power in a safe and orderly manner.

Third, pushing for industrial upgrading and optimization. We must seize the opportunities presented by a new revolution in science, technology and industry, promote further integration of green and low-carbon industries with emerging technologies such as the internet, big data, artificial intelligence, and 5G, build green manufacturing and service systems, and increase the proportion of green and low-carbon industries in the economy.

We should impose strict control over the carbon emissions of new projects, and resolutely curb the blind development of energy-intensive projects with high emissions and outdated technology. We will work hard to upgrade traditional industries such as steel, non-ferrous metals, petrochemicals, chemicals, and building materials, and accelerate the pace of low-carbon technology innovation and the digital transformation of industry. We will make greater efforts to turn waste into resources, boost the circular economy, and reduce waste in the use of energy and resources.

We will coordinate efforts to build a low-carbon transport system and facilitate quality low-carbon development in both urban and rural areas. Integrated conservation and management of mountain, river, forest, farmland, lake, grassland and desert ecosystems will consolidate and increase the carbon sink capacity of the environment.

We will advocate a healthy lifestyle that is simple, moderate, green, and low-carbon, encourage green and low-carbon consumption, promote the use of green transport services, launch green action plans and pilot programs targeting a low-carbon society, and increase the public awareness of conservation and eco-environmental protection.

Fourth, speeding up the green and low-carbon scientific and technological revolution. We will do everything within our capacity to make breakthroughs in green technologies and accelerate R&D and application of advanced and applicable technologies. We will set up a sound system for green and low-carbon technology assessment and trading to speed up the application of innovation results. We will apply new approaches to the training of professionals and encourage universities and colleges to accelerate the development of relevant disciplines.

Fifth, improving green and low-carbon policies. We will further improve the system for dual control over the volume and intensity of energy use. Consumption of newly added renewable energy and raw material energy is not to be included in the control of total energy use.

We will improve standards for peak carbon and carbon neutrality, build a unified and standardized calculation system for carbon emissions, and transition from dual control over the volume and intensity of energy use to dual control over the volume and intensity of carbon emissions.

We will improve laws and regulations, and fiscal, tax, price, investment and financial policies. We need to expand the capacity of the market, improve the carbon pricing mechanism, and increase coordination between trading in carbon emissions rights, trading in energy use permits, and electricity trading.

Sixth, actively participating in global climate governance and steering its course. Committed to the vision of a global community of shared future, we will participate more actively in setting the agenda of global climate negotiations and the formulation of international rules, to help build a fair and rational global climate governance system directed towards cooperation and win-win results.

We must strengthen the Party's leadership over the work towards peak carbon and carbon neutrality. We should intensify overall planning and coordination, exercise strict supervision and assessment, and form synergy at work. Both the Party and the government should assume responsibilities and play their part. Carbon assessment indicators will be a part of the comprehensive evaluation system for regional economic and social development, and more weight will be given to these assessments in order to strengthen the binding effect of indicators. Leading officials at all levels must devote more time to the study of the basics, approaches, and requirements for this work, so that they can achieve a better understanding and apply what they have learned in practice properly. This should be an important part of the training for officials, so that they become better equipped to lead in green and low-carbon development.

Notes

[1] These are actions: for achieving green and low-carbon energy transition; for saving energy, reducing carbon dioxide emissions, and improving efficiency; for reaching peak carbon dioxide emissions in the industrial sector; for realizing peak

carbon dioxide emissions in urban and rural development; for promoting green and low-carbon transport; for facilitating reduction of carbon dioxide emissions through the circular economy; for advancing innovation in green and low-carbon technology; for consolidating and improving carbon sink capacity; for advocating a green and low-carbon lifestyle nationwide; and for achieving peak carbon dioxide emissions by different regions in a structured and orderly manner.

Strong Armed Forces

Meet the Centenary Goal of the Armed Forces[*]

July 30, 2021

The CPC Central Committee and the Central Military Commission have set the centenary goal of the People's Liberation Army (PLA) to be achieved by 2027. This is an important task that bears on China's national security and overall development. This centenary goal is the most crucial of the three steps to modernize China's national defense and the military in the new era[1]. To realize this goal as scheduled we must maintain firm resolve and a strong sense of urgency, and do solid work.

Through a century of struggle, the Party has reached a key conclusion – that the Party must command the gun and build up the people's armed forces. This is a conclusion drawn from the war of blood and fire during the revolutionary years. Throughout the years of revolution, construction and reform, the people's armed forces, under the Party's leadership, have always borne in mind their original aspiration, founding mission, nature and purpose. They have forced a path through brambles and thorns, won one victory after another, and achieved extraordinary feats for the Party and the people. As long as the people's armed forces progress under the absolute leadership of the Party, they will continue to grow in strength and provide firm support for the undertakings of our Party and our people.

A strong country must have strong armed forces, and only strong armed forces can keep the country safe. Since the 18th CPC National Congress in 2012, the Central Committee and the Central Military Commission have made strategic plans to accelerate modernization of

---

* Main points of the speech at the 32nd group study session of the Political Bureau of the 19th CPC Central Committee.

national defense and the military, leading the armed forces to reach a new stage of development. On the path towards the Second Centenary Goal of building China into a modern socialist country in all respects, we must give greater weight to boosting national defense and building a strong military.

The development plan for the armed forces during the 14th Five-year Plan period (2021-2025) has set the tasks for achieving the centenary goal of the armed forces. To build greater strategic capabilities, we must maintain the authority of the plan, coordinate all our efforts, focus on priority tasks, and press ahead with our work more efficiently and effectively. We will strengthen our military in line with the requirements of the battlefield. We will coordinate our overall development of the military with efforts to prepare our forces for the possibility of military action and to ensure combat readiness.

The centenary goal of the armed forces calls for profound military reform.

We should emphasize innovation, update our development philosophy, create new development models, and take a stronger initiative to ensure high-quality development.

We should strive for greater strength and self-reliance in science and technology, make breakthroughs in core technologies, and accelerate the development of strategic technologies, frontier technologies, and disruptive technologies, so that technological innovation provides crucial support for the development of our military.

We should drive deeper reform of national defense and the armed forces, in order to adapt to global military development trends and respond to the requirement of greater strategic capabilities of our military.

We should launch military management reform centered on strategic management, so that our military system can function more efficiently and our defense resources are utilized more effectively.

We should strengthen strategic planning with new ideas and measures, to enable all-round improvements in the quality, structure, deployment, development and management of our military personnel.

Achieving the centenary goal of the armed forces is the shared responsibility of all members of the military, the Party, and the country. Central Party and government departments, along with local Party committees and governments, must raise their awareness of national defense, meet the requirements of military reform, and fulfill their duties in national defense. We must take into full account military needs in our social and economic development, reinforce the defense functions of major infrastructure projects, and support the construction of important combat training projects. We will help with providing employment for spouses of our military personnel in the vicinity of their deployments, ensuring their children have access to education, resettling demobilized veterans, and guaranteeing other benefits and services for eligible recipients.

Notes

[1] This refers to the following three steps: realizing the centenary goal of the armed forces by 2027, achieving basic modernization of national defense and the military by 2035, and transforming the military into world-class armed forces by the mid-21st century.

Build a Talent-Strong Military in the New Era[*]

November 26, 2021

Cultivating competent personnel is key to building a strong military. Talent is essential for our armed forces to achieve high-quality development, stand out in military competition, and seize the initiative in future wars. This is a real and urgent requirement in building our military into a world-class armed force and will have a far-reaching influence on its development. Following the guiding principles of this year's Central Conference on Talent, we must further implement the strategy of strengthening the military by cultivating competent personnel for the new era. This strategy will provide solid support for realizing the centenary goal of our armed forces and ensure that the general level of our military personnel will be raised to the level of the most powerful countries.

At the Sixth Plenary Session of the 19th CPC Central Committee in 2021, the Party summarized its major achievements and successful experience of a century's endeavor. It emphasized upholding Party leadership over talent management, implementing the strategy of invigorating the country by cultivating talent in the new era, building China into the world's leading talent center and innovation frontier, and assembling the best minds across the world. In accordance with the above guidelines, we will plan carefully to develop capable service personnel for the new era.

Since the 18th CPC National Congress in 2012, the CPC Central Committee and the Central Military Commission have implemented a strategy to build a talent-strong military. Keeping to the correct political direction and focusing on training for combat readiness, we have

* Main points of the speech at the Central Military Commission Conference on Talent.

optimized the structure of our military staff for a modern armed force, furthered the reform of policy framework, and promoted open and inclusive management of service personnel. Through the above efforts, our military has made historic progress in this endeavor.

As the world is undergoing an accelerating rate of change on a scale unseen in a century, new technology and military revolutions are taking place with each passing day. Our military is marching towards its centenary goal by implementing the new three-step strategy for the modernization of national defense and the army. The armed forces must develop a stronger sense of mission and urgency in developing a solid base of competent personnel, create better plans, and act upon them faster. We must ensure that outstanding people buttress the effort to strengthen our military.

In building a talent-strong military, we must implement the Party's philosophy on strengthening the military and our military strategy for the new era, and follow the strategic guidelines for modernizing national defense and the army. We must work hard to realize the centenary goal of the armed forces. To this end, we will upgrade the qualities and capabilities, structure and distribution, and cultivation and management of our military personnel; we will train high-caliber military personnel of both ability and integrity; we will ensure major progress across the whole army and breakthroughs in key areas.

In building a talent-strong military, we must ensure that the Party exercises absolute leadership over personnel management in the armed forces in every respect and throughout the whole process; we must focus on the ability to fight and win; we must look at the frontiers of global military development, meet the major needs of national security, and serve the task of national defense and military modernization; we must provide comprehensive training, and put talent to the right posts under a reformed policy framework for service personnel.

In building a talent-strong military, we must coordinate all endeavors, covering training, job placement, evaluation, service, support, and motivation, and make breakthroughs in priority areas. We must develop military talent within the framework of state-level planning on talent, and orient relevant plans, policies and work towards meeting military requirements, leading to efficient management of military personnel.

Political commitment is the most important criterion and political integrity an essential requirement for our military personnel. We will strengthen education on political integrity and commitment in the military, and conduct evaluation of service personnel from a political perspective so as to ensure their absolute loyalty to the Party and the state.

We will pursue independent development of competent personnel, mainly by the armed forces and also through other channels, and build a distinctive Chinese model to foster more soldiers with greater warfighting capabilities. We will redouble our efforts to improve the technological knowhow of our military staff, so that they can fight and win in modern wars. We will implement education guidelines appropriate to the new era, prioritize the development of military schooling, and develop first-class military academies and military talent. We encourage our service personnel to temper their body and character in drills and operations.

We will make effective and flexible use of talent in all fields, and ensure precise and efficient allocation of human resources, so that they can best play their role in the most suitable positions. We will adopt different policies for different fields, improve the training and performance of commanders for joint operations, new types of combat personnel, and high-caliber personnel for technological innovation and for strategic management, and leverage the strengths of both service members and civilian staff in the armed forces.

We will find right ways to foster military personnel, identify their diverse needs for career development, and update our philosophy and approaches towards specialized, detailed and well-conceived management. We will restructure the policy framework for military human resources, and improve support policies and systems. With trust, respect, support and care from the military, our servicemen and servicewomen will be more active and creative in work.

The Central Military Commission must strengthen its leadership over human resources, and Party committees in the military must fulfill their principal responsibilities. Leading officials, particularly senior officials, must be adept at identifying and cultivating talent. Central Party and government departments, along with local Party committees and governments, must act in concert to support the military in this field.

Run the Military in Accordance with the Law*

March 7, 2022

Running the military in accordance with the law is our Party's basic strategy in building and running the military, and a necessary requirement for achieving the Party's goal of building a stronger military for the new era. This strategy must be implemented to strengthen the rule of law in national defense and the armed forces and provide a strong legal guarantee for the building of a strong army.

Over the last year, the military has resolutely implemented the decisions and instructions of the Party Central Committee and the Central Military Commission and engaged in military actions, training and development, providing strong support for a good start to the 14th Five-year Plan (2021-2025), and for the cause of the Party and the country.

Since the 18th CPC National Congress in 2012, the Central Committee has incorporated its strategy of law-based governance of the military into the country's overall plan for law-based governance. The 18th CPC Central Committee made important plans for running the military in accordance with the law at its Fourth Plenary Session in 2014. The Central Military Commission made a special decision on the subject of running the military with strict discipline in accordance with the law in new circumstances. After an unremitting effort, major progress has been made in this field. At its Sixth Plenary Session in 2021, the 19th CPC Central Committee decided to implement this strategy. This is an important decision made by the Party Central

---

* Main points of the speech at the plenary meeting of the delegation of the People's Liberation Army and the Chinese People's Armed Police Force during the Fifth Plenary Session of the 13th National People's Congress.

Committee based on the characteristics of the new era and the overall need to build a stronger military.

It is essential to fully understand the strategy of running the military in accordance with the law. We must implement the Party's philosophy on strengthening the military and the thought on Chinese socialist rule of law for the new era. Taking into consideration the need to build a regular army that is revolutionary and modern in every respect, we should work on a military legal system with Chinese characteristics, and accelerate the fundamental changes required to apply that system. We must improve law-based governance in building our national defense and the military.

We must uphold the principle of the Party's absolute leadership, take combat capability as the sole and fundamental criterion for our work, and build a military legal system with Chinese characteristics. We should always run the military with strict discipline in accordance with the law. We should give prominence to the scrutiny of the "key few" commanding officers and uphold the principal position of the men and women in uniform. All of this should be part of our overall effort to implement law-based governance in the whole country.

The implementation of the strategy requires integrated systems engineering. We should highlight priorities while taking a holistic approach, and promote all-round progress with breakthroughs in key areas.

We should accelerate legislative work related to the military, improve relevant policies and systems, increase the quality of legislation, and make sure that it is systematic, integrated and coordinated.

We should implement rules and regulations properly, especially those concerning joint military operations. We should carry out law-based management over military training, and conduct the training according to set programs. To ensure effective implementation of our programs and plans in building the military, we must intensify the management of troops in strict accordance with the rules and regulations.

To ensure effective implementation of rules and regulations, we should intensify supervision of the implementation process, clarify the subjects of responsibility, define evaluation criteria, improve the supervision mechanism, and tighten the accountability system.

When conducting foreign-related military affairs, we should emphasize the rule of law, coordinate the planning of military operations and battles on the legal front. We should update foreign-related laws and regulations concerning the military and better protect our national interests.

We should pool our strengths to implement the strategy of running the military in accordance with the law. The Central Military Commission should exercise the best possible leadership, units at all levels must conscientiously perform their duties and fulfill their responsibilities, the legal affairs departments should perform their functions with diligence, and commanding officers should take the lead in fulfilling their duties in accordance with the law. Central Party and government departments and local Party committees and governments at all levels should raise their awareness of the importance of national defense, conscientiously perform their statutory duties for national defense, and provide strong support for military operations, building up the armed forces, and protecting the legitimate rights and interests of military personnel in accordance with the law.

The military should make unremitting efforts to strengthen military preparedness, provide assistance to local governments in maintaining overall social stability, handle all kinds of emergencies promptly and effectively, maintain national security and stability, and complete all the tasks entrusted by the Party and the people.

Development and Security

Pursue a Holistic Approach to National Security*

December 11, 2020

National security, a key area for the Party's governance of China, is extremely important in ensuring prosperity and peace. To guarantee national security in the new era we must pursue a holistic approach, seize the development opportunities presented during this strategic period, and make good use of them. We must guarantee national security in all respects and through all the work of the Party and the country, and take it into consideration together with social and economic development in our planning and dispositions. We will persevere with systems thinking to establish a complete security architecture and promote international security and world peace, so as to ensure success in building a modern socialist country.

The Recommendations of the Central Committee of the Communist Party of China for Formulating the 14th Five-Year Plan for Economic and Social Development and Long-Range Objectives Through the Year 2035 were adopted at the Fifth Plenary Session of the 19th CPC Central Committee on October 29, 2020. This was the first time that coordinating development and national security had been incorporated in the guiding principles for economic and social development during the 14th Five-year Plan period (2021-2025). A chapter in the Recommendations is devoted to relevant strategies and plans, highlighting the significance of national security in the overall work of the Party and the country. This is the logical outcome of China's stage of development and the situation and tasks it faces in safeguarding national security.

* Main points of the speech at the 26th group study session of the Political Bureau of the 19th CPC Central Committee.

Our Party was established at a time when the nation was beset by domestic crises and exposed to multiple threats and foreign aggression, so it knows only too well the importance of national security. Since the founding of the PRC in 1949, the Central Committee has attached great importance to the country's development and security, and safeguarding national security has always been one of its main concerns.

Since the 18th National Congress of the Party in 2012, the Central Committee has strengthened its centralized, unified leadership over national security. It has incorporated a holistic approach to national security into the basic policy that underpins our endeavors to uphold and develop socialism with Chinese characteristics, and made major decisions and plans in this area from an overall and strategic perspective. The central leadership has improved top-level design for national security, policies in key areas, and relevant laws and regulations, and by so doing has effectively addressed major risks and challenges and brought stability to the country's security.

I would like to make the following 10 points on how to implement the holistic approach to national security.

First, we must uphold the Party's absolute leadership and the Central Committee's centralized, unified leadership over national security. With overall planning and effective coordination, we must ensure the Party's leadership in all areas of work relating to national security, and urge Party committees and Party leadership groups at all levels to fulfill their responsibilities in this area.

Second, we must follow a path with Chinese features and pursue a holistic approach to national security. We consider political security, the people's security, and the supremacy of national interests as three essential elements of an indivisible whole. The people's security, political security, and economic security are of great importance in maintaining national security. We will safeguard China's sovereignty and territorial integrity, guard against and defuse major security risks, and provide strong safeguards for realizing our national rejuvenation.

Third, we must take the people's security as our purpose. Everything we do to maintain national security is for the people and supported by the people. We should make the best use of people's enthusiasm and creativity to safeguard their security rights and interests. We should always regard the people as the fundamental force for national security, and will pool all the strengths and resources across the country to ensure it.

Fourth, we must consider development and security as of equal importance, and work to achieve mutually beneficial interaction between high-quality development and high-level security. We will improve our ability to maintain national security through development, and at the same time try to create a safe environment conducive to social and economic development through innovations in the approach, mechanisms and methods for ensuring national security. Taking greater account of security factors in pursuing development, we will try to achieve a dynamic balance and increase our capacity to perform our duties for national security.

Fifth, we must assign the highest priority to political security. This means that we must ensure the security of our state power and political system, and carry out all relevant work more proactively.

Sixth, we must promote security in all areas and respond to conventional and non-conventional challenges in a coordinated manner. We will coordinate national security activities and make good use of relevant policy tools.

Seventh, we must highlight the prevention and resolution of national security risks, and reinforce our ability to anticipate risks, so as to nip in the bud any latent danger that may cause a major threat.

Eighth, we must continue to promote global security for all. Upholding the principles of cooperation, innovation, the rule of law, and win-win results, we will contribute our part to the international endeavor to adopt a global vision of common, comprehensive, cooperative and sustainable security. We will strengthen international security cooperation and improve the global security governance system, so as to build a global community of shared future marked by universal security.

Ninth, we must continue to modernize our systems and capacity for maintaining national security. Supported by reform and innovation, we will bear in mind the rule of law and set up a well-conceived, well-developed, procedure-based and effective framework of systems for maintaining national security. We need to increase our ability to apply science and technology in safeguarding national security, as well as our ability to create positive momentum.

Tenth, we must strengthen our national security teams and Party leadership in this field, and make them an invincible force with strong political commitment.

Develop China on More Secure and Reliable Foundations*

December 16, 2020

While taking a holistic approach to the domestic and international situation and coordinating epidemic response and economic and social development, we have gained a deeper understanding of how to grow the economy in the face of severe challenges and have summed up the factors contributing to our achievements as follows:

First, the authority of the CPC Central Committee is the fundamental guarantee for the whole Party and all the people in overcoming difficulties at critical moments.

Our national realities and the system of socialism with Chinese characteristics determine that in order to achieve our goals and meet the challenges on our way forward, we must uphold the centralized, unified leadership of the Party and the authority of its Central Committee.

Past experience shows clearly that at critical historical junctures or in the face of major tests, the ability to lead is the most important factor, while the Central Committee's capacity to conduct assessments, make decisions and take action plays a key role. As long as we uphold the leadership of the Party and the authority of its Central Committee and unite the people closely around the Party, we will be able to move forward against all hardships and obstacles.

Second, putting the people first is the fundamental prerequisite for us to make correct decisions.

To address this most serious crisis, the Party maintains its stance which determines the direction and order of its action. Our Party

* Part of the speech at the Central Conference on Economic Work.

represents the fundamental interests of the people and is committed to serving the public good and exercising power in the interests
of the people. Since the start of the coronavirus pandemic, we have
assigned high priority to people and their lives, and defined the optimal process – first control the epidemic spread; then resume work in
some areas; and finally return to normal across the country.

Experience has proved once again that we can make correct decisions and overcome all difficulties as long as we put the people at the
center of our concerns, regard their interests as the top priority, and
always rely on their support.

Third, institutional strength provides a fundamental guarantee for
us to unite to overcome difficulties and remove obstacles.

Success comes to those who share in one purpose. In the face of
major disasters and crises, we have shown no fear and have united as
one. We have brought into full play the political strengths of Party
leadership and the socialist system. We can mobilize and coordinate
resources from all regions, departments, sectors and fields, forming a
level of synergy that has enabled us to overcome all these difficulties.

Experience has proved once again that we can unite the whole
Party and all the people into a strong force to overcome difficulties and advance our cause, as long as we maintain confidence in
China's socialist path, theory, system and culture, and take advantage
of our great political strength – the ability to mobilize resources and
complete major missions.

Fourth, rational decision-making and creativity are the essential
means to turn crisis into opportunity.

Extraordinary measures are needed to respond to extraordinary
challenges. The present crisis, unlike the Great Depression of 1929
or the global financial crisis of 2008, is marked by the coincidence of
supply disruption and falling demand, posing unprecedented challenges. Combining design of strategies with application of tactics, we have
adopted both economic and social policies, stimulated supply and
demand, leveraged our complete industrial system, increased material
supply, and carried out cross-cyclical planning and counter-cyclical

regulation, thus maximizing the results at a reasonable cost.

Experience has proved once again that we can create opportunities and remain invincible in our response to major risks, as long as we correctly understand and effectively respond to the situation, take action to make changes, bear in mind the general picture in making decisions, and implement them just as the arms employ the fingers without any difficulty.

Fifth, strength and self-reliance in science and technology are the fundamental support for development.

In our response to Covid-19, to changes in the external economic environment, and to pressure from foreign forces, we have paid more attention to the important role of science and technology. To protect people's lives and health, we have applied science in preventing and controlling the spread of the virus and treating the disease. We have ensured the smooth functioning of industrial and supply chains through technological innovation. And we have made rapid breakthroughs in core technologies to clear bottlenecks in order to ensure economic security and promote high-quality development.

Experience has proved once again that we can build more secure and reliable foundations for our country's development, as long as we develop a scientific mindset, follow the laws of science, and carry forward independent innovation.

Keep Food Security in Our Own Hands[*]

December 28, 2020

"Grain sustains life and is vital to the nation."[1] I have often said that adjusting the food supply is a tactical move, while ensuring food security is of strategic importance – a point amply illustrated by the huge role that the abundant supply of food and key agro-products played in the response to Covid-19 epidemic this year.

The tight balance between grain supply and demand in our country has not changed, and as we are setting out to address structural problems, the problem of insufficient grain supply has become prominent again. As the demand for food will continue to increase in the years to come, the pressure on food supply will grow accordingly. At the same time, in view of the complex and disturbing international situation, we cannot relax for a moment in ensuring food security. We would rather produce and store more food, as the pressure of having too much food is entirely different from that of not having enough. We should never relax our efforts in grain production, and we should make sure that grain acreage and output do not decrease and that supply and market problems do not occur.

As an ancient statesman said, "Without farming, no food can be produced. And without arable land, no crops can grow."[2] Arable land is the lifeblood of food production. As early as 2013, I said that arable land must be protected in the same way as giant pandas, and that the total area of China's farmland must stay above the red line of 120 million hectares. Over the years, I have given instructions to remove residences and non-agricultural commercial facilities illegally built on cultivated land, and curb the use of cultivated land for purposes

* Part of the speech at the Central Conference on Rural Work.

other than farming and for non-grain production. Relevant departments have introduced a set of targeted and coordinated policies and measures. However, arable land abuses have persisted.

For example, basic cropland in some places has been used for afforestation or ornamental lakes, and green belts dozens or even hundreds of meters wide have been created on fertile land along roads, railways and canals in some other places. We do have a lot of land, but it is a scarce resource compared with the needs of 1.4 billion people. Land is needed for building cities, developing industries, and introducing eco-environmental projects, and this requires careful planning and use of land against properly defined criteria. We must not engage in afforestation of cultivated land or go against the laws of nature. All provinces, autonomous regions and municipalities must maintain their existing farmland for food production and cannot reduce it any further.

In addition to ensuring the quantity of arable land, we also need to improve its quality. The cultivation of high-standard farmland is an important measure that should be taken consistently, in order to improve farmland standard and quality and achieve high and stable yields even in times of drought or flood. We must have the determination to do so and should not cut corners on the budget required. We should attach great importance to the conservation of chernozem soil, maintain it, and make good use of it. We must apply the strictest and most effective system to protect cultivated land, for which we must adopt compulsory measures with real teeth. Those who fail to carry out orders, who engage in or continue with expressly prohibited acts, or who fail in their duties, must be investigated and held accountable.

The amount of cultivated land is limited, so the fundamental route to stabilizing and increasing production lies in science and technology. A new round of scientific and technological revolution in agriculture characterized by biotechnology and information technology is generating major breakthroughs, and all countries are trying to gain an edge in this revolution. As a large agricultural country, we must not lag behind. Instead, we should be more self-reliant in agricultural science and technology, and master core technologies as soon as possible.

After much reflection, I think one point must be made clear – seeds are the foundation of modern agriculture. I highlighted this point at the recent Central Conference on Economic Work. Even if we have all kinds of sophisticated equipment and favorable conditions, it is still difficult to achieve agricultural modernization without good seeds. The question of quality seeds for crops like soybeans has been a problem for years, and progress has not been satisfactory. We need to have the drive to break technological bottlenecks, know the direction and goals full well, speed up the implementation of major biological breeding projects, and bring seed resources for major agro-products under our own control as early as possible. Relevant departments should accelerate the R&D and application of biological breeding, conditional on strict supervision and risk control.

We need to bring science and technology faster to villages and households, making full use of both public services from the government and market services. We will use modern information technologies such as the internet of things and big data to develop smart agriculture. At the same time, we will speed up efforts to remedy our weak links in modern agricultural equipment such as drying and storage equipment, cold-chain preservation facilities, and agricultural machinery. In particular, we will increase our independent R&D capacity for important agricultural equipment, and improve the animal and plant quarantine system as well as the disaster prevention and mitigation system.

The key to incentivizing farmers to grow grain is to make sure they get a return from their effort. In recent years, the cost of growing grain has increased, while the cost effectiveness has been low, and farmers in many places have even suffered losses. In this context, we should stabilize and increase subsidies for grain producers, increase our capacity for adjusting grain purchase and storage, improve the minimum purchase price policy, and expand the scope of insurance programs covering total production costs and incomes. One of the weak points in grain production is high costs. The solution is to develop new operating models for agriculture – fostering family farms and farmers' cooperatives, developing agricultural operations on an appropriate scale, and improving specialized and commercial services to handle tasks that are not cost-effective or feasible for a single household. Training farmers in production skills and management should also be strengthened to modernize management.

Party committees and governments at all levels should assume political responsibility for food security. In recent years, China's grain production has been significantly concentrated in major producing areas, which makes sense, but excessive concentration also brings risks. If everyone everywhere only wants to eat grain and meat, and does not want to grow grain or raise hogs, then who will guarantee the supply? Food should not be treated only as a commodity – it is wrong to focus only on immediate economic gains or losses and ignore the political and long-term interests of the country as a whole.

All areas, whether major producers, major markets, or regions with balanced production and consumption, must ensure adequate acreage and output for food production, and they should jointly shoulder the responsibility for food security, as it is a major issue concerning fundamental national interests.

Party and government officials should both be accountable for food security – for instance, the governor and the Party secretary of a province are jointly responsible for the "rice bag" of their province.

Over the years, major grain-producing provinces, cities and counties have made an important contribution to our food security, which should be commended. For this reason, we will improve the mechanism for compensating major grain-producing areas, increase rewards and subsidies, and ensure that those who value agriculture and grain production do not suffer economic losses.

The food consumption patterns of urban and rural residents are constantly moving up market. In the future, the supply of agro-products should be guaranteed not only in quantity, but also in variety and quality. Supply-side structural reform in agriculture should aim to foster superior varieties, improve quality, build brands, and standardize production. We should continue to support the recovery and the steady development of hog production. We should make well-thought-out plans for the production of bulk agro-products, such as soybeans, cotton, corn and wheat, as soon as possible, and expand the output where necessary. This is a matter of national security, and we must not let others hold us in check.

We should make the best use of agricultural trade, but the key is to control risks, have alternative products and solutions, and prepare contingency plans. We should implement the strategy of diversifying agricultural imports, support enterprises in going global, improve their control over key logistics nodes, and make supply chains more resilient to risk. To ensure food security, we must conduct in-depth research into farm produce item by item, formulate plans, and implement them for each and every product. There has been good progress recently in the fight against food waste. We must continue this battle for a long time to come, and encourage the whole of society to practice frugality.

Notes

[1] Jia Sixie: *Important Arts for the People's Welfare* (*Qi Min Yao Shu*). Jia Sixie (dates unknown) was an agronomist in the Northern Wei Dynasty (386-534).

[2] *Guan Zi.*

Build a Strong National Shield
Against Biosecurity Threats*

September 29, 2021

Biosecurity is vital to the lives and health of our people, to the long-term peace and order of our country, and to the future of the Chinese nation. It is an essential component of overall national security that might affect and even reshape the global landscape. Therefore we must fully recognize the significance and urgency of strengthening biosecurity management. We should adopt a holistic approach to national security, enforce the Biosecurity Law, and coordinate development and security. Following the principles of people first, risk prevention, category-based management, and coordination, we will take stronger measures to prevent and curb biosecurity risks, improve the system and capacity for national biosecurity governance, and build a strong and effective national shield against biosecurity threats.

Since the 18th CPC National Congress in 2012, the central leadership has prioritized biosecurity management on its agenda and included it in the national security strategy. The Biosecurity Law has been promulgated and implemented, policies and strategies on national biosecurity have been developed, and systems and mechanisms for biosecurity management have been improved. The central leadership has actively responded to major biosecurity risks and strengthened efforts to better protect and utilize biological resources. It has mobilized the entire Party, country and society to wage a people's war against the Covid-19 epidemic. Our early awareness and preemptive capability against biothreats have improved, our foundations for safeguarding

* Main points of the speech at the 33rd group study session of the Political Bureau of the 19th CPC Central Committee.

biosecurity have been constantly reinforced, and our efforts to ensure biosecurity have yielded results of historic significance.

Today, due to the overlap of traditional problems and new risks concerning biosecurity, together with the presence of overseas biothreats combined with domestic risks, new facets of biosecurity protection are becoming apparent. In addition, there are shortcomings and weaknesses in our risk management and governance system against biothreats. This requires that we conduct a science-based analysis of the situation, accurately identify the risks and challenges we face, adopt a right approach to stronger biosecurity management, and apply corresponding measures.

We should reinforce the national biosecurity governance system by planning and conducting strategic and forward-looking studies, and by improving the nation's biosecurity strategy. Refinements should be made to the governance mechanism under which Party committees exercise leadership, governments assume responsibility, non-governmental actors provide assistance, the public are involved, and legal support is in place, and to the mechanism for coordinating biosecurity-related activities at all levels. We will make an all-out effort to improve legislation, law enforcement, judicature, legal education, and observance of the law. This means we need to improve the legal system and institutional guarantees, carry out a public education program on relevant laws and regulations as well as the basics of biosecurity, and raise public awareness of biosecurity risks. The grassroots foundations will be reinforced to create a prevention and control mechanism involving governments at all levels and the whole of society.

We should strengthen systematic governance and whole-process prevention and control by adopting systems thinking, taking science-based measures, making comprehensive plans, and ensuring whole-process management. We need to build a sound network and a solid system for risk monitoring and early warning, with a focus on building monitoring facilities at the grassroots and strengthening their ability to identify risks. Potential threats from new and unexpected infectious diseases, outbreaks of serious diseases in plants and animals, drug resistance of microorganisms, and the impact of biotechnology on the environment should be detected and identified at an early stage, thus enabling a timely warning and response. We will establish sound contingency plans for biosecurity emergencies to improve the rapid response mechanism, and expand the reserve of emergency supply and industrial capacity. We will take proactive measures to prevent and control animal diseases in order to cut down the transmission of zoonoses at source. To achieve more targeted and effective prevention of animal and plant diseases, we need to ensure proper functioning of grassroots prevention and control mechanisms, clarify the functions of relevant institutions, and improve their professional competence.

We should focus on the sectors most exposed to biosecurity risks and remain alert to worst-case scenarios and potential risks. It is important to strengthen oversight of biological resource security, and devise a catalog of biological and human genetic resources and keep it up to date. To ensure our borders and passes are defended well, we should adopt stricter border quarantine measures, analyze potential risks, and punish all violations. We should accurately identify inbound biohazards that have caused serious harm in our country, and take targeted measures to eliminate them one by one. We must strengthen biosecurity management of pathogenic microorganism laboratories, requiring them to strictly follow all relevant standards and norms and to strictly manage samples, animals and waste associated with related experiments. Management must be intensified over the use and residues of antimicrobial drugs.

We should accelerate innovation and industrial application of biotechnology for greater self-reliance in biosecurity-related science and technology, and strengthen our scientific and technological capabilities to implement the national biosecurity strategy. We should improve the mechanism for key scientific research projects, strictly oversee the research, development and application of biotechnology, and strengthen management of biological laboratories. We should carry out strict ethical reviews of research projects and provide ethical education to scientists. To ensure sound development of biotechnology we will encourage industrial application of bio-breeding and bio-pharmaceutical technologies in an orderly manner, on the preconditions that science is respected, strict oversight is in place, laws and regulations are observed, and safety is guaranteed. Useful traditional concepts should be integrated into modern biotechnology, and traditional Chinese medicine be combined with Western medicine. We should popularize the technologies and models of biological and eco-friendly pest and disease control, and regulate the use of antibiotic medicines, so as to promote harmonious coexistence between humanity and nature.

We should actively participate in global biosecurity governance. China will work with the international community to address mounting challenges in this area, and reinforce bilateral and multilateral cooperation and exchanges in policy-making, risk assessment, emergency response, information sharing, and capacity building. We will ensure the smooth hosting of the 15th meeting of the Conference of the Parties to the Convention on Biological Diversity and facilitate the formulation of the Post-2020 Global Biodiversity Framework, offering Chinese ideas and approaches to the international community. We advocate origin-tracing of the novel coronavirus based on scientific principles and rules.

Strengthening our biosecurity management will be a long and arduous task requiring constant and concrete efforts. Party committees, Party leadership groups, and governments at all levels must effectively align their thinking and actions with the decisions and plans of the central Party leadership. They must ensure accountability for biosecurity, and fulfill their responsibilities and missions with dedication. We will increase investment, improve relevant policies and measures, and guarantee the functioning of key elements, so that we will achieve tangible results, build a modern risk management and governance system, and keep the biosecurity of our country firmly in our own hands. We must persevere in the fight against Covid-19, remaining vigilant, avoiding slackening our efforts and taking chances, and strictly enforcing prevention and control measures, so that our hard-won gains will not be lost.

One Country, Two Systems and National Reunification

Uphold the Principle of Patriots Governing Hong Kong to Secure the Success of the One Country, Two Systems Policy*

January 27 and December 22, 2021

I

In line with the requirements of Covid-19 control, I have listened to your 2020 work report via video link. First of all, I would like to communicate my sincere concern to all residents in the Hong Kong Special Administrative Region (HKSAR). Covid-19 has exerted a massive impact on the world over the past year and more, and Hong Kong, a highly-open international metropolis, has not been spared. I was deeply concerned when the fourth wave of the pandemic swept Hong Kong not long ago, posing a serious threat to the safety and health of Hong Kong residents and affecting their lives and their work. The central government has taken and will continue to take all necessary measures to support the HKSAR in fighting the disease. I hope all of you will remain confident and stay united in the battle. Hong Kong always has the strong backing of the motherland, and can surely overcome the difficulties at hand.

Over the past year, you and the HKSAR government have dealt calmly with multiple serious challenges brought by the turbulence over the proposed ordinance amendments, the Covid-19 pandemic, and adverse changes in the external environment. A significant degree

* Main points in response to the work reports from Carrie Lam Cheng Yuet-ngor, chief executive of the Hong Kong Special Administrative Region.

of success has been achieved in maintaining order, fighting the virus, addressing people's difficulties, and reviving the economy. What should be noted is that since the Standing Committee of the National People's Congress (NPC) adopted the Hong Kong national security law, you have led the HKSAR government in resolutely enforcing the law to end violence and chaos and bring Hong Kong back on track. On major issues of principle such as national security, you have taken a firm stand and shouldered your responsibilities, demonstrating your love for and strong sense of responsibility to the country and Hong Kong. The central authorities fully appreciate how you and the HKSAR government have performed in fulfilling your duties.

The restoration of order and stability in Hong Kong has demonstrated once again that we must always uphold the principle of patriots governing Hong Kong to secure steady and continued success of the One Country, Two Systems policy. It is a fundamental principle critical to the sovereignty, security, development interests of our country, and to long-term prosperity and stability in Hong Kong. Only by applying this principle can the central government's overall jurisdiction over the HKSAR be effectively exercised and the constitutional order as established by the Constitution and the Basic Law be effectively maintained. This will enable Hong Kong to solve its deepseated problems, achieve durable stability and security, and contribute to national rejuvenation.

(from a virtual meeting with HKSAR Chief Executive Carrie Lam Cheng Yuet-ngor, who reported on her work in 2020, January 27, 2021)

II

Over the past year, Hong Kong has consolidated its achievements in restoring order and the situation has steadily improved. Notable results have been achieved in the Covid-19 response, in economic recovery, and in maintaining social stability.

Under the leadership of Chief Executive Carrie Lam Cheng Yuet-ngor, the HKSAR government has made systematic modifications to Hong Kong's electoral system in accordance with the decision of the NPC and the legislation of the NPC Standing Committee. It has held the elections of the Election Committee and the Legislative Council with success, and taken solid steps to advance democracy in Hong Kong in line with its realities. It has resolutely implemented the National Security Law of Hong Kong to end violence and chaos, restore order, and ensure a turn for the better in the region, and upheld the authority and dignity of the rule of law. It has also taken active measures to integrate Hong Kong into the country's overall development and expand exchanges and cooperation with the mainland in all areas.

The central authorities fully appreciate the work of the Chief Executive and the HKSAR government.

Several days ago, the election of the Seventh Legislative Council of the HKSAR was held. Under the new electoral system, the elections of the Election Committee and the Seventh Legislative Council were both successful. Our compatriots in Hong Kong exercised their democratic rights as the masters of the region and upheld the principle of patriots governing Hong Kong, and a political landscape with extensive and balanced participation of all social sectors and constituencies was created. The new electoral system embodies the One Country, Two Systems policy and fits Hong Kong's realities. It is a good system that will provide strong institutional support for the implementation of the One Country, Two Systems policy and for enduring prosperity and stability in the region.

This year marks the centenary of the CPC. At its Sixth Plenary Session, the 19th CPC Central Committee adopted a resolution on the major achievements and historical experience of the Party over the past century. The resolution highlights the One Country, Two Systems policy as a historic achievement of the Party. The extraordinary experience over the past two decades and more since the return of Hong Kong has proved that the One Country, Two Systems policy serves the best interests of the country, the HKSAR, and our Hong Kong compatriots. The central authorities will continue to firmly implement the policy, and we have full confidence that its strengths will become more evident as the relevant systems are improved. Our compatriots in Hong Kong will certainly carry on their honorable tradition of loving the country and Hong Kong, and strive for the rejuvenation of the Chinese nation shoulder to shoulder with the people of the rest of the country.

(from a meeting with HKSAR Chief Executive Carrie Lam Cheng Yuet-ngor, who reported on her work during a visit to Beijing, December 22, 2021)

Build on Macao's Success
with the One Country, Two Systems Policy[*]

January 27 and December 22, 2021

I

In line with the requirements of Covid-19 control, I have listened to your report on the work of the Macao Special Administrative Region (MSAR) government in 2020 via video link. This was the first year of your term in office and also of the new MSAR government. You have tamed the Covid-19 epidemic in Macao in a fairly short period, as a result of a quick response and forceful measures. No new local infections have been reported for more than 300 days. You have earned high praise for your efforts from the citizens of Macao and other relevant sectors. While containing the virus, you have also taken effective measures to enable economic recovery and help relieve the people of difficulties and hardships. These measures have achieved positive results and promoted social harmony in Macao. The central authorities fully acknowledge the work you and the MSAR government have done.

The central authorities always concern ourselves with the wellbeing of our Macao compatriots and the development of the MSAR. We will continue to support the MSAR government's efforts to coordinate epidemic response with economic and social development, to improve its legal system and corresponding enforcement mechanisms for safeguarding national security, to promote an appropriate level

---

[*] Main points in response to the work reports from Ho Iat Seng, chief executive of the Macao Special Administrative Region.

of diversity in its economy, and to integrate into the country's overall development, so as to further advance Macao's success with the One Country, Two Systems policy.

(from a virtual meeting with MSAR Chief Executive Ho Iat Seng,
who reported on his work in 2020, January 27, 2021)

II

On December 20, the MSAR held activities to celebrate the 22nd anniversary of Macao's return to the motherland. On this occasion, I would like to extend my festive greetings and best wishes to all compatriots in Macao.

Over the past year, Macao has maintained stability and sustained strong momentum in development. You have continued normal people-to-people exchanges with the mainland while effectively taming Covid-19 and achieving zero infection. Macao has made a gradual economic recovery, with struggling groups and micro and small businesses receiving support and assistance. The legal system and enforcement mechanisms for safeguarding national security have continued to improve. The region successfully completed the election of its seventh Legislative Assembly, and the principle of patriots governing Macao has been implemented. The central authorities have issued a general plan for building a Guangdong-Macao in-depth cooperation zone in Hengqin, creating new momentum for Macao to integrate into overall national development. The central authorities fully acknowledge the work that you, Chief Executive Ho Iat Seng, and the MSAR government have done.

Covid-19 is still spreading and has had a severe impact on society and the economy across the world. The pandemic has also given the various sectors of Macao a clearer understanding of the structural problems in the city's economy and prompted deeper reflection on its path of development. The motherland will always provide the strongest backing for Macao in maintaining long-term prosperity and stability. Adhering to the One Country, Two Systems policy, the central authorities will continue to enable the city to diversify its economy, and open a new chapter in the practice of One Country, Two Systems with Macao characteristics.

(from a meeting with MSAR Chief Executive Ho Iat Seng, who reported on his work during a visit to Beijing, December 22, 2021)

Join Hands to Achieve Complete Reunification and National Rejuvenation*

October 9, 2021

Dr Sun Yat-sen once said, "Unification is the hope of all Chinese nationals. If China can be unified, all Chinese will enjoy a happy life; if it cannot, all will suffer."[1] The Taiwan question arose as a result of weakness and chaos in our nation, and it will be resolved as national rejuvenation becomes a reality. This is determined by the general trend of Chinese history, but more importantly, it is the common will of all Chinese people. As Dr Sun observed, "The tide of the times is mighty; those who follow it will prosper while those who resist it will perish."[2]

National reunification by peaceful means best serves the interests of the Chinese nation as a whole, including our compatriots in Taiwan. We will adhere to the basic principles of peaceful reunification and One Country, Two Systems, uphold the one-China principle and the 1992 Consensus, and work for the peaceful development of cross-Straits relations. Compatriots on both sides of the Taiwan Straits should stand on the right side of history and join hands to achieve China's complete reunification and national rejuvenation.

The Chinese nation has an honorable tradition of opposing division and safeguarding unity. Secessionism directed towards "Taiwan independence" is the greatest obstacle to national reunification and a grave danger to national rejuvenation. Those who forget their roots, betray their motherland, and seek to split the country will come to no good end; they will be condemned by the people and indicted by

---

* Part of the speech at a meeting marking the 110th anniversary of the Revolution of 1911.

history. The Taiwan question is an internal matter for China and China alone, one which brooks no external interference. No one should underestimate the resolve, the will, and the ability of the Chinese people to defend our national sovereignty and territorial integrity. The complete reunification of our country can be and will be realized.

Notes

[1] Sun Yat-sen: "An Interview with a Japanese Journalist", *Complete Works of Sun Yat-sen*, Vol. VIII, Chin. ed., People's Publishing House, Beijing, 2015, p. 730.

[2] Sun Yat-sen: "An Inscription After Viewing the Qiantang River Tidal Bore in Haining on September 15, 1916", *Complete Works of Sun Yat-sen*, Vol. XV, Chin. ed., People's Publishing House, Beijing, 2015, p. 120.

Delivering a keynote speech while chairing the Extraordinary China-Africa Summit on Solidarity Against Covid-19 via video link from Beijing, June 17, 2020.

Delivering a speech at the 27th APEC Economic Leaders' Meeting via video link from Beijing, November 20, 2020.

Delivering a keynote speech while chairing the China-CEEC Summit via video link from Beijing, February 9, 2021.

Delivering a speech upon the invitation of US President Joe Biden at the Leaders Summit on Climate via video link from Beijing, April 22, 2021.

Delivering a keynote speech at the CPC and World Political Parties Summit via video link from Beijing, July 6, 2021.

Delivering a speech at the 21st Meeting of the Council of Heads of State of the Shanghai Cooperation Organization via video link from Beijing, September 17, 2021.

Delivering a speech at the conference in Beijing marking the 50th anniversary of the restoration of the lawful seat of the People's Republic of China in the United Nations, October 25, 2021.

Attending the opening ceremony of the China-Laos Railway with Thongloun Sisoulith, general secretary of the Central Committee of the Lao People's Revolutionary Party and Lao president, via video link from Beijing, December 3, 2021.

Chairing and addressing the virtual summit from Beijing to celebrate the 30th anniversary of the establishment of diplomatic relations between China and the five Central Asian countries (Kazakhstan, Kyrgyzstan, Tajikistan, Turkmenistan and Uzbekistan), January 25, 2022.

Declaring the 24th Winter Olympic Games open at the National Stadium in Beijing, February 4, 2022.

Xi and his wife Peng Liyuan (5th right, 1st row), with international guests who had come to attend the opening ceremony of the Beijing 2022 Winter Olympic Games, before a welcome banquet in the Great Hall of the People, Beijing, February 5, 2022.

Meeting in the Great Hall of the People with UN Secretary-General António Guterres, who had come to attend the Beijing 2022 Winter Olympic Games, Beijing, February 5, 2022.

A Global Community of
Shared Future

Work Together to Protect the Lives and Health of All[*]

May 18, 2020

The history of human civilization is one of fighting disease and disaster. Viruses are no respecters of border, race or nationality. Confronted by the ravages of Covid-19, the international community has not flinched, and the people of all countries have risen to the challenge. Around the world, people have pulled together as one, helping each other as best we can. With love and compassion, we have forged extraordinary synergy in the battle against Covid-19.

In China, after painstaking efforts and enormous sacrifice, we have turned the tide of the battle and succeeded in protecting the lives and health of our people. All along, we have acted with openness, transparency and responsibility. We have provided information to the World Health Organization (WHO) and other affected countries in a most timely fashion. We have released the genome sequence at the earliest possible time. We have shared our experience of control and treatment with the rest of the world without reservation. We have done everything in our power to support and assist countries in need.

Even as we meet, the virus is still raging, and more must be done to bring it under control. To this end, I want to make the following proposals:

First, we must do everything we can to prevent and contain the spread of the virus. This is a most urgent task. We must always put the people first, for nothing in the world is more precious than people's lives. We need to deploy medical expertise and critical supplies in

* Part of the speech at the opening ceremony of the virtual 73rd World Health Assembly.

places where they are most needed. We need to take strong measures in key areas such as prevention, quarantine, detection, treatment and tracing. We need to move as fast as we can to curb the global spread of the virus and do our best to stem cross-border transmission. We need to step up information sharing, learn from each other's experience and best practices, and pursue international cooperation on testing methods, clinical treatment, and research and development of vaccines and medicines. We also need to continue supporting global research by scientists on the source and transmission routes of the virus.

Second, the WHO should lead the global response. Under the leadership of Director General Tedros Adhanom Ghebreyesus, the WHO has made a major contribution in leading and advancing the global response to Covid-19. Its good work has been applauded by the international community. At this crucial juncture, to support the WHO is to support international cooperation and the battle for saving lives. China calls on the international community to increase political and financial support for the WHO so as to mobilize resources worldwide to defeat the virus.

Third, we must provide greater support for Africa. Developing countries, those in Africa in particular, have weaker public health systems. Helping them to build capacity must be a top priority in our Covid-19 response. The world needs to provide more material, technological and manpower support for African countries. China has sent tremendous quantities of medical supplies and offered assistance to over 50 African countries and the African Union. Five teams of Chinese health and medical experts have been sent to the African continent in support of its Covid-19 response. For the past seven decades, a total of over 200 million people in Africa have received care and treatment from Chinese medical teams. At present, 46 resident Chinese medical teams are in Africa helping with local Covid-19 containment efforts.

Fourth, we must strengthen global public health governance. Humanity will eventually prevail over the coronavirus. Yet this will not be the last time we are confronted by a major public health emergency. In view of the weaknesses and deficiencies exposed by Covid-19, we need to improve the system of governance for public health security. We need to respond more quickly to public health emergencies and establish global and regional centers of anti-epidemic reserves. China supports the idea of conducting a comprehensive review of the global response to Covid-19 once it has been brought under control, to take stock of experience and lessons learned and address deficiencies. This should be based on science and professionalism, led by the WHO and conducted in an objective and impartial manner.

Fifth, we must restore economic and social development. While working on an ongoing basis to contain the virus, countries may reopen businesses and schools where conditions permit, in an orderly fashion and in accordance with the WHO's professional recommendations. In the meantime, coordination of international macroeconomic policy should be stepped up, and global industrial and supply chains should be kept open and stable, if we are to restore growth to the world economy.

Sixth, we must strengthen international cooperation. Humanity shares a common future. Solidarity and cooperation are our most powerful weapons to defeat the virus. This is a key lesson the world has learned from fighting HIV/AIDS, Ebola, avian influenza, influenza A (H1N1) and other major epidemics. And solidarity and cooperation offer a sure method through which we, the people of the world, can defeat this novel coronavirus.

China stands for the vision of building a global community of shared future. China considers it has a responsibility to ensure the lives and health of its own citizens, and also to safeguard global public health. In order to boost international cooperation against Covid-19, I hereby announce the following:

– China will provide US$2 billion over two years to help with the Covid-19 response and with economic and social development in affected countries, especially developing countries.

– China will work with the UN to set up a global humanitarian response depot and hub in China, to ensure the operation of anti-epidemic supply chains, and to foster "green corridors" for fast-track transport and customs clearance.

– China will establish a cooperation mechanism for its hospitals to pair up with 30 African hospitals. We will accelerate the building of the Africa CDC headquarters and help the continent ramp up its capacity for disease prevention and control.

– Covid-19 vaccines, once they have been developed and applied in China, will be made available as a global public good. This will be China's contribution to ensuring access to affordable vaccines in developing countries.

– China will work with other G20 members to implement the Debt Service Suspension Initiative for the poorest countries. China is also ready to work with the international community to boost support for the worst-affected countries that are struggling the hardest to service their debt, and help them emerge from their current difficulties.

To conclude, I call on all of us to come together and work as one. Let us make a concerted effort to protect the lives and health of all people in all countries. Let us work together to safeguard planet earth, our common home. Let us work together to build a global community of health for all.

Boost China-Arab Cooperation and Move Forward Together*

July 6, 2020

At the Eighth Ministerial Conference of the China-Arab States Cooperation Forum (CASCF) held in 2018, I announced the establishment of the China-Arab strategic partnership, and proposed building a China-Arab community of shared future as part of our endeavors to build a global community of shared future. This initiative has been warmly received by the Arab countries. Over the past two years, our two sides have strengthened coordination on strategic affairs and concrete actions, consolidated mutual political trust, delivered solid outcomes in Belt and Road cooperation, and increased and enriched our people-to-people exchanges. Working together, we have raised to a new level the China-Arab future-oriented strategic partnership of comprehensive cooperation and common development.

In the battle against Covid-19, China and the Arab countries have stood firmly together and increased mutual support and cooperation. This vividly demonstrates the close bond that binds us. Now, more than ever, we need to increase cooperation to navigate this trying time and move forward together. Both sides should take the opportunity presented by this conference to reinforce consultation on our strategies in various fields and boost cooperation on our response to Covid-19. Let us work together to build an ever-stronger China-Arab community of shared future, and deliver greater benefits to our peoples.

---

* Main part of the congratulatory letter to the Ninth Ministerial Conference of the China-Arab States Cooperation Forum.

Work Together for Asia-Pacific Prosperity*

November 20, 2020

Both the world and the Asia-Pacific are experiencing profound change, a process accelerated by Covid-19. The world economy is in a downturn. Economic globalization is encountering headwinds. Unilateralism and protectionism are on the rise. Balancing equity and efficiency, growth and distribution, and technological development and employment is becoming more difficult. The wealth gap remains widespread. The global governance system faces new challenges. For the first time in decades, the Asia-Pacific as a whole has registered negative economic growth. Protecting people's health and reviving the economy are two formidable challenges we face.

Which way should Asia-Pacific cooperation be heading? The answer will have a profound impact on the development of our region, the wellbeing of our people, and the future of the world.

One priority on this year's agenda of Asia-Pacific Economic Cooperation (APEC) is to unveil the post-2020 vision, a pathway towards our goal of building an Asia-Pacific community. This should be pursued as a new starting point for us to begin another phase in Asia-Pacific cooperation, to sustain the strong momentum of development in our region, and to embrace a future of shared prosperity. Together, we can build an Asia-Pacific community of shared future, one of openness, inclusiveness, innovation-driven growth, greater connectivity, and mutually beneficial cooperation.

First, we need to stay open and inclusive.

The global economy is like the nearby Pacific Ocean – it admits water from various rivers, and connects different parts of the world.

---

* Part of the speech at the 27th APEC Economic Leaders' Meeting.

This gives it an immense capacity and enormous vitality. We should pursue cooperation on the basis of equality and dissolve differences with mutual respect because this is essential to delivering economic development and prosperity in our region.

Over the years, APEC has remained committed to regional economic integration and made significant gains in implementing the Bogor Goals. It has also played an important role in steering the development of the multilateral trading system. However, free and open trade and investment are not something that can be achieved overnight. It is important that the Asia-Pacific nations continue to take the lead in safeguarding peace and stability, upholding multilateralism, and fostering an open world economy.

We must stay as determined as ever in our support to the multilateral trading system with the World Trade Organization at its core, promote free and open trade and investment, and steer economic globalization in such a way that will make the global economy more open, inclusive, balanced and beneficial to all. Continued efforts are needed to step up regional economic integration towards the early realization of a Free Trade Area of the Asia-Pacific.

China welcomes the signing of the Regional Comprehensive Economic Partnership, and will favorably consider joining the Comprehensive and Progressive Agreement for Trans-Pacific Partnership.

As we continue to promote free and open trade, we should pay no less attention to economic and technical cooperation. We need to further implement the APEC Strategy for Strengthening Quality Growth and the Action Agenda on Advancing Economic, Financial and Social Inclusion, and address the concerns of developing members. In particular, we need to respond to the special needs of women and other groups, and support micro, small and medium-sized enterprises (MSMEs). Such efforts will contribute to inclusive and sustainable growth.

China will host a seminar on advancing economic inclusion through trade and investment, where we can expect to hear proposals on how trade and investment policies can deliver great benefits to all the people. China looks forward to working with all parties to follow up on proposals to be made at the seminar.

Second, we need to pursue innovation-driven growth.

The digital economy represents the future of global development, and innovation will drive the economic takeoff of the Asia-Pacific. We need to seize the opportunities of our times and make full use of our region's abundant human resources, solid technological foundations, and enormous market potential to gain a new competitive edge and open up new possibilities for bettering our people's lives.

The APEC Internet and Digital Economy Roadmap should be implemented in full to encourage the dissemination and application of new technologies, strengthen digital infrastructure, and close the digital divide. We need to improve economic governance and foster an open, fair, equitable and nondiscriminatory environment for businesses. This year, China has conducted an APEC case study on smart cities, which we hope will contribute to the formulation of guidelines on smart cities and offer an example for pursuing innovative urban development across the region.

China calls for sharing practices among APEC members on how to respond to Covid-19 and achieve economic recovery with digital technologies. China also calls for improving the digital business environment to energize market entities and tap the potential of the digital market. These efforts will add new impetus to economic recovery in our region. Next year, China will host a workshop on digital technology-enabled poverty alleviation to leverage the role of digital technologies in eradicating poverty in our region.

Third, we need to strengthen connectivity.

Connectivity is vital for both regional economic integration and interconnected global development. The pandemic confronting us further highlights the importance of connectivity. We need to continue to implement the APEC Connectivity Blueprint to facilitate a smooth, safe and orderly flow of people, goods, capital and data, and to achieve a seamlessly connected Asia-Pacific. China has opened fast tracks with other APEC members including Indonesia, the Republic of Korea, and Singapore to facilitate the movement of people during the pandemic, and we will do more to build a network of facilitation arrangements.

To this end, it is important to promote the mutual recognition of Covid-related health information for international travelers. China is ready to take active and well-considered steps with all other parties to set up "green lanes" for goods, make customs clearance more efficient, remove bottlenecks, and reconnect disrupted links. We are ready to promote the creation of international cooperation platforms on industrial and supply chains to ensure their safe and smooth operation in our region and beyond.

We need to integrate development plans and connectivity initiatives of different parties to create greater synergy. On its part, China will work with all partners to pursue high-quality Belt and Road cooperation. We believe this will provide a larger platform for increasing connectivity in the Asia-Pacific and inject stronger momentum into the economy of our region and the wider world.

Fourth, we need to promote mutually beneficial cooperation.

We APEC members are highly complementary in terms of development, and our interests are deeply intertwined. Economic cooperation among us has never been a zero-sum political game in which one gains at the expense of others. Rather, our cooperation has provided us with a development platform that delivers gains to us all. As a Malaysian saying goes, we should climb the hill and cross the ravine together. This aptly captures what defines us as an Asia-Pacific family. Covid-19 also reminds us that only with solidarity and cooperation can we meet challenges.

We need to forge stronger Asia-Pacific partnerships based on mutual trust, inclusiveness, and mutually beneficial cooperation, and act on the principles of extensive consultation, joint contribution, and shared benefits. We need to upgrade and expand regional cooperation to deliver prosperity for the whole region. It is important that we advance results-oriented cooperation on the basis of consensus, properly manage differences and disagreements, and steer Asia-Pacific cooperation in the right direction to ensure APEC's sound long-term development.

Beating Covid-19 is the most pressing task facing us all. We must step up research and development of vaccines and exchanges, work harder to make vaccines a global public good, and improve their accessibility and affordability in developing countries. With this in mind, China has joined the Covid-19 Vaccines Global Access (COVAX) Facility.

We support APEC in strengthening policy exchanges and capacity building in the areas of public health and MSMEs. China has proposed a telemedicine initiative to give people in poor and remote areas access to timely and quality medical services. We hope these efforts will contribute to anti-pandemic cooperation and economic recovery.

China values the role of APEC. We will continue to support the organization, and with our roots struck deep in the Asia-Pacific, we will continue to serve its development and prosperity.

Strengthen Cooperation Among World Political Parties to Benefit the People[*]

July 6, 2021

Your Excellencies Leaders of Political Parties,
Ladies and gentlemen,
Friends,

Today as the CPC reaches its 100th anniversary, it gives me great pleasure to join you, the leaders of more than 500 political parties and organizations from over 160 countries, as well as the 10,000 and more representatives assembled at this cloud event, to discuss the important question of "the responsibility of political parties in working for the benefit of the people". In recent weeks, over 600 political parties and organizations from over 170 countries have sent more than 1,500 congratulatory messages and letters conveying their goodwill and best wishes to the CPC. I wish to take this opportunity to express to all of you, on behalf of the Communist Party of China, our heartfelt thanks.

A few days ago we celebrated our Party's centenary with a grand gathering. Over the past hundred years, the CPC has united the Chinese people and led them in working towards the tremendous transformation of the Chinese nation, from standing up and becoming better off to growing in strength. Over the past hundred years, the CPC has always believed that the Chinese people and other peoples of the world have a shared future. Respecting international trends and flowing with international currents, it has steered the course of China's development and supported the development and prosperity of all countries.

---

* Keynote speech at the CPC and World Political Parties Summit.

The historic achievements of the CPC and the Chinese people would not have been possible without the generous support of others.

Here, on behalf of the CPC and the Chinese people, I would like to express my heartfelt gratitude to peoples, political parties, and friends from all countries who have given their attention, support and assistance to the CPC and the revolution, construction, and reform in China.

Ladies and gentlemen,

Friends,

The world today is undergoing change on a scale unseen in a century. Although countries are increasingly interconnected and inter-dependent, support for multi-polarity and economic globalization is volatile. The international community has made strenuous efforts to deal with Covid-19, revive the global economy, and safeguard world stability. Political parties in many countries have exhibited a strong sense of responsibility by actively exploring ways to address existing problems. At the same time wars and conflicts are still raging in some places, famine and disease are affecting many people, estrangement increases, and confrontations arise. The call for a better life from all peoples, whatever their country, is becoming ever louder and clearer.

Today, human society has once again found itself at a historic crossroads. Will we choose hostile confrontation or mutual respect? Will we choose isolation and decoupling or openness and coopera-tion? Will we choose zero-sum game or win-win results? The choice is in our hands, and the responsibility falls on our shoulders.

The human race is one single global community and the planet earth its homeland. No person or country can remain cloistered from the common challenges we face. The only solution is to work together in harmony. As an important force behind human progress, political parties need to set the right course. They need to assume their historic responsibility to work for the benefit of the people. I believe that political parties need to work even harder on the following:

First, we need to lead the way in seizing and shaping the shared future of humanity. People aspire to affluence and contentment. They yearn for fairness and justice. Great times call for a grand strategy, and a grand strategy calls for great vision. Viewed from the perspective of "my own country first", the world is a cramped and crowded place mired in fierce competition. Viewed from the perspective of a common destiny, the world is a vast and broad place full of cooperation opportunities. We need to heed the voices of the people, follow the trends of the times, and strengthen coordination and cooperation. In doing so, we can keep the interests of every people in line with all others, and work together to realize the global community of shared future.

Second, we need to build consensus by upholding and promoting the common values of humanity. Despite the differences between countries in history, culture, social system, and level of development, their peoples do subscribe to the common values of peace, development, equality, justice, democracy and freedom. With a strong sense of our responsibility for the future of all humanity, we need to champion common human values, foster broad-minded understanding of the values of other civilizations, and respect the choice of every nation for its pathway to realizing its values. In this way, the common values of humanity will be translated into concrete and pragmatic actions by individual countries that serve the interests of their own peoples.

Third, we need to promote development by delivering greater benefits to all in a fairer manner. Development holds the key to the wellbeing of all humankind, and no country or nation should be left behind on this road. All countries and nations have an equal right to access and realize development opportunities. We need to face up squarely to major problems such as the wealth gap and the development divide, giving particular care and attention to underdeveloped countries and regions and impoverished people, so that hope prevails in every corner of the world. As a Ming-dynasty scholar said, "Those who seek comfort only for themselves will ultimately be denounced, while those who sacrifice their own interests for the success of others will be hailed."[1] Development is the right of all, not an exclusive privilege of the few. We need to enable all countries to step up cooperation and share the fruits of development. We need to bring greater equity, higher efficiency, and stronger synergy to global development, and jointly oppose technology blockades, widening gaps, and decoupling. I believe that in the final analysis, any political manipulation designed to hinder the development of other countries and undermine the livelihood of other peoples will win little support and prove futile.

Fourth, we need to strengthen cooperation by working together to address global risks and challenges. In the face of the ongoing Covid-19 pandemic, we need to continue with a science-based response and advocate solidarity and cooperation so as to close the immunization gap. We must oppose any attempt to politicize the pandemic or assign the virus with geographical labels. We need to work together to build a global community of health for all. In the face of terrorism and other common enemies of humankind, we need to pursue security and stability through cooperation so as to tighten our defenses together. In defense of a fragile eco-environment, we need to respect and protect Mother Nature and follow her laws, so as to build a green homeland together. Confronted by the severe challenges to human existence and development posed by climate change, we need to be bold in our responses and work as one to find the way to harmonious coexistence with nature.

Fifth, we need to improve governance by strengthening our capacity to ensure the people's wellbeing. There are different ways to a good life. Every country and its people should be entitled to choose their own development path and governance model. This, in itself, is what a good life means. In the same vein, democracy is the right of all peoples, rather than an exclusive privilege of the few. There is no single model of democracy; there are multiple ways and means by which it can be realized. A country's democratic credentials should be judged by its own people, not by a small number of outsiders. To advance democracy in a way that is adapted to the national conditions of a country, we need to strengthen exchanges and mutual learning, improve mechanisms for communication, be fully aware of public opinion, create and consolidate sound institutions, and strengthen our capacity in governance. This will make us more effective in improving the people's wellbeing.

Ladies and gentlemen,

Friends,

Working for the people's wellbeing was the original aspiration of the CPC and has always been a cherished aim. Having achieved the goal of all-round moderate prosperity, China has embarked on a new journey towards building a modern socialist country. The Chinese people overflow with an increasing sense of gain, fulfillment, and security. The unswerving objectives of the CPC are to run our own country well, ensure a happy life for more than 1.4 billion Chinese people, and advance the lofty cause of promoting peace and development for all humankind. The CPC will continue to uphold the philosophy of people-centered development, reflect upon the overarching issues of national rejuvenation and human progress in the greater context of time and space, and lead all the people of China in creating an even better tomorrow through perseverance and an enterprising spirit.

As history has taught us, we can only embrace the future when we embrace the world, and we can only travel safe and far when we walk together. The CPC stands ready to work with political parties throughout the world to turn our dreams into reality. Let us always be builders of world peace, advocates for global development, and guardians of the international order.

– The CPC will unite and lead the Chinese people to advance China's modernization while contributing to human progress.

Proceeding from reality in all it does, the CPC has led the Chinese people to the path of socialism with Chinese characteristics. History and our experience have proved and will continue to prove that this is the path that works and the path that pays off. We will continue to follow this path to ensure that development is pursued both for our own good and for the benefit of the world. There is no fixed model for the path to modernization, and the one that suits you well will serve you well. Cutting your foot to fit a shoe will not work. Every effort by any country to find its own path to modernization is worthy of respect. The CPC is willing to share its experience with political parties of all countries and work together with them to broaden paths to modernization so as to ensure the wellbeing of their own and other peoples.

– The CPC will unite the Chinese people and lead them in deeper reform and opening up to share its development and prosperity with all countries.

Despite considerable headwinds, economic globalization is making good headway. On the whole, the headway is prevailing over the head-winds – the trend towards opening up and cooperation in all countries is and will remain unchanged. The CPC is ready to boost communication with world political parties in steering economic globalization towards greater openness, inclusiveness, balance, and win-win results. We stand ready to work with the international community to increase global connectivity and high-quality Belt and Road cooperation, so that more countries and peoples can share the fruits of development.

– The CPC will shoulder its responsibilities as a major political party in a major country to improve human wellbeing.

The eradication of poverty has long been a common aspiration of all peoples in all countries, and an important objective that all political parties strive to achieve. Since the 18th National Congress of the CPC in 2012, all of China's 99 million rural residents living below the current poverty line have been lifted out of extreme poverty, enabling us to meet the poverty reduction target set out in the UN 2030 Agenda for Sustainable Development 10 years ahead of schedule. The CPC is willing to contribute more Chinese solutions and Chinese strength to the poverty reduction process worldwide. China will spare no effort to support international cooperation against Covid-19 and to increase the accessibility and affordability of vaccines in developing countries.

China will deliver on its promises to achieve peak carbon dioxide emissions and carbon neutrality and contribute more to the global fight against climate change. China will host the 15th meeting of the Conference of the Parties to the Convention on Biological Diversity, where parties will discuss new strategies and embark on a new journey of global biodiversity governance.

– The CPC will actively improve global governance to support humanity's joint response to common challenges.

Multilateralism is at the core of the current international system and order. The better it is practiced, the faster humanity's common problems will be resolved. International rules should be based on universally recognized norms rather than the rules of the few. Countries should cooperate to serve all of humanity instead of seeking hegemony by way of bloc politics. We should stand in opposition to the practice of unilateralism disguised as multilateralism and say no to hegemony and power politics. Upholding the purposes and principles of the UN Charter, China is of the view that matters concerning all should be handled through joint consultation, so that the international order and system will be fairer and more equitable. I wish to reiterate that China will always be part of the developing world, and is committed to strengthening its representation and voice in the global governance system. China will never seek hegemony, expansion or spheres of influence. The CPC will work with political parties of all countries to promote state-to-state coordination and cooperation through party-to-party consultation, and promote their role in global governance.

Ladies and gentlemen,

Friends,

Our journey will be long and arduous. But as long as we persevere on the road ahead, there will be much to anticipate. Our road will never be straight or smooth, but hopes abound. The CPC stands ready to continue to work with political parties and organizations of all countries to support the right side of history and the progressive cause of humanity. Let us make an even greater contribution to building a global community of shared future and a better world.

Thank you.

Notes

[1] Fang Xiaoru: "Thoughts on Items in Daily Life" (Za Ming). Fang Xiaoru (1357-1402) was an orthodox Confucian scholar of the Ming Dynasty.

Build a Stronger Shanghai Cooperation Organization*

September 17, 2021

The past 20 years have seen an evolving international environment and a profound reshaping of the global governance system. These years have also witnessed the vigorous growth of the Shanghai Cooperation Organization (SCO) and fruitful, mutually beneficial cooperation among its member states. Over the past two decades, the SCO has been guided by the Shanghai Spirit of mutual trust, mutual benefit, equality, consultation, respect for diversity of civilizations, and pursuit of common development. It has endeavored to promote world peace, development and human progress, and it has explored new ground, both in theory and in practice, to build a new model of international relations and a global community of shared future.

– We have promoted mutual political trust.

We have signed the Treaty on Long-Term Good-Neighborliness, Friendship and Cooperation and created a new model based on partnership and dialogue rather than alliance or confrontation. We have supported each other on issues which involve our respective core interests and are of major concern to us. And we have provided reliable and strong support to each other in our pursuit of development.

– We have ensured security and stability.

We were the first to issue a call to arms against terrorism, separatism and extremism. We have taken tough actions to curb the spread of drug trafficking, cybercrime, and transnational organized crime, and held joint counter-terrorism exercises and border control operations.

* Part of the speech at the 21st Meeting of the Council of Heads of State of the Shanghai Cooperation Organization.

We call for political settlement of international and regional flash-points. Thus, we have erected a powerful defense to uphold peace and tranquility in our region.

– We have jointly pursued prosperity and development.

We have intensified cooperation in our region. People-to-people programs such as art festivals, the SCO University, and the SCO Forum on Traditional Medicine have been launched. With SCO speed and SCO efficiency, as evidenced by the 12 percent annual growth of the total GDP and foreign trade of SCO member states and a mani-fold increase in the number of mutual visits, we have moved faster to deliver a decent life for people in SCO countries.

– We have upheld international justice.

We have advocated multilateralism and the common values of humanity and spoken out against hegemony and power politics. We have maintained close coordination with SCO observer states and dialogue partners as well as international and regional organizations which share the SCO's purposes and principles. And we have worked with other members of the international community in quest of a shared future.

The SCO has now reached a new historic starting point. We should stay committed to the Shanghai Spirit, keep to the right direction, promote democracy in international relations, and pursue our own development as part of our efforts to promote common development for humanity. Together, we can build a closer SCO communi-ty of shared future and contribute even more to durable global peace and common prosperity. To this end, it is imperative that we do the following:

First, we need to strengthen solidarity and cooperation.

To keep the SCO on a steady course of development, we should make the most of the meeting mechanisms and platforms at vari-ous levels, and step up policy dialogue, consultation and coordina-tion. And we should respect each other's legitimate concerns, and promptly resolve issues that may arise and affect our cooperation. We should maintain firm confidence in our systems, reject condescending lectures, and firmly support countries in exploring the development paths and governance models that are compatible with their national conditions. We should support each other in steadily advancing important political agendas such as domestic elections. We must never allow any external interference in the domestic affairs of countries in our region under whatever pretext. In short, we should keep our countries' development and future firmly in our own hands.

Fighting Covid-19 remains the most pressing task facing us all. We should follow the principle of putting people and their lives first and respect science. We need to expand international cooperation against the virus, promote fair and equitable distribution of vaccines, and firmly oppose any attempt to politicize Covid-19 origin tracing. To protect the lives and health of people across the world, China has provided close to 1.2 billion doses of finished and bulk vaccines to over 100 countries and international organizations, which means it is the biggest vaccine provider in the world. China will provide a total of 2 billion doses to other countries in the course of this year. We will expand anti-Covid-19 cooperation with other developing countries, and make good use of China's US$100 million donation to COVAX. Together, we humanity will ultimately beat the virus.

Second, we need to uphold our common security.

Faced with complex and fluid security dynamics in the region, we need to pursue common, comprehensive, cooperative and sustainable security, and take tough actions against terrorism, separatism and extremism, including the East Turkestan Islamic Movement. We need to strengthen cooperation in counter-narcotics, border control, and security for major events, and speedily improve the SCO's security cooperation mechanism. We need to fully implement the Convention on Countering Extremism and other legal instruments, and boost the capacity of competent SCO government authorities to maintain stability and respond to emergencies.

Afghanistan has experienced a period of dramatic change. With the withdrawal of foreign troops, a new page has been opened in its history. But Afghanistan still faces many daunting challenges, and it needs the support and assistance of the international community, particularly countries in our region. We SCO member states need to step up coordination, make full use of platforms such as the SCO-Afghanistan Contact Group, and facilitate a smooth transition in Afghanistan. We need to encourage Afghanistan to put in place a broad-based and inclusive political framework, adopt prudent and moderate domestic and foreign policies, resolutely fight terrorism in all its forms, live in amity with its neighbors, and truly embark on a path of peace, stability and development.

Third, we need to promote openness and integration.

We SCO countries are all at a critical stage of development. Being close to each other and sharing common interests are our unique strengths. We need to make full use of these strengths, stay committed to openness and cooperation, and pursue our shared goal of development and rejuvenation. We need to continue to promote trade and investment liberalization and facilitation, and ensure secure and orderly flow of people, goods, capital and data. We should create growth drivers that promote cooperation, such as the digital economy, green energy and modern agriculture. Belt and Road cooperation is a major platform for promoting development for us all. We need to strengthen complementarity between the Belt and Road Initiative and the development strategies of SCO countries, and with regional cooperation initiatives such as the Eurasian Economic Union. We should keep industrial and supply chains functioning smoothly, promote economic integration and interconnected development of all countries, and deliver shared benefits to all.

To facilitate post-Covid economic recovery in SCO countries, China will continue to share its market opportunities with other countries. In the next five years we will work to achieve the goal of US$2.3 trillion in cumulative trade with you, our fellow SCO countries, and we will improve the structure and balance of China's trade with you. China will open a China-SCO Business and Trade Institute to promote multilateral business and trade cooperation among SCO countries. Phase one of the RMB30 billion equivalent special lending facility set up by China in 2018 within the SCO framework will soon be completed, and China will then launch the second phase to promote Belt and Road cooperation. This lending facility is earmarked mainly for projects on modern connectivity, infrastructure development, and green, low-carbon and sustainable development.

Fourth, we need to draw on each other's strengths.

The most solid foundation for the SCO's development lies in mutual learning among civilizations, and its greatest strength lies in people-to-people bonds. We need to encourage exchanges, dialogue, harmony and coexistence between civilizations. We should launch more popular and practical projects in such areas as science and technology, education, culture, health and poverty alleviation. We should fully tap into platforms including the youth exchange camp, women's forum, media forum, and forum on people-to-people friendship, and give full rein to social organizations such as the Good-neighborliness, Friendship and Cooperation Commission. With these efforts, we can build a bridge of mutual understanding and friendship between the peoples of the SCO countries.

In the next three years, China will provide 1,000 training opportunities on poverty alleviation for other SCO countries, open 10 Lu Ban[1] Workshops, and launch 30 cooperation projects within the framework of the Silk Road Community Building Initiative in areas such as health, poverty alleviation, culture and education. This will help those countries in need build capacity and improve the lives of their people. China will host an SCO youth forum on technology and innovation next year to help unleash the creativity of young people in SCO countries. China proposes to establish an SCO alliance of traditional medicine industries to explore new ways of cooperation in this field. China welcomes the participation of all countries in the Beijing 2022 Olympic and Paralympic Winter Games. Together, we can deliver a streamlined, safe and splendid Olympic Games.

Fifth, we need to uphold equity and justice.

"The powerful may get the upper hand for the time being, but justice will ultimately prevail."[2] Acting from an assumed position of strength is not the way to handle international affairs; hegemonic and domineering actions should be firmly rejected, as should the abuse of the weak by the strong. In handling international relations, we should abide by the purposes and principles of the UN Charter and follow the principles of extensive consultation, joint contribution, and shared benefits. We must practice true multilateralism and oppose actions that use spurious rules as a pretext to undermine the international order and cause confrontation and division. We should boost mutually beneficial cooperation, remove barriers that impede trade, investment and technological exchanges, and promote inclusive development that delivers benefits to all.

Notes

¹ Lu Ban (507-444 BC) was a civil engineer and inventor in the Spring and Autumn Period. – *Tr.*

² Feng Menglong: *Romance of the States in Eastern Zhou (Dong Zhou Lie Guo Zhi).* Feng Menglong (1574-1646) was a writer and thinker of the Ming Dynasty.

Protect the Earth for Sustainable Development*

October 12, 2021

"All beings flourish when they live in harmony and receive nourishment from nature."[1] Biodiversity fills the earth with vigor and vitality, and lays the foundation for human survival and development. Protecting biodiversity helps protect the earth, our common homeland, and contributes to humanity's sustainable development.

The Kunming conference, on the theme of "Ecological Civilization: Building a Shared Future for All Life on Earth", is of great significance. It will work for the conclusion of the Post-2020 Global Biodiversity Framework, and identify targets and pathways for global biodiversity protection in the future. In this context, the international community must increase cooperation, build consensus, and pool strength to build a community of all life on earth.

Humanity and nature need to coexist in harmony. When we take care to protect nature, nature rewards us generously; when we exploit nature ruthlessly, it punishes us without mercy. We need to have a deep reverence for nature, respect nature's needs, follow nature's laws, and protect nature, so as to build a homeland where humanity and nature coexist in harmony.

Clear waters and green mountains are invaluable assets. A sound eco-environment is not just a natural asset, but also an economic asset, and has a critical impact on the potential and sustainability of economic and social development. We need to speed up efforts to foster a green approach to development and secure both economic growth and environmental protection, so as to build a homeland of

---

* Main part of the keynote speech at the leaders' summit of the 15th meeting of the Conference of the Parties to the Convention on Biological Diversity.

coordinated progress in the economy and the environment.

The Covid-19 pandemic has cast a shadow over global development and compounded challenges to the UN 2030 Agenda for Sustainable Development. Faced with the dual tasks of economic recovery and eco-environmental protection, developing countries need all the more help and support. We need to strengthen solidarity to overcome difficulties and let people across countries benefit in a broadly inclusive and fair way from development outcomes and a sound eco-environment, so as to build a homeland of common development of all countries.

We are living in an era fraught with dangers and yet brimming with hopes. As long as we press ahead and persevere, a bright future beckons. For the sake of our common future, we need to join hands and start a new journey of high-quality development for humanity.

First, it is important to harmonize the relationship between humanity and nature through stronger eco-environmental protection. We need to solve the problems brought by industrial civilization, keep human activities within the carrying capacity of the eco-environment, and carry out holistic conservation and systematic governance of mountains, rivers, forests, farmlands, lakes, grasslands and deserts.

Second, it is important to promote global sustainable development by adopting a green approach to growth. We need to develop a green, low-carbon and circular economy, translate eco-environmental strengths into development strengths, and bring out the enormous benefits that clear waters and green mountains can offer. We also need to step up international cooperation and share the fruits of green development among all countries.

Third, it is important to promote social equity and justice with a focus on improving the people's wellbeing. We need to keep in mind the people's aspirations for a better life, pursue win-win results in environmental protection, economic development, job creation, poverty elimination and other endeavors, and increase the sense of gain, fulfillment and security of all people in all countries.

Fourth, it is important to uphold a fair and equitable international governance system based on international law. We need to practice true multilateralism, and respect and comply with international rules, which are not to be exploited or discarded at one's convenience. The new targets of environmental protection we set must be ambitious on the one hand and pragmatic and balanced on the other, so as to make the global environmental governance system fairer and more equitable.

China has made remarkable progress in ecological conservation and environmental protection. The recent northward travel and return of a herd of elephants in Yunnan Province in southwest China is a vivid example of our endeavor and success in protecting wild animals. China will continue to advance eco-environmental protection, stay committed to the philosophy of innovative, coordinated, green, open and shared development, and build a beautiful China.

On this occasion, I wish to announce a new initiative from China – to establish a Kunming Biodiversity Fund in support of biodiversity protection in developing countries. And we will take the lead by contributing RMB1.5 billion. China also welcomes and calls for contributions from other parties to the fund.

To strengthen its biodiversity protection, China is making rapid progress in establishing a nature reserve system mainly consisting of national parks. Over time, areas of the greatest importance to the natural ecosystems, with the most unique natural landscapes, with the most valuable natural heritage, and with the greatest biodiversity will be included in the national parks system.

China has officially designated its first group of national parks. They include the Three-River-Source National Park, the Giant Panda National Park, the Northeast China Tiger and Leopard National Park, the National Park of Hainan Tropical Rainforest, and the Wuyishan National Park. The land area under protection extends to 230,000 square kilometers, and these parks are home to nearly 30 percent of the key terrestrial wildlife species found in China. In the meantime, acting on the principle of balancing in-situ and ex-situ conservation, China has started building a system of national botanical gardens in places such as Beijing and Guangzhou.

To achieve peak carbon dioxide emissions and carbon neutrality, China will release action plans for peak carbon emissions in key areas and sectors as well as a series of support measures, and will put in place a "1+N" policy framework for achieving its carbon goals. China will continue to readjust its industrial structure and energy mix, vigorously develop renewable energy, and make faster progress in planning and developing large wind power and photovoltaic bases in sandy areas, rocky areas and deserts. We are now making smooth progress on construction of the first phase of projects with an installed capacity of approximately 100,000 megawatts.

If we humans do not fail nature, nature will not fail us. Eco-environmental protection represents the optimal path for human civilization. Let us come together to protect our ecosystems and the environment, and shoulder our responsibility for future generations. Let us make a joint effort to build a community of all life on earth, and a clean and beautiful world for us all.

Notes

[1] *Xun Zi*. This is a book written by Xun Kuang. Xun Kuang (c. 313-238 BC), also known as Xun Zi, was a philosopher, thinker and educator in the Warring States Period.

Deliver a Great Future for China-ASEAN Relations*

November 22, 2021

Your Majesty Sultan Hassanal of Brunei Darussalam,
Colleagues,

It gives me great pleasure to meet you online to celebrate the 30th anniversary of China-ASEAN Dialogue Relations, review what we have accomplished together, summarize experience, and draw up a blueprint for the future.

China-ASEAN Dialogue Relations have come a long way over the past three decades. During these 30 years, we have witnessed the advance of economic globalization and profound changes in the international landscape. During these 30 years, China and ASEAN have seized opportunities and achieved leapfrog development in our relationship. We have cast aside the shadow of the Cold War and ensured stability in our region. We have spearheaded economic integration in East Asia, promoted common development and prosperity, and delivered a better life to a population of over 2 billion people. We have embarked on a path of good-neighborliness and win-win cooperation, taken strides towards a closer community of shared future, and made an important contribution to human progress.

Today, we jointly declare the establishment of a China-ASEAN comprehensive strategic partnership. This is a new milestone in our relations and will inject new impetus into our endeavors to promote peace, stability, prosperity and development both in our region and globally.

Colleagues,

We owe gains in China-ASEAN cooperation over the past 30

* Speech at the Special Summit to Commemorate the 30th Anniversary of China-ASEAN Dialogue Relations.

years to our unique geographical proximity and cultural affinity, to the fact that we have actively embraced the trend of our times and made the right historic choices.

First, we respect each other, and we have observed the basic norms governing international relations.

We people in the East believe in "not doing to others what we would not have done to ourselves"[1]. Equality and harmonious coexistence are values that we share. We were the first to put forward the Five Principles of Peaceful Coexistence and the Bandung Spirit[2]. China was the first among ASEAN's dialogue partners to join the Treaty of Amity and Cooperation in Southeast Asia. We accommodate each other's major concerns, and respect each other's choice of development paths. We have increased understanding and trust through sincere dialogue, and properly handled disagreement and problems by seeking common ground while shelving differences, thus upholding and promoting Asian values.

Second, we have promoted cooperation to deliver win-win outcomes as we pursue peaceful development.

China and ASEAN countries have similar historical experiences and share the same goals of securing stability for our countries and happiness for our peoples. We are firm in maintaining regional peace and stability. We have stayed focused on development, taken the lead in establishing free trade areas, promoted high-quality Belt and Road cooperation, and concluded and signed the Regional Comprehensive Economic Partnership (RCEP). We have thus promoted integrated development of the region and the wellbeing of our peoples.

Third, we have reached out to help each other in accordance with the principle of amity, sincerity, mutual benefit and inclusiveness.

China and ASEAN are neighbors, and mutual assistance is our shared tradition. China and Brunei both have proverbs that express the idea of sharing bliss and misfortune together. Our exchanges are as frequent as those between relatives. We value friendship and credibility. We rejoice together in good times, and help each other out in hard times. We have stood with each other through the Asian financial crisis, international financial crisis, Covid-19 and other challenges, thus forging a stronger sense of a community of shared future.

Fourth, we are committed to inclusiveness, mutual learning and open regionalism.

China and ASEAN have diverse ethnic groups, cultures and religions. Respect for diversity and mutual accommodation are in our blood. Drawing inspiration from the East Asian civilization, we have steered regional economic integration with an open mind, advanced ASEAN-led regional cooperation through consultation on an equal footing, and forged friendship that is open and non-exclusive in accordance with the principles of extensive consultation, joint contribution and shared benefits.

The valuable experience we have gained over the past 30 years is the shared asset of China and ASEAN. It has laid the foundations and provided the guidelines for forging our comprehensive strategic partnership. We should doubly cherish, retain, and continue to enrich and develop this experience as we go forward.

Colleagues,

As a Chinese proverb goes, "Just as distance tests a horse's strength, time reveals a person's sincerity." China has been and will remain a good neighbor, good friend and good partner of ASEAN. I wish to reaffirm that ASEAN will always be a high priority in China's neighborhood diplomacy. China will continue to support ASEAN unity, the ASEAN Community, and ASEAN centrality in the regional architecture, and it will continue to support ASEAN in playing a bigger role both in our region and internationally.

Not long ago, the Communist Party of China convened the Sixth Plenary Session of its 19th Central Committee, during which it conducted a comprehensive review of its major achievements and experience over the century. Full of confidence, we Chinese are marching forward on the new journey towards a modern socialist country in all respects. China's development will provide more opportunities for and a strong boost to both our region and the wider world. China is ready to work with ASEAN to navigate the global environment, remove interference, share opportunities, and promote common prosperity. We will strengthen our comprehensive strategic partnership and make new strides towards a closer China-ASEAN community of shared future.

Here, I call for five steps to deliver a great future for China-ASEAN relations:

First, we should build a peaceful home together.

Without peace, nothing is possible. Maintaining peace is our greatest common interest and the most cherished aspiration of people of all countries. We need to serve as the builders and guardians of peace in the region. We need to pursue dialogue instead of confrontation, build partnerships instead of alliances, and make a concerted effort to address the various negative factors that might threaten or undermine peace. We need to practice true multilateralism and act on the principle that international and regional affairs be handled through discussion among us all. China opposes hegemony and power politics. It pursues long-term and friendly coexistence with its neighbors and plays its part in the common efforts to secure lasting peace in our region. China will never seek hegemony, still less will it abuse smaller countries. It supports ASEAN in its efforts to build a nuclear weapon-free zone, and is prepared to sign the Protocol to the Treaty on the Southeast Asia Nuclear Weapon-Free Zone at an early date.

Second, we should build a safe and secure home together.

Once again, the Covid-19 pandemic has shown that no place on earth is an insulated island enjoying absolute security, and that only security for all can truly ensure security. China is ready to work with ASEAN countries to build a "health shield" for the region. Under this initiative, China will donate an additional 150 million doses of Covid vaccines to ASEAN countries to raise their vaccination rates. It will contribute an additional US$5 million to the Covid-19 ASEAN Response Fund, step up joint vaccine production and technology transfer, and collaborate with ASEAN on research and development of essential medicines, so as to help ASEAN increase its self-reliance. It will support ASEAN in strengthening community-level public health systems and training competent personnel to increase its capacity to respond to major public health emergencies.

In addition to Covid-19, our region faces various traditional and non-traditional security challenges. In addressing these challenges, it is important for us to pursue common, comprehensive, cooperative and sustainable security, and expand cooperation in areas such as defense, counter-terrorism, joint maritime search, rescue and exercise, countering transnational crime, and disaster management. We should jointly safeguard stability in the South China Sea and make it a sea of peace, friendship and cooperation.

Third, we should build a home of prosperity together.

I recently proposed the Global Development Initiative, which is a call for the international community to jointly meet challenges, promote global economic recovery, and accelerate implementation of the UN 2030 Agenda for Sustainable Development. This initiative is well-aligned with ASEAN Community Vision 2025, and it can contribute to the efforts of ASEAN countries to meet their development needs. China is ready to provide ASEAN with another US$1.5 billion of development assistance in the next three years to support their fight against Covid-19 and the region's economic recovery. China is also ready to engage in international development cooperation with ASEAN and launch negotiations on an agreement in this area. We support the establishment of a China-ASEAN Knowledge Network for Development. China will strengthen exchanges and cooperation with ASEAN on poverty reduction to promote balanced and inclusive development.

We need to fully leverage the role of the RCEP, begin work to upgrade the China-ASEAN Free Trade Area at an early date, and promote trade and investment liberalization and facilitation. We need to expand cooperation in new areas like the digital and green economy and build joint demonstration zones on innovative economic development. China has a vast domestic market, and this market will remain open to ASEAN countries. It is ready to import more quality products from ASEAN countries, including buying up to US$150 billion worth of agricultural products from ASEAN in the next five years. We will promote high-quality Belt and Road cooperation with ASEAN Outlook on the Indo-Pacific. China will continue to develop demonstration zones for high-quality Belt and Road international cooperation in industrial capacity and welcomes ASEAN countries' participation in building a new international land-sea trade corridor. China will launch the China-ASEAN Science, Technology and Innovation Enhancing Program, provide 1,000 items of advanced and applicable technology to ASEAN, and support 300 young scientists from ASEAN to come to China for exchanges in the next five years. We propose a China-ASEAN Digital Governance Dialogue to expand innovative application of digital technology.

Fourth, we should build a beautiful home together.

Humanity can only enjoy sustainable development if we work together in harmony with nature. China is ready to open a dialogue with ASEAN on climate response, increase policy communication and experience sharing, and synergize our plans for sustainable development.

We can work together on regional energy transition, discuss the establishment of a China-ASEAN clean energy cooperation center, and increase technology sharing in renewable energies. We need to intensify cooperation on green finance and investment to support regional low-carbon and sustainable development. China is ready to launch the Action Plan on China-ASEAN Green Agriculture to make our countries' agricultural sector more resilient and sustainable. We can also energize the China-ASEAN Countries Joint Research and Development Center of Marine Science and Technology, build up the Partnership on Blue Economy, and promote sustainable marine development.

Fifth, we should build a home of good will together.

We should advocate peace, development, equity, justice, democracy and freedom, which are the common values of humanity, increase exchanges and mutual learning between civilizations, and fully leverage our region's unique strength of cultural diversity. We should consider an orderly resumption of flows of people in the post-Covid-19 era and continue to promote exchanges in areas such as culture, tourism, think tanks, the media, and women's issues, to expand mutual understanding and friendship and form one big family between our peoples. Young people represent the future of both China and ASEAN. China will expand cooperation with ASEAN in vocational education and mutual recognition of diplomas, provide more China-ASEAN Young Leaders Scholarship opportunities, and organize events like youth camps. Next year, China will host both the Beijing 2022 Winter Olympics and Paralympics and the Hangzhou Asian Games, which will offer good opportunities for further sports exchanges and cooperation between China and ASEAN countries.

Colleagues,

As an ancient Chinese statesman observed, "Designs for justice prevail, and actions to benefit the people succeed."[3] Let us keep in mind our peoples' desire for a better life, and shoulder the mission of our times to safeguard peace and promote development. Let us join hands in building on what we have achieved, work towards a closer China-ASEAN community of shared future, and deliver greater prosperity to both our region and the wider world.

Notes

[1] *The Analects of Confucius* (*Lun Yu*). This is one of the Confucian classics compiled by the disciples of Confucius. It records the words and deeds of Confucius, and also comprises dialogues between Confucius and his disciples. Confucius (551-479 BC), also known as Kong Qiu or Zhongni, was a philosopher, educator, and statesman in the Spring and Autumn Period and the founder of Confucianism.

[2] Embodying unity, friendship and cooperation, this spirit was formed through the Bandung Conference in Indonesia in April 1955, attended by representatives from 29 Asian and African countries and regions. – Tr.

[3] *Annals of Master Yan* (*Yan Zi Chun Qiu*). This is a book that records the words and deeds of Yan Ying. Yan Ying (?-500 BC), also known as Yan Zi, was a statesman of the State of Qi during the Spring and Autumn Period.

Promote Friendly Cooperation Between China and Africa*

November 29, 2021

This year marks the 65th anniversary of the start of diplomatic relations between China and African countries. Over the past 65 years, China and Africa have forged unbreakable bonds in our struggle against imperialism and colonialism, and embarked on a distinctive path of cooperation in our journey towards development and revitalization. Together, we have written a splendid chapter of mutual assistance in a world of complexity and change, and set a shining example for building a new model of international relations.

Why do China and Africa have such a close relationship and such a deep bond of friendship? The key lies in an everlasting spirit of China-Africa friendship and cooperation forged between the two sides, characterized by sincere friendship and equality, mutual benefit and common development, fairness and justice, openness and inclusiveness, and progress with the times. This truly captures the story of China and Africa working together in good times and hardship over the past decades, and provides a source of strength for the continuous growth of friendly China-Africa relations.

This year marks the 50th anniversary of the restoration of China's lawful seat in the United Nations. Here, let me express sincere appreciation to the many African friends who supported China back then. Let me also make it clear that China will never forget the profound friendship of African countries and will remain guided by the principles of sincerity, amity, good faith, real results, and pursuing the

---

* Main part of the keynote speech at the opening ceremony of the Eighth Ministerial Conference of the Forum on China-Africa Cooperation.

greater good and shared interests. China will work together with African friends to carry forward the spirit of China-Africa friendship and cooperation from generation to generation.

At the 2018 Beijing Summit of the Forum on China-Africa Cooperation (FOCAC), I proposed that we build an even stronger China-Africa community of shared future. The proposal was unanimously endorsed by African leaders. Over the past three years and more, China and Africa have worked together to fully implement the eight major initiatives[1] and other outcomes of the Beijing Summit, and completed a large number of priority cooperation projects. China-Africa trade and China's investment in Africa have seen a steady rise. Almost all African members of FOCAC have joined the great family of Belt and Road cooperation. All of this has added strong momentum to the China-Africa comprehensive strategic and cooperative partnership.

A journey of a thousand miles begins with the first step. As we stand at the historic starting point of building a China-Africa community of shared future in the new era, I wish to make the following four proposals:

First, fighting Covid-19 with solidarity. We need to put people and lives first and be guided by science. We should be ready to waive intellectual property rights on Covid-19 vaccines, and ensure that vaccines are accessible and affordable in Africa to bridge the immunization gap.

Second, expanding practical cooperation. We need to open up new prospects for China-Africa cooperation, expand trade and investment, share experience on poverty reduction and elimination, strengthen cooperation on the digital economy, and promote entrepreneurship by young Africans and the development of small and medium-sized enterprises (SMEs). At the UN General Assembly this year, I proposed the Global Development Initiative, which shares similar goals with the African Union's Agenda 2063 and the UN's 2030 Agenda for Sustainable Development. We welcome the active support of African countries and their participation.

Third, promoting green development. In the face of climate change, a major challenge to all of humanity, we need to advocate green and low-carbon development, actively promote solar, wind and other sources of renewable energy, work for effective implementation of the Paris Agreement on climate change, and continue to strengthen our capacity for sustainable development.

Fourth, upholding equity and justice. The world needs true multilateralism. Peace, development, equity, justice, democracy and freedom are common values of humanity and represent the abiding aspirations of both China and Africa. We both advocate a development path suited to our national conditions and are both committed to safeguarding the rights and interests of developing countries. We both oppose intervention in domestic affairs, racial discrimination, and unilateral sanctions. We need to take an unequivocal stance on the just propositions of developing countries and translate our common aspirations and interests into joint action.

In the run-up to this Conference, our two sides have prepared the China-Africa Cooperation Vision 2035. Under the first three-year plan of the Vision, China will work closely with African countries to implement nine programs:

First, the medical and health program. To help the African Union (AU) achieve its goal of vaccinating 60 percent of the African population by 2022, I announce that China will provide another 1 billion doses of vaccine to Africa. Of these, 600 million doses will be donated, and 400 million doses will be jointly manufactured by Chinese and African enterprises. In addition, China will undertake 10 medical and health projects for African countries, and send 1,500 medical personnel and public health experts to Africa.

Second, the poverty reduction and agricultural development program. China will undertake 10 poverty reduction and agricultural projects, and send 500 agricultural experts to Africa. China will set up a number of China-Africa centers for modern agro-technology exchanges, demonstration and training in China, encourage Chinese institutions and companies to build demonstration villages for China-

Africa cooperation on agricultural development and poverty reduction in Africa, and support the Alliance of Chinese Business in Africa for Social Responsibilities in launching the initiative of "100 Companies in 1,000 Villages".

Third, the trade promotion program. China will open up fast-track channels for African agricultural exports to China, speed up the inspection and quarantine procedures, and further increase the scope of products enjoying zero-tariff treatment for the least developed countries (LDCs) who have diplomatic relations with China, in a bid to reach US$300 billion in total imports from Africa in the next three years. China will provide US$10 billion of trade finance to support African exports, and build in China a pioneering zone for in-depth China-Africa trade and economic cooperation and a China-Africa industrial park for Belt and Road cooperation. China will undertake 10 connectivity projects for Africa, form an expert group on economic cooperation with the secretariat of the African Continental Free Trade Area (AfCFTA), and give continued support to the development of the AfCFTA.

Fourth, the investment promotion program. China will encourage its businesses to invest no less than US$10 billion in Africa in the next three years, and will establish a platform for China-Africa private investment promotion. China will undertake 10 industrialization and employment promotion projects for Africa, provide credit facilities of US$10 billion to African financial institutions, support the development of African SMEs on a priority basis, and establish a China-Africa cross-border Renminbi service center. China will exempt African LDCs from debt incurred in the form of interest-free Chinese government loans due by the end of 2021. China is ready to channel to African countries US$10 billion from its share of the International Monetary Fund's new allocation of special drawing rights.

Fifth, the digital innovation program. China will undertake 10 digital economy projects for Africa, set up centers for China-Africa cooperation on satellite remote-sensing applications, and support the development of China-Africa joint laboratories, partner institutes, and scientific and technological innovation and cooperation bases. China will work with African countries to expand Silk Road e-commerce cooperation, hold online shopping festivals presenting quality African products and undertaking tourism e-commerce promotion activities, and launch a campaign to market 100 African stores and 1,000 African products on e-commerce platforms.

Sixth, the green development program. China will undertake 10 green development, environmental protection and climate action projects for Africa, support the development of the Great Green Wall, and build centers of excellence on low-carbon development and climate change adaptation in Africa.

Seventh, the capacity building program. China will help build or upgrade 10 schools in Africa, and invite 10,000 high-level African professionals to seminars and workshops. We will implement Future of Africa – a project for China-Africa cooperation on vocational education, and start an employment "through train" initiative for African students in China. China will continue to work with African countries to set up Lu Ban Workshops, and encourage Chinese companies in Africa to create at least 800,000 local jobs.

Eighth, the cultural and people-to-people exchange program. All African countries which have diplomatic ties with China are encouraged to become destinations for Chinese tourist groups. We will hold African film festivals in China and Chinese film festivals in Africa, as well as a China-Africa youth services forum, and a China-Africa women's forum.

Ninth, the peace and security program. China will undertake 10 peace and security projects for Africa. We will continue to deliver military assistance to the AU, support African countries' efforts to independently maintain regional security and fight terrorism, and conduct joint exercises and on-site training between Chinese and African peacekeeping troops and cooperation on small arms and light weapons control.

Senegal's first President Léopold Sédar Senghor once wrote, "Let us answer 'present' at the rebirth of the world."[2] I am convinced that the concerted efforts of China and Africa will make this FOCAC conference a full success, one that pools the might of the 2.7 billion Chinese and Africans and guides us towards a high-level China-Africa community of shared future.

Notes

[1] This refers to industrial development, infrastructure connectivity, trade facilitation, green development, capacity building, health care, cultural and people-to-people exchanges, and peace and security.

[2] Léopold Sédar Senghor: "Prayer to the Masks" (Prière aux masques).

Usher in a New Era for China-CELAC Relations[*]

December 3, 2021

During the seven years since 2014 when the Forum of China and the Community of Latin American and Caribbean States (CELAC) was established, our two sides have stayed true to its founding mission of strengthening solidarity, improving policy coordination, and advancing South-South cooperation. We have turned the forum into a mutually beneficial platform and brought China-CELAC relations into a new era of equality, mutual benefit, innovation, and openness – one that will deliver real benefits to our peoples.

The world now finds itself in a new period of turbulence. Both China and CELAC are faced with a common challenge – promoting post-pandemic recovery and working for a better life for the people. We welcome an active CELAC participation in the Global Development Initiative. I hope China and CELAC will work together to overcome difficulties, create opportunities, and build a global community of shared development.

History tells us that peaceful development, fairness and justice, and win-win cooperation are the right way forward for humanity. As developing countries, China and CELAC members are partners in all-round cooperation based on equality, mutual benefit, and shared development. Our shared dream of maintaining independence, pursuing development, and achieving revitalization has brought us together. Let us draw up a blueprint for growing China-CELAC relations, add momentum to our cooperation, and make a new contribution to the wellbeing of our peoples and the cause of human progress.

---

* Main points of the speech via video link at the Third Ministerial Meeting of the Forum of China and the Community of Latin American and Caribbean States.

Maintain World Peace and Stability[*]

April 21, 2022

"Stability brings a country prosperity while instability may well plunge it into poverty."[1] Security underpins development. Humanity is a community of indivisible security. A Cold War mindset can only disrupt the global peace framework, hegemonism and power politics can only endanger world peace, and confrontation between blocs can only exacerbate threats to security in the 21st century. All this has been proved time and again. To promote security for all the world, China proposes a Global Security Initiative:

We should stay committed to the vision of common, comprehensive, cooperative and sustainable security, and work together to maintain world peace and security.

We should respect the sovereignty and territorial integrity of all countries, oppose interference in internal affairs, and recognize the independent choice of development paths and social systems made by peoples of different countries.

We should abide by the purposes and principles of the UN Charter, reject the Cold War mentality, and oppose unilateralism, group politics and bloc rivalry.

We should address the legitimate security concerns of all countries, uphold the principle of indivisible security, build a balanced, effective and sustainable security architecture, and oppose any attempt by any country to ensure its own security at the expense of the security of others.

We should resolve differences and disputes between countries

* Part of the keynote speech at the opening ceremony of the Boao Forum for Asia Annual Conference 2022.

through dialogue, consultation and other peaceful means, support all efforts for peaceful settlement of crises, reject double standards, and oppose any abuse of unilateral sanctions and long-arm jurisdiction.

We should maintain security in both traditional and non-traditional domains, and jointly resolve regional disputes and global issues such as terrorism, climate change, cybersecurity and biosecurity.

Notes

[1] *Guan Zi.*

Global Governance and Multilateralism

Stay True to Multilateralism and Contribute to World Prosperity*

November 17, 2020

Across the world, Covid-19 is posing a grave threat to people's lives and health. The global public health system is facing a severe test. Human society is experiencing the most serious pandemic in the past century. International trade and investment have shrunk considerably. The flow of people and goods is impeded. Uncertainty and instability are mounting. The world economy has been hit by the worst recession since the Great Depression in the 1930s. Unilateralism, protectionism and abuse of the weak by the strong have intensified, and the deficit in governance, trust, development and peace is growing.

Despite all these challenges, we remain convinced that the under-lying trend of our times – peace and development – has not changed, and that the trend towards multi-polarity and economic globalization is irreversible. We must keep people's wellbeing close to our hearts and strive to build a global community of shared future. With concrete actions, we can make the world a better place for everyone.

First, we need to stay true to multilateralism, and safeguard global peace and stability.

History teaches us that multilateralism, equity and justice will keep war and conflict at bay, while unilateralism and power politics can only foment dispute and exacerbate confrontation. Flouting rules and laws, pursuing unilateralism, abusing the weak, and withdrawing from international organizations and agreements run counter to the will of the people of the world and trample on the legitimate rights and dignity of all countries.

---

* Part of the speech at the 12th BRICS Summit.

Facing the choice between multilateralism and unilateralism, and between justice and hegemony, we BRICS countries must stand up for equity and justice. We must uphold multilateralism and the purposes and principles of the Charter of the United Nations. We must endeavor to safeguard the UN-centered international system and the international order underpinned by international law. It is important that countries rise above ideology and respect each other's choice of social system, economic model, and development path that suit their national conditions. We should pursue common, comprehensive, cooperative and sustainable security. We should address differences through consultation and negotiation. We should oppose interference in others' internal affairs, unilateral sanctions, and overreach in cross-border jurisdiction. With concerted efforts, we can foster a peaceful and stable environment for development.

Second, we should reinforce solidarity and coordination and meet the Covid-19 challenge together.

Covid-19 is still wreaking havoc in many places, and waves of infection are resurging. Securing a global victory against the pandemic remains a daunting challenge. Close to one year into the battle, many countries have gained valuable experience in pandemic containment and made encouraging advances in drugs and vaccine research and development. Our fight over these past months demonstrates that as long as we stand in unity and follow the guidance of science, we can stem the spread of the virus and minimize its impact.

We should put people's lives and health first, pool all available resources, and do everything we can to protect people's safety and wellbeing. We should step up international coordination and response, and share information and epidemic control experience to stop the transmission of the virus. We should also support the WHO's crucial leadership role in this endeavor.

As I speak, Chinese companies are working with their Russian and Brazilian partners on phase-III clinical trials of vaccines, and we are prepared to cooperate with South Africa and India as well. China has joined the COVAX Facility, a platform on which we will share vaccines with other countries, developing countries in particular. We will actively consider providing vaccines to BRICS countries when the need arises. To support the development of the BRICS Vaccine R&D Center, China has set up its national center. We will work with other BRICS countries both online and offline to advance collective vaccine research and trials, build plants, authorize production, and recognize each other's standards. I propose that we convene a BRICS symposium on traditional medicine to explore its role in Covid-19 prevention and treatment. This will boost the global arsenal against Covid-19.

Recent events have shown that politicization, stigmatization, blame-shifting and scapegoating only serve to disrupt overall global cooperation in the fight against the virus. We need to eliminate division through unity, replace bias with reasoning, and stamp out the "politicization of the virus". By doing so, we will build a powerful global synergy to beat the virus.

Third, we need to remain open, encourage innovation, and promote global economic recovery.

The International Monetary Fund predicts that the world economy will shrink by 4.4 percent this year, and that emerging markets and developing countries will experience negative growth for the first time in 60 years. To stabilize the economy while responding to the pandemic is a pressing task facing all countries. While ensuring safety, we need to promote economic recovery and carry out economic and social activities in an orderly manner as we carry out virus control as part of our regular work. To resume business activities and pursue economic recovery in our countries, we need to strengthen macroeconomic policy coordination, facilitate cross-border flows of people and goods, and keep industrial and supply chains reliable and unimpeded.

Those who exploit the pandemic in pursuit of deglobalization or clamor for economic decoupling or parallel systems will only end up hurting their own interests and the common interests of all. Now, more than ever, we need to stand firm for building an open world economy. We need to uphold the multilateral trading system with the WTO at its core and reject protectionism under the pretext of so-called national security. We need to begin with new business forms and models triggered by the pandemic, strengthen cooperation in scientific and technological innovation, and nurture an open, fair, equitable and nondiscriminatory business environment. This will enable us to achieve common development of greater resilience and higher quality.

China will work with you to accelerate the establishment of the BRICS Partnership on New Industrial Revolution. We will open in Xiamen, Fujian Province, an innovation center of the partnership, to advance cooperation in policy coordination, personnel training, and project development, and our fellow BRICS countries are welcome to join us. Not long ago, China launched a Global Initiative on Data Security, which aims to foster a peaceful, secure, open, cooperative and orderly cyberspace to enable sound growth of the digital economy. We hope our fellow BRICS countries will support this initiative.

Fourth, we need to prioritize people's wellbeing in our efforts for sustainable global development.

Development holds the key to resolving all problems. All our efforts, whether eliminating the impact of Covid-19, getting back to a normal life, or ending conflicts and humanitarian crises, ultimately depend on people-centered development. According to a World Bank forecast, global per capita income will drop 3.6 percent this year, and 88 million to 115 million people will be pushed into extreme poverty by the pandemic.

Covid-19 is a challenge we must face head-on. We should call on the international community to implement the 2030 Agenda for Sustainable Development as a top priority in international cooperation. Poverty eradication must be our primary goal, and more resources must be channeled to poverty reduction, education, public health, and infrastructure. We need to support the UN in playing a coordinating role and foster an equality-based global partnership for more balanced development, so that the fruits will be shared by more developing countries and the needs of underprivileged groups will be better addressed.

Fifth, we need to pursue green and low-carbon development, and promote harmony between humanity and nature.

Global warming will not stop just because of Covid-19. To respond to climate change, we must never relax our efforts. We need to implement the Paris Agreement in good faith, stick to the principle of common but differentiated responsibilities, and provide more help to developing countries, particularly the small island developing states. China is ready to assume its international responsibilities as far as its current level of development permits, and will continue to make every effort to address climate change. I recently announced at the UN China's initiative to scale up our nationally determined contributions and adopt more forceful policies and measures to achieve peak carbon dioxide emissions before 2030 and carbon neutrality before 2060. China will keep its promise.

Light Up Our Way Forward with Multilateralism[*]

January 25, 2021

Professor Klaus Schwab,
Ladies and gentlemen,
Friends,

The past year was marked by the sudden attack of the Covid-19 pandemic. Global public health faced a severe threat, and the world economy was mired in deep recession. Humanity encountered multiple crises on a scale unseen in history.

The past year also witnessed the enormous resolve and courage of people around the world in battling the deadly coronavirus. Guided by science, reason, and a humanitarian spirit, the world has achieved initial progress in fighting Covid-19. That said, the pandemic is far from over. The recent resurgence in Covid cases reminds us that we must carry on the fight. Yet we remain convinced that winter cannot stop the arrival of spring, and darkness can never shroud the light of dawn. There is no doubt that humanity will prevail over the virus and emerge even stronger from this disaster.

Ladies and gentlemen,

Friends,

Time moves on, and the world will not go back to what it was. Every choice and move we make today will shape the world of the future. It is therefore important that we properly address the following four topics of our time.

The first is to step up macroeconomic policy coordination and jointly promote strong, sustainable, balanced and inclusive growth of the world economy.

---

* Special address at the World Economic Forum Virtual Event of the Davos Agenda.

We are going through the worst recession since the end of World War II. For the first time in history, the economies of all regions have been hit hard at the same time, with global industrial and supply chains disrupted and trade and investment stagnating.

Despite the trillions of dollars in relief packages worldwide, the global recovery is unstable, and the outlook remains uncertain. We need to focus on current priorities and balance Covid response and economic development. Macroeconomic policy support should be stepped up to bring the global economy back on track as early as possible. More importantly, we need to look beyond the horizon and strengthen our will and resolve for change. We need to shift the driving forces and growth models of the global economy and improve its structure, so as to set the course for long-term, sound and steady development.

The second is to abandon ideological prejudice and jointly follow a path of peaceful coexistence, mutual benefit, and win-win cooperation.

No two leaves in the world are identical; the same holds true for our histories, cultures and social systems. Each country is unique, with its own history, culture and social system, and none is superior to others. What is important is whether a country's social system fits its national conditions, enjoys public endorsement and support, serves to deliver political stability, social progress and better lives, and contributes to human progress.

The differences in our histories, cultures and systems are as old as human societies themselves; they are the intrinsic characteristics of human civilization, which would have long perished without diversity. Diversity is an objective reality and this will not change. Difference in itself is no cause for concern. What does sound the alarm is arrogance, prejudice and hatred; it is the attempt to impose a hierarchy on human civilization or force one's own historical experience, culture and social system upon others. All countries should pursue peaceful coexistence on the basis of mutual respect, seek common ground while shelving differences, and promote exchanges and mutual learning. This will give impetus to the development of human civilization.

The third is to close the divide between developed and developing countries and jointly bring about growth and prosperity for all.

Today, inequality continues to grow, the North-South gap remains unbridged, and sustainable development faces severe challenges. As countries grapple with the pandemic, their economic recovery is following divergent trajectories, and there is a risk that the North-South gap will widen further or even be perpetuated. Developing countries are aspiring to obtain more resources and space for development, and they are calling for stronger representation and a louder voice in global economic governance.

We should recognize that the growth of developing countries will put global prosperity and stability on a more solid footing, and developed countries will stand to benefit from such growth. The international community should keep its eye on the long term, honor its commitments, provide necessary support to developing countries, and safeguard their legitimate development interests. Equal rights, equal opportunities and equal rules should be strengthened, so that all countries will benefit from the opportunities and fruits of development.

The fourth is to come together against global challenges and jointly create a better future for humanity.

In this era of economic globalization, public health emergencies like Covid-19 may very well recur, and global public health governance needs to be reinforced. The earth is our one and only home. The future of humanity depends on our scaling up efforts to address climate change and promote sustainable development. No global problem can be solved by any one country alone. There must be global action, global response and global cooperation.

Ladies and gentlemen,

Friends,

The problems confronting the world are intricate and complex. Their solutions will come through upholding multilateralism and building a global community of shared future.

– We should stay committed to openness and inclusiveness and avoid closure and exclusion.

Multilateralism is about having international affairs addressed through consultation and the future of the world decided by everyone working together. To create exclusive circles or start a new Cold War, to reject, threaten or intimidate others, to grant oneself the right to engage in arbitrary decoupling, supply disruption or sanctions, and to create isolation or estrangement will only push the world into division and eventual confrontation. We cannot tackle common challenges in a divided world, and confrontation will lead us nowhere. Humanity has learned the lesson the hard way, and that history is not long gone. We must not return to the path of the past.

The right approach is to act on the vision of a global community of shared future. We should uphold the common values of humanity – peace, development, equity, justice, democracy and freedom, rise above ideological prejudice, make the mechanisms, principles and policies of our cooperation as open and inclusive as possible, and jointly safeguard world peace and stability.

We should build an open world economy, uphold the multilateral trading system, discard discriminatory and exclusionary standards, rules and systems, and break down barriers to trade, investment and exchanges of technology. We should strengthen the G20 as the premier forum for global economic governance, engage in closer macroeconomic policy coordination, and keep the global industrial and supply chains open and stable. We should ensure the sound operation of the global financial system, promote structural reform and expand global aggregate demand in an effort to strive for higher quality and stronger resilience in global economic development.

– We should stay committed to international law and international rules instead of seeking supremacy.

The ancient Chinese believed that "the law is the very foundation of governance"[1]. International governance should be based on rules agreed and consensus reached by all, not on the order imposed by one or the few. The Charter of the United Nations provides the basic and universally recognized norms governing state-to-state relations. Without international law and international rules that are formed and recognized by the global community, the world may return to the law of the jungle, and the consequence would be devastating for humanity.

We need to be resolute in championing the international rule of law, and steadfast in our resolve to safeguard the international system centered on the UN and the international order based on international law. Multilateral institutions provide the platforms for putting multilateralism into action, and they are the basic architecture underpinning multilateralism. Their authority and effectiveness should be respected and safeguarded. State-to-state relations should be coordinated and regulated through proper institutions and rules. The strong should not abuse the weak. Decisions should not be forced through by a display of strong muscles or by waving a big fist. Multilateralism should not be used as a pretext for acts of unilateralism. Principles should be observed and rules, once made, should be followed by all. "Selective multilateralism" should not be an option.

– We should stay committed to consultation and cooperation rather than conflict and confrontation.

Differences in history, culture and social system should not be an excuse for antagonism or confrontation, but rather an incentive for cooperation. We should respect and accommodate differences, avoid meddling in other countries' internal affairs, and resolve disagreements through consultation and dialogue. History and our experience have made it clear, time and again, that the misguided approach of antagonism and confrontation, be it in the form of cold war, hot war, trade war or tech war, will eventually hurt all countries' interests and undermine everyone's wellbeing.

We should reject the outdated Cold War and zero-sum game mentality, adhere to mutual respect and mutual accommodation, and reinforce political trust through strategic communication. It is important that we stick to the cooperation concept based on mutual benefit, say no to narrow-minded, selfish beggar-thy-neighbor policies, and stop the practice of keeping to oneself all advantages gained in development. Equal rights to development should be guaranteed for all countries to promote common development and prosperity. We should advocate fair competition, like competing with each other for excellence on a racing track, not attacking each other in a life-or-death fight.

– We should stay committed to keeping up with the times.

The world is undergoing change on a scale unseen in a century, and now is the time for major development and major transformation. To uphold multilateralism in the 21st century, we should promote its best traditions, take on new perspectives, and look to the future. We must stand by the core values and basic principles of multilateralism. We should also adapt to the changing international landscape, respond to global challenges as they arise, and reform and improve the system of global governance on the basis of extensive consultation and building consensus.

We must give full play to the role of the World Health Organization in building a global community of health for all. We should advance reform of the World Trade Organization and the international financial and monetary system in a way that boosts global economic growth and protects the development rights, interests and opportunities of developing countries. We should adopt a people-centered and facts-based approach when we make policies and develop international rules on global digital governance. We should deliver on the Paris Agreement on climate change and promote green development. We should continuously prioritize development, implement the 2030 Agenda for Sustainable Development, and see that all countries, especially developing ones, are able to enjoy the fruits of global development.

Ladies and gentlemen,

Friends,

After decades of strenuous effort by all its people, China is on course to finish building a moderately prosperous society in all respects. We have achieved historic gains in ending extreme poverty, and have embarked on a new journey towards building a modern socialist country. As China enters a new development stage, we will follow a new development philosophy and create a double development dynamic with the domestic economy as the mainstay and the domestic economy and international engagement providing mutual reinforcement. China will work with other countries to build an open, inclusive, clean and beautiful world that enjoys lasting peace, universal security, and common prosperity.

– China will continue to take an active part in international cooperation on Covid-19.

Containing the coronavirus is the most pressing task for the international community. This is because people and lives must always come before anything else. It is also what it takes to stabilize and revive the economy. Greater solidarity, closer cooperation, more information sharing, and a stronger global response are what we need to defeat Covid-19 across the world. It is especially important to scale up cooperation on the R&D, production and distribution of vaccines, and make them a public good that is easily accessible and affordable for people in all countries.

To date, China has provided assistance to over 150 countries and 13 international organizations, and sent 36 teams of health and medical experts to countries in need. China is strongly supportive of and actively engaged in international cooperation on Covid vaccines. China will continue to share its experience with other countries, do its best to assist countries and regions that are less prepared for the pandemic, and work to make Covid vaccines more accessible and affordable in developing countries. We hope these efforts will contribute to an early and complete victory over the coronavirus throughout the world.

– China will continue to implement a win-win strategy of opening up.

Economic globalization meets the requirements of growing social productivity and is a natural outcome of scientific and technological progress. It serves no one's interest to use the pandemic as a pretext to reverse globalization in favor of seclusion and decoupling.

As a longstanding supporter of economic globalization, China is committed to following through on its fundamental policy of opening up. China will continue to liberalize and facilitate trade and investment, help keep global industrial and supply chains smooth and stable, and advance high-quality Belt and Road cooperation. China will promote institutional opening up that covers rules, regulations, management and standards. We will foster a business environment that is based on market principles and governed by law, and meets international standards, and we will unleash the potential of the huge China market and enormous domestic demand. We hope these efforts will bring more cooperation opportunities to other countries and add further impetus to global economic recovery and growth.

– China will continue to promote sustainable development.

China will implement, in full, the 2030 Agenda for Sustainable Development. We will do more on the eco-environmental front by transforming and improving our industrial structure and energy mix at a faster pace and promoting green, low-carbon ways of life and work.

I have announced China's goals to achieve peak carbon dioxide emissions before 2030 and carbon neutrality before 2060. We must make a tremendous effort to meet these targets. We always believe that when the interests of the whole of humanity are at stake, China must step forward, take action, and get the job done. China is already drawing up action plans and taking specific measures to make sure we meet the set targets. We are doing this as a concrete action to uphold multilateralism and as a contribution to protecting our shared home and realizing sustainable development.

– China will continue to advance science, technology and innovation.

Science, technology and innovation are the key engines for human progress. They are a powerful weapon to overcome many global challenges, and they provide the only way for China to foster the new development dynamic and achieve high-quality development.

China will invest more in science and technology, develop an enabling system for innovation as a priority, turn breakthroughs in science and technology into productive forces at a faster pace, and strengthen protection of intellectual property rights, all with the goal of fostering innovation-driven, higher-quality growth.

Scientific and technological advances should benefit all of humanity rather than be used to curb and contain the development of other countries. China will be more open in its thinking and actions with regard to international exchanges and cooperation on science and technology. We will work with other countries to create an open, fair, equitable and nondiscriminatory environment for scientific and technological progress that is beneficial to all and shared by all.

– China will continue to promote a new model of international relations.

The Chinese people do not believe in the zero-sum game or winner-takes-all thinking. As a staunch follower of an independent foreign policy of peace, China is working hard to bridge differences through dialogue and resolve disputes through negotiation and to pursue friendly and cooperative relations with other countries on the basis of equality, mutual respect, and mutual benefit.

As a steadfast member of the developing world, China will further expand South-South cooperation, and contribute to the efforts of other developing countries to eradicate poverty, ease their debt burden, and achieve more growth. China will become more actively engaged in global economic governance and push for an economic globalization that is more open, inclusive, balanced and beneficial to all.

Ladies and gentlemen,

Friends,

There is only one earth and one shared future for humanity. As we deal with the current crises and endeavor to make a better day for everyone, we need to stand united and work together. History demonstrates time and again that to beggar thy neighbor, to go it alone, or to slip into arrogant isolation will always fail. Let us all join hands and let multilateralism light our way towards a global community of shared future.

Thank you.

Notes

[1] *Xun Zi.*

Increase Confidence and Overcome Difficulties to Build a Better World*

September 21, 2021

Mr President,

The year 2021 is a truly remarkable one for the Chinese people. It marks the centenary of the Communist Party of China. It is also the 50th anniversary of the restoration of the lawful seat of the People's Republic of China in the United Nations (UN), a historic event which will be solemnly commemorated by China. We will continue our active efforts to raise China's cooperation with the UN to a new level and make new and greater contributions to advancing the noble cause of the UN.

Mr President,

A year ago, global leaders attended the high-level meetings marking the 75th anniversary of the UN and issued a declaration pledging to fight Covid-19 in solidarity, tackle challenges together, uphold multilateralism, strengthen the role of the UN, and work for the common future of present and future generations.

One year on, our world is facing the impact of change on a scale unseen in a century, together with the Covid-19 pandemic. In all countries, people long for peace and development more than ever before, their call for equity and justice is growing stronger, and they are more determined to pursue win-win cooperation.

Right now, Covid-19 is still raging around the world, and profound changes are taking place in human society. The world has entered a

---

* Speech at the general debate of the 76th Session of the United Nations General Assembly.

new period of turbulence and transformation. It falls on each and every responsible political leader to answer the questions of our times and make a historic choice with confidence, courage, and a sense of mission.

First, we must beat Covid-19 and win this decisive fight that is crucial to the future of humanity. The history of world civilization is also one of fighting pandemics. Rising to the challenge, humanity has always triumphed and achieved greater development and progress. The current pandemic may appear overwhelming, but we will surely overcome it and prevail.

We should always put people and their lives first, and care about the life, value and dignity of every individual. We need a spirit, an attitude, and an approach of scientific inquiry to coordinate regular and targeted epidemic prevention and control with emergency response, and coordinate epidemic prevention and control with economic and social development. We need to reinforce the coordinated global Covid-19 response and minimize the risk of cross-border virus transmission.

Vaccination is our powerful weapon against Covid-19. I have emphasized on many occasions the need to make vaccines a global public good and ensure vaccine accessibility and affordability in developing countries. Of pressing urgency is to ensure a fair and equitable distribution of vaccines globally. China will do its best to provide a total of 2 billion doses of vaccine to the world by the end of this year. In addition to donating US$100 million to COVAX, China will donate 100 million doses of vaccine to other developing countries in the course of this year. China will continue to support and engage in global science-based tracing of Covid-19 origins and stand firmly opposed to political maneuvering in whatever form.

Second, we must revitalize the economy and pursue more robust, greener and more balanced global development. Development holds the key to human wellbeing. Facing the severe shock of Covid-19, we need to work together to steer global development towards a new stage of balanced, coordinated and inclusive growth. To this end, I would like to propose a Global Development Initiative:

– Committed to development as a priority. We need to put development high on the global macro policy agenda, strengthen policy coordination among major economies, and ensure policy continuity, consistency, and sustainability. We need to foster global development partnerships that are more equal and balanced, forge greater synergy among multilateral development cooperation processes, and speed up the implementation of the UN 2030 Agenda for Sustainable Development.

– Committed to a people-centered approach. We should safeguard and improve people's livelihoods and protect and promote human rights through development, and make sure that development is for the people and by the people, and that its fruits are shared among all the people. We should continue our work so that the people will have a greater sense of gain, fulfillment and security, and achieve well-rounded development.

– Committed to benefits for all. We should direct our attention to the special needs of developing countries. We may employ such means as debt suspension and development aid to help developing countries, particularly vulnerable countries facing exceptional difficulties, with the emphasis on addressing imbalanced and insufficient development between and within countries.

– Committed to innovation-driven development. We need to seize the historic opportunities created by the new revolution in science, technology and industry, redouble our efforts to harness technological achievements to boost productivity, and foster an open, fair, equitable and nondiscriminatory environment for the development of science and technology. We should foster new drivers of economic growth in the post-Covid era and jointly pursue leapfrog development.

– Committed to harmony between humanity and nature. We need to improve global environmental governance, actively respond to climate change, and create a community of life for humanity and nature. We need to accelerate the transition to a green and low-carbon economy and achieve green recovery and development. China will strive to achieve peak carbon dioxide emissions before 2030 and carbon neutrality before 2060. This requires tremendous hard work, and we will make every effort to meet these goals. China will step up support for other developing countries in developing green and low-carbon energy, and will not build new coal-fired power projects abroad.

– Committed to results-oriented actions. We need to increase input and financing in development, and prioritize cooperation in areas such as poverty reduction, food security, Covid-19 response and vaccines, climate change, green development, industrialization, the digital economy, and connectivity. We must also accelerate implementation of the UN 2030 Agenda for Sustainable Development, so as to build a global community of shared development. China has pledged an additional US$3 billion of international assistance in the next three years to support other developing countries in responding to Covid-19 and promoting economic and social recovery.

Third, we must strengthen solidarity and promote mutual respect and win-win cooperation in international relations. A world of peace and development should embrace civilizations of all forms, and must accommodate diverse paths to modernization. Democracy is not a special right reserved to individual countries, but a right for the people of all countries to enjoy. Recent developments in the world show once again that external military intervention and so-called democratic transformation lead to nothing but harm. We need to advocate peace, development, equity, justice, democracy, and freedom, which are the common values of humanity, and reject any leaning towards exclusive circles or zero-sum games.

Differences and problems among countries are hardly avoidable, and they need to be handled through dialogue and cooperation on the basis of equality and mutual respect. One country's success does not have to come at the expense of another's failure, and the world is big enough to accommodate common development and progress among all countries. We need to pursue dialogue and inclusiveness rather than confrontation and exclusion. We need to build a new model of international relations based on mutual respect, equity, justice and win-win cooperation, and do the best we can to expand the convergence of our interests and achieve the greatest synergy possible.

The Chinese people have always celebrated peace, amity and harmony and striven to pursue that vision. China has never invaded or abused others or sought hegemony, and will never do so. China has consistently been a builder of world peace, a contributor to global development, a defender of the international order, and a provider of public goods, and China will continue to bring the world new opportunities through its own development.

Fourth, we must improve global governance and practice true multilateralism. There is only one international system in the world – the international system with the UN at its core. There is only one international order – the international order underpinned by international law. And there is only one set of rules – the basic norms governing international relations underpinned by the purposes and principles of the UN Charter.

The UN should uphold true multilateralism and serve as the central platform for countries to safeguard universal security, share development achievements, and chart the future course of the world. The UN should remain committed to ensuring a stable international order, increasing the representation and say of developing countries in international affairs, and taking the lead in advancing democracy and the rule of law in international relations. The UN should seek balanced progress in the three key areas of security, development and human rights. It should set a common agenda, highlight pressing issues, and focus on real actions, and ensure that commitments made by all parties to multilateralism are truly delivered.

Mr President,

The world is once again at a historic crossroads. I am convinced that the trend of peace, development and progress for humanity is irresistible. Let us gird our loins, jointly address global threats and challenges, and work together to build a global community of shared future and a better world for all.

Speech at the Conference Marking the 50th Anniversary of the Restoration of the Lawful Seat of the People's Republic of China in the United Nations

October 25, 2021

Your Excellency Secretary-General António Guterres,
Your Excellencies Diplomatic Envoys and Representatives of
    International Organizations,
Ladies and gentlemen,
Friends,
Comrades,

Fifty years ago today at its 26th Session, the General Assembly of the United Nations adopted Resolution 2758 by an overwhelming majority, and the decision was made to restore all the rights of the People's Republic of China in the United Nations and to recognize the representatives of the Government of the People's Republic of China as the only legitimate representatives of China to the United Nations. It was a victory for the Chinese people and a victory for all the people of the world.

Today, on this special date, we are gathered here to review the past and look to the future, and that makes our gathering all the more significant.

The restoration of the lawful seat of the PRC in the UN was a momentous event for the world and the UN. It came as the result of a combined effort by all the peace-loving countries that stood up for justice in the world. It marked the return of the people of China, or one-fourth of the world's population, back to the UN. The event was significant and far-reaching for both China and the wider world.

On this occasion, I wish to express, on behalf of the Chinese government and the Chinese people, our heartfelt gratitude to all the countries that co-sponsored and supported UN General Assembly Resolution 2758, and to pay tribute to all the countries and people who stand on the side of justice.

Ladies and gentlemen,

Friends,

Comrades,

The past five decades since the restoration of the PRC's lawful seat in the United Nations have witnessed China's peaceful development and its commitment and dedication to the wellbeing of all humanity.

– For these 50 years, the Chinese people have demonstrated an untiring spirit and kept to the right direction amid changing circumstances, writing an epic chapter in the story of China and humanity.

Building on achievements in national construction and development after the founding of the People's Republic, the Chinese people started a new period of reform and opening up, succeeded in founding and developing socialism with Chinese characteristics, and focused on unleashing and developing the productive forces and raising their living standards. China has achieved the historic transformation from a country with relatively backward productive forces to the world's second largest economy. Through hard work, the Chinese people have completed the goal of building a moderately prosperous society in all respects on the vast land of China, and won the battle against poverty, thus securing a historic success in eradicating absolute poverty in China. We have now embarked on a new journey towards a modern socialist country that presents brighter prospects for the rejuvenation of the Chinese nation.

– For these 50 years, the Chinese people have stood in solidarity and cooperation with other peoples around the world and upheld international equity and justice, contributing significantly to world peace and development.

The Chinese people love peace and know well the value of peace and stability. We have followed and never deviated from an independent foreign policy of peace. We have stood firm for fairness and justice, and resolutely opposed hegemony and power politics. The Chinese people are strong supporters of other developing countries in their just struggle to safeguard their sovereignty, security and development interests.

The Chinese people are committed to promoting common development. From the Tazara Railway to the Belt and Road Initiative, we have done what we could to help other developing countries, and have offered the world new opportunities through our own development.

During the challenging times of the Covid-19 pandemic, China has shared its Covid response experience with the rest of the world without reservation, sent large quantities of supplies, vaccines and medicines to other countries, and engaged deeply in science-based cooperation on tracing Covid-19 origins, all in a sincere and proactive effort to contribute to humanity's final victory over the pandemic.

– For these 50 years, the Chinese people have upheld the authority and sanctity of the UN and practiced multilateralism, and China's cooperation with the UN has steadily expanded.

China has faithfully fulfilled its missions and responsibilities as a permanent member of the UN Security Council, stayed true to the purposes and principles of the UN Charter, and upheld the central role of the UN in international affairs.

China has all along advocated peaceful and diplomatic settlement of disputes. It has sent over 50,000 peacekeepers to UN peacekeeping operations, and is now the second largest financial contributor to both the UN and its peacekeeping operations.

China is among the first countries to have met the UN Millennium Development Goals. It has taken the lead in implementing the 2030 Agenda for Sustainable Development, and contributed to over 70 percent of global poverty reduction.

China has stood by the spirit of the UN Charter and the Universal Declaration of Human Rights, and earnestly applied the universality of human rights in the Chinese context. It has blazed a path of protection and promotion of human rights that is consistent with the trend of the times and bears distinct Chinese features, thus making a major contribution to the progress of human rights in China and to the international cause of human rights.

Ladies and gentlemen,

Friends,

Comrades,

The tide of the times is mighty; those who follow it will prosper while those who resist it will perish. Over the past 50 years, in spite of times of trouble and turmoil, the world has remained stable as a whole, thanks to the concerted efforts of the peoples of all countries. The global economy has grown rapidly, and innovations in science and technology have continued to open new ground. A large number of developing countries have grown stronger, over a billion people have emerged from poverty, and several billion are moving towards modernization.

In the world today, change on a scale unseen in a century is accelerating, and the forces for peace, development and progress have continued to grow. It falls upon us to follow the prevailing trend of history, and choose cooperation over confrontation, openness over isolation, and mutual benefit over zero-sum games. We must be firm in opposing all forms of hegemony and power politics, as well as all forms of unilateralism and protectionism.

– We should vigorously advocate peace, development, equity, justice, democracy and freedom, which are common values of humanity, and work together to provide the right philosophy for building a better world.

Peace and development are our common cause, equity and justice our common aspiration, and democracy and freedom our common goal. Our world is characterized above all by diversity. It is diversity that makes human civilization what it is. It provides us a constant source of vitality and a driving force for world development.

As Liu Kai of the Qing Dynasty said, "Only by learning from

hundred schools of thoughts and drawing on their strength can one develop and establish one's own distinct style."[1] No civilization in the world is superior to others; every civilization is special and unique to its own region. Civilizations can achieve harmony only through communication, and can make progress only through harmonization. The success of a country's path of development is judged first and foremost by whether it fits the country's conditions, whether it follows the trends of the times, whether it brings economic growth, social progress, stability, and better lives, whether it has the people's endorsement and support, and whether it contributes to human progress.

– We should join together to build a global community of shared future, and work together to build an open, inclusive, clean and beautiful world that enjoys lasting peace, universal security, and common prosperity.

The human race is an integral community, and the earth is our common homeland. No individual or country can thrive in isolation. Humanity should stand together in solidarity and pursue common development in harmony. We should keep moving towards a global community of shared future, and jointly create a better tomorrow. Building a global community of shared future does not mean replacing one system or civilization with another. Rather, it is about countries with different social systems, ideologies, histories, cultures, and levels of development coming together to further shared interests, shared rights, and shared responsibilities in global affairs, and creating the greatest synergy for building a better world.

– We should remain committed to mutual benefit and win-win results, and work together to promote economic and social development for the greater benefit of our people.

As an ancient Chinese once observed, "The essence of governance is livelihood, and the essence of livelihood is sufficiency."[2] Development and happy lives are the common aspirations of people in all countries. Development is meaningful only when it advances the people's interests, and can be sustained only when it is driven by the people. Countries should put their people first, and strive to realize development of greater quality, efficiency, equity, sustainability and security. It is important to resolve the problem of imbalanced and insufficient development, and make development more coordinated and inclusive. It is also important to strengthen the people's capacity for development, foster an environment where everyone takes part and has a share, and create a dynamic where the outcome of development benefits every person in every country in a fair way.

Not long ago, at the 76th Session of the UN General Assembly, I proposed a Global Development Initiative, in the hope that countries will work together to overcome the impact of Covid-19, accelerate implementation of the 2030 Agenda for Sustainable Development, and build a global community of shared development.

– We should step up cooperation, and work together to address the global challenges and issues facing humanity.

The international community is confronted by regional disputes as well as global issues such as terrorism, climate change, cybersecurity, and biosecurity. Only with more inclusive global governance, more effective multilateral mechanisms, and more active regional cooperation can these issues be addressed effectively.

Climate change is nature's warning to humanity. Countries need to take concrete actions to protect Mother Nature. We need to encourage green recovery, green production, and green consumption, promote healthy and positive lifestyles, foster harmony between humanity and nature, protect the eco-environment, and make it an inexhaustible source of sustainable development.

– We should resolutely uphold the authority and sanctity of the UN, and work together to practice true multilateralism. Building a global community of shared future requires a strong UN, and calls for reform and improvement of the global governance system. Countries should uphold the international system with the UN at its core, the international order underpinned by international law, and the basic norms of international relations based on the purposes and principles of the UN Charter.

International rules can only be made by the 193 UN member states together, and not decided by any individual country or by power blocs. International rules should be observed by the 193 UN member states, and there is no exception and should be no exception. Countries should respect the UN, take good care of the UN family, refrain from exploiting the organization – still less abandon it for self-serving reasons – and make sure that the UN plays an ever more positive role in advancing humanity's noble cause of peace and development. China is ready to work with all countries under the principles of extensive consultation, joint contribution, and shared benefits, to explore new ideas and new models of cooperation, and to continue enriching the practice of multilateralism under new circumstances.

Ladies and gentlemen,

Friends,

Comrades,

A review of the past can light the way forward. Standing at a new historical starting point, China will stay committed to the path of peaceful development and always be a builder of world peace. China will stay committed to the path of reform and opening up and always be a contributor to global development. China will stay committed to the path of multilateralism and always be a defender of the international order.

As a Chinese poem reads, "Green hills bathe in the same cloud and rain. The same moon lights up towns however far away."[3] Let us join hands, stand on the right side of history and the side of human progress, and work tirelessly for the lasting and peaceful development of the world and for a global community of shared future.

Thank you.

Notes

[1] Liu Kai: "A Discussion on Literature with Sir Ruan Yuntai, the Deputy Security Advisor to the Crown Prince" (Yu Ruan Yun Tai Gong Bao Lun Wen Shu). Liu Kai (1784-1824) was an essayist of the Qing Dynasty.

[2] *Huai Nan Zi.*

[3] Wang Changling: "Seeing Off Imperial Censor Chai" (Song Chai Shi Yu). Wang Changling (?-756) was a renowned poet of the Tang Dynasty.

Uphold Openness, Inclusiveness, Win-Win Cooperation and Multilateralism*

October 30, 2021

Faced with changes and a pandemic, both on a scale unseen in a century, the G20, the premier forum for international economic cooperation, must shoulder its responsibilities, consider the future of humanity and the wellbeing of the people, uphold openness, inclusiveness and win-win cooperation, practice true multilateralism, and promote the building of a global community of shared future. I would like to suggest that we work in the following five specific areas.

First, work in solidarity to combat Covid-19.

With the coronavirus ravaging the whole world, none of us can stay safe on our own. Solidarity and cooperation are the most powerful weapons. The international community must work in concert to confront and defeat the pandemic with a science-based approach. Stigmatization around the issue of the virus and politicization of origin tracing both run counter to the spirit of solidarity against the pandemic. We need to step up cooperation on prevention, control, diagnosis and treatment, and be more ready for major public health emergencies. The G20 includes the world's major economies and should therefore play a leading role in building consensus, mobilizing resources, and promoting cooperation.

At the early stage of the pandemic, I called for Covid-19 vaccines to be made a global public good. To this end, I would like to propose here a Global Vaccine Cooperation Action Initiative:

One, we need to strengthen vaccine R&D cooperation and

* Part of the speech at Session I of the 16th G20 Leaders' Summit.

support vaccine companies in conducting joint R&D and production with developing countries.

Two, we need to uphold equity and justice, and provide more vaccines to developing countries to meet the global vaccination target for 2022 as set by the World Health Organization (WHO).

Three, we need to support the World Trade Organization (WTO) in making an early decision on waiving intellectual property rights on Covid-19 vaccines, and encourage vaccine companies to transfer technology to developing countries.

Four, we need to scale up cross-border trade cooperation to ensure smooth passage of vaccines and related raw and auxiliary materials.

Five, we need to treat different vaccines equally and advance mutual recognition of vaccines in accordance with the WHO's Emergency Use Listing.

Six, we need to provide financial support for global vaccine cooperation, especially for developing countries to access vaccines.

To date, China has provided over 1.6 billion doses of vaccine to more than 100 countries and international organizations, and will provide over 2 billion doses to the world in the course of this year. China is conducting joint vaccine production with 16 countries, with an initial capacity of 700 million doses per year. The International Forum on Covid-19 Vaccine Cooperation that I proposed in May at the Global Health Summit was held successfully in August. The participating countries reached intended agreements amounting to more than 1.5 billion doses for this year. China, together with 30 other countries, has also launched an Initiative for Belt and Road Partnership on Covid-19 Vaccine Cooperation, calling on the international community to promote fair distribution of vaccines around the world. China is ready to work with all parties to increase vaccine accessibility and affordability in developing countries and make a positive contribution to building a global line of defense through vaccination.

Second, strengthen coordination to promote recovery.

Covid-19 has had a complex and far-reaching impact on the global economy. It is imperative that we apply the right prescriptions to address both symptoms and root causes of the problems we face. We should step up macroeconomic policy coordination and ensure the continuity, consistency and sustainability of our policies. Major economies should adopt responsible macroeconomic policies, prevent their domestic measures from causing a rise in inflation, exchange rate fluctuations, or mounting debt, avoid negative fallout on developing countries, and ensure the sound functioning of the international economic and financial system.

At the same time, we should take a long-term perspective, improve the global economic governance system and rules, and make up for the relevant governance deficit. We should continue to push for the scheduled conclusion of the 16th General Review of Quotas of the International Monetary Fund (IMF) to buttress the global financial safety net. China supports the early launch of negotiations on the 20th replenishment process of the International Development Association, and maintains that the relevant Voting Rights Review should faithfully reflect the changes in the international economic landscape and amplify the voice of developing countries. China welcomes the IMF's decision on the new allocation of Special Drawing Rights totaling US$650 billion, and stands ready to lend the new allocation to low-income countries that are seriously affected by Covid-19.

We should safeguard the multilateral trading system with the WTO at its core and build an open world economy. The G20 should continue to provide political guidance on the reform of the WTO, uphold its core values and basic principles, and protect developing countries' rights, interests and development space. It is imperative to restore, as quickly as possible, the normal operation of the dispute settlement mechanism, and work for positive results at the 12th WTO Ministerial Conference. We should keep industrial and supply chains secure and stable, and ensure the smooth functioning of the global economy. China proposes to hold an international forum on resilient and stable industrial and supply chains, and welcomes the active participation of

G20 members and relevant international organizations.

Infrastructure development plays an important role in propelling economic growth. China has made unremitting efforts in this regard through Belt and Road cooperation and other initiatives. China is prepared to work with all sides to uphold the principles of extensive consultation, joint contribution, and shared benefits. China will stay committed to the vision of open, green and clean cooperation, and pursue the goal of high-standard and sustainable development for the benefits of the people, so as to deliver more fruitful outcomes from high-quality Belt and Road cooperation.

Third, embrace inclusiveness to achieve common development.

The pandemic has created multiple crises around the world, and hit developing countries particularly hard. The number of people living in hunger has reached around 800 million. Implementation of the 2030 Agenda for Sustainable Development is facing unprecedented challenges. In this context, we must take a people-centered approach and make global development more equitable, effective and inclusive, so that no country will be left behind.

The G20 should prioritize development in macro policy coordination, ensure sound implementation of the Action Plan on the 2030 Agenda for Sustainable Development, move forward with the Initiative on Supporting Industrialization in Africa and Least Developed Countries, and promote synergy among the existing mechanisms for development cooperation. Advanced economies should fulfill their pledges on official development assistance and provide more resources for developing countries.

Not long ago, I proposed a Global Development Initiative at the United Nations and called on the international community to strengthen cooperation in poverty alleviation, food security, Covid-19 response and vaccines, development financing, climate change and green development, industrialization, the digital economy and connectivity, so as to accelerate the implementation of the 2030 Agenda for Sustainable Development and achieve more robust, greener and more balanced global development. This initiative is closely compatible with the G20's priority goal of promoting global development. We welcome the active participation of more countries in the initiative.

Fourth, pursue innovation to tap growth potential.

Innovation is a decisive factor in economic and social development and in addressing common challenges to humanity. The G20 should join forces to unleash the potential for innovation-driven growth and draw up rules based on extensive participation and broad-based consensus to foster an enabling environment for innovation-driven development. Forming exclusive blocs and drawing ideological boundaries will only cause division and create more obstacles, which will do only harm to scientific and technological innovation.

The digital economy is an important frontier of scientific and technological innovation. The G20 should shoulder its responsibilities in the digital era, accelerate the development of new types of digital infrastructure, promote deeper integration of digital technologies with the real economy, and help developing countries eliminate the digital divide. China has proposed the Global Initiative on Data Security. We may discuss and develop international rules for digital governance that reflect the will and respect the interests of all sides, and actively foster an open, fair, just and nondiscriminatory environment for digital development. China attaches great importance to international cooperation on the digital economy, and has decided to apply to join the Digital Economy Partnership Agreement. China stands ready to work with all parties for the healthy and orderly development of the digital economy.

Fifth, promote harmonious coexistence to achieve green and sustainable development.

The G20 must uphold the principle of common but differentiated responsibilities. It must push for the full implementation of the Paris Agreement on climate change, and support a successful COP26 of the United Nations Framework Convention on Climate Change and a fruitful COP15 of the Convention on Biological Diversity. Developed countries must lead by example on emissions reduction, fully accommodate the special difficulties and concerns of developing countries, deliver on their commitments in climate financing, and provide technology, capacity-building, and other support for developing countries. This is critical to the success of the upcoming COP26.

China has all along undertaken the international responsibilities commensurate with its national conditions. We have actively advanced the green transition of our economy and raised the targets of our climate actions on our own initiative. In the past 10 years, China has phased out 120 million kilowatts of installed coal-fired power generation capacity. The construction of a first batch of wind and photovoltaic power stations, with a total installed capacity of about 100 million kilowatts, has proceeded according to schedule. China will strive to achieve peak carbon dioxide emissions before 2030 and carbon neutrality before 2060. We will honor our words with actions and work with all countries to pursue a path of green, low-carbon and sustainable development.

Create a Better Post-Covid World*

January 17, 2022

The world today is undergoing change on a scale unseen in a century. This process, not limited to a particular moment, event, country or region, highlights the profound and sweeping changes of our times. As they combine with a once-in-a-century pandemic, the world finds itself in a new period of turbulence and transformation. How do we beat the pandemic and build the post-Covid world? These are major issues of common concern to people throughout the world. They are also urgent questions to which we must provide answers.

As a Song-dynasty philosopher observed, "The momentum of the world either flourishes or declines; the governance of the world either progresses or regresses."[1] The world is always developing through the interplay of opposites; without this interplay, nothing would exist. The history of humanity is one of achieving growth by meeting various tests and of developing by resolving various crises. We need to move forward by following the logic of history, and develop by keeping pace with the trend of our times.

Whatever the trials and tribulations, humanity will move on. We need to learn by comparing and analyzing long cycles of history, and see the change in things through the subtle and the minute. We need to foster new opportunities amid crises, open up new horizons on a shifting landscape, and pool great strengths to overcome difficulties and challenges.

First, we need to embrace cooperation and jointly defeat the pandemic.

Confronted by this unprecedented pandemic, which is going to

* Part of the speech at a virtual session of the 2022 World Economic Forum.

significantly affect the future of humanity, the international community has fought a tenacious battle. Reality has once again proved that amid the raging torrents of a global crisis, countries are not riding separately in some 190 small boats, but are rather all in a giant ship, on which our shared destiny depends. Small boats cannot survive a storm, but a giant ship is strong enough to withstand it. Thanks to the concerted efforts of the international community, marked progress has been made in the global battle against the pandemic. This said, the pandemic is proving a stubborn opponent, resurging with more variants and spreading faster than before. It poses a serious threat to public safety and health, and is exerting a profound impact on the global economy.

Strong confidence and cooperation represent the only way to defeat the pandemic. Hindering each other's efforts or casting around for targets to blame only causes needless delay in our response and distract us from the overall objective. Countries need to strengthen international cooperation against Covid-19, carry out joint research and development of medicines, build multiple lines of defense against the coronavirus, and speed up efforts to build a global community of health for all. Of particular importance is to fully leverage vaccines as a powerful weapon, ensure their equitable distribution, accelerate the vaccination process, and close the global immunization gap, so as to truly safeguard people's lives, health and livelihoods.

China is a country that delivers on its promises. China has already sent over 2 billion doses of vaccine to more than 120 countries and international organizations. And China will provide a further 1 billion doses to African countries – including 600 million donated doses – and will also donate 150 million doses to ASEAN countries.

Second, we need to address a number of risks and promote a steady recovery of the global economy.

The global economy is emerging from the trough, yet it is still subject to many constraints. Global industrial and supply chains have been disrupted. Commodity prices continue to rise. Energy supply remains tight. These and other stresses compound one another and heighten uncertainty about economic recovery. The low inflation environment has changed considerably, and the risk of rising inflation driven by multiple factors is surfacing. If major economies slam on the brakes or take a sudden turn in their monetary policies, there will be serious negative spillovers. They will present a threat to global economic and financial stability, and developing countries will bear the brunt. In responding to the ongoing Covid-19 crisis we need to explore new drivers of economic growth, new social models, and new pathways for people-to-people exchange, in a bid to facilitate cross-border trade, keep industrial and supply chains secure and smooth, and promote steady and solid progress in global economic recovery.

Economic globalization is the trend of the times. Though countercurrents are sure to exist in a river, none can stop it from flowing to the sea. The weight of the water boosts the river's momentum, and eddies of resistance may yet strengthen its overall flow. Despite the countercurrents and dangerous shoals along the way, economic globalization has never veered off course and never will.

All countries should uphold true multilateralism. We should remove barriers, not erect walls. We should open up, not close down. We should seek integration, not decoupling. This is the way to build an open world economy. We should guide reform of the global governance system in accordance with the principles of fairness and justice, and uphold the multilateral trading system with the World Trade Organization at its center. We should establish generally accepted and effective rules for artificial intelligence and the digital economy on the basis of full consultation, and create an open, just and nondiscriminatory environment for scientific and technological innovation. This is the way to make economic globalization more open, inclusive, balanced and beneficial to all, and to fully unleash the vitality of the global economy.

There is a common understanding that to steer the world economy from crisis to recovery, it is imperative to strengthen macro policy coordination. Major economies should see the world as a single community, apply systems thinking, increase policy transparency and information sharing, and coordinate the objectives, intensity and pace of fiscal and monetary policies, so as to prevent the world economy from faltering again. Major developed countries should adopt responsible economic policies, manage policy spillovers, and avoid severe impacts on developing countries. International economic and financial institutions should play a constructive role to build global consensus, enhance policy synergy, and prevent systemic risks.

Third, we need to bridge the development divide and revitalize global development.

The process of global development is suffering from severe disruption, exacerbating prominent problems such as a widening North-South gap, diverging recovery trajectories, development fault lines, and a technological divide. The Human Development Index has declined for the first time in 30 years. The world's poor population has increased by more than 100 million. Nearly 800 million people live in hunger. Difficulties are mounting in food security, education, employment, medicine, health and other areas critical to people's wellbeing. Some developing countries have fallen back into poverty and instability due to the pandemic. Many in developed countries are also experiencing difficulties.

Whatever difficulties may come our way, we must adhere to a people-centered philosophy of development, place development and people's wellbeing front and center in global macro policies, realize the UN 2030 Agenda for Sustainable Development, and build greater synergy among existing mechanisms of development cooperation to promote balanced development worldwide.

We should uphold the principle of common but differentiated responsibilities, promote international cooperation on climate change in the context of development, and follow up on the outcomes of COP26 of the United Nations Framework Convention on Climate Change. Developed economies should take the lead in honoring their emissions reduction responsibilities, deliver on their commitments to financial and technological support, and create the necessary conditions for developing countries to address climate change and achieve sustainable development.

Last year, I proposed a Global Development Initiative at the UN General Assembly to draw international attention to the pressing challenges faced by developing countries. The initiative is a public good, open to the whole world, designed to form synergy with the 2030 Agenda for Sustainable Development and boost common development across the world. China stands ready to work with all partners to translate the initiative into concrete actions and make sure that no country is left behind in this process.

Fourth, we need to discard the Cold War mentality and seek peaceful coexistence and win-win outcomes.

Our world today is far from tranquil; rhetoric that stokes hatred and prejudice is widespread. The resultant acts of containment, suppression or confrontation do harm to all; they do not in any way advance world peace and security. History has proved time and again that confrontation does not solve problems; it only invites catastrophic consequences. Protectionism and unilateralism can protect no one; they ultimately hurt one's own interests as well as damaging the interests of others. Even worse are the practice of hegemony and the strong abusing the weak, which run counter to the tide of history.

It is inevitable that countries will experience differences of opinion and disagreements, but a zero-sum approach that seeks to enlarge one's own gain at the expense of others will not help. Stubbornly creating "walled-in courtyards" or parallel systems, zealously putting together exclusive circles or blocs that polarize the world, overstretching the concept of national security to hold back economic and technological progress in other countries, fanning ideological antagonism, and politicizing or weaponizing economic, scientific and technological issues – all of these will gravely undermine international efforts to tackle common challenges.

The right way forward for humanity is peaceful development and win-win cooperation. Different countries and civilizations can prosper together on the basis of mutual respect, and seek common ground and win-win outcomes by setting aside differences.

We should follow the trend of history, work for a stable international order, champion the common values of humanity, and build a global community of shared future. We should choose dialogue over confrontation and inclusiveness over exclusion, and we should take a stand against all forms of unilateralism, protectionism, hegemonism and power politics.

Notes

[1] Lü Zuqian: *Essays on Zuo's Commentary on the Spring and Autumn Annals* (*Dong Lai Bo Yi*). Lü Zuqian (1137-1181) was a writer and neo-Confucian philosopher of the Southern Song Dynasty.

High-Quality
Belt and Road Cooperation

A Path of Cooperation, Health, Recovery and Growth*

June 18, 2020

The sudden onslaught of Covid-19 represents a grave threat to the health and lives of people around the world. It has taken a heavy toll on the global economy, posing a tough economic and social challenge to many countries – developing countries in particular.

To contain the epidemic, countries affected have taken robust and effective measures based on their national conditions, and achieved encouraging results. While addressing the Covid-19 outbreak, many countries are also striving to revive the economy and get social development back on track.

China always puts the people and their lives front and center and will do what it can to bring about an early global victory against Covid-19 and an early economic recovery worldwide.

The epidemic is a stark reminder that the destinies of all nations are closely connected, and we humans rise and fall together. Be it in taming the virus or achieving economic recovery, we cannot succeed without solidarity, cooperation and multilateralism.

Greater connectivity, openness and inclusiveness are essential if we are to overcome global crises of this kind and achieve long-term development.

This is where Belt and Road international cooperation can make a difference.

China is committed to peaceful development and mutually beneficial cooperation. We stand ready to work with all partners to build

---

* Main points of the written message to the High-level Video Conference on Belt and Road International Cooperation.

the Belt and Road and make it a path of cooperation in addressing common challenges, a path of health for protecting people's health and safety, a path of economic recovery and social development, and a path of growth to achieve our full development potential.

Let us join hands to strengthen high-quality Belt and Road cooperation and build a global community of shared future.

Build a Closer Belt and Road Partnership[*]

April 20, 2021

I have emphasized on various occasions that the Belt and Road Initiative (BRI) is a public road open to all, not a private path owned by one single party. All interested countries are welcome to take part in cooperation and share in its benefits. Belt and Road cooperation targets development and mutual benefits, and conveys a message of hope.

Going forward, we will continue to work with other parties on high-quality Belt and Road cooperation. We will follow the principles of extensive consultation, joint contribution, and shared benefits, and champion the philosophy of open, green and clean cooperation. We will ensure that Belt and Road cooperation is people-centered and sustainable, and meets high standards.

– We will build a closer partnership in health. Chinese businesses have already started joint vaccine production in BRI countries such as Indonesia, Brazil, the United Arab Emirates, Malaysia, Pakistan and Turkey. We will expand cooperation with various parties in areas such as infectious disease control, public health, and traditional medicine, to protect the lives and health of people in all countries.

– We will build a closer partnership in connectivity. China will work actively with all partners to promote "hard connectivity" in infrastructure and "soft connectivity" through harmonized rules and standards, to ensure unimpeded channels for cooperation in trade and investment, and to develop Silk Road e-commerce. All of this is designed to ensure bright prospects for integrated development.

* Part of the keynote speech at the opening ceremony of the Boao Forum for Asia Annual Conference 2021 via video link.

– We will build a closer partnership in green development. We will strengthen cooperation in green infrastructure, green energy, and green finance, and improve the BRI International Green Development Coalition, the Green Investment Principles for the Belt and Road Development, and other multilateral cooperation platforms to make "green" a defining feature of Belt and Road cooperation.

– We will build a closer partnership in openness and inclusiveness. A World Bank study suggests that by 2030 Belt and Road projects will have helped to lift 7.6 million people from extreme poverty and 32 million people from moderate poverty across the world. Acting in the spirit of openness and inclusiveness, we will work with all BRI participants to build the Belt and Road into a pathway to poverty reduction and economic growth, and contribute to common prosperity for all.

Strive for New Progress in High-Quality Belt and Road Development[*]

November 19, 2021

We must apply the new development philosophy in full, to the letter and in all fields, and pursue high-quality, sustainable and people-centered growth through the Belt and Road Initiative (BRI). We must consolidate the foundations for connectivity, expand areas of international cooperation, and strengthen the network of risk prevention and control. To make new progress in high-quality Belt and Road development, we need to implement higher standards in cooperation, work for better deliverables from investment, ensure higher-quality supply, and build stronger resilience in development.

Over the past eight years, under the strong leadership of the Party Central Committee, we have stepped up the overall planning and made coordinated progress in promoting high-quality development, fostering a new development dynamic, and advancing BRI cooperation.

Committed to the principles of extensive consultation, joint contribution, and shared benefits, we have achieved significant and tangible results by strengthening "hard connectivity" in infrastructure, "soft connectivity" through harmonized rules and standards, and people-to-people connectivity.

BRI cooperation has helped regions across the country to open wider to the world. More sectors have joined, and new progress has been made in opening up on the institutional level. We have made more friends across the world and found new paths of common development, realizing mutual benefit with participating countries.

---

* Main points of the speech at the third meeting on the Belt and Road Initiative.

To further BRI cooperation, we need to work on the following:

– Have a clear understanding of the new circumstances we are facing.

On the whole, peace and development remain the main themes of our times, the general direction of economic globalization has not changed, and shifts in the international strategic landscape are favorable for our country. This affords great opportunities for BRI cooperation.

However, the international situation is becoming increasingly complex for BRI, as we face an accelerating rate of change on a scale unseen in a century. A new revolution in science, technology and industry has led to fierce competition, while climate change, Covid-19 and other global problems have had a severe impact on society.

In response, we must maintain strategic resolve and seize strategic opportunities. We need to balance development and security, domestic and international imperatives, cooperation and competition, projects in the execution and planning stages, and broader considerations and specific priorities, so as to meet challenges with a proactive approach, exploit positive factors, and avoid adverse impacts.

– Consolidate the foundations for Belt and Road cooperation.

We must expand mutual political trust and strengthen policy coordination to guide and facilitate cooperation. We must explore and establish more cooperation mechanisms and turn political consensus into concrete actions, and shared vision into tangible results.

We will strengthen infrastructure connectivity and build a better network that spans land, sea, air and cyberspace. We will intensify cooperation in both traditional and new-type infrastructure projects, and strengthen the "soft connectivity" through harmonized rules and standards among participating countries, to contribute to global connectivity.

We will promote unimpeded trade. We will expand trade with neighboring countries, encourage more imports of high-quality products, and facilitate free trade and investment, making trade more balanced and mutually beneficial.

We will continue to expand third-party and multiparty market cooperation, and cooperation with other countries in building industrial capacity.

We will strengthen financial connectivity. We will work towards extensive participation by multilateral development agencies and financial institutions from developed countries in BRI cooperation. We will improve the framework for diversified investment and financing.

We will encourage more people-to-people and cultural exchanges, and facilitate multifaceted interaction.

– Expand areas of cooperation.

We will foster new areas of cooperation and strengthen cooperation in health, green development, the digital economy, and innovation.

We will continue to engage in international cooperation on the Covid-19 response, and offer assistance within our capacity to BRI participating countries. We will support other developing countries in the development of green and low-carbon energy, promote capacity building, share related information, and expand cooperation in eco-environmental protection and climate governance.

We will increase cooperation in the digital economy by promoting Silk Road e-commerce, and foster an environment favorable to this cooperation.

We will implement the action plan for sci-tech innovation and strengthen international cooperation in protecting intellectual property rights, so as to create an open, fair, equitable and nondiscriminatory environment for sci-tech progress.

– Contribute to a new development dynamic.

We must coordinate a new development dynamic with BRI cooperation, with a focus on building new connections and creating new drivers of growth.

We will accelerate the construction of land transport routes that are safe and smooth and complement each other with their respective advantages, and improve maritime transport routes, so that these transport networks will give a boost to domestic and global economic flows.

We must do what is needed to ensure supply chains are smoothly connected with industrial chains and to diversify sources of supply. We will complete some high-quality flagship projects. We will also launch high-quality landmark projects for improving quality of life as this can be an effective way to increase sense of fulfillment in BRI participating countries. We must make proper plans to ensure that these projects meet the practical needs of local people, and win their support.

– Strengthen risk prevention and control across the board.

We must strictly enforce risk control systems and see that enterprises take on their primary responsibilities, and relevant departments effectively perform their administrative duties.

We will develop a comprehensive early warning and risk assessment platform for overseas projects that operates round-the-clock services and issues early warnings whenever necessary, while providing risk assessments on a regular basis. We must build greater synergy between the mechanisms for security control, the fight against international terrorism, and the protection of our overseas interests.

We must balance the Covid-19 response and BRI cooperation to protect the lives and health of Chinese workers abroad. We must take targeted measures to guarantee material supplies and financial support, meet the demand for labor, and ensure rotation of staff and workers stationed abroad. We should also educate and guide our citizens and enterprises working abroad to conscientiously observe local laws and customs.

In addition, we should move faster to develop well-conceived laws and regulations to combat foreign-related corruption, and step up efforts to eliminate cross-border corruption. Enterprises must regulate their business activities. Never will we ever allow any action that could damage China's image abroad. Any violation of the law or disciplinary norms will be subject to severe punishment.

– Strengthen overall planning and coordination.

We must uphold the centralized, unified leadership of the Party. The BRI leading group should coordinate and follow up on major plans, policies, projects, issues and key annual tasks. Relevant departments must keep BRI-related work high on their agenda, and shoulder their responsibilities in implementing overseas projects and controlling risks associated with them. Local governments must be clear about their roles in promoting the BRI.

It is important to cultivate public opinion favorable to BRI cooperation. We can do so through communication and outreach, explaining the philosophy, principles and operating mechanisms of the BRI and telling accurate and engaging stories of BRI cooperation.

Party Self-Reform for Social Transformation

Implement the Party's Organizational Guideline for the New Era*

June 29, 2020

It takes the efforts of the whole Party to fully implement its organizational guideline for the new era. We must have a thorough understanding of its rich content and requirements. In implementing the guideline, we should stay true to our goal, adopt a problem-solving approach and deliver results.

First, we should uphold and improve the Party's leadership and follow and develop socialism with Chinese characteristics. The Party's organizational guideline is determined by its sound political guideline, and serves to ensure that the sound political guideline is implemented properly. The Party exercises overall leadership over all areas of endeavor in our country. This is the most important guideline the Party has developed in leading the people in the course of revolution, construction and reform.

The fundamental purpose of strengthening the Party's organizations is to uphold and improve overall Party leadership and provide a strong guarantee for advancing the cause of socialism with Chinese characteristics. During the War of Liberation, the Party Central Committee called for the preparation of a well-trained force for the day when political power would be won nationwide. In less than three months, the Party's organizational departments at all levels sent 53,000 Party officials to work in the newly liberated areas. In the years from 1952 to 1954, in order to carry out large-scale economic construction,

---

* Part of the speech at the 21st group study session of the Political Bureau of the 19th CPC Central Committee.

more than 160,000 people were transferred to the industrial sector across the country, among whom more than 3,000 assumed leading positions in key Soviet-aided factories and mines. In 1956, the Party Central Committee issued a call to encourage intellectuals to dedicate themselves to socialist development. By the end of June 1957, more than 17,500 of 110,000 senior intellectuals in China had joined the Party. Many scientists of the older generation such as Li Siguang[1] and Qian Xuesen[2] joined the Party in the 1950s.

Now, we expect to accomplish the First Centenary Goal and embark on a new journey towards the Second Centenary Goal of building a modern socialist country in all respects. Today's world is going through profound and complex changes, and we are faced with risks and challenges, both foreseeable and unforeseeable. We should be fully aware of this complexity and these challenges, and we should pursue the goal of national rejuvenation in the context of a world facing a scale of change unseen in a century. If we are to respond effectively to daunting challenges, defuse risks, remove major obstacles and resolve serious problems, and if we are to succeed in our great historic struggle with many new features and achieve the rejuvenation of the Chinese nation, we must ensure the leadership of the Party.

Upholding Party leadership first and foremost means upholding the authority of the Party Central Committee and its centralized, unified leadership. We should see to it that all Party members closely follow the Party's central leadership in thinking, action and political orientation. We should also see to it that Party committees and Party leadership groups at all levels as well as primary-level Party organizations in all sectors perform their political and organizational functions. We should unite and energize Party members, officials, professionals and the general public so that they will come together and become a powerful force to build socialism with Chinese characteristics for the new era.

Second, we should arm all Party members with the Party's sound theories. The Party's organization is the body, while its vision is the soul, so to speak. To strengthen the Party's organization, we should build up the body, and more importantly, shape its soul. The Party has succeeded in accomplishing a mission that no other political force in modern China was able to complete, and it has led the people in making great achievements in revolution, construction and reform. What has made this possible is that the Party has always followed Marxism as its guide to action, and informed all its members about the latest achievement in adapting Marxism to China's realities. And this has created a shared vision, a strong will, great strength, and a powerful capacity to act in concert in our Party.

As the largest political party in the world, our Party should act in a way commensurate with its status, although it faces various problems that come with size. It is especially difficult for the whole Party to maintain a high degree of unity in thinking and theory. We must arm the Party with Marxism, especially the Thought on Socialism with Chinese Characteristics for a New Era. Party organizations at all levels, Party members and officials, and especially we leading officials, should know how to use the theoretical weapons of Marxism, improve our ability to apply theory in practice, and turn the Party's new thinking into a force for advancing the cause of socialism with Chinese characteristics in the new era. We in Party committees at all levels and our organizational departments should take the Party's sound theories as the guide to consolidating the Party's organizations. We should promote reform and open new ground under new conditions, move ahead with the times, gain a good understanding of how to conduct the Party's organizational work, and be creative in our work. This will provide a strong organizational base for accomplishing the Party's historic mission in the new era.

Third, we should improve the Party's organizational system. A well-knit organizational system is the source of strength of a Marxist political party. Lenin said, "The proletariat can, and inevitably will, become an invincible force only through its ideological unification on the principles of Marxism being reinforced by the material unity of organization."[3] Our Party has established a well-functioning organizational structure consisting of the central, local and primary level units. This comprises 3,200 local Party committees, 145,000 Party leadership groups and Party working committees, and 4.68 million primary-level Party organizations.

This is a strength no other political party in the world has. The strength of the Party's organizational system can be fully unleashed only when our central, local and primary-level Party units maintain their strengths and play their roles. Only with a tight-knit organizational system where Party units at all levels are well-developed, well-functioning, closely connected, and competent in policy implementation can the Party exercise effective leadership, just as the brain directs the arms and the arms employ the fingers[4]. This is why we emphasize that priority should be given to strengthening the organizational system in implementing the Party's organizational guideline for the new era.

Since the 18th CPC National Congress, we have worked to strengthen the Party's organizations as a priority. We have done this, first and foremost, by strengthening the Central Committee, and the Political Bureau and its standing committee. In the Party regulations we have formulated, high standards are set for comrades in the central leadership team. This requires them to play an exemplary role for the rest of the Party in observing the Party's discipline and rules, and fulfilling their political responsibility for exercising governance over the Party.

Central Party and government departments should take the lead in implementing the decisions and action plans of the Central Committee, and must not erect any roadblocks. We must implement the regulations on the work of Party leadership groups and on the Party's working bodies, so as to turn central Party and government departments into models in keeping political commitment, observing discipline, taking responsibilities seriously, and carrying out duties effectively.

Local Party committees are the main channel in implementing the Central Committee's decisions and action plans, and this channel must not be impeded. We must fully implement the regulations on the work of local Party committees, to build them into strong organizations that resolutely follow the lead of the Central Committee, exercise strict and effective self-governance and supervision, maintain high cohesion, and have a high degree of integrity.

The primary-level Party organizations are the "last mile" in implementing the Central Committee's decisions and action plans, and they must not be allowed to drag feet or take no action. We must pay greater attention to strengthening primary-level Party organizations, rectify the weak and the slack ones, address shortcomings in their work, and ensure Party organizations and their work cover all sectors. This will enable these organizations in different sectors to play a key role in exercising Party leadership.

At the same time, we must recruit new high-caliber Party members, strengthen the commitment of all Party members and keep them well managed so that they can be the vanguard and the models in advancing reform and development and ensuring stability. We in the Party organizations at all levels should continue to strengthen our ability to provide political leadership and theoretical guidance and to organize and inspire the people. We can thus rally all the people closely around the Party.

Fourth, we should build a core contingent of administrative officials and talent of all disciplines. As an ancient Chinese philosopher observed, "If a country has a huge pool of talent, good governance is ensured; otherwise, poor governance is unavoidable."[5] Managing human resources, including officials and talent, is essentially a matter of how to put people to good use. To respond to changes, create new opportunities, and open new horizons to rejuvenate our country, the key is for us to strengthen the Party's leadership teams at all levels and train high-caliber officials. As I have said before, great decisions and implementation plans will come to nothing if they are not implemented by competent people. The Party's organizational guideline for the new era requires that officials be selected on the basis of both integrity and competence, with greater emphasis on the former. Officials with competence but no integrity will ruin our cause; those with integrity but no competence will weaken our cause; only those with both integrity and competence can ensure the success of our cause.

Our Party emphasized at the Fourth Plenary Session of its 19th Central Committee that strengthening the governance capacity of officials is a major task in the new era. We should give officials more training in theory to strengthen their political commitment, hone their skills, and give them more hands-on practice. We should urge all officials to perform their duties and exercise their power in strict accordance with all relevant regulations. We in the Party organizations at all levels should set high standards of political commitment and integrity for officials. We should not allow anyone with a dubious political stance or lack of integrity to present themselves as an effective performer. We must also set strict standards of qualification and competence for officials, appoint leadership teams, and use capable officials with passion and vigor to meet the needs of development. This way, we can identify and appoint officials who are enterprising, devoted to their jobs, and able to deliver results. We should select and train younger officials from among the best, focusing on the quality of candidates. We should not be impatient as if trying to help shoots grow by pulling them up, still less should we lower our standards for officials. High-caliber younger officials, once selected, need to be properly trained and managed. We should strengthen political and professional training of officials, so that they will honor their political commitment, and have a good command of theory and the professional skills and knowhow to respond to the call of our times.

We should reform the human resources management system, and improve the supervision mechanism with a view to ensuring that our officials keep their political commitment, perform their duties properly, practice the code of conduct and observe discipline. This reform should aim for greater career mobility, providing opportunities for officials to move up or down and in or out, and promoting the competent and awarding the high performers, while demoting the mediocre and dismissing the poorest performers. We should build and improve incentive and protection mechanisms to encourage officials to fulfill their duties, live up to their responsibilities, and resolve tough issues, and we should provide them with proper support.

We should accelerate the reform of institutions and mechanisms for managing human resources and remove institutional obstacles to recruiting, training, using, evaluating, rotating and motivating staff. We should implement a more proactive, open and effective human resources policy to form a sound human resources system with international competitiveness, to pool competent people of all disciplines and put them to the best use.

Fifth, we should improve the Party's organizational system. Democratic centralism is the fundamental organizational and leadership principle of our Party. Since the 18th CPC National Congress, the Central Committee has formulated and revised a range of Party rules and regulations. They include guidelines for internal Party activities under new circumstances, and regulations on the work of Party leadership groups, on the work of local Party committees, on the Party's working bodies, on the work of Party branches, and on the work of primary-level Party organizations in rural areas, state-owned enterprises, and Party and government departments.

At its Fourth Plenary Session, the 19th Central Committee incorporated into the state and governance systems the principle that optimizing and safeguarding the Party's centralized, unified organizational system is an important means of upholding and improving the Party's leadership system.

The competent departments of the Central Committee and Party committees and Party leadership groups at all levels should take concrete steps to implement the Party's organizational rules and regulations, and meet the requirements of the Central Committee in light of their specific conditions. Efforts should be made to establish a complete and sound set of systems and institutions, including those for the setup, operation, management and supervision of Party organizations.

Efforts should also be made to improve and enforce the system under which Party committees and Party leadership groups assume primary responsibility in strictly enforcing Party discipline. All these efforts to strengthen the Party's organizations should be institutionalized, standardized and well-conceived.

Notes

[1] Li Siguang (1889-1971) was a Chinese geologist, and one of the founders of China's geomechanics.

[2] Qian Xuesen (1911-2009) was a Chinese physicist, and the pioneer of engineering cybernetics, mechanics, aerospace engineering, systems science, and systems engineering in China.

[3] V. I. Lenin: "One Step Forward, Two Steps Back", *V. I. Lenin: Collected Works*, Vol. 7, Eng. ed., Progress Publishers, Moscow, 1961, p. 412.

[4] Lü Zhong: *Records of Major Events of the Dynasty* (*Lei Bian Huang Chao Da Shi Ji Jiang Yi*). Lü Zhong (dates unknown) was a scholar of the Southern Song Dynasty (1127-1279).

[5] *Mo Zi.*

The Battle Against Corruption Is First and Foremost a Political Issue*

January 22, 2021

I

Since the 18th CPC National Congress in 2012, I have reiterated that the battle against corruption is first and foremost a political issue. There are five reasons:

First, corruption is the worst of the factors that most seriously undermine the foundations of our Party's governance. It can bring about the most serious damage and harm, and may even lead to the loss of power. It is the most dangerous threat to the Party. The fight against corruption is a major political struggle that we cannot and must not lose. We must go all out and win it.

Second, our Party has taken a clear political stance against corruption and in favor of building clean government. This is an essential requirement for upholding its nature and purpose, and a major and long-term political task for its self-reform. We must declare our Party's resolute opposition to corruption and leave no place for corrupt officials to hide within the Party.

Third, political corruption is the most serious form of corruption. We must eliminate all hidden political threats from within the Party, and resolutely prevent vested interest groups from arising within the Party. If they usurp Party power, or if leading Party officials become

---

* Excerpts from the speech at the Fifth Plenary Session of the 19th CPC Central Commission for Discipline Inspection.

their agents or even form their own cliques, the nature of our socialist country will change.

Fourth, the people's support is of paramount importance in governance. The people resent corruption most. If we let a few hundred corrupt officials slip through the cracks, we are letting down all 1.4 billion Chinese people. This is the simple arithmetic of politics and popular support. If we are to unite the Party, the military, and the people, and lay solid political foundations for the Party's governance, we must intensify our effort to improve Party conduct, enforce Party discipline, and fight corruption.

Fifth, we are engaged in an ongoing drive to improve Party conduct, build clean government, and combat corruption. We must take resolute and sustained action to win this prolonged battle in the spirit of "leaving our mark in the steel we grasp and our print on the stone we tread", so that our Party will maintain its political integrity.

II

From the perspective of improving Party conduct, building clean government, and combating corruption, we must increase our political acumen. This means: taking China's political security as the top priority, putting the people first, and upholding and developing Chinese socialism as the fundamental principle; thoroughly understanding the political nature and hazards of various types of corruption, and discerning between right and wrong; effectively guarding against risks and overcoming challenges to keep our country from changing its nature.

We must reinforce our political understanding. This means: having a thorough understanding of the Central Committee's efforts to improve Party conduct, build clean government, and combat corruption; having a sound understanding of the Central Committee's major policies, principles and actions on strict governance over the Party; conscientiously keeping in alignment with the Central Committee.

We must also strengthen our political capacity to deliver. This means: improving Party conduct and combating corruption in the direction determined by the Central Committee; conducting regular self-examination against our goals and standards and promptly rectifying any deviation; strengthening our sense of responsibility to ensure full implementation of all measures.

Focus of the Education Campaign on CPC History[*]

February 20, 2021

The CPC Central Committee has set clear guidelines in its notice to launch this education campaign, requiring Party members to study Party history for deeper understanding, firmer commitment, greater integrity, and stronger action. The campaign seeks to help Party members, through studying Party history, to better understand the theories it espouses, work effectively, and achieve new successes.

First, the campaign will help Party members better appreciate and proactively apply the Party's innovative theories. Theories and ideas give people power. Theoretical thinking and guidance are pivotal for a nation to be ahead of the times. At a moment of great peril for modern China, China's Communists rescued the country with Marxism-Leninism and went on to adapt it to the Chinese context. Through the truths of Marxism, the millennia-old Chinese civilization has revived and become a great source of inspiration. Our experience has shown that Marxism offers an inexhaustible theoretical wellspring for us to seek truth, understand the world and its laws, and transform it. Therefore, Marxism must always be the guiding philosophy of the Party and the state.

The lifeline of a theory lies in innovation. Marxism has profoundly changed the course of China's history, which has in turn developed and enriched Marxism. Over the past century, our Party has sought truth from facts while freeing the mind, and broken new ground while maintaining its orientation and consolidating its foundations. In this way, it has broadened the dimensions of Marxism with Mao Zedong

---

[*] Part of the speech at the preparatory meeting for the education campaign on CPC history.

Thought, Deng Xiaoping Theory, the Theory of Three Represents, the Scientific Outlook on Development, and the Thought on Socialism with Chinese Characteristics for a New Era, providing sound guidance for the Party and the people. The Party's history embodies an ongoing process of adapting Marxism to the Chinese context and exploring innovative theories and ideas.

The campaign will help Party members to gain insight from the Party's epic journey into the profound changes that Marxism has brought to China and the wider world, appreciate the philosophical and practical power of Marxism, and recognize both theoretical continuity and innovation in adapting Marxism to the Chinese context. With a focus on reviewing the historic successes and changes in the Party and the country since the 18th CPC National Congress in 2012, the campaign aims to deliver a better understanding of the Party's innovative theories for the new era and encourage sustained efforts to study the latest theoretical developments and apply them to our future work.

Second, the campaign will help Party members to better understand the general laws and trends of history and steer the course of the Party and the state. History indeed has its laws, but this does not mean that people are completely passive. As long as we follow the general laws and trends of history, and leverage opportunities for change accordingly, we can achieve greater success.

More than 170 years ago, Marx and Engels systematically revealed the historical law that socialism would eventually replace capitalism. This general trend of human society is irreversible, but it is a lengthy process, during which we need to be rooted firmly in reality, control the course of each stage, and make solid and steady progress.

By analyzing historical trends against the basic tenets of Marxism, the Party has properly handled the relationship between China and the world in general, and made good use of every opportunity available over the past century.

Our Party was born in response to the call of history when socialism gained global momentum following the victory of Russia's October

Revolution. Since then, the Party has been at the forefront of the times.

Acting upon the call to save the country and fight against fascism during the War of Resistance Against Japanese Aggression (1931-1945) and Global War Against Fascism, the Party pushed for a national united front against Japanese aggression and led the Chinese people to total victory over the aggressors.

The founding and consolidation of the PRC was a result of conforming to the times, as socialism was gaining greater traction and national liberation movements were surging in Asia, Africa and Latin America. The new republic established a firm foothold as righteous revolutionary causes carried the day around the world.

Thanks to our thorough understanding of the prevailing trends of the times, we made the major decision to reform and open up in 1978. Then, the world was experiencing rapid economic and technological development, while the gap between China and the advanced countries was widening. Deng Xiaoping noted, "We must keep abreast of the times; that is the purpose of our reform."[1] Based on a sound assessment of the prevailing trends, the central authorities decided to shift the focus of the Party and the country onto economic development, and therefore proceeded with the landmark policy of reform and opening up.

"It is wiser to avail oneself of a favorable situation than to rely on one's mere wisdom."[2] We cannot see far or advance further, if we do not know and understand history. This education campaign will help all Party members to be clear about China's strategy of realizing national rejuvenation within the context of a wider world that is undergoing change on a scale unseen in a century, to establish a comprehensive and balanced view of history, to understand the dynamics of evolution and the laws of history by analyzing history, the times and the world from a broader perspective, and to devise systematic, forward-looking and innovative strategies as appropriate.

Third, the campaign will help CPC members better understand the Party's nature and purpose, and maintain its distinctive features as a

Marxist party. Our Party comes from the people, with its roots in the people and its lifeline sustained by the people. Our Party was born for the people and has prospered because of the people. It is the ultimate goal of the Party to always stand together with the people and work for their interests.

Our Party's history records a century-long journey to fulfill its original aspiration and founding mission, and to dedicate its mind and soul to the people and share their weal and woe.

Among more than 300,000 revolutionaries who died after the failure of the Great Revolution (1924-1927), most were supporters of the CPC. During the Red Army period (1927-1937), the people built a formidable defense in support of our Party and the Red Army. During the War of Resistance Against Japanese Aggression, the Party mobilized the masses and overwhelmed the enemy with a vast people's war. The Party won the Huai-Hai Campaign (1948-1949) with supplies transported in wheelbarrows by the people. It won the Nanjing-Shanghai-Hangzhou Campaign across the Yangtze River in 1949 with boats provided and rowed by the people.

Progress in socialist revolution and construction was realized through the people's hard work. And it is also the people who have played the main role in the great program of reform and opening up.

History has made it clear to us that the country is the people and the people are the country. Winning public support is vital to our Party's survival. The Party can conquer any difficulties and become invincible if it wins the people's trust and support. Otherwise, it will achieve nothing or even be doomed to failure.

The Party Constitution states in its first line that the Communist Party of China is the vanguard of the Chinese working class, the Chinese people, and the Chinese nation. It also prescribes the principles of serving the people wholeheartedly, always putting the interests of the people above anything else, sharing weal and woe with them, and maintaining the closest possible ties with them.

To uphold these principles, we must respect the people's principal role in making history, which represents the law of social development.

We must pursue the lofty goal of communism and accomplish the Party's work, all in the interests of the people. We must always engage with the people, sharing weal and woe, and stand together with them through thick and thin.

We must educate and guide all Party members so that they will have a better understanding of the Party's nature and purpose. We do everything for the people and rely on them for everything we do. It is important to always put the people first and meet their expectation for a better life as our abiding goal. We should work to ensure that reform and development offer greater benefits to all the people in a fair way and that further substantial progress is achieved in the pursuit of common prosperity, so that our 1.4 billion people can come together as a mighty force for the rejuvenation of the Chinese nation.

Fourth, the campaign will help CPC members improve their capacity to address risks and challenges through studying Party history. Drawing on past experience to build a greater capacity to defuse risks and meet challenges has been a key to our Party's success.

The Party's experience has come neither out of thin air nor from any textbook; rather, the Party has accumulated its experience in trials and tribulations and through successes and failures over the years. It attests to the hard work, sacrifice, fortitude and wisdom of Party members.

At present, China is facing unprecedented risks and challenges – both at home and abroad, both conventional and unconventional – in politics, the economy, culture, social affairs, and the eco-environment. The situation can be exacerbated by the sudden occurrence of "black swan" and "grey rhino" events. To better deal with foreseeable and unforeseeable risks and challenges on our way forward, we need to draw inspiration from history and search the past for optimal solutions.

When reviewing the Party's revolutionary experience, Mao Zedong listed the united front, armed struggle, and strengthening the Party as the "three principal magic weapons" of the Party. These "magic weapons" played an important role in our victory in the New Democratic Revolution (1919-1949), and they are still playing a crucial role to this day.

On several important occasions, including the 95th anniversary of the CPC, the 40th anniversary of the launch of reform and opening up, and the 70th anniversary of the PRC, I have summarized the Party's experience from multiple perspectives.

Approaching the Party's centenary, we should seize this critical opportunity to push forward the great historic struggle by grasping its new features and applying the full wealth of experience we have accumulated during different periods in countering risks and meeting challenges. We should be prepared, in both thought and deed, to respond to long-term changes in the external environment. We must reinforce our commitment, enrich our experience, and build up our ability to meet challenges head-on. While building up our governance capacity, we must have plans in place for the worst possible scenarios as we strive for the best results.

It is easier to breach a fortress from within. In this sense, degeneracy, corruption and betrayal from within the Party have been the gravest threat since its founding. The Party would lose the people's support if it betrays its political character as a Marxist party and its fundamental purpose. Over its century-long journey, our Party has stayed alert to risks of corruption and disintegration, and maintained its progressive and wholesome nature.

Through education and guidance, all Party members should learn from history how to address problems in relation to strengthening the Party, improve the Party's leadership and governance, and reinforce its ability to resist corruption and withstand threats. This will ensure that the Party always remains ahead of the times as the world progresses and profound changes occur. This will also ensure that the Party always remains the spine of the nation as China responds to risks and challenges at home and abroad, and a strong leader as the country continues to uphold and advance socialism with Chinese characteristics.

Fifth, the campaign will inspire Party members to carry forward the revolutionary spirit. It will give them motivation and the will to always work hard with great enthusiasm. "As you move on, the road ahead is bound to be strewn with difficulties and obstacles."[3] The Party has experienced countless trials and hardships, and made sacrifices on a scale that few other political parties in the world could endure.

On its arduous 100-year journey, our Party has tempered its character with the courage to vanquish formidable enemies, counter serious threats, and fight and win victories. This has become the Party's defining quality and character.

The past hundred years have witnessed the extraordinary, tenacious and unwavering efforts of generations of China's Communists, spearheaded by dauntless revolutionary martyrs, hardworking heroes, and devoted role models. These efforts have given rise to the revolutionary spirit of the Jinggangshan, the Long March, and the Zunyi Meeting; to the revolutionary spirit of Yan'an, Xibaipo, and Hongyan; to the spirit demonstrated in the War to Resist US Aggression and Aid Korea, in the development of China's first atomic and hydrogen bombs, missile, and man-made satellite and in the experimentation with special economic zones; to the spirit forged in battles against floods, earthquakes and other natural disasters and in the fight against Covid-19. Together, these constitute a long line of principles inspiring China's Communists. In short, it is this revolutionary spirit and selfless dedication that hold the key to the Party's lasting vigor and vitality through all the trials and tribulations of the past hundred years.

These invaluable principles endure and transcend time and space. They manifest the Party's firm convictions, defining purpose, and finest traditions, and epitomize the hardworking, selfless and pioneering character of Party members. They have been instilled into the lifeblood of the Party and the Chinese nation, and have provided a powerful driving force for the Party to survive, prosper and grow in strength.

We should be conscious of the risk that the Party's extensive term in governance and the enduring peace in our country might dilute the drive of some Party members and officials. Some rest on the status quo, thinking the time is right to slow down and take things easy, and lacking the drive to make progress or take on responsibilities. Some rest on their laurels or make a token effort in their work, assuming that they have reached the finish line of their career. Some concern themselves too much with personal gains and losses, and pursue pleasure, fame and fortune instead of taking on their due responsibilities. Some lack the will and courage to meet challenges head-on, and tend to evade problems and pass the buck to higher-ups, accustomed as they are to playing the role of a conduit.

I have emphasized on many occasions that Communists should instill in themselves the spirit of carrying the revolution through to the end, and emulate the resolve and determination of the older generation of revolutionaries, who chased down the last remnant of the enemy till the whole land was liberated, rather than giving up halfway. We Communists should carry forward the dauntless spirit in our efforts to create a new China. I have underlined this for a reason. Just imagine how difficult it is for a country with 1.4 billion people to realize socialist modernization, and the significance of that achievement. All Party members should be required to pass down the revolutionary faith and tradition, maintain the source of their strength and the dauntless spirit to prevail, and embark with drive and enthusiasm on a new journey to achieve our goals for the new era.

Sixth, the campaign will bolster the unity and solidarity of the Party and ensure concerted action. Taking a clear political stance and ensuring the Party's unity and solidarity are its lifeblood and the key to its historic successes over the past century. History has demonstrated that the whole Party acting with one mind can rally all the Chinese people and build them into an invincible force that will defeat the most powerful enemy and overcome the most daunting obstacle.

The top and long-term priority in reinforcing the Party's political foundations is to ensure that the whole Party defers to the Central Committee and upholds its authority and centralized, unified leadership.

The Zunyi Meeting in 1935 marked a turning point in the Party's history. It was convened at a critical moment when the Long March had just begun, after the Red Army had failed to break the Kuomintang's fifth campaign of encirclement and suppression and had suffered grcat losses. At the meeting, Mao Zedong was affirmed as the leader of the Central Committee and the Red Army. The meeting also laid the groundwork for establishing the leading position within the Central Committee of the correct Marxist line chiefly represented by Mao Zedong, as well as for the formation of the first generation of the central collective leadership with Mao Zedong at its core. The meeting opened a new chapter in which the Party would set its own course to address practical problems concerning the Chinese revolution. At a moment of great peril, the meeting saved the Party, the Red Army, and the Chinese revolution.

After the Zunyi Meeting, however, it took a long time for the whole Party to fully realize the importance of upholding the authority of the Central Committee and its centralized, unified leadership and to turn this realization into conscious action. During the Long March, when solidarity was most called for, Zhang Guotao set up a second central committee, relying on the strength of his troops, and attempted to split the Party and the Red Army. Again, in the early days of the War of Resistance Against Japanese Aggression, Wang Ming formed self-serving factions, ignored Party discipline, and disobeyed the Central Committee. This once again taught us a bitter lesson. During its Yan'an period (1935-1948), the Party launched a large-scale rectification movement to address divisions and factionalism within the Party. The movement was exceptionally effective in strengthening solidarity and unity throughout the Party, and laid solid ideological and political foundations for winning the war against Japanese aggression and realizing national liberation.

"As long as the fundamental principles are upheld, all work will fall in place."[4] Since the 18th CPC National Congress, we have made an all-out effort to reinforce the Party's political foundations, improve the systems for upholding the authority of the Central Committee and its centralized, unified leadership, and consolidate the unity of the Party.

Nevertheless, we should take note that some Party members and officials still lack political awareness and acuity, and fail to observe and solve problems from a political perspective. They do not care about matters of fundamental national interest and pay little attention to the Party's political requirements, rules and discipline. Nor do they concern themselves with the adverse political implications of various problems. They only make a perfunctory effort to implement the policies and guidelines of the Central Committee. They have yet to translate the Party's political requirements into their own initiative.

Upholding the authority of the Central Committee and its centralized, unified leadership requires action rather than empty talk. The whole Party should learn from both the successful experience and bitter lessons of the past, act consistently with the Central Committee, and strengthen their political acumen, understanding and capacity to deliver. They should strengthen their commitment to the Four Consciousnesses, the Four-sphere Confidence, and the Two Upholds. All Party members should keep in line with the Central Committee in thinking, action and political orientation, to ensure that the whole Party pulls together towards the same goal with one mind.

Notes

¹ Deng Xiaoping: "We Shall Speed Up Reform", *Selected Works of Deng Xiaoping*, Vol. III, Eng. ed., Foreign Languages Press, Beijing, 1994, p. 239.

² *The Mencius (Meng Zi)*. This is one of the Confucian classics written by Mencius and his disciples. Mencius (c. 372-289 BC), also known as Meng Ke or Ziyu, was a philosopher, thinker and educator in the Warring States Period.

³ Yuan Haowen: "To the Hall of Destiny of Li Yanren in Linfen" (Lin Fen Li Shi Ren Yun Tang). Yuan Haowen (1190-1257) was a writer and historian of the Jin Dynasty.

⁴ *Lü's Spring and Autumn Annals (Lü Shi Chun Qiu)*. This is a collection of works from different schools of thoughts compiled by the followers of Lü Buwei (?-235 BC), chief minister of the State of Qin during the Warring States Period.

Study Party History to Generate Understanding, Commitment, Integrity and Action*

March 22-July 23, 2021

I

Fujian is an old revolutionary base area, a place where many events in the Party's history took place, and a place that is home to many revolutionary forefathers. Its wealth of revolutionary resources gives it unique advantages as a venue for studying Party history and conducting related educational activities. Through studying history we can have a better understanding of our cause, which is the premise to boost our commitment, integrity and action.

From the Party's splendid achievements, arduous journeys, historical experience and fine traditions, we can have a good understanding of the capability of our Party, the practicality of Marxism, and the strengths of socialism with Chinese characteristics. We can draw from the historical, theoretical and practical background, understand the necessity to uphold Party leadership from a historical perspective, and strengthen our confidence in it. We can comprehend the truth of Marxism and the innovative theories developed by our Party in the process of adapting Marxism to the Chinese context, and be proactive and resolute in applying these theories. We can develop a profound understanding of the reason why socialism with Chinese characteristics is right for China and why it is the only right choice for us to make. We will strengthen grassroots Party organizations. We

---

* Excerpts from speeches made between March 22 and July 23, 2021.

must continuously strengthen the fight against corruption to ensure that our officials dare not, cannot, and will not engage in corruption, and we must continue to consolidate and develop a healthy political ecosystem.

(from the speech during a visit to Fujian Province,
March 22-25, 2021)

II

Guangxi is rich in revolutionary resources. It should make full use of these resources in the education campaign on CPC history and ensure that Party members affirm their political commitment. In other words, through studying Party history, we will have stronger faith, firmer convictions, and greater confidence, which will inspire us to overcome difficulties, defeat enemies, and secure victories.

We should reinforce our faith in Marxism and communism, and guide Party members and officials to draw strength for our faith from the Party's endeavors over the past century, maintain a strong will, and prevail over severe challenges. We should strengthen our faith in socialism with Chinese characteristics, and guide Party members and officials to fully understand that socialism with Chinese characteristics is the logical result of China's historical development, the only way to develop China, and a truth that has been tested in practice. We should remain confident in the path, theory, system and culture of Chinese socialism.

We should build greater confidence in the prospects for national rejuvenation. We should guide Party members and officials to stay true to the Party's original aspiration and founding mission, to have confidence in the Party's capability to unite the people and lead them in realizing the rejuvenation of the Chinese nation along the path of Chinese socialism, and to realize the historic achievements required of this generation in the new era.

Faith and convictions are the most effective weapons against corruption. We should continue to improve Party conduct and build clean government. We should set more institutional barriers to ensure that our officials dare not, cannot, and will not engage in corruption.

(from the speech during a visit to Guangxi Zhuang Autonomous
Region, April 25-27, 2021)

III

In its endeavors over the past century, our Party has fostered a distinctive set of revolutionary traditions. Epitomizing the Party's firm belief, fundamental purpose, and fine conduct, they are invaluable assets that have inspired us to firmly press ahead. To boost their integrity through the education campaign on CPC history, we need to guide Party members and officials to carry forward the Party's revolutionary legacy and build strength of character.

First, we should value loyalty to the Party. Party members and officials should never forget their oath of admission to the Party. We should stay committed to Party undertakings, and follow the Party's leadership with resolution and without second thoughts.

Second, we should value the determination to work for the well-being of the people. Party members and officials must always stand with the people and share weal and woe with them. We should take on responsibilities, act decisively, and consider improving people's lives to be our most fundamental duty.

Third, we should promote strict self-discipline. Party members and officials should strengthen self-discipline and guard against temptations, and be clean and honest in office and daily life, so that they will become honorable and wholesome individuals who are of moral integrity, above base interests, and of value to the people.

(from the speech during a visit to Qinghai Province, June 7-9, 2021)

IV

Putting what one has learned into action is the purpose of the education campaign on CPC history. A better understanding of our cause, firmer commitment to our ideals, and higher standards of integrity gained from studying history should be converted into concrete actions to transform our objective and subjective worlds.

We should strengthen our commitment to the Party with action. We should educate and guide Party members and officials to carry forward the best of our Party's traditions, pass down its revolutionary legacy, and strengthen their commitment to the Party by drawing on the great founding spirit of the Party. Party members and officials should have firm ideals and convictions. We should constantly strengthen our political acumen, understanding and capacity to deliver, and bear in mind the country's most fundamental interests. We should cultivate and discipline ourselves in accordance with Party principles, and with our moral character as Party members, win the trust of the people and guide them.

We should take stronger actions to serve the people. We should educate and guide Party members and officials to hold the people dearest in their hearts. We should become the people's trustworthy and caring friends as well as their guides. We should work hard to help people overcome difficulties, ease their concerns and solve their most urgent problems with heart and soul, and make more notable and substantive progress towards common prosperity.

We should make greater efforts to promote development. We should encourage Party members and officials to combine studying Party history with their work, to be pragmatic, to assume responsibilities, and to creatively implement the decisions and plans of the Party Central Committee. We should focus on resolving problems and cultivating new strengths, and achieve new successes that merit the trust of the Party and the people and that are worthy of history and our times.

(from the speech during a visit to Tibet Autonomous Region,
July 21-23, 2021)

Be the Spine of Our Party[*]

September 1, 2021

This year marks the centenary of our Party, and at present all Party members are engaged in the education campaign on CPC history. It is necessary for you to systematically study Party theories to consolidate your political commitment here at the Central Party School. Every time since 2013, I have come and talked to the younger officials at the opening ceremony of this training program. Today, I would like to talk with you and set some expectations.

First, you must have firm ideals and convictions in Marxism, communism and Chinese socialism, and be loyal to the Party. Since our Party's 18th National Congress in 2012, I have emphasized on many occasions that Party members and officials must strengthen their ideals and convictions. The reason for this is that during a period of time in the past, quite a number of Party members and officials lost their ideals and beliefs under the influence of erroneous and misguided thinking, and sought to obtain material gain and indulge in selfish desires.

Since its founding a hundred years ago, the CPC has always possessed lofty ideals and firm convictions. These are its belief in Marxism, in the long-term goal of communism, and in the common ideal of socialism with Chinese characteristics. As the source of strength and political soul of China's Communists, these are the ideological basis for maintaining the Party's solidarity and unity. I have always emphasized that we must be unequivocal and confident

* Main part of the speech at the opening ceremony of a training program for younger officials at the Central Party School (National Academy of Governance) during its 2021 fall semester.

when talking about the ideals and convictions of our Party. Do not be ambiguous about this; do not be hesitant. Once a communist party loses its ideals, it is no different from other political parties. Without this motivating force and inner bond, it will become a disjointed group, doomed to failure. This is why I keep saying that ideals and convictions are as essential for a Communist as calcium is for bones. Without this compound they will be deficient in mind. The core of their being will suffer; they will inevitably become politically, financially and morally corrupt; they will pursue a degenerate lifestyle.

How Party members and officials think and act is determined by whether they hold firm ideals and convictions, or pursue personal gain and selfish desires. Only when they are strong in mind and belief, will they be able to stand fast in the face of any test, and achieve steady and continued progress; in contrast, if they are lacking or weak in ideals and convictions, they will not hold their ground when confronting challenges. They will be overwhelmed by desires and selfish interests or worse still, abandon their responsibility at critical moments.

In real life, some Party members and officials are enslaved by addiction to material enjoyment. Their inner world is barren and they lack drive. They worship money, renown and pleasure, and consider these to be the ultimate goal of life. A few of them use the power bestowed by the Party and the people as a passport to personal gain, falling disgracefully into the abyss of corruption. All this is caused by a loss of ideals and convictions.

I have said on many occasions that we Communists should temper our mind and character, integrating our learning, thinking and practice, and seeking unity between what we learn, what we believe in, and what we do. The main goal for Party members and officials is to consolidate their ideals and convictions and strengthen their commitment to the Party. We cannot forge firm convictions at a stroke, nor is this a one-time effort. Whether we are true to them does not depend on what we think, but is judged by what we do when facing the harshest or most protracted tests throughout our life.

Countless martyrs took the road of revolution because they found

Marxism and communism when they went out in search of truth and the ultimate way to save the country and the people. The recent TV series *The Age of Awakening*, which you may have watched, vividly narrates the story of how our Party's early leaders fixed on Marxism and communism in the face of extreme difficulties and many competing ideologies. Li Dazhao once said, "Our purpose in living is to make something of our life, but there is a moment when we must sacrifice our lives for that purpose.... A lofty life is often characterized by a heroic death."[1] Facing the executioner's blade, he welcomed death as a true hero, fulfilling his commitment to his ideals with action.

Over the Party's hundred-year history, a great many of its members carried through their ideals to the end, shedding blood in the fire of war and standing the test of life and death. Countless gave their precious lives to defend their faith. However, there were also many who wavered and betrayed the cause, tired of a hard life or fearful of the cruel struggle. Among the 13 delegates to the First CPC National Congress in 1921, five – Wang Jinmei, Li Hanjun, Deng Enming, He Shuheng and Chen Tanqiu – laid down their lives for the revolution; some left the Party; and Chen Gongbo, Zhou Fohai and Zhang Guotao betrayed the Party. History has proved that vacillating elements will be sifted out by the revolutionary tide, just as Lu Xun wrote, "Because of the difference in ultimate aims, during the struggle some may drop out, take flight, grow decadent, or turn renegade. But so long as the rest keep advancing, as time goes by their force will grow finer and better trained."[2]

Younger officials should bear in mind that ideals and beliefs are a lifelong commitment, and regular reinforcement is a requisite. Beliefs are to be upheld for life. Any change of heart, falling by the wayside, or betrayal will have major consequences.

A strong faith is closely connected to loyalty to the Party. Only with firm ideals and convictions can one stay loyal to the Party, and fidelity to the Party interprets these beliefs best.

Liu Guozhi (1921-1949), the real-life model for Liu Siyang in the novel *Red Crag*, was born into a wealthy family in Sichuan Province.

He was arrested and thrown into jail because of the treachery of a renegade. The enemy promised to release him if he would provide information on the Party organization and announce in a newspaper his withdrawal from the Party. But he remained resolute and decisive, saying "I will never die as long as the Party lives; what would be the meaning of my life if I sell out the Party?"

Chen Yi[3] had a life motto: "A strong faith is central to revolution." Although he was not there when the first gunshots were fired in the Nanchang Uprising in 1927, he overcame all difficulties and caught up with the main force, which was reduced to only 800 men upon arriving at Tianxinxu in Jiangxi Province. He assisted Zhu De[4] to rally the remaining troops, and said to them, "It is easy to be a hero in victory, but much harder to be one in adversity. Only one who has experienced failures can be a real hero. We should be heroes in a time of defeat." This is true loyalty to the Party. No matter the circumstances, members must follow the Party to the end even it costs their lives.

In the revolutionary years, the criterion of loyalty was whether one would fight for and sacrifice oneself for the cause of the Party and the people. In times of peace there are also clear standards of assessment. These include:

- whether one can uphold Party leadership, safeguard the authority of the Central Committee and its centralized, unified leadership, and keep in line with the Party's central leadership in thinking, action and political orientation;
- whether one can faithfully follow the Party's theories, guidelines, principles and policies, and implement the decisions and plans of the Central Committee to the letter;
- whether one can strictly abide by the Party's political discipline and rules, be honest with the Party, and take a clear political stance;
- whether one can put the cause of the Party and the people above anything else, execute the decisions of Party organizations, and accept any assignment given.

Our Party has a long and cherished tradition – whatever the Party tells us to do, we do; wherever the Party wants us to go, we go; wherever there is a task to fulfill, we settle there to do the job. No hesitation, no complaint. We must carry forward this tradition. Now, some officials prefer to work only in big cities like Beijing, Shanghai and Guangzhou, and are reluctant to go to remote and less developed places like Xinjiang, Tibet and Lanzhou. With this kind of attitude, they cannot be said to be strong in faith or loyal to the Party. In a spirit of trust, Party organizations delegate younger officials to work in tough and outlying places, to temper them and prepare them for more senior roles. They should be proud and eager to take up such challenges, rather than seeking to avoid heavy tasks, worrying about personal gains and losses, or trying to wheel and deal. Those who are reluctant to accept their assignments and think too much about themselves will not be put in important positions, as they will no doubt fail the Party at critical moments. Adversity makes one stronger and helps one to succeed, just as the whetstone makes a knife sharper. Only through meeting challenges and experiencing frustrations can we become extraordinary.

Second, you should be pragmatic and realistic. Basing everything on reality is our fundamental approach when addressing issues, making decisions and taking action. Mao Zedong pointed out, "The most fundamental method of work which all Communists must firmly bear in mind is to determine our working policies according to actual conditions. When we study the causes of the mistakes we have made, we find that they all arose because we departed from the actual situation at a given time and place and were subjective in our working policies."[5]

His words strike to the heart of the matter. It is for this precise reason that I require all Party members to be strict with themselves in self-cultivation, in the exercise of power, and in self-discipline, and to act in good faith when performing official duties, undertaking initiatives, and interacting with others. And it is for this reason that the Party Central Committee launched a special education campaign on this theme throughout the Party after the 18th CPC National

Congress. The Central Committee also issued many instructions, which you must follow faithfully.

In order to do everything in line with reality, we should first go to the grassroots to find out the real situation. This is the only way to truth. It is also true that only when we have the right attitude – seeking truth from facts – will we direct the necessary attention to going to the grassroots to find out the real situation. To do this well, we must develop our basic skills in fact-finding and in-depth study. Now we know these are important, we must do more and better. The key is to address the issue thoroughly; a cursory visit or going through the motions will not do. Go to villages; go to communities. Go there often. Visit those close by and those far afield; see the real situation, good or bad. We should listen to both praise and criticism from the public. That is how we get to grips with what is really going on. Modern technology has made communication easy. We can obtain much information by making phone calls, sending WeChat messages, and reading reports, but this will never compare to on-site visits, face-to-face talks, and free discussions where anyone can take part.

Many fact-finding methods that proved effective in the past still work today, like staying at the grassroots to gain firsthand experience and conducting case studies. Our practice of extending successful pilot projects nationwide is in fact a case-study method. Mere visits are not enough, you should devote all your attention to the work. Listen to what people say, find out the real situation, study problems thoroughly and identify genuine difficulties. We cannot make cursory visits just for show or restrict ourselves to observing only positive things. It is completely unacceptable to set out with "no intention of seeking truth from facts, but only a desire to curry favor by claptrap"[6]. This kind of conduct is a typical example of favoring form over substance and bureaucratism.

We should invest hard efforts in in-depth analysis, discarding what is worthless and false and seeking out what is valuable and true, and proceeding from the one to the other and from the outside to the inside, so that we can discern the essence of things and the rules behind phenomena, and work out solutions to problems. In this process, we should exchange ideas, compare notes, double-check actual problems, respect different points of view including minority and opposition opinions, conduct analyses from different angles, and think carefully before we act. Do not present yourselves as infallible, nor be over-confident based on a smattering of knowledge. Listen to both sides and you will be enlightened; heed only one side and you will be ill-informed. It is not a bad thing to hear conflicting voices. Only through several rounds of negating the negation can our ideas and decisions reflect reality.

My proposal for targeted poverty alleviation was based on fact-finding and in-depth study. Shaking off poverty is the earnest desire of every sufferer, and a longstanding wish of revolutionaries of the older generation. If we cannot do this job properly, we will have let down the people living in impoverished areas and also failed those revolutionaries.

Soon after the closing of the 18th CPC National Congress, I went to Fuping County in Hebei Province to observe poverty elimination work. After that, I continued to visit all 14 contiguous poverty-stricken areas on a regular basis. Every year, I called on poor households to see their real lives for myself and to help those in real need. I sought opinions face-to-face from officials and individuals in impoverished areas and constantly sought to improve ideas and measures involving poverty alleviation. I pushed the relevant work forward, with a deep devotion to the people and a promise to serve them wholeheartedly. Through the joint efforts of all Party members and all people across the country, the battle against poverty has been won. Those living in previously impoverished areas are happy, and the departed revolutionaries can rest in peace.

Basing our work on reality and seeking truth from facts is not just a way of thinking, it is also a test of officials' commitment to the Party. The first step in making our officials realistic and practical is to raise their commitment to the Party.

My father once said, "Our Party emphasizes commitment to the

Party. In my opinion, seeking truth from facts is the most important component of this commitment." In 1943, a strict campaign was launched to examine officials' personal histories. This was necessary at that particular moment, as the Kuomintang were trying every means to infiltrate the revolutionary bases. However, the severity of threat was overestimated. Kang Sheng, who was put in charge of the work, applied an ultra-Left approach, extracting confessions through duress and using them as evidence. The consequence was that grave errors were made that resulted in a large number of unjust and false charges.

My father was secretary of the CPC Suide Prefectural Committee. Learning that many students at Suide Normal School had given false confessions under physical abuse and coercion, he was very troubled. After a careful investigation, he said that political awareness should be distinguished from political stance, and an erroneous extension of the campaign should be stopped. He reported the real situation to the CPC Central Committee and its Northwest Bureau, and suggested that the Central Committee should put an end to extorting confessions promptly and correct the "Leftist" mistakes. At that time, this involved a significant political risk. The reason my father was willing to take the risk was that he believed that loyalty to the Party means not lying to the Party.

Gu Wenchang, an exemplary county Party secretary, was another faithful follower of the principle of seeking truth from facts. Dongshan County in Fujian Province was not liberated from the Kuomintang until May 1950. Before retreating to Taiwan, the Kuomintang press-ganged a large number of young and middle-aged men, including 4,700 from Dongshan, a place with only around 10,000 households. After liberation in 1949, the family members of these press-ganged soldiers were classified as "families of the enemy and puppet troops". Serving at the time as secretary of the Working Committee of the First District of Dongshan County, Gu Wenchang advised his superiors to change their descriptor to "families scourged by war" as they were victims of the Kuomintang's atrocities. Accepting this suggestion, the higher authorities decided to accord these families fair and equitable political status and financial help, provide relief to those in need, and take care of elderly persons without family support. One day in July 1953, more than 10,000 Kuomintang troops carried out a raid on Dongshan, which was guarded by only 1,000 soldiers. In spite of such a huge disparity in numbers, the defending troops and civilians in the county united as one, forged an impregnable barrier, and finally secured victory. The families of the press-ganged men also joined in the defense. One said, "The Kuomintang took away our men by force, while the Communist Party treats us like family. We are ready to die to defend the island." It was precisely because of its respect for facts that the Party won popular support.

Although there are a number of standards by which we judge whether an official seeks truth from facts, the most fundamental criterion is whether he or she speaks the truth and does honest work for concrete outcomes. Today, we have other types of officials: Some vacillate like a weathercock, some conceal problems and pretend everything is going well, some indulge in showy display and do nothing practical, and some are obsessed with status and crave instant success – none of these are true adherents of philosophical materialism, but are victims of self-centered thinking.

You younger officials must always keep commitment to the Party to the fore in your conduct and your duties, and reinforce it by being honest and truthful and doing solid work. Have the courage to uphold truth, be an independent thinker, and work in a pragmatic manner. This will benefit the Party and the people, and you will achieve personal growth. Honesty is not folly, and no one will lose out by doing practical and concrete work. Betrayal of the Party and dishonesty will make officials opportunistic and self-seeking, which will tempt them into building covert political connections, buying promotions, and trading power for money, and ultimately lead to their undoing.

Third, you should shoulder your responsibilities and act on your duties. Fulfilling tasks and taking responsibilities are the bound duty of officials; this is where your value lies. The Party assigns officials to different positions to take responsibilities and perform duties, not to see you acting like lords and indulging in luxury. There is much work to be done in promoting reform, development and stability. Any official who wants to do it well must act. Without a sense of responsibility and a will to act, without enforcement and effectiveness, you will fail in your duties.

Earnest and down-to-earth efforts are essential for performing one's duties; empty rhetoric and inaction will not lead to success. I have shared many times how the longwinded scholars of the Western and Eastern Jin dynasties (265-420) cost their country its future. Wang Yan (256-311) was a typical example. He was so good at talking that no one could debate with him at the time. During the final years of the Western Jin, Shi Le (274-333) of the nomadic Jie tribe led an army to attack Luoyang, the Jin's capital. As the top military adviser to the Jin emperor, Wang followed the imperial army to put down the rebellion, but was defeated and captured. When Shi asked him the reasons for Jin's defeat, he tried every means to evade responsibility, saying he had not attended to state affairs since a young age. Shi retorted, "Your fame spreads throughout the empire. You have served in the court since your youth, and are still entrusted with great responsibilities even now when your head is grey. How can you say you have not attended to state affairs? You are entirely to blame for the havoc around the country."[7] Soon after this encounter Shi had him killed. Before his death, Wang Yan bewailed his misfortune and attributed it to his shallow, empty talk and lack of real effort.

We also have people like him today. Some are great talkers, not doers. They work by shouting slogans and making verbal commitments. Some seek form over substance. They indulge in wasteful and extravagant projects, but make only a perfunctory effort to carry out real tasks. Some remain inactive and muddle through if nobody presses them to do things. Some even disobey orders from their superiors and violate their prohibitions, conceal the true state of affairs from both superiors and subordinates, and engage in fraud. We have found some officials who did not make genuine and concrete efforts to fulfill their responsibilities. This is a significant problem, and it explains why there were shortcomings in so many fields this year, such as epidemic control, natural disaster response, eco-environmental protection, and workplace safety.

Shouldering responsibilities and performing duties cannot be separated. Failure to perform duties constitutes neglect of responsibilities, and a sense of responsibility is essential to the execution of duties. Anything we do carries a level of risk. Exactly what, in the world, is risk-free and completely goes as planned? This is why we need the courage to take on responsibility. If all work was easy and everyone could perform well, then why is courage so precious? It is always like this: The more you fear getting into trouble, the more likely that things will go wrong; the more you want to avoid problems, the more likely it is that they will stand in your way. Problems will only be solved when you have the courage and determination to invest in real effort and take risks, knowing the danger but still forging ahead.

When I worked in Fujian, a province rich in forest resources, I saw the farmers leading a hard life due to unclear ownership of the green mountains outside their doors. To help them, I launched a reform to address unclear forest tenure and other institutional and structural problems.

At that time it was a risky move, as the central authorities had suspended the contracting of hills to households due to destructive logging in some areas in the 1980s. We were uncertain whether we could resume this policy after more than 20 years. But after careful consideration, I concluded that since forest tenure concerned the people's immediate interests, conflict would eventually erupt if the issue remained unresolved. We should address it as early as possible. Also, rapid economic growth and better quality of life for rural people had reduced the need for destructive logging. As long as we formulated a sensible policy and applied effective methods, we could keep risks under control. The decision reached, we carried out extensive research and full analyses on four key problems – how to distribute forestland, how to plan for logging, how to make the necessary funds available to farmers, and how to integrate scattered pieces of forestland operated by individual households. Then we introduced reform measures tailored to local conditions, and formulated our country's first tenure reform policy for collectively owned forests at the provincial level. The central authorities included all of Fujian's experience in its No.10 document of 2008.

We should be bold and resolute in work, and fulfill our duties when in office. Anything that benefits the Party and the people, no matter how hard it might be, must be done. And it is our responsibility to do it. Just be bold and act. As a famous line by Lin Zexu goes, "I am willing to sacrifice my life for my country. How then should I shrink from lesser possible harm?"[8]

In advancing our cause and promoting reform, we will certainly touch upon many vested interests and provoke disagreement. Such disapproval or attack is inevitable if we want to do things, change things, and set things right. Throwing a stone into the water will create ripples; all the more so carrying out a great undertaking. Hesitation in performing bound duties in the face of disapproval is not the attitude that a Communist should have.

We should remain calm and carry out a rational analysis of opposition. If we are sure of the things we do and have been proved correct, we should move forward without any thought of turning back even if we are unjustly criticized, accused, or blamed. We should explain things well and build consensus to gain maximum understanding and support. We should accept fair criticism with an open mind and improve our plans and policies accordingly. It is important to have willpower, perseverance, and self-discipline, and essential to be bold and resourceful. If we persevere and ultimately achieve success, much opposition will vanish into thin air.

Fourth, you should uphold principles and be ready for challenges. Sticking to principles is an important characteristic of Communists, and a primary criterion to judge whether an official is well qualified. There is now a misunderstanding about harmony among some officials. They abuse this cherished value and misinterpret broad-mindedness, adopt a "nice guy" approach in their work, and fail to take a clear-cut stance on political principles. They are "open-minded" on cardinal issues of right and wrong, and let misconduct go unchecked. Some are unctuous in social relations and tack along with every breeze. What they say and do depends on whom they are talking to or dealing with, and what their superiors and coworkers support. Some just follow others, caring naught for right or wrong. All this runs contrary to Party principles and must be corrected.

For Communists, the "nice guy" in the workplace is not a good person. Such people are self-centered and self-serving, devoid of ethics and without the public good in mind. They believe that upholding principles will provoke strife, that resolving thorny problems will cause conflict, that not taking risks brings a great many benefits, and that utilitarian socializing helps make friends.

Their kind has been treated with disdain since ancient times. Confucius said, "The 'honest villager' spoils true virtue."[9] The "honest villager" here is a person who, devoid of any sense of right and wrong, tries to please everyone in the village. Mencius denounced such people for "just following the herd and being in concord with the filthy world"[10]. A sentence in *A Dream of Red Mansions* portrays them in a penetrating way as "doing things to serve their own ends while trying not to create any waves".

Pandering without principle does not stem from good intentions, because it is done for one's own benefit at the cost of healthy progress and greater undertakings. It has been repeatedly proved that this is one of the fundamental reasons why in some regions and departments the forces of right are waning while malign influences are spreading. This is why no breakthroughs are made in work, and conflicts and problems are piling up.

Our Party always values unity, which is attained through positive, healthy criticism and self-criticism, rather than keeping on good terms with everyone at the expense of principles. In order to uphold commitment to the Party and its principles, we Communists must engage in criticism and self-criticism. We must be resolute and make no concessions on matters of principle; otherwise we will fail the Party and the people or even commit serious mistakes tantamount to breaking the law.

In addition to cardinal issues of right and wrong, we must also adhere to principle on less important things. The Chinese people set great store by personal connections. We live in this society, and we all have relatives, friends, acquaintances, colleagues, superiors and subordinates. We often have to make a choice between principles and our family and friends when performing duties and addressing problems. It is of course ideal if the two are in concord; but we must never compromise a principle for any person when we are not able to serve both.

Huang Kecheng once served as the executive secretary of the Party's Central Commission for Discipline Inspection. He said that to improve conduct, one should "dare to offend others". When a previous subordinate of many years had a banquet paid out of public funds at Jingxi Hotel, he handled the issue in line with discipline and in disregard of past fellowship. The then minister of commerce entertained guests at Fengzeyuan Restaurant but asked for an unreasonable discount for the meal. After investigation, Huang circulated a notice of criticism across the Party and publicized the matter in the *People's Daily*. Party officials must be strictly impartial, upright and selfless, focusing on principle and commitment to the Party rather than connections and personal favors.

We must be ready to fight malign influences and tendencies at any time and in any place. Today, as the world is experiencing an accelerating rate of change on a scale unseen in a century, and as our mission of national rejuvenation enters a critical stage, the risks and challenges we face are increasing. It is unrealistic to expect days free from troubles and struggles. More than ever, Communists should have backbone, integrity and the courage to overcome any fear and any evil.

Fifth, you must strictly observe the rules and never cross red lines. I have repeated this too many times, but today I still need to remind you again. It is not easy for our Party to train a well-qualified official. If he or she is tempted onto an erroneous path, and violates discipline and laws, all their training will be for nothing and they fail the Party's trust. It pains me to see how some leading officials have decayed. I feel truly sorry for them. Not long ago, I read a report about how some young public servants went astray and became involved in corruption as soon as they gained some seniority in their departments or took up a leadership position. They failed to maintain integrity even at an early stage. You should draw lessons from them, and always bear discipline and rules in mind.

In order to observe the rules and keep ourselves within the lines, we should first hold them in total respect. Only with such awareness will we be able to set limits on what we say and do. Since the Party's 18th National Congress, the Central Committee has maintained a tough stance on corruption, imposed tight constraints for long-term deterrence, and ensured that there is no such thing as a no-go area. No ground is left unturned, and no tolerance is shown for corruption.

In disregard of all this, some officials still violate discipline. This is not because they do not know what discipline and rules require, but because they do not hold them in total respect. Which offence have they committed that is not prohibited by explicit Party discipline and state laws? Which mistake have they made that does not have a prior example? As a Ming-dynasty thinker said, "With awe in mind, one will be prudent in word and deed, and therefore cultivate virtue; without awe in mind, one will act rashly, and therefore bring disaster to oneself."[11]

Those who do not respect discipline and rules will do evil and commit horrifying crimes. Our officials must always hold the Party, the people, the law, and Party discipline in total respect, and never cross the line. Do not deceive yourselves that no one will know of your misdeeds; do not allow yourselves to be overwhelmed by the sweet talk of those offering bribes; do not take chances because you believe "money and power come from taking risks"; do not act recklessly under the misapprehension that the law cannot cope when wrongdoers are too numerous.

Only with stringent moral standards can one be strict with oneself. Only when officials maintain a sound worldview, positive values, and a healthy outlook on life, and foster a noble mind and a strong moral character, can they rise above temptation. They might have been held back from taking bribes by fear before, but now they are free from such lowly desires. Xue Xuan, a neo-Confucian philosopher of the Ming Dynasty (1368-1644), divided officials of honesty and integrity into three levels: The best are those who do not accept gifts because they know they should not; in the center are those who do not lower themselves for money because they value honor; the lowest are those who dare not to take bribes because they want to hold on to their official post and fear punishment.

We Communists are committed to the public good, justice and the greater self. Therefore, we should always be upright and honorable. We should always place the people at the center and in the forefront of our hearts, devote ourselves to the public interest, and remain righteous and incorruptible.

Yang Shanzhou was an exemplary prefectural Party secretary, who dedicated his whole life to serving the people selflessly. In the 1970s and 1980s, when many people in rural areas had built wood-and-brick and tile-roofed houses, his family still lived in a thatched hut, which leaked on rainy days. He told his family, "I can't afford to repair our house. You'll have to make do with it for now. Buy some earthen jars to catch the rain from the roof." In 1992, the Daliangshan Forest Farm he co-founded built its first brick-and-tile house. He allocated it to a newly-arrived technician, while he himself lived in a shack made of tarred sheets. Another time he visited a village and stayed in a farmer's home. He paid for his food and accommodation in line with regulations. But the host family felt uncomfortable about the poor food, and secretly returned 20 cents into his bag. When he found it, he traveled more than 50 kilometers back to the village that night and gave those 20 cents back to the host. In some people's eyes, he was a "fool" who paid no attention to what to eat and wear, where to live, or how to travel. He said, "Some say I go out of my way to seek hardship, but they don't know how happy I am.... If Communists have an occupational disease, it must be a zeal for putting up with any difficulty for the benefit of the people."

The mindset that cherishes hard work and arduous struggle will never be obsolete, and we must always encourage it. Being a Party official, you must not make too much of fame, social status, or individual interests. An official who "does everything he can to seek a government post just for good food and clothes" – as a saying goes – will not accomplish anything.

Sixth, you should continue to develop yourselves through diligent study and painstaking training. As an ancient Chinese philosopher observed, "A small bag cannot hold large things; a short rope cannot reach a deep well."[12] We are in an era of unprecedented change and we are trying to accomplish things that have never been done before. Unless we expand our knowledge, broaden our horizons, and increase our ability, success will never come our way. Younger officials are energetic and active in thinking, and you are fast learners. You are at an ideal stage to hone your skills and improve your abilities, so you must cherish every minute and never idle away your youth. You should study with great eagerness and improve yourselves ceaselessly.

Books can increase your knowledge and teach you skills. Mao Zedong once said, "Unlike eating and sleeping, reading is indispensable every day." With a heavy schedule, he made use of every moment to read, even while having his hair cut. He said with humor to his barber, "You do your job and I'll do mine, and we'll leave each other be."

We should follow his example and employ every second of time to study intensively, read more and read selectively, and draw wisdom and intellectual nourishment from books. We must not feel too pleased with ourselves to bother with study, or relax our studies on the pretext that we are too busy, or take a perfunctory attitude towards study as if putting on a show.

We must know what and how to study. There is a limit to one's energy, and one cannot learn everything. What officials should learn is based on the demands of their work and the gaps in their knowledge. We should study Marxism, especially our Party's innovative theories in the new era, and the history of the CPC, the PRC, reform and opening up, and the development of socialism. We should build a basic knowledge of economics, politics, law, culture, social sciences, management, the environment, international relations and other fields. We should add new knowledge and skills that we need in work, establishing a complete knowledge system that is necessary for fulfilling duties.

Practice brings us true knowledge and makes us more capable. The undertakings of the Party and the country cover a wide range of fields. Leading officials will not always work in one position, and they cannot possibly be ready and fully prepared in knowledge and skills every time they are transferred to a new position. To learn at work and then apply what we have learned is the only way for officials to cultivate talent and grow.

During the early days of the PRC, the central leadership appointed Xiao Jingguang as the commander-in-chief for the newly established navy. Xiao had never been involved with the navy before, and he could not even swim. He learned what he needed through his work, and accomplished the task assigned by the central leadership, building from scratch a navy that quickly grew stronger. This was also how many older revolutionaries developed the necessary expertise in economics, science and technology, diplomacy, and other fields. As our ancestors pointed out, "Through learning we improve ability, as through the whetstone knives are honed."[13]

Just as a seasoned coworker noted, the more you work at something, the better you become at it and the more you want to improve. Of course, the gains and progress you draw from study depend on how diligent you are and whether you are good at thinking and summing up experience. If you merely busy yourselves with mechanical effort, and allow yourselves to become bogged down in the quagmire of trivial and routine matters, you will hardly improve your knowledge and skills.

All of these points are critical for the healthy growth of younger officials. Living in a great age, you are a vital new force for the Party and the country. I hope you will add to your capabilities and become more confident and competitive. Do not go astray, fall behind, or drop out. I expect you to become the spine of our Party, to work in important positions and undertake great responsibilities for meeting the Second Centenary Goal. The Party and the people trust you, and look forward to the results of your hard work.

Notes

[1] Li Dazhao: "Sacrifice", *Collected Works of Li Dazhao*, Vol. 3, Chin. ed., People's Publishing House, Beijing, 2013, p. 107.

[2] Lu Xun: "Unrevolutionary Eagerness for Revolution", *Complete Works of Lu Xun*, Vol. IV. Chin. ed., People's Literature Publishing House, Beijing, 2005, p. 231.

[3] Chen Yi (1901-1972) was a Chinese proletarian revolutionary, military commander and political leader, one of the founders and leaders of the People's Liberation Army and one of the marshals of the People's Republic of China. – Tr.

[4] Zhu De (1886-1976) was one of the main founders of the PLA and served as its commander-in-chief. He was an important member of the first generation of the CPC central collective leadership with Mao Zedong at the core. – Tr.

[5] Mao Zedong: "Speech at a Conference of Cadres in the Shansi-Suiyuan Liberated Area", *Selected Works of Mao Zedong*, Vol. IV, Eng. ed., Foreign Languages Press, Beijing, 1961, pp. 229-230.

[6] Mao Zedong: "Reform Our Study", *Selected Works of Mao Zedong*, Vol. III, Eng. ed., Foreign Languages Press, 1965, p. 21.

[7] Fang Xuanling *et. al.*: *Book of Jin (Jin Shu)*.

[8] Lin Zexu: *Farewell to My Family on My Way to Exile (Fu Shu Deng Cheng Kou Zhan Shi Jia Ren)*. Lin Zexu (1785-1850) was a patriot and statesman of the Qing Dynasty who advocated resistance to Western invasion and a ban on the non-medicinal consumption of opium during the Opium War of 1840.

[9] See note 1, p. 516.

[10] See note 2, p. 601.

[11] Lü Kun: *Groans from My Sickbed (Shen Yin Yu)*. Lü Kun (1536-1618) was a writer and thinker of the Ming Dynasty.

[12] *Zhuang Zi.*

[13] Liu Xiang: *Garden of Stories (Shuo Yuan)*.

New Vision, Strategy and Measures for Talent Development in the New Era[*]

September 27, 2021

Since the 18th CPC National Congress in 2012, the Central Committee has answered a series of important theoretical and practical questions about building a talent-strong country, including why and how to achieve it. It has put forward a new vision, a new strategy and a range of measures for talent development.

First, we should uphold the Party's overall leadership over talent-related work. This is the fundamental guarantee for developing a contingent of people of high caliber.

The future of a country depends on talent. By exercising leadership over the management and development of talent, the Party should strengthen self-reliance in science and technology through the strategy of building a talent-strong country. We should provide strong political guidance as well as all-round support and assistance, and explore all avenues to nurture talent. We should value talented people, select them, put them in suitable posts, and stay engaged with them. This will enable us to attract capable people from both within and outside the Party and from both China and abroad to join us in the great cause of the Party and the people. We must train the right combination of high-caliber people in large numbers.

Second, we should ensure that talent plays a strategic role in driving development, which is a major strategy for building a contingent of people of high caliber.

Talent is the primary driver of innovation. Talented people are a key strength that will enable China to prevail in fierce international

---

[*] Part of the speech at the Central Conference on Talent.

competition. Innovation-driven development is, in essence, talent-driven development. As we are in a new development stage, we should apply the new development philosophy, create a new development dynamic, and promote high-quality development. In pursuing this goal, we must give top priority to human resources, cultivate a strategic talent pool, and thus lay a solid foundation for innovation-driven development.

Third, we should target global scientific and technological frontiers, serve the economy, meet major national needs, and strive to improve people's lives and health. This is the goal for developing a contingent of people of high caliber.

We must support and encourage our scientists and engineers to keep abreast of global advances in science and technology and achieve first-class research outcomes. To meet the urgent and long-term needs of China's development, they should boldly put forward new theories, explore new frontiers, and map out new routes. They should deliver more outcomes of strategic significance in key fields, and make breakthroughs in developing core technologies. They should explore the unknown in science and technology, and apply research findings to socialist modernization.

Fourth, we should provide well-rounded training for talent and tap into their full potential. This is the top priority in developing a contingent of people of high caliber.

We must be confident in our capacity to nurture talent, develop top-notch personnel and teams for innovation, and cultivate a reserve of young scientists and engineers who are internationally competitive. We should assign talent to suitable posts, and make sure they are managed, supported and rewarded in the right ways. We should promote competent young people, and give full play to their creativity and capacity for innovation. We must broaden our vision in selecting talent and put them in the right posts regardless of their background.

Fifth, we should expand the institutional reform of talent development. This is an important guarantee for developing a contingent of people of high caliber.

We must remove all institutional barriers in training, posting, evaluating, supporting and incentivizing talent. We should discard the criteria that overemphasize research papers, academic titles, educational backgrounds, and awards. Instead, we should give more say to employers, and create an accommodating environment for talent development. We should turn our institutional strengths into competitive strengths in talent and technology. We should put in place effective training, hiring, incentive and competition mechanisms that enable talent to pursue excellence. We should free researchers from pointless formalities and bureaucratic constraints in their work.

Sixth, we should search for the best minds and give full rein to their expertise, which is crucial for developing a contingent of people of high caliber.

China welcomes talent from all countries to participate in its development and offers opportunities for their career development. We should introduce talent recruitment policies that are more robust, open and effective, make the best use of innovative resources across the world, and adopt targeted measures to bring in urgently needed talent. We should develop an institutional framework that is appealing and internationally competitive. We should move faster to build China into a global talent and innovation center.

Seventh, we should create an enabling environment for identifying, respecting, cherishing and giving full play to talent, which will create the social conditions necessary for developing a contingent of people of high caliber.

We must foster a social environment of respecting and valuing talent, an institutional environment that promotes fairness and equality and that facilitates the selection of the best among competitors, and a living environment with satisfactory support and appropriate benefits. In short, we should create the best conditions possible for talent to fully devote themselves to their work, and foster a culture that encourages creativity and innovation throughout society.

Eighth, we should promote the ethos of scientists as a source of inspiration for developing a contingent of people of high caliber.

We should champion patriotism expressed by honoring the country and serving the people. We should pursue innovation by meeting challenges and breaking new ground. We should advocate a truth-seeking approach and a scrupulous attitude to scholarly work. We should encourage dedication and commitment and resist the temptations of fame and fortune. We should encourage teamwork and collaboration to pool wisdom to tackle tough problems. We should encourage seasoned talent to impart their knowledge and experience to help young people achieve success. We should inspire people in various sectors to blaze new trails for innovation and work hard for the country.

These eight principles encapsulate our understanding of talent development. We should continue to implement and enrich these principles.

Self-Reform: The Second Answer to Breaking the Cycle of Rise and Fall*

November 11, 2021

Self-reform is key to ensuring our Party never betrays its nature and mission. In my speech at the ceremony marking the centenary of the CPC, I pointed out that the Party has never represented any individual interest group, power group, or privileged stratum. The resolution adopted at this plenary session reiterated that point. This is a response to any attempt to divide our Party from the people or set the people against our Party by those with ulterior motives, and also a reminder to the whole Party that we must remain firm and clear-headed: For whom do we govern, for whom do we exercise power, and for whom do we seek benefit?

Ours is a very large party with 100 years of history, and we have governed this country since 1949. How can we break the historical cycle of rise and fall? Mao Zedong offered the first answer to the question in Yan'an back in 1947. He said, "The government will not dare slacken its effort only under the people's scrutiny."[1] Now, after a century of exploring the path, especially with a new approach since the Party's 18th National Congress in 2012, our Party has given the second answer: by carrying out self-reform.

The courage to engage in self-reform is a distinctive feature that differentiates our Party from other political parties. Mao Zedong said, "Conscientious practice of self-criticism is still another hallmark distinguishing our Party from all other political parties."[2] It is this character that has enabled our Party to rise time and again at critical moments,

* Part of the speech at the second full assembly of the Sixth Plenary Session of the 19th CPC Central Committee.

to bring order out of chaos after making mistakes, and to become a Marxist party that still stands strong despite setbacks. For any political party, remembering the founding mission and never having a change of heart, even in toughest times, is always the most difficult part.

"Selflessness in governance creates social equity."[3] Our Party has no interests of its own – this is the source of our courage and strength in self-reform. It is because of this that we have regularly examined our conduct and reflected on mistakes from a purely materialist perspective. It is because of this that we have been able to overcome attempts by individual interest groups, power groups, and privileged strata to corrupt us. We have been able to seek out and punish Party members who have done wrong under the influence of these groups.

Ours is a great party not because we do not make mistakes, but because we never conceal mistakes. We face up to them and reform ourselves. We have upheld truth in the guiding principles, correcting mistakes such as the Right opportunist leadership of Chen Duxiu after the failure of the Great Revolution (1924-1927), the "Leftist" mistakes of rash action and adventurism during the Agrarian Revolutionary War (1927-1937), the "Leftist" dogmatism during Wang Ming's leadership when the Party was headquartered in Yan'an (1935-1948), and the Cultural Revolution (1966-1976) which was completely repudiated after the Third Plenary Session of the 11th CPC Central Committee in 1978.

Through the movement to rectify Party conduct in the Yan'an period, the campaigns to improve Party conduct and fight corruption, waste and bureaucratism in the early years of the PRC, the Party-wide rectification and the many education campaigns following the launch of reform and opening up, we have addressed prominent problems of unwholesome thinking, organization and conduct, and lack of political commitment.

We have resolutely fought corruption. Liu Qingshan and Zhang Zishan – two senior Party officials who took large bribes in the early 1950s – were given capital sentences. Prioritizing the battle against corruption and the fight to improve Party conduct since 1978, we have established a framework for preventing and punishing corruption, and forged a strong resistance to corruption among officials.

Since the Party's 18th National Congress, we have shown unprecedented courage and resolve in implementing full and rigorous self-governance, and developed a complete set of rules and regulations for the Party to cleanse, improve and reform itself. In response to the Seven Malpractices[4] and other prominent problems undermining the Party's image, authority, and ties with the people, we have enforced strict discipline, supervision, and accountability, and focused on key senior officials to make our Party stronger.

Just as it takes a heavy dose of medicine to treat a serious disease and stringent laws to address disorder, we have been determined to "take out tigers", "swat flies", and "hunt down foxes", removing potential dangers in the Party, the state, and the military even though it means pain for the time being. How many of the world's political parties can match our resolve and scale in fighting corruption? Some extol the multiparty rule of the West and their separation of powers, refusing to believe that our Party is capable of thorough self-reform. But reality has taught them otherwise.

Our Party has won wide acclaim for its achievements over the past hundred years. We cannot lose ourselves in self-congratulation; we should carry on with self-reform. As an ancient Chinese philosopher said, "One should not be seduced by praise, nor should one fear opprobrium."[5] All Party members must always be ready for self-reform, and be aware that there is no end to full and rigorous governance of the Party. We must not feel complacent about our progress so far. The major corruption cases recently investigated have warned us that we should never slacken our efforts in improving Party conduct and fighting corruption.

Members of the Central Committee and Party officials at all levels should keep a clear head, and know the real situation regarding the mindset, organization, conduct, and clean governance. We must have the courage to face up to problems and carry out self-reform through vigorous self-examination. If you are sick, go to the doctor. Take medicine if needed, and have surgery if necessary. We will not hold back on punishing corruption. Whoever commits a crime will be investigated and we will turn a blind eye in no case. We will not relent in cleansing the viruses that damage the health of the Party and undermine its progressive and wholesome nature. There will be no leniency for anyone who damages the interests of the country and the people, encroaches upon the Party's governing foundations, or weakens the socialist state power. There will be no tolerance for anyone trying to form political factions, cliques or interest groups inside the Party.

When we celebrate our centenary, a milestone of success, we must keep alert against the possibility that as an organization we might one day become fragile and feeble. We must not forget the setbacks in our past, or the times we lost our way, or the hard lessons of the governments around the world that have failed due to complacency. We cannot be halfhearted or soft-handed in dealing with our problems – that will only lead to our demise. We should guide social transformation with self-reform and advance self-reform through social transformation, to ensure that the Party continues to exercise strong leadership in building socialism with Chinese characteristics in the new era.

Notes

[1] From Mao Zedong's conversation with Huang Yanpei in July 1945. See *Chronicle of Mao Zedong (1893-1949)*, Vol. II, Chin. ed., Central Party Literature Publishing House, Beijing, 2013, p. 611.

[2] Mao Zedong: "On Coalition Government", *Selected Works of Mao Zedong*, Vol. III, Eng. ed., Foreign Languages Press, Beijing, 1965, p. 266.

[3] *Classic of Loyalty (Zhong Jing)*. This is a book attributed to Ma Rong. Ma Rong (79-166) was a Confucian scholar of the Eastern Han Dynasty.

[4] This was put forward by Xi Jinping at the second full assembly of the Fourth Plenary Session of the 18th CPC Central Committee in October 2014. In order

to seek promotion and greater power, some officials, ignoring the Party's political discipline and rules, have engaged in one or more of these malpractices: (1) making appointments based on favoritism and discriminating against those who hold different views; (2) ganging together to form self-serving factions; (3) making anonymous and false allegations against others and spreading rumors; (4) buying support and votes; (5) promising high positions in exchange for favors and relying on cronyism for promotion; (6) feigning compliance while opposing in action and going their own way; (7) failing to comply with or even making baseless criticisms of Central Committee decisions.

[5] *Xun Zi.*

Build Confidence, Unity and Fighting Spirit*

December 27-28, 2021

This is a fruitful meeting as we have exchanged ideas, examined problems, and set the direction for the future, which are the results we, members of the Political Bureau, have achieved in the education campaign on CPC history. This is very important to our preparation for the upcoming 20th National Congress of the Party. Your comments and proposals will be very helpful to improving our work.

Over the century since its founding in 1921, our Party has united the people and led them to remarkable achievements, and accumulated invaluable experience. The history of our Party is like a most lively and convincing textbook. Our Party has always attached great importance to the study of its past. The more we learn about its journey, the more deeply we understand the laws of history, the more insights we gain, and the better we can steer future development. The Central Committee made a decision early this year to launch an education campaign on CPC history in the whole Party and society to review, study and promote the Party's history. Through this campaign, Party members will have a better understanding of our cause, firmer commitment to our ideals, higher standards of integrity, and greater determination to turn what has been learned into concrete actions. This education campaign is designed to help build confidence, unity and fighting spirit.

Whether we are able to maintain excellent performance on our new journey essentially depends on whether we have firm confidence.

---

* Main points of the speech at a criticism and self-criticism meeting on the education campaign on CPC history, among members of the Political Bureau of the 19th CPC Central Committee.

Over the past century, our Party has been dedicated to working for the wellbeing of the Chinese people and rejuvenation of the Chinese nation, and to pursuing progress for humanity and great harmony for the world. Our commitment to the common good leads us on the right path to a better future for humanity. This is the greatest source of confidence that underpins our Party's long-term governance of China and its capacity to rally the people and lead them forward into the future. Today, we can claim with full confidence that the CPC has been worthy of the choice of history and the people.

Our confidence is grounded in a full and accurate understanding of history. Since the 18th CPC National Congress in 2012, faithful to historical materialism and a rational outlook on Party history, we have made considerable progress in ending confusion and resolving misunderstandings over certain major questions in relation to the history of the Party and the country. At the same time, we know full well that to have a good understanding of our past, it is still necessary for our Party to conduct a serious, comprehensive and authoritative review of its history, followed by an enduring campaign to study and publicize it. In this way, more and more people will get a proper perspective on Party history, and the general public will have a clear understanding of the official account of Party history. We will encourage Party members, officials and the general public, particularly young people, to bear in mind our past experiences and have full confidence in our journey ahead.

Unity is the lifeline of our Party. Our Party is experienced in unifying thinking and taking concerted action through reviewing history. This unity is, first and foremost, political unity, which has reached new heights with the joint efforts of the whole Party since the 18th CPC National Congress. The 19th Central Committee decided that Chinese socialism in the new era should be highlighted in the resolution adopted at its Sixth Plenary Session in 2021. This is of tremendous significance for our Party to unify thinking and take concerted action on major theoretical and practical questions, and to rally the Chinese people of all ethnic groups and lead them towards the victory of socialism with Chinese characteristics in the new era.

Our Party comes from the people, has its roots among the people, and is dedicated to serving the people. The resolution adopted at the Sixth Plenary Session was the third on the history of our Party. Its purpose is to remind all Party members that we should remain true to our original aspiration and founding mission in the new era; properly answer the essential questions of where we have come from and where we are going; always maintain close ties with the people; and guide the people to study our Party's century-long history, fully understand its nature, and follow its leadership.

The emergence and development of Marxism and socialist countries is a story of hardship and struggle. During the New Democratic Revolution (1919-1949), we endured unprecedented difficulties and made enormous sacrifices. After the founding of the PRC in 1949, particularly after the 18th CPC National Congress, we addressed many major risks and challenges through courageous and tenacious struggle. In the new era, we will review and make good use of this experience, always be ready to respond to worst-case scenarios, and guard against potential dangers. We will maintain our fighting spirit, identify proper methods or approaches, and develop the capacity to solve problems. We will be dauntless and forge ahead no matter what difficulties may arise. We will respond effectively to risks and challenges on the way forward, both foreseeable and unexpected, while steering the ship of Chinese socialism onward through the waves.

The Political Bureau should draw wisdom and strength from our Party's century-long history of struggle to improve itself. We, as members of the Political Bureau, must conscientiously turn the original aspiration into action, have a broad vision and foresight, show concern for the country and the people, make long-term and practical plans, avoid seeking personal gain, position or privilege, always focus on the cause of the Party and the people, and be forever close to the people and work by their side through thick and thin. We should play an exemplary role in strengthening commitment to the Party's ideals and convictions. These ideals and convictions will be a beacon for us to observe the general situation, respond to change, and learn about future prospects; a source of strength for hard work and constant improvement; a source of political wisdom for us to distinguish between right and wrong and avoid confusion; a source of strong antibodies for us to resist unhealthy tendencies and decadence.

We, as members of the Political Bureau, must be firm and clear-headed ourselves and take the lead in upholding the authority and centralized, unified leadership of the Central Committee. In addition, we must also make a conscious effort to encourage all Party members to do likewise. In particular, we must prevent and reverse unhealthy trends. We must have keen and farsighted strategic vision, focus on new issues as they emerge, give broad rein to democracy, draw on collective wisdom, and put forward advice that is in line with reality for sound decision-making. We must set an example in fully implementing the decisions and plans of the Central Committee, and we must urge people in the sectors and departments for which we are responsible to study earnestly and understand thoroughly the Central Committee's decisions and plans, which are of the greatest significance to our country, and ensure that they are implemented to the letter.

The top priority of the Political Bureau next year is to convene the 20th CPC National Congress. We, as members of the Political Bureau, must perform our duties in earnest and do our best with a strong sense of responsibility and mission. Leadership elections will take place this year and the next. Senior leaders must strictly observe political discipline and rules and abide by organizational discipline and election regulations. We must guide leading officials to correctly understand the decisions of our Party, appraise themselves honestly, subordinate themselves to overall interests, and defer to the decisions of the organization. We must all gird up our loins as Communists and devote all our energy to work.

At this meeting, many valuable comments and suggestions have been made on the work of the Central Committee, and of the central and local governments. These must be examined immediately after the meeting with measures to improve our work and deliver concrete results.

Make Further Progress in Party Self-Governance*

January 18, 2022

The year 2021 marks the centenary of the founding of the Communist Party of China. The CPC Central Committee's efforts to enforce strict Party self-governance have provided a strong political base for building a modern socialist country.

Ten years have passed since the 18th CPC National Congress held in 2012. A blacksmith in the past would spend 10 years forging a perfect sword. Likewise, over the past decade, the Central Committee has incorporated strict Party self-governance into the Four-pronged Comprehensive Strategy, and pressed forward with unprecedented courage and determination to improve Party conduct, build clean government, and fight corruption.

Some malfeasances that had not been checked for many years have been curbed, intractable problems of long standing have been resolved, and serious hidden dangers within the Party, the state and the armed forces have been removed. Lax and weak governance in the Party has been fundamentally reversed, and we have chosen to rely on the Party's self-reform to avoid the historical cycle of rise and fall.

Since 2012, historic and groundbreaking achievements have been made in strengthening the Party's self-governance; this has had a profound impact in multiple dimensions. We should continue this process in the long term and make steady progress.

Over the past 100 years, the Party has ensured its lasting vitality and robust growth by relying on developing people's democracy and accepting public scrutiny from outside the Party, and on strengthening

---

* Main points of the speech at the Sixth Plenary Session of the 19th CPC Central Commission for Discipline Inspection.

self-governance and self-reform within the Party. It has had the courage and determination to uphold the truth and correct mistakes. Strict self-governance, a significant element of the Party's self-reform in the new era, has opened up a new realm for our century-old Party.

To succeed in self-reform we must:

- reinforce the Party's political foundations as the overarching principle and self-reform as the political direction;
- improve ideological work, which is essential to the development of the Party, and make it a powerful tool for self-reform;
- implement the Central Committee's Eight Rules[1] to improve Party conduct with strict discipline, and introduce more measures of self-reform;
- fight corruption and punish wrongdoers with decisive measures, to prepare for a tough and protracted process of self-reform;
- strengthen the political function, organization and cohesion of the Party to build a force that is bold in self-reform and knows how to do it well;
- establish a system of rules and regulations that will help the Party cleanse, improve and reform itself, to provide an institutional guarantee for self-reform.

Since 2012, based on the Marxist theory of political party development, we have reviewed and applied the experience of our Party gained over one century to further innovations in the theory, practice, and system of Party governance. Our understanding of how to build a Marxist political party fit to rule in the long term, and of what steps must be taken, has risen to a new level. It includes:

- upholding the centralized, unified leadership of the CPC Central Committee;
- ensuring that the Party exercises effective self-supervision and strict self-governance;
- reinforcing the Party's political foundations;
- maintaining a resolute stance on matters concerning strict self-discipline;
- working tenaciously to improve Party conduct;

- showing zero tolerance for corruption;
- eliminating all forms of corruption and misconduct that harm the interests of the people;
- focusing on those in leading positions so that they can lead by example in these areas;
- improving the supervisory systems of the Party and the state to form an effective supervision mechanism that covers all areas.

We must consolidate what we have achieved during the education campaign on CPC history, stay true to our original aspiration and founding mission, and open up new prospects for development. We need to study and implement the decisions made at the Sixth Plenary Session of the 19th CPC Central Committee in 2021, strengthen education and presentation of Party history, and increase the confidence in the Party, so that our original aspiration and founding mission will truly take root in the hearts of Party members. We should encourage Party members to carry forward the Party's fine traditions and conduct, stay loyal to the Party and the people through concrete actions, and remain committed to them, so as to achieve greater success on the new journey.

We need to strengthen political oversight to ensure that the new development philosophy is implemented in full, to the letter and in all fields. We must apply the new development philosophy, ground our efforts in the new development stage, create a new development dynamic, and focus on high-quality development. We should guide Party members and officials to fully understand the major policies and decisions of the Central Committee, act consistently with them, and implement them in full. Neither half measures nor superficial compliance should be allowed in enforcement. We must overcome the silo mentality and regional protectionism, and stamp out political calculation, petty scheming for personal gain, and acts in disregard of the rules, so as to ensure that the Central Committee's decisions and plans are carried out strictly and faithfully.

We must be resolute in the battle against corruption and succeed in our strategic goal of ensuring that our officials dare not, cannot, and will not engage in corruption. We must be soberly aware that the battle against corruption is still fierce and is shifting to unfamiliar terrain. We are facing a formidable task to guard against collusion among malevolent interest groups seeking to tempt and corrupt officials by various means. We are also facing a formidable task to deal effectively with new forms of corruption that are difficult to detect. We must eradicate the breeding ground for corruption and bring about a corruption-free political environment. We must also clean up systemic corruption, defuse risks, and remove hidden dangers. We still have a long way to go.

We need to keep a clear head and bear in mind that the battle against corruption is a protracted one, and we should be ready for fight at any time. As long as the soil and conditions for corruption exist, it will never be eradicated and our struggle will never end. Leading officials should sharpen their political acumen and discernment. Leading officials, those in the higher ranks in particular, should take the lead in implementing directives on strengthening political integrity in the new era, consolidate the foundations of sound values, reinforce their commitment to the Party, and build up their capacity to resist corruption and venality. They should also nurture a healthy family culture and set a good example for their family members through integrity and honest behavior.

The Eight Rules must be reinforced to correct the Four Malfeasances of favoring form over substance, bureaucratism, hedonism, and extravagance, and foster healthy and positive practices. Favoring form over substance and bureaucratism are the archenemies of the healthy growth of our Party and the state. We need to start with leading officials, especially those at the higher levels, and urge them to adopt the right view on job performance, respect reality and the needs of the people, and strengthen systems thinking and rational planning, so as to serve and benefit the people. They must not fail to put an end to favoring form over substance, going through the motions, or launching expensive and ill-considered projects. We must implement the system for evaluating officials and inspecting their work in order to have them better perform their duties.

We must strengthen scrutiny over the implementation of Central Committee policies that bring benefits and security to the people, and address their key concerns in areas such as education, health care, old-age insurance, social security, environmental protection, workplace safety, and food and drug security. We must consolidate what we have achieved in the fight against criminal gangs and organized crime, and in the education and rectification drive for judicial, prosecuting and public security teams, so that people can see that equity and justice are served in every judicial case.

We will strengthen education, management and supervision of younger officials, and train and guide them to be honest and loyal to the Party and the people. They should be strictly and thoroughly educated, managed, and supervised, so as to firm up their ideals and convictions and encourage them to keep in mind the Party's original aspiration and founding mission. They must exercise power in the right way, maintain self-respect, conduct self-examination, strictly observe discipline, laws and regulations, and start their political career as they mean to carry on. Younger officials must constantly review the Party's Constitution, regulations and discipline, its theories, guidelines, principles and policies, and our Party's original aspiration and founding mission, and use these as their yardstick to judge whether any action can and should be taken, so as to guard against corruption and decadence.

We must reinforce the system for overseeing the exercise of state power and improve supervision over discipline compliance and law enforcement, to make supervision more standardized, forceful and effective. Party committees and Party leadership groups at all levels should take primary responsibility for internal supervision and strengthen supervision over senior officials, especially those in command and the leadership teams. Discipline inspection and supervision departments should assist Party committees in strictly governing the Party and realizing effective coordination between internal Party supervision and other types of supervision. We must implement the principle of the Party supervising officials, strengthening scrutiny of election of a new leadership, and ensuring that Party organizations reinforce their leadership and supervision in evaluating the performance of officials, especially in terms of political commitment and clean governance.

Departments and officials engaged in discipline inspection and supervision should always be loyal to the Party, the people, and their duties, play their due role in the Party's self-reform, and carry forward the Party's best practices and finest conduct established over the past century. Focusing on the overall work of the Party and the state, they should perform their supervisory role for more effective implementation of the strategic plans, objectives and tasks of the Party and the state. Discipline inspection and supervision teams must hold themselves to stricter standards and discipline to sharpen their minds and capabilities. They should strengthen their commitment to the Party, be upright, impartial and prudent in exercising their power, and constantly build up their immunity against corruption. They should readily subject themselves to supervision from the Party and all sectors of society, and always be loyal guardians of the Party and the people.

Notes

[1] The Eight Rules were set by the Political Bureau of the 18th CPC Central Committee to urge all officials to improve their ways of doing things and maintain close ties with the people. They are summarized as follows: improving investigation and fact-finding trips, streamlining meetings and other activities, reducing documents and briefings, standardizing arrangements for visits abroad, improving security procedures, improving media reports, imposing restrictions on publishing their own works, and practicing diligence and frugality.

Unity for Strength and Hard Work for a Bright Future[*]

January 30, 2022

Over the past hundred years, the CPC has secured historic achievements on behalf of the Chinese people. Today, it is rallying the people and leading them on a new journey towards the Second Centenary Goal.

All that the Party and the people have achieved over the past century derives from unity of effort, which is the most distinctive tradition of the CPC and the Chinese people. The Party's century-long history has shown that unity means strength and that hard work leads to a bright future. Unity of effort is what a nation relies on to build its future and what a political party counts on to remain resolute. Our century-long history has also revealed that unity under a clear goal is the strongest and that endeavor based on complete unity is the most powerful.

We have relied on unity of effort to create a glorious history, and we will continue to do so to shape a bright future. As long as more than 1.4 billion Chinese people join forces and work together for a shared future, as long as over 95 million Party members stay truly connected with the people and strive together with them for a shared future, we will be certain to achieve even greater successes that continue to astonish the world.

Working for the good of the public is the greatest joy in the world. We have the people in our heart and the truth on our side, and we are marching on the right track – this is what makes us strong and confident. No matter how the world changes, no matter what daunt-

* Part of the speech at a Spring Festival gathering in 2022.

ing challenges lie ahead, we will always carry forward the Party's great founding spirit, while bearing in mind the wisdom of our forebears that "one prospers in hardship and adversity, and perishes in ease and comfort".

We must see things from a long-term and strategic perspective and remain mindful of potential dangers. We must unite as one and work relentlessly to advance our historic mission of national rejuvenation.

The best way to celebrate our century-long history is to write a new page for the future. In the second half of this year, our Party will convene its 20th National Congress to review its work over the past five years and draw up a blueprint for future development. In the run-up to the congress and beyond, we must take a holistic approach to imperatives at home and abroad, and implement the Five-sphere Integrated Plan and the Four-pronged Comprehensive Strategy. We must balance development with security, and the Covid-19 response with economic and social development.

Under the general principle of pursuing progress while securing stability, we must apply our new development philosophy in full, to the letter and in all fields, and move faster to create a new development dynamic. We must expand reform and opening up across the board, promote high-quality development, and continue to ensure and improve the people's wellbeing.

By all these means, we will strive to maintain a stable and healthy economy, a prosperous and peaceful society, and a clean and wholesome political environment. We must deliver new achievements to usher in the 20th CPC National Congress.

Index

图书在版编目 (CIP) 数据

习近平谈治国理政. 第四卷：英文 / 习近平著；
英文翻译组译. – 北京：外文出版社, 2022.6
ISBN 978-7-119-13094-1

I. ①习… II. ①习… ②英… III. ①习近平 – 讲话
– 学习参考资料 – 英文②习近平新时代中国特色社会主义
思想 – 学习参考资料 – 英文 IV. ① D2-0 ② D610.4

中国版本图书馆 CIP 数据核字 (2022) 第 098517 号

习近平谈治国理政
第 四 卷

© 外文出版社有限责任公司
外文出版社有限责任公司出版发行
（中国北京百万庄大街 24 号）
邮政编码：100037
http://www.flp.com.cn
北京中科印刷有限公司印刷
2022 年 6 月（小 16 开）第 1 版
2022 年 6 月第 1 版第 1 次印刷
（英文）
ISBN 978-7-119-13094-1
08000（平）